Moving from the Millennium to the Sustainable Development Goals

Sefa Awaworyi Churchill
Editor

Moving from the Millennium to the Sustainable Development Goals

Lessons and Recommendations

palgrave
macmillan

Editor
Sefa Awaworyi Churchill
School of Economics, Finance and Marketing
RMIT University
Melbourne, VIC, Australia

ISBN 978-981-15-1555-2   ISBN 978-981-15-1556-9   (eBook)
https://doi.org/10.1007/978-981-15-1556-9

This Palgrave Macmillan imprint is published by the registered company Springer Nature Singapore Pte Ltd.
The registered company address is: 152 Beach Road, #21-01/04 Gateway East, Singapore 189721, Singapore

Contents

Notes on Contributors

Khalid Ahmed is an Associate Professor of Economics in the Department of Business Administration, Sukkur IBA University. His area of interest falls within applied economics with focus on sustainable development and related policy. He has published in international peer-reviewed journals including *Energy Economics, Applied Economics, Journal of Cleaner Production, Resources Policy, Renewable and Sustainable Energy Reviews* and *Social Indicators Research*, among others. He has also secured several national and international grants and has been on visiting positions at University of Cambridge, University of Gottingen and Korea Institute for International Economic Policy (KIEP).

Samuelson Appau is a Lecturer in Marketing at RMIT University. He holds a PhD from the University of Melbourne. His research focuses on the impact of marketing, religion, culture and poverty on individual and group well-being and marketplace engagement. Samuelson's research sits at the intersection of transformative consumer research, development economics and consumer culture theory. His scholarly research has appeared in reputable scholarly outlets, such as the *Journal of Public Policy & Marketing, Journal of Business Research, Applied Economics* and *Empirical Economics*.

Sefa Awaworyi Churchill is a principal research fellow with the School of Economics, Finance and Marketing at RMIT University, Australia. He holds a PhD in Economics from Monash University. His interdisciplinary research focuses on development economics, addictive behaviour, ethnic diversity, well-being and other issues related to sociology, health and economics. He has experiences working on consultancy projects for various policy agencies and international development organisations.

Mita Bhattacharya is a Senior Lecturer in Economics at Monash University. Mita specialises in applied economics research focusing on energy, environment and trade. Mita has published widely in peer-reviewed journals including in *Energy Economics, International Journal of Industrial Organisation, International Journal of Production Economics, World Economy, Review of Industrial Organisation* and *Applied Energy*. She has held visiting positions at Australian National University, Curtin University, Doshisha University, University of East Anglia and the Organisation for Economic Co-operation and Development. Mita has received numerous grants including from sources such as the Australian Research Council, Tyre Australia and National Science Council (Taiwan).

Festival Godwin Boateng holds a BA (Hons) degree in Sociology and Social Work from the Kwame Nkrumah University of Science and Technology (KNUST), Ghana, and an MA in Global Studies and International Development Studies from Roskilde University, Denmark. He is a PhD candidate at the School of Global, Urban and Social Studies, RMIT University, Australia, where his research focuses on the political economy of building collapse in developing countries.

Shanaz Broermann is a public financial management officer at the Collaborative Africa Budget Reform Initiative (CABRI) and an Overseas Development Institute (ODI) fellow. She has previously worked in academia where she taught economics and research methods. She has extensive in country experience working in several African countries. She completed her PhD at University of Greenwich on economic growth in low-income countries, with specific reference to sub-Saharan Africa.

Chei Bukari is a demonstrator at the Department of Applied Economics, School of Economics, University of Cape Coast, Ghana. He holds an MPhil (Economics) degree from University of Cape Coast, Ghana. His research interests include poverty, inequality, finance and corruption. He has also worked as a research assistant in the Directorate of Research, Innovation and Consultancy (DRIC) at the University of Cape Coast (UCC) for close to three years.

Meg Elkins is a Senior Lecturer in Economics at RMIT University. She holds a PhD in Economics from La Trobe University. She is an applied economist with a focus on well-being, and cultural economics. Meg's research methods include microeconomic analysis to evaluate programmes and policies in the areas of international development, social protection, homelessness, youth curiosity and arts programmes. Meg has published in high-quality research journals in the area of development and communications. She has received research grants to conduct research for the City of Melbourne and Higher Education Research and Development Society of Australia (HERDSA).

Lisa Farrell is Professor and Deputy Dean Research and Innovation in the School of Economics, Finance and Marketing at RMIT University. Her research field is in the area of applied microeconomics, with a particular focus on important contemporary social issues such as subjective well-being, decision making under uncertainty and lifestyle choice behaviours. Her work has spanned both the theoretical and microeconometric aspects of risk and well-being and the academic impact of this work is clear from the important contributions she has made leading to publications in high quality international economic journals.

Simon Feeny is a Professor in development economics at RMIT University, Melbourne, Australia. He has published nearly 80 books, book chapters and journal articles in a wide range of fields and undertaken a number of research-based consultancies for organisations including the Department for Foreign Affairs and Trade, World Vision International, Oxfam Australia, Plan International, the Fred Hollows Foundation and the Association of Southeast Asian Nations (ASEAN) Secretariat. He has led large research projects valued at almost $2 million and which have included extensive research fieldwork in developing countries.

Isaac Koomson is a PhD candidate (Applied Econometrics) in the UNE Business School, University of New England, Australia. He holds an MPhil (Economics) degree from University of Cape Coast, Ghana, and has eight years of graduate teaching experience. His research interest is multidisciplinary and includes development economics, small businesses, agricultural economics and finance. Isaac is the lead economist/consultant for the Network for Socioeconomic Research and Advancement (NESRA), Accra, Ghana, and has consulted for the World Bank, the United Nations University Institute for Natural Resources in Africa (UNU-INRA) and other agencies.

Matthew Gmalifo Mabefam is a tutor and PhD candidate in the School of Social and Political Sciences at the University of Melbourne. Matthew has experiences with local and international non-governmental organisations in Ghana and Australia. In the past decade, he has engaged in mobilising and advocating for and with local communities, and groups in negotiating spaces for their well-being. His research focuses on the impact of the relationship between development actors, both state and non-state actors and the well-being of people in Africa. His work lies at the intersection of well-being of vulnerable groups, especially women who have been displaced from their communities as a result of violent ethnic, chieftaincy and cultural conflicts.

Vijaya Bhaskar Marisetty is Professor of Finance at the University of Hyderabad. He holds a PhD from Monash University. Earlier, he worked as faculty at Monash University, RMIT University and Indian Institute of Management (IIM), Bangalore. His research interests include financial regulation and investor welfare. He has published in top tier journals, including *Journal of Financial Markets*, *Journal of Banking and Finance*, *World Bank Economic Review* and *Auditing: Journal of Practice and Theory*. He has received several best paper awards, including, CFA Institute best paper award, Pacific-Basin Finance Journal best paper award and Emerald publishers citation excellence award.

Ankita Mishra is a Senior Lecturer in the School of Economics, Finance and Marketing, at RMIT University, Australia. She holds a PhD from the Indira Gandhi Institute of Development Research, India. She mainly teaches courses in macroeconomics ranging from introductory units to advanced postgraduate units. Her main research expertise lies in applied macroeconomics and development economics, with a focus on policy-relevant issues. She has published extensively in leading international journals in her areas of expertise. Prior to joining academia, Ankita worked in industry as a research associate with Morgan Stanley, India.

Musharavati Ephraim Munyanyi is a PhD candidate in the School of Economics, Finance and Marketing at RMIT University, Australia. He holds an MA (Economics) degree from the Istanbul Medeniyet University, Turkey. He has experiences working for non-governmental organisations, government ministries and research institutions. His research interest is multidisciplinary and includes development economics, macroeconomics and monetary economics.

Ahmed Salim Nuhu is a PhD candidate in the dual programme of Economics and Agricultural, Food, and Resource Economics (AFRE) at Michigan State University. His research revolves around the use of experimental methods to evaluate development intervention programmes, household, firm and farm-level choices as well as outcomes. He holds a master's degree in economics from Eastern Illinois University and a bachelor's degree in economics from the Kwame Nkrumah University of Science and Technology, Ghana.

Janet Exornam Ocloo holds a master's degree in public health promotion from Leeds Beckett University. She has over 15 years of experience working in the health sector in Ghana. She is working with the Korle-Bu Teaching Hospital, Accra. Her research focuses on issues of public health. Much of her current research focuses on determinants of subjective well-being and health in general.

Ahmed Skali is a Lecturer in Economics with the School of Economics, Finance and Marketing at RMIT. His research focuses on understanding political institutions and social norms, from their roots in human behaviour to their consequences on socioeconomic outcomes, using insights and methods from economics, psychology and across the social sciences. His research has appeared in the *European Economic Review*, *The Leadership Quarterly* and the *Journal of Economic Psychology*. He is deputy chair of the Behavioural Business Lab and a member of the International Development and Trade Group at RMIT.

Russell Smyth is Professor of Economics and Deputy Dean (Academic Resourcing) in the Monash Business School, Monash University, Australia. He holds honours degrees in Economics and Law from Monash University and a PhD in Economics from University of London. His research interests include energy economics, empirical legal studies and subjective well-being. Much of his work has a geographic focus on China. He has published widely on these topics in a variety of outlets.

List of Figures

List of Tables

13.4 Shaping machine operations

Figure 13.6(*a*) shows how the cutting tools are held on a shaping machine and how the *clapper box* allows the tool to lift and ride over the work on the return stroke of the ram, thus preventing wear on the cutting edge. The settings to produce a plane surface parallel to the worktable of a shaping machine are shown in Fig. 13.6(*b*), where it can be seen that the machine head is in the vertical position and that the clapper box is centralised.

For the production of surfaces perpendicular to the shaping machine table the machine head remains vertical but the clapper box is off-set to swing the tool towards the surface being machined as shown in Fig. 13.6(*c*).

For the production of inclined surfaces both the machine head and the clapper box are off-set as shown in Fig. 13.6(*d*). Again, the clapper box is off-set so as to swing the tool towards the surface being machined.

The stroke of the ram should be adjusted so that the cutting tool only just clears the work at each end of the stroke. This ensures that the tool is only moving slowly as it strikes and leaves the work. It also avoids wasting time and energy 'cutting fresh air'. The ram achieves its maximum cutting and return speeds at the mid-point of its travel for any given setting.

13.5 Some typical applications of the shaping machine

The most simple job which can be performed on the shaping machine is that of squaring up a blank ready for further machining operations. The corrrct sequence of operations for squaring up a blank is set out in Fig. 13.7, where it can be seen that the top surface of the vice slides and the face of the fixed jaw provide the datum surfaces for these operations. It is essential that these datum surfaces are square to each other and correctly aligned to the surface of the machine worktable.

The shaping machine can also be used to machine slots, steps and chamfers. The relative settings of the tool slide and clapper box when machining such surfaces have already been discussed in section 13.4.

A component exploiting these movements is shown in Fig. 13.8(*a*), whilst the operations to produce this more complex component are outlined in Fig. 13.8(*b*). It can be assumed that the blank has been previously squared-up.

To machine the step, slot and chamfer, this component would be held in the machine vice so that it is perpendicular to the movement of the ram. Thus the first operation would be to place a ground parallel strip in the vice and check that the vice is correctly set using a dial test indicator as shown in Fig. 13.8(*b*), operation 1. Next, the tool slide would need to be set perpendicular using a dial test indicator and try-square. Normally the slide would be set to the machine table, but since the component is being held in the machine vice, the moving jaw slideways are being used as the horizontal datum in this instance. The table rise and fall cannot be used for machining the step and the slot as the vertical feed mechanism is not sufficiently sensitive or accurate.

1

Hitting the Right Targets: Understanding What Works in the Development Process

Sefa Awaworyi Churchill

1 Background

Between 2000 and 2015, the Millennium Development Goals (MDGs) remained the overarching development framework that governed the international development community. Many countries incorporated the MDGs into their development plans and implemented specific projects intended to achieve various development targets. After a decade and half of commitment to the MDGs, the framework is widely considered a success. For instance, according to the United Nations (2015a), the number of people living in extreme poverty have declined by more than half, reducing from 1.9 billion in 1990 to 836 million in 2015. With regards to education, the average primary school enrolment rates across developing countries have increased from 83 percent in 2000 to 91 percent in

S. Awaworyi Churchill (✉)
School of Economics, Finance and Marketing, RMIT University,
Melbourne, VIC, Australia
e-mail: sefa.churchill@rmit.edu.au

© The Author(s) 2020
S. Awaworyi Churchill (ed.), *Moving from the Millennium to the Sustainable Development Goals*, https://doi.org/10.1007/978-981-15-1556-9_1

2015, while the number of out-of-school children of school-going age fell from an estimated 100 million in 2000 to about 57 million in 2015.

Substantial progress has been made regarding gender equality, however, gender gaps in areas of opportunities, economic and political empowerment, and other areas of wellbeing persist in many developed and developing countries (Klasen, 2018). For instance, while many more girls are now enrolled in school and the percentage of women with vulnerable jobs as a share of total female employment has declined, female parliamentary representation has not seen much increase. Gender gaps in wages persist as well. Child mortality and maternal mortality rates have declined by more than half and about half, respectively. However, children from the poorest households are more likely to suffer from malnutrition. Mortality rates are also about twice as high for these children compared to those from the wealthiest households. Improvements in access to improving water sources do not extend to the majority of people in rural areas (United Nations, 2015a).

Despite the success that has been reported across countries, progress has been uneven. Specifically, the recorded achievements have also been accompanied by uneven shortfalls across many countries and areas. With the introduction of the Sustainable Development Goals (SDGs), perhaps the most important questions on the minds of most policymakers pertain to what factors contributed to the MDGs progress, and what is likely to explain the uneven progress across countries. Answering these questions is important for assessing the ongoing progress of the SDGs and identifying key policy areas to focus on. This book presents a collection of chapters that examine various dimensions of the MDGs and development goals in general. It provides insights that are relevant to understanding the factors that influence development.

The new overarching international development framework may not be successful or present the best opportunities for the desired global change without a better understanding of factors that contributed the most or the least to the attainment of the MDGs. The chapters presented in this book provide discussions and insights into understanding these factors better. They represent a collection of scholarship that addresses some of the important questions in international development that have remained unanswered. They adopt a wide range of research methods to provide insight into what works, and what does not, in promoting the stipulated development goals.

2 Summary of Chapters in the Book

The individual chapters in this book focus on a wide range of development issues ranging from the focus on specific development goals to more general discussions on development. Five chapters focus on single countries to present sub-national (i.e., household- or individual-level) evidence on factors that influence development outcomes, while another five focus on cross-country evidence. Two chapters provide descriptive accounts based on qualitative analysis, while one chapter provides a much needed review of existing literature.

Sefa Awaworyi Churchill, Ahmed Salim Nuhu and Russell Smyth reflect on the importance of financial inclusion as a tool for poverty alleviation. The United Nations and the World Bank have declared universal financial inclusion as a strategic priority to address poverty (World Bank, 2018). Financial inclusion is believed to promote inclusive growth, financial deepening and economic development (Aghion & Bolton, 1997; Galor & Zeira, 1993). The expansion of poor people's access to finance is argued to increase their economic opportunities, thus helping alleviate poverty (Ellis & Lemma, 2010; Ghosh & Vinod, 2017). The general acceptance of the importance of financial inclusion has led to the adoption of various programs by governments around the world to promote financial inclusion. Several governments have also committed to global frameworks such as the principles proposed in the Maya Declaration, which is an initiative for promoting sustainable financial inclusion made by a group of developing nations during the Alliance for Financial Inclusion's 2011 Global Policy Forum held in Mexico.

Awaworyi Churchill, Nuhu and Smyth use data from the Financial Inclusion Insights (FII) program for Nigeria, one of the first nations to commit to the Maya Declaration, to present evidence on the effects of financial inclusion on household poverty. Their study is timely and their focus on Nigeria is also particularly relevant. With the World Bank's target date for the declaration of universal financial inclusion by 2020 almost due, understanding whether financial inclusion has made a difference in the lives of poor households, especially in countries such as Nigeria that are committed to the financial inclusion agenda, is important. Nigeria hosts Africa's largest economy but is also one of the poorest. More importantly, Awaworyi Churchill, Nuhu and Smyth discuss the relevance of drawing on evidence from a country such as Nigeria for policy, given that it hosts the largest financial inclusion program in Africa. They measure financial inclusion multi-dimensionally to reflect access to banks, access to credit and access to insurance, and find that financial inclusion alleviates poverty. The chapter reveals interesting insights on the importance of financial inclusion, and which dimension of financial inclusion in the most effective.

Chei Bukari and Isaac Koomson provide evidence on the potential link between mobile money adoption and household health outcomes. Mobile money is believed to have advanced financial inclusion in many developing countries (Donovan, 2012; Hughes & Lonie, 2007). Mobile money is widely viewed as a financial technology that offers the opportunity for people to spend, save and transfer money using a cell phone. Thus, for those who are unable to open accounts with a bank for various reasons, having a phone and an active SIM card ensures that basic financial transactions are executed. This model of financial inclusion is championed by several mobile network providers in developing countries. Bukari and Koomson focus on SDG 3, which aims at *ensuring healthy lives and promoting wellbeing for all at all ages*. With emphasis on the sub-target of achieving universal health coverage, they examine the effect of mobile money adoption on healthcare spending and utilization of rural households in Ghana. Their findings show that mobile money adoption enhances healthcare utilization and improves the ability of rural households to spend on healthcare. This finding is more so pronounced in the case of female-headed households.

Sefa Awaworyi Churchill, Lisa Farrell and Vijaya Marisetty also focus on the impact of various dimensions of mobile money, but with emphasis on the gender equality and the women's empowerment aspect of the SDGs. The United Nations describes gender equality as a fundamental human right that is a relevant foundation for development in general. Providing women and girls with equal representation in economic and household-decision making processes is argued to fuel sustainable econo-mies that will help alleviate poverty and other social and economic ills (Diebolt & Perrin, 2013; Duflo, 2012). Awaworyi Churchill, Farrell and Marisetty, thus, focus on examining how the knowledge of, and adoption of, mobile money influence female empowerment in India. They focused on five different indicators of empowerment and found limited evidence to support the idea that mobile money promotes female empowerment. They, however, identify important areas of interest for policy.

Ankita Mishra and Sefa Awaworyi Churchill provide a unique per-spective to the debate on factors that influence the attainment of the health goals, specifically the child health target of the SDGs. The impor-tance of understanding which factors influence child health and nutri-tion is evident in the United Nations statistics that, each year, more than five million children die before their fifth birthday. Mishra and Awaworyi Churchill contribute to the discourse on factors that influence child nutrition by examining the role of fertility gap. Using data from India, they examine the impact of fertility gap on child nutritional outcomes. Their findings suggest that the odds of having malnourished children are higher for women who exceed their fertility target compared to those who have achieved or underachieved it. This finding emphasizes the importance of lower fertility on development and thus calls for policies that are aimed at achieving this.

With approximately 37 million people living with HIV globally as at 2017, the importance of understanding risk factors cannot be overstated. Sefa Awaworyi Churchill, Lisa Farrell and Janet Exornam Ocloo examine if individual sexual orientation and sexual behavior are risk factors, and how they influence people's perception of HIV risks and the prevalence of other sexually transmissible infections. They focus on evidence from the United Kingdom, and argue that some development goals including those related to health and gender equality should be a concern not just for developing countries but also for developed countries. Their results show that both sexual orientation and sexual behavior increase the odds of having a sexually transmissible infection. Their findings highlight the need for policies that advance education on how to promote responsible sexual behavior regardless of sexual orientation, especially among youth who experience significant risks.

Shanaz Broermann presents cross-country evidence that offers insight into why trade-led growth may be a path to sustainable development in Sub-Saharan Africa. Broermann's study not only provides evidence on how to attain SDG 8 of economic growth but also draws out policy implications that are relevant to attain other development goals. Broermann estimates a demand-led growth model for 22 African economies, and finds evidence to support trade as an important tool for economic growth.

Sefa Awaworyi Churchill, Meg Elkins and Simon Feeny examine the impact of ethnic diversity, an important social and cultural factor, on development. They provide discussions on why and how ethnic diversity is likely to influence various development goals. Using data on 119 countries, they show that cross-country differences in ethnic diversity can explain differences in development levels and progress made toward the MDGs across countries. Specifically, findings from their study show that ethnic diversity hinders development and MDG progress, and this is consistent across the MDG targets employed in the study. Policy-wise, their study shows that ethnic diversity is important in understanding progress made toward development and thus it should be a factor of interest when strategizing and implementing development projects across countries.

Musharavati Ephraim Munyanyi, Sefa Awaworyi Churchill and Ahmed Skali examine the impact of foreign aid on development. The discourse on the effectiveness of foreign aid has a long history in the development literature. Against the background of the United Nation's declaration of increased foreign aid as an important approach to achieve the SDGs (United Nations, 2015b), Munyanyi, Awaworyi Churchill and Skali revisit the evidence on effect of foreign aid on development outcomes. They examine the impact of foreign aid on various indicators of development and find evidence of a negative effect of aid on the prevalence of HIV and child mortality, although an increase in foreign aid has no visible effect on development outcomes relating to poverty, hunger, education and maternal mortality, among others. Their study also confirms the importance of an enabling environment characterized by economic development and good institutions for aid to be effective.

Khalid Ahmed and Mita Bhattacharya contribute to how to achieve SDG 13 relating to climate change. Specifically, Ahmed and Bhattacharya examine the role of institutional quality in mitigating carbon dioxide (CO_2) emissions for a panel of eight countries included in the Association of Southeast Asian Nations (ASEAN-8). They used bureaucratic quality, democratic accountability and corruption as proxies for institutional quality, and found that good institutions tend to help reduce CO_2 emissions. Their findings emphasize that the effect of different institutional elements is heterogeneous across countries. Thus, policymakers need to target country-specific institutional element in combating emissions.

Advocates of social protection argue that it is crucial in assisting the vulnerable and poor manage risk as this can prevent them from sliding into destitution. Social protection is also purported to raise human capital, as well as improve livelihoods and development outcomes in general (Barrientos & Hulme, 2009; Guillaumont & Chauvet, 2001). It is therefore considered an important tool in the development process, although these claims are not substantiated with empirical evidence. Meg Elkins, Simon Feeny and Sefa Awaworyi Churchill fill an important gap in the literature by providing evidence on the relationship between social protection and the progress they made toward the Millennium Development Goals (MDGs). Using cross-country data on 101 developing countries, their results suggest that social protection coverage is positively associated with progress toward many of the MDGs.

Sub-Saharan Africa is the poorest region in the world, but it is also one of the most religious. Past and current development efforts at poverty alleviation have often overlooked the immutable role of religion. Samuelson Appau and Matthew Gmalifo Mabefam provide unique insights into how Pentecostalism and its associated message in Africa influence poverty and the development process. Appau and Mabefam discuss the role of what is referred to as the "prosperity gospel" or "wealth and health gospel" in alleviating or exacerbating issues of poverty.

Godwin Festival Boateng contributes to the discourse on SDG 11 of sustainable cities and communities. Building collapses are becoming a common, tragic occurrence in cities in developing countries, particularly in Africa and Asia. Despite its adverse implications for sustainable urban life and development in general, the phenomenon has remained very much under-researched. As a first step to gaining a deeper understanding, and to provide direction for future research, Boateng provides a much-needed discussion on how building safer infrastructure can play an important role in development and ensure sustainable urban life as proposed by SDG 11.

While the microfinance industry has attained considerable growth around the world with the promise of helping alleviate poverty, the truth behind its ability to alleviate poverty is still a subject of public discourse. Donors (both prospective and current), government agencies, policy-makers and stakeholders are showing much interest in understanding what works and what does not work in microfinance. Awaworyi Churchill, thus, conducts a systematic review of the literature that examines the impact of microfinance on poverty and microenterprise performance. He finds no robust evidence of any significant impact on the performance of microenterprises. With regards to impact on poverty, findings suggest some positive effects, but this effect is weak. The findings from this chapter suggest that the question of whether microfinance is a viable development tool in improving the well-being of the poor needs to be revisited and considered seriously.

In the concluding chapter, Simon Feeny summarizes the lessons from the global experience of the MDGs and discusses the extent to which these lessons have been applied to the evolution of the SDGs. Feeny demonstrates that while some of the critiques of the MDGs have been addressed, unfortunately some of the insights we learnt from the MDGs were not applied to the SDG agenda. He provides important recommendations toward the achievement of the SGDs.

References

Aghion, P., & Bolton, P. (1997). A theory of trickle-down growth and development. *The Review of Economic Studies, 64*(2), 151–172. https://doi.org/10.2307/2971707

Barrientos, A., & Hulme, D. (2009). Social protection for the poor and poorest in developing countries: Reflections on a quiet revolution: Commentary. *Oxford Development Studies, 37*(4), 439–456.

Diebolt, C., & Perrin, F. (2013). From stagnation to sustained growth: The role of female empowerment. *American Economic Review, 103*(3), 545–549.

Donovan, K. (2012). Mobile money for financial inclusion. *Information and Communications for Development, 61*(1), 61–73.

Duflo, E. (2012). Women empowerment and economic development. *Journal of Economic Literature, 50*(4), 1051–1079.

Ellis, K., & Lemma, A. (2010). Financial inclusion, household investment and growth in Kenya and Tanzania. *ODI Project Briefing, 43*, 1–4.

Galor, O., & Zeira, J. (1993). Income distribution and macroeconomics. *The Review of Economic Studies, 60*(1), 35–52. https://doi.org/10.2307/2297811

Ghosh, S., & Vinod, D. (2017). What constrains financial inclusion for women? Evidence from Indian micro data. *World Development, 92*, 60–81.

Guillaumont, P., & Chauvet, L. (2001). Aid and performance: A reassessment. *Journal of Development Studies, 37*(6), 66–92.

Hughes, N., & Lonie, S. (2007). M-PESA: Mobile money for the "unbanked" turning cellphones into 24-hour tellers in Kenya. *Innovations: Technology, Governance, Globalization, 2*(1–2), 63–81.

Klasen, S. (2018). The impact of gender inequality on economic performance in developing countries. *Annual Review of Resource Economics, 10*, 279–298.

United Nations. (2015a). *The Millennium Development Goals Report.* New York.

United Nations. (2015b). *Transforming our world: The 2030 agenda for sustainable development.* New York: United Nations.

World Bank. (2018). UFA2020 overview: Universal financial access by 2020. Retrieved July 11, 2019, from https://www.worldbank.org/en/topic/financialinclusion/brief/achieving-universal-financial-access-by-2020

2

Financial Inclusion and Poverty: Micro-level Evidence from Nigeria

Sefa Awaworyi Churchill, Ahmed Salim Nuhu, and Russell Smyth

1 Introduction

There has been a major expansion in access to financial services across developing countries. In 2017, the share of the global adult population with a bank or mobile money account was 69%, which is a significant improvement over the corresponding figure of 51% in 2011. This includes about 515 million adults who have opened new accounts since 2014. In sub-Saharan

S. Awaworyi Churchill (✉)
School of Economics, Finance and Marketing, RMIT University, Melbourne, VIC, Australia
e-mail: sefa.churchill@rmit.edu.au

A. S. Nuhu
Department of Agricultural, Food and Resource Economics, Michigan State University, East Lansing, MI, USA
e-mail: nuhuahme@msu.edu

R. Smyth
Department of Economics, Monash University, Melbourne, VIC, Australia
e-mail: russell.smyth@monash.edu

© The Author(s) 2020
S. Awaworyi Churchill (ed.), *Moving from the Millennium to the Sustainable Development Goals*, https://doi.org/10.1007/978-981-15-1556-9_2

Africa, about 21% of the adult population now has access to mobile money services—the highest in any region of the world (Demirguc-Kunt, Klapper, Singer, Ansar, & Hess, 2018). This observed upward trend in financial inclusion has been largely driven by innovations in financial services delivery as well as initiatives by governments and international agencies to promote financial inclusion. Following the World Bank's declaration of universal financial inclusion by 2020 as a strategic priority, governments around the world have developed various programs to promote financial inclusion. Thus, in most countries, the provision of financial services through mobile phones, and other digital platforms has become a key approach to promoting financial inclusion and improving economic outcomes for poor households and firms (Chauvet & Jacolin, 2017; Demirguc-Kunt, Klapper, & Singer, 2017; Ibrahim & Alagidede, 2017).

However, the precise impact of financial inclusion on economic outcomes is not settled (see, e.g., Aghion & Bolton, 1997; Ang, 2008; Galor & Zeira, 1993; King & Levine, 1993; Levine, 2005; Van Rooyen, Stewart, & De Wet, 2012). One strand of literature posits that financial inclusion provides a sustainable pathway for poor households to escape poverty, by significantly lowering price and non-price barriers. Studies belonging to this strand of the literature suggest that financial inclusion relaxes firm and household credit constraints for the poor who are usually more credit constrained, thus enhancing investment in human capital and income-generating activities (see, e.g., Galor & Zeira, 1993). Financial inclusion provides poor households with opportunities to access credit, make investments, build savings and hedge against unforeseen shocks (see, e.g., Beck, Demirgüç-Kunt, & Honohan, 2009; Ellis & Lemma, 2010; Ghosh & Vinod, 2017). Access to finance is also likely to reduce information and transaction costs, which can enhance savings and investment decisions, technological innovation and, consequently, economic growth in the long-run (Beck et al., 2009). Additionally, it is argued, that in settings in which government welfare programs exist, financial inclusion can help households to more reliably access these services.

On the other hand, another strand of the literature argues that access to financial services could generate negative outcomes for poor households (see, Galor & Zeira, 1993). This strand of the literature suggests that poor households end up being caught in a debt-trap in an attempt to keep up with consumption (Awaworyi Churchill & Nuhu, 2016; Frank,

Levine, & Dijk, 2014). Thus, according to this alternative view, financial inclusion acts as an incentive for borrowing for consumption purposes, as opposed to saving and investing in capital accumulation.

In this chapter, we examine the impact of financial inclusion on poverty in Nigeria using survey data from the 2016 Financial Inclusion Insights (FII) program. To do this, we construct a composite measure of financial inclusion that captures the banking, credit and insurance dimensions of financial inclusion. We use various measures of poverty including the Poverty Probability Index (PPI), household deprivation and a measure of poverty reflecting the poverty line. The relationship between financial inclusion and poverty is potentially endogenous. On the one hand, while having access to financial services could improve household's ability to save, access credit and invest in income-generating activities, thus influencing poverty, it is also plausible that poor households are less likely to pursue financial services, due to entry costs and other barriers that may significantly impact on the level of participation of poor households in financial markets.

To address the issue of endogeneity, we consider the average time (in minutes) taken to reach the nearest financial institution as a source of exogenous variation in the financial inclusion variable. To do so, we take advantage of the fact that in Nigeria, banks are fairly evenly distributed across rural and urban areas. Specifically, households that are reasonably closer to financial institutions are more likely to access financial services than households that are farther away, all things equal. However, the time taken to reach a financial institution does not directly affect the poverty status of households, thus satisfying the exclusion restriction. Our two-stage least squares (2SLS) estimates suggest that endogeneity biases our estimates downwards, reducing the magnitude of the impact. Specifically, using average time (in minutes) taken to reach the nearest financial institution as our external instrument, we find that a standard deviation increase in financial inclusion is associated with a decline in poverty of between 0.277 and 0.672 standard deviations, depending on how poverty is measured. We complement our 2SLS estimates with propensity score matching (PSM), using a range of matching techniques. In robustness checks, we apply our external instrument to rural and urban samples separately and adopt a heteroskedasticity-based identification strategy.

Across all estimation methods, we find significant poverty-reducing effects of financial inclusion.

Nigeria makes for an important case study for at least two reasons. It hosts the largest financial inclusion program in Africa and has the highest number of people in poverty. Not only is Nigeria Africa's largest economy, but it is also the poorest in Africa, and, indeed, one of the poorest in the world. Of the 87 million people in Nigeria, evidence from the FII program suggests that 60% of Nigerians live below the poverty line of $2.50 per day (FII, 2018; Roser & Ortiz-Ospina, 2018). Further, Nigeria currently has a negative poverty escape rate of −5.6% (World Poverty Clock, 2018), suggesting that rather than escaping poverty, more people are actually falling into poverty.

Nigeria was one of the first countries globally to commit to the Maya Declaration,[1] and since making this commitment, the Nigerian government launched the National Financial Inclusion Strategy in 2012, with the objective of reducing the number of people who are financially excluded to 20% by 2020 (Central Bank of Nigeria, 2012). However, since the implementation of this strategy, no study has examined the impact of financial inclusion in Nigeria. The FII survey is a unique dataset designed to measure national trends on key indicators of financial inclusion since 2013, the year after Nigeria launched the National Financial Inclusion Strategy, and is, thus, well-suited for this study.

Most of the existing literature on financial inclusion and poverty is at the macro-level (see, e.g., Beck, Demirgüç-Kunt, & Levine, 2007; Beck, Demirguc-Kunt, Laeven, & Levine, 2008; Chibba, 2009; Giné & Townsend, 2004; Levine, 1998). Related studies at the micro-level have typically used microfinance as a proxy for financial inclusion, and have examined the relationship between microfinance and outcomes such as poverty and income (e.g., Imai, Gaiha, Thapa, & Annim, 2012; Khandker, 2005; Zhang, 2017). We have very little evidence on the impact of specific financial inclusion interventions on development outcomes and what we do know is largely restricted to South Asia (see, e.g., Binswanger

---

[1] The Maya Declaration is a statement of common principles regarding the development of financial inclusion policy made by a group of developing nations during the Alliance for Financial Inclusion's 2011 Global Policy Forum held in Mexico.

& Khandker, 1995; Burgess & Pande, 2005). We contribute to the literature on financial inclusion and poverty by providing evidence on the efficacy of Africa's largest financial inclusion program on alleviating poverty in one of the poorest countries in the world.

We also contribute to a small related literature that has examined the implications of financial inclusion and access to microcredit in Nigeria. A few studies have examined the impact of access to finance or microfinance on consumption and expenditure (see, Aideyan, 2009; Dimova & Adebowale, 2018; Seck, Naiya, & Muhammad, 2017). In a related study, using cross-sectional data from the General Household Surveys for Nigeria, Dimova and Adebowale (2018) find evidence to suggest that access to finance improves household welfare, but increases income inequality. We extend this literature to examine the impact of financial inclusion on household poverty in Nigeria.

The rest of the chapter is set out as follows. The next section describes the data and variables used. Section 3 explains the empirical method. Section 4 presents the results and Sect. 5 concludes.

2 Data and Variables

We use data from the InterMedia Financial Inclusion Insights (FII) program. The FII program conducts nationally representative surveys in selected countries across Asia and Africa, including Nigeria. Commencing in 2013, the FII surveys have included modules that highlight trends in financial inclusion and the use of financial technologies and services with sections on the usage of mobile phones, mobile money, banks and non-bank financial institutions. Each module of the survey explores various dimensions of awareness, access and use of financial services. Our study draws on wave 4 of the survey for Nigeria conducted in 2016, which seeks to measure national trends in key indicators of financial inclusion since 2013, one year after Nigeria launched its National Financial Inclusion Strategy. The survey covers 6352 adults aged 15 years and above and includes information on household demographics, financial behavior, assets and poverty indicators among others.

Poverty

Based on information available in the FII survey, we employ three measures of poverty which enables us to examine the robustness of our results to alternative ways of measuring poverty. The first measure of poverty is the Poverty Probability Index (PPI). The PPI, commissioned by the Grameen Foundation, provides scores for households based on household characteristics to determine the likelihood of a household living below the national poverty line, which is set at $2.50 per day and takes into account current country conditions.[2] The scores on the PPI range between zero and 100, where a score of zero represents the household most likely to be poor and 100 represents the household least likely to be poor. Our second measure of poverty is a dummy variable set to equal one if the household lives below the poverty line of $2.50 per day.

Our third measure of poverty is a multi-dimensional poverty index (MPI) following the approach developed by the Oxford Poverty and Human Development Initiative (OPHI) (Alkire & Santos, 2010). We consider three equally-weighted dimensions in the poverty index; namely, education, health and living standards with multiple indicators under each dimension as shown in Appendix Table 2.6. Equal weights are assigned to each indicator under a dimension, and, thus, with two indicators each under the health and education dimensions, we assign a weight of 1/6 to each indicator, while for each of the six indicators under the living standard dimension we assign equal weights of 1/18. We use a poverty deprivation score derived from these indicators. The deprivation score per household is the weighted sum of the number of deprivations calculated as follows:

$$d_i = w_1 I_1 + w_2 I_2 + \ldots + w_n I_n, \tag{2.1}$$

where d_i is the household deprivation score, $I_i = 1$ if a household is deprived in indicator i and $I_i = 0$ otherwise. w_i is the weight attached to indicator i with $\sum_{i=1}^{d} w_i = 1$. Table 2.6 provides full details of how the household deprivation scores are assigned.

---

[2] See https://www.povertyindex.org/about-ppi for details on the construction of the PPI.

Financial Inclusion

Our measure of financial inclusion is a multi-dimensional financial inclusion index using an approach similar to that in Eq. (2.1). The index reflects a holistic view of financial inclusion based on various definitions of financial inclusion as proposed by the World Bank and the existing literature. According to the World Bank, a household or individual is financially included if they have access to affordable financial products that meet the needs associated with transactions and payment, savings, credit and insurance (World Bank, 2018a). Thus, the existing literature has often considered measures such as access to credit, access to savings, access to banking and access to insurance as the core pillars of financial inclusion (Mialou, Amidzic, & Massara, 2017; Park & Mercado, 2015).

In our multi-dimensional financial inclusion index, we consider three dimensions of financial inclusion; namely, access to banks, access to credit and access to insurance.[3] We assign each dimension an equal weight of 1/3 and develop a household financial deprivation score based on Eq. (2.1). Following Zhang & Posso (2019), we adopt a threshold of 0.5, where our measure of financial inclusion is a dummy variable set equal to one if the household financial deprivation score is less than 0.5, and zero otherwise. As a robustness test, we also use the individual indicators (access to bank, access to credit and access to insurance).

Covariates

Consistent with the household poverty literature, we control for household characteristics as well as the characteristics of a household reference person including household size, household asset ownership, age, gender, marital status, education, employment status, religion, household location (rural vs. urban) and number of children living in the household. Appendix Table 2.8 provides a description and summary statistics of variables included in our analysis.

---

[3] In the FII survey, access to banking services captures households that have either checking, savings or fixed deposit accounts, and thus our chosen indicators also reflect the savings dimension of financial inclusion. Table 2.7 presents details of the indicators used.

3   Empirical Specification and Methods

Our baseline estimates employ the following cross-section model for household poverty:

$$P_i = \beta F_i + \gamma X_i + \alpha_i + \varepsilon_i, \tag{2.2}$$

where P_i is poverty status or level of household i. F_i is the measure of financial inclusion and X_i is a vector of covariates correlated with household poverty. The variable α_i is a state-level dummy variable that controls for unobserved state-level fixed effects, while ε_i is a normally distributed error term. For our baseline results, we use ordinary least squares (OLS) for PPI and deprivation score regressions, while we use logit regressions for poverty line regressions.

We also employ 2SLS and PSM to address endogeneity arising from reverse causation and potential measurement error issues. In 2SLS regressions, we instrument for financial inclusion using the average time (in minutes) taken by a household member to get to the nearest financial institution providing financial inclusion services. Intuitively, time taken to reach the nearest financial institution should be correlated with financial inclusion, given the longer the time taken to reach the nearest financial institution, the less likely households will be able to avail financial services. This conjecture is consistent with the findings of studies that have examined the relationship between financial inclusion and distance to nearest banks (Brown, Guin, & Kirschenmann, 2016; Demirgüç-Kunt & Klapper, 2012). This time variable, however, only affects poverty through its effects on access to financial services, which are essentially measures of financial inclusion. One may be concerned about the validity of this instrument if the distribution of financial institutions across rural and urban areas in Nigeria were uneven. For instance, if the majority of financial institutions were in urban areas, and poverty was higher in rural areas than urban areas due to factors other than distance to financial institutions, distance to financial institutions might be correlated with poverty through other channels. We do not believe this is an issue in our case given that there has been an increase in the number, and distribution, of banks in rural areas since the introduction of Nigeria's Rural Banking Scheme (RBS) in 1977. However, to ensure that our choice of instrument is not sensitive to the geographic location of respondents (i.e., urban vs. rural), in a robustness check, we also conduct 2SLS results in which we split our sample based on an urban/rural split.

We also follow a growing body of literature that has used PSM to address endogeneity in non-experimental data (see, e.g., Campello, Graham, & Harvey, 2010; Maertens & Swinnen, 2009; Zhang & Posso, 2019). We define the treatment as households that are financially included, and examine the average effect of this treatment on poverty by applying the PSM technique in Rosenbaum and Rubin (1983). In order to draw causal inferences about the effect of financial inclusion on poverty using PSM, we ask the question: What is the outcome (in terms of poverty) for a household that is treated (i.e., financially included), relative to the hypothetical outcome that would have prevailed if the same household was financially excluded? We estimate the average treatment effect as follows:

$$
\tau = \{E\{E\{O_1 - O_0 \quad B = 1, p(W)\}\} \\
E\{O_1 - O_0 \quad B = 1\} \\
E\{E\{O_1 \quad B = 1, p(W) - E\{O_0 \quad B = 0, p(W)\} \quad B = 1\}
$$

,

where τ is the average effect of the treatment, B is a binary variable equal to one for a financially included household and zero otherwise, O represents poverty outcomes including household PPI scores, deprivation scores and poverty line, and W is a vector of pre-treatment characteristics represented by relevant covariates. The propensity score, $p(W)$, captures the probability of being poorer given pre-treatment characteristics (W). We use different matching methods, including nearest neighbour, radius, kernel and local linear regression matching methods.

4 Empirical Results

Table 2.1 presents the baseline results for the relationship between financial inclusion and household poverty. Column 1 presents results for household PPI scores, Column 2 presents results for household deprivation scores and Column 3 reports results for the poverty line.

Table 2.1 Financial inclusion and poverty (baseline results)

	(1)	(2)	(3)
Variables	PPI score	Deprivation	Poverty line
Financial inclusion	0.061***	−0.041***	−1.148***
	(0.008)	(0.011)	(0.246)
	[0.066]	[−0.031]	[−0.431]
Male	−0.007***	−0.004	0.085
	(0.003)	(0.005)	(0.077)
	[−0.022]	[−0.007]	[0.086]
Age	0.001***	0.000	−0.007**
	(0.000)	(0.000)	(0.003)
	[0.057]	[0.017]	[−0.226]
Rural	−0.076***	0.052***	1.367***
	(0.004)	(0.006)	(0.097)
	[−0.200]	[0.094]	[0.249]
Married	0.009***	−0.011**	−0.038
	(0.003)	(0.005)	(0.082)
	[0.027]	[−0.023]	[−0.039]
Children	−0.017***	0.012***	0.350***
	(0.001)	(0.002)	(0.037)
	[−0.185]	[0.091]	[0.316]
Household size	−0.014***	0.011***	0.157***
	(0.001)	(0.002)	(0.027)
	[−0.206]	[0.113]	[0.793]
Primary	0.038***	−0.282***	−0.681***
	(0.004)	(0.007)	(0.124)
	[0.087]	[−0.438]	[−0.534]
Secondary	0.088***	−0.335***	−1.630***
	(0.004)	(0.007)	(0.117)
	[0.252]	[−0.657]	[−1.615]
Tertiary	0.152***	−0.399***	−2.599***
	(0.006)	(0.009)	(0.152)
	[0.306]	[−0.549]	[−0.808]
Farm land	−0.037***	0.021***	0.701***
	(0.003)	(0.005)	(0.085)
	[−0.103]	[0.041]	[0.682]
Employed	0.017***	−0.026***	−0.492***
	(0.004)	(0.007)	(0.112)
	[0.036]	[−0.038]	[−0.366]
Self-employed	−0.003	−0.005	−0.161*
	(0.003)	(0.005)	(0.089)
	[−0.007]	[−0.011]	[−0.160]
Christian	0.019	−0.078***	−0.313
	(0.014)	(0.026)	(0.481)
	[0.055]	[−0.158]	[−0.318]

(*continued*)

Table 2.1 (continued)

Variables	(1) PPI score	(2) Deprivation	(3) Poverty line
Muslim	0.016	−0.086***	−0.112
	(0.015)	(0.027)	(0.488)
	[0.046]	[−0.173]	[−0.114]
Constant	0.677***	0.627***	−1.606***
	(0.019)	(0.033)	(0.573)
State fixed effect	Yes	Yes	Yes
Observations	6352	6352	6352
R-squared	0.645	0.528	−

Notes: Reference category for marital status is single/divorced/widowed, education status is no formal education, for employment, status is unemployed, for religion is other religions. Robust standard errors in parentheses. Standardized coefficients in brackets. ***$p < 0.01$, **$p < 0.05$, *$p < 0.1$

In Column 1, a standard deviation increase in financial inclusion is associated with a 0.066 standard deviation increase in household PPI scores, while, in Column 2, a standard deviation increase in financial inclusion is associated with a 0.031 standard deviation decrease in household deprivation scores. In Column 3, a standard deviation increase in financial inclusion is associated with a decline of 0.431 standard deviations in the number of people below the poverty line. These results, viewed together, suggest that financial inclusion is associated with poverty alleviation. Further, compared to other covariates, the effects of financial inclusion on poverty is relatively stronger than factors such as gender, age, marital status and employment status of household reference persons.

Panel A of Table 2.2 presents 2SLS results for the association between financial inclusion and poverty using average time to the nearest bank as the instrument. From the first stage, consistent with expectations, we find that an increase in the time taken to reach the nearest bank is associated with a decline in financial inclusion. The F statistics, which are greater than 10, imply that our instruments are not weakly correlated with financial inclusion (Stock & Yogo, 2005). The 2SLS results suggest that endogeneity of financial inclusion causes a downward bias in our baseline estimates given that the 2SLS estimates are considerably higher than estimates from our baseline models. Specifically, a standard

Table 2.2 Financial inclusion and poverty (IV results)

Variables	(1) PPI score	(2) Deprivation	(3) Poverty line
Panel A: Full sample			
Financial inclusion	4.253*	−3.569*	−4.904***
	(2.229)	(1.923)	(0.053)
	[0.371]	[−0.277]	[−0.672]
State fixed effect	Yes	Yes	Yes
Observations	4555	4555	4555
First stage			
Time to bank	−0.007*		
	(0.004)		
Partial *R*-squared	0.1257		
F-statistic	18.11		
Panel B: Urban sample			
Financial inclusion	1.969**	−1.101*	−7.193*
	(0.994)	(0.661)	(4.018)
	[0.221]	[−0.212]	[−0.432]
State fixed effect	Yes	Yes	Yes
Observations	1533	1533	1533
First stage			
Time to bank	−0.020**		
	(0.009)		
Partial *R*-squared	0.1129		
F-statistic	8.97		
Panel C: Rural sample			
Financial inclusion	3.803**	−4.310**	−7.361**
	(1.806)	(2.094)	(3.578)
	[0.375]	[−0.365]	[−0.566]
State fixed effect	Yes	Yes	Yes
Observations	3022	3022	3022
First stage			
Time to bank	−0.009**		
	(0.004)		
Partial *R*-squared	0.1863		
F-statistic	14.30		

Notes: All regressions include the relevant control variables. Robust standard errors in parentheses. Standardized coefficients in brackets. ***$p < 0.01$, **$p < 0.05$, *$p < 0.1$

deviation increase in financial inclusion is associated with an increase of 0.371 standard deviations in household PPI scores, and declines of 0.277 and 0.672 standard deviations in household deprivation scores and the number of households below the poverty line, respectively.

Panels B and C of Table 2.2 report 2SLS results for the urban and rural sub-samples, respectively. In Panel B, a standard deviation increase in financial inclusion is associated with an increase of 0.221 standard deviations in household PPI scores, and declines of 0.212 and 0.432 standard deviations in household deprivation scores and the number of households below the poverty line, respectively. In Panel C, a standard deviation increase in financial inclusion is associated with an increase of 0.375 standard deviations in household PPI scores and declines of 0.365 and 0.566 standard deviations in household deprivation scores and the number of households below the poverty line, respectively. These results are consistent with our baseline results and 2SLS results based on the full sample, although results for the urban sub-sample (Panel B) should be treated with caution given that the reported F-statistics are marginally below the Stock and Yogo (2005) critical value of 10.

Table 2.3 reports results for the effects of financial inclusion on poverty using PSM. Here, the treatment comprises households that are financially included, given that our baseline results suggest that financial inclusion is associated with better livelihoods. The PSM results suggest that, on average, poverty is lower for households that are financially included. This finding is consistent across all matching methods used and also consistent with our baselines and 2SLS results.

Table 2.3 PSM results with different matching methods

Matching method	ATT (average treatment effect on the treated)		
	PPI score	Deprivation	Poverty level
1—Nearest neighbor (one-to-one)	0.061***	−0.033***	−0.123***
	(0.003)	(0.006)	(0.026)
4—Nearest neighbor	0.063***	−0.037***	−0.118***
	(0.006)	(0.011)	(0.001)
Radius	0.070***	−0.044***	−0.148***
	(0.011)	(0.001)	(0.012)
Kernel	0.082***	−0.061***	−0.179***
	(0.013)	(0.001)	(0.007)
Local linear regression	0.073***	−0.048***	−0.156***
	(0.011)	(0.005)	(0.013)

Notes: ***represent significant at the 1% level. Bootstrapped standard errors in parentheses

Robustness Checks

In this section, we conduct a series of test to examine the sensitivity of our results. First, we examine the robustness of our 2SLS estimates using the Lewbel (2012) 2SLS approach in which we combine internally generated instruments with the time variable. Heteroskedasticity-based identification has a relatively long history as a complementary identification strategy to using external instruments (see, e.g., Klein & Vella, 2010). The Lewbel (2012) approach relies on heteroskedasticity of the error term. Because it relies on higher moments, it is less reliable than the standard IV approach, but it has still been widely used as a robustness check on 2SLS findings with external instruments (see, e.g., Brown, Martinez-Gutierrez, & Navab, 2014; Dang & Rogers, 2015; Denny & Oppedisano, 2013; Mallick, 2012; Mishra & Smyth, 2015; Sabia, 2007; Xue, 2018). In particular, several studies have combined Lewbel's method with an external instrument as a robustness check (see, e.g., Dang & Rogers, 2015; Denny & Oppedisano, 2013; Xue, 2018). The advantage of so doing is that it can enhance efficiency of estimation and create over-identification to test the validity of the instruments (Xue, 2018).

To employ the Lewbel (2012) approach, we estimate the following two equations:

$$Y_1 = X^I \beta_1 + Y_2 \Upsilon_1 + \xi_1, \quad \xi_1 = \alpha_1 U + V_1 \tag{2.3}$$

$$Y_2 = X^I \beta_2 + \xi_2, \quad \xi_2 = \alpha_2 U + V_2 \tag{2.4}$$

Y_1 is our measure of poverty, Y_2 is financial inclusion and U denotes unobserved characteristics, which affect both financial inclusion and poverty. V_1 and V_2 are idiosyncratic errors. Lewbel (2012) suggests that one can take a vector Z of observed exogenous variables and use $\left[Z - E(Z) \right] \xi_2$ as an instrument, provided that $E(X \xi_1) = 0$, $E(X \xi_2)$, $cov(Z, \xi_1, \xi_2) = 0$ and that there is at least some heteroskedasticity in ξ_j. The intuition is that $\left[Z - E(Z) \right] \xi_2$ is a valid instrument because identification depends on having regressors that are not correlated with the product of the heteroskedastic errors. Lewbel (2012) suggests that, where instruments (such as time taken to reach the nearest financial institution) exist, we can estimate

Eqs. (2.3) and (2.4) using 2SLS with both time taken to reach the nearest financial institution and an estimate of $\left[Z - E(Z)\right]\xi_2$ as instruments. As ξ_2 is a population parameter, and it cannot be directly observed, we use its sample estimate $\hat{e}_2$, obtained from the first stage regression and consequently use the vector $\left[Z - E(Z)\right]\hat{e}_2$ as instruments.

The main assumption of the Lewbel (2012) approach is that there is heteroskedasticity in ξ_j. The exact form of heteroskedasticity requirement as derived in Lewbel (2012) is $cov\left(Z,\xi_2^{\;2}\right) \neq 0$. As an approximation, Lewbel (2012) suggests using the estimate of the sample covariance between Z and squared residuals from the first stage regression linear regression on X to test for this requirement, using the Breusch and Pagan test for heteroskedasticity. As noted by Lewbel (2012, p. 71), "if $cov\left(Z,\xi_2^{\;2}\right)$ is close to or equal to zero, then $\left[Z - E(Z)\right]\xi_2$ will be a weak or useless instrument, and this problem will be evident in the form of imprecise estimates with large standard errors". The other assumptions that $E\left(X\,\xi_1\right) = 0$, $E\left(X\,\xi_2\right)$, $cov\left(Z,\xi_1,\xi_2\right) = 0$ are premised on population parameters and are non-testable. But, there is nothing unusual about these assumptions. As Lewbel (2012, p. 69) puts it: "These are all standard assumptions, except that one usually either imposes homoscedasticity or allows for heteroskedasticity, rather than requiring heteroskedasticity". This means, therefore, that the only non-standard required assumption by Lewbel (2012) is heteroskedasticity.

Table 2.4 reports findings from Lewbel 2SLS regressions. Panel A reports findings from regressions that use only internally generated instruments, while Panel B reports findings from regressions that combine time to the nearest bank with internally generated instruments. The Breusch and Pagan test for heteroskedasticity confirms that the heteroskedasticity assumption for the Lewbel (2012) approach is satisfied in our data. The first stage F statistics are consistently greater than 10 (Stock & Yogo, 2005). Further, we do not reject the null hypothesis for the over-identifying restriction test for regressions, suggesting that the instruments are not over-identified in the first stage.

In Panel A, we find that the effect of financial inclusion is significant across all columns. Specifically, a standard deviation increase in financial inclusion is associated with an increase of 0.059 standard deviations in household PPI scores, and decreases of 0.020 and 0.037 standard deviations in household deprivation scores and the number of households below

Table 2.4 Financial inclusion and poverty (Lewbel 2SLS results)

Variables	(1) PPI score	(2) Deprivation	(3) Poverty line
Panel A: Lewbel 2SLS with internal instruments			
Financial inclusion	0.054***	−0.028**	−0.100***
	(0.009)	(0.012)	(0.029)
	[0.059]	[−0.020]	[−0.037]
State fixed effect	Yes	Yes	Yes
Observations	6352	6352	6352
First stage			
Partial *R*-squared	0.8224	0.8224	0.8224
F-statistic	381.31	381.31	381.31
J *p*-value	0.1512	0.1415	0.2276
Panel B: Lewbel 2SLS with external & internal instruments			
Financial inclusion	0.053***	−0.019	−0.104***
	(0.009)	(0.012)	(0.030)
	[0.067]	[−0.017]	[−0.045]
State fixed effect	Yes	Yes	Yes
Observations	4555	4555	4555
First stage			
Time to bank	−0.007***		
	(0.002)		
Partial *R*-squared	0.7891		
F-statistic	282.09		

Notes: All regressions include the relevant control variables. Robust standard errors in parentheses. Standardized coefficients in brackets. ***$p < 0.01$, **$p < 0.05$

the poverty line, respectively. In Panel B, while the effect of financial inclusion on the household deprivation score is statistically insignificant, a standard deviation increase in financial inclusion is associated with an increase of 0.067 standard deviations in household PPI scores, and a decrease of 0.045 standard deviations in the number of households below the poverty line. These results are generally consistent with the baseline results in Table 2.1 and the instrumented results in Table 2.2. The coefficients in both Panels A and B are much closer to the baseline estimates than the estimates just using the external instrument and the coefficients in Panel B are slightly higher than those in Panel B, consistent with most previous studies that have employed the Lewbel method (see Mishra & Smyth, 2015).

We next examine the robustness of results to a sub-sample of our dataset. The common trend in the household poverty literature is to control for characteristics of a household reference person. While the reference person is defined differently in the literature, in most cases, it corresponds with the household head or household member with the highest income. In the FII survey, not all household reference persons are household heads (or at least all household reference persons interviewed did not state that they were household heads). We examine the sensitivity of our results to a sub-sample which restricts our sample to household heads only, thus allowing us to control for the characteristics of household heads alone. Panel A of Table 2.4 reports results for the association between financial inclusion and poverty using this sub-sample. The results are consistent with our baseline estimates for financial inclusion reported in Table 2.1.

Next, we examine the robustness of our results to each component of financial inclusion that is used in our multi-dimensional financial inclusion index. Specifically, we examine the effects of access to banks, access to credit and access to insurance on poverty. Panel B of Table 2.5 reports results for the effects for access to banks, while Panel C reports results for access to credit. Panel D reports results for access to insurance. These results are generally consistent with our baseline results and thus the effects of financial inclusion are not sensitive to how financial inclusion is measured. We do, however, find that the association between access to banks and poverty is stronger than the association between either access to credit and insurance and poverty.

The stronger effect of access to banks could be because access to a bank account is considered the first and most important step toward financial inclusion (Sen & De, 2018). Nigeria has pursued a bank-led financial inclusion strategy (Wanga & Schueth, 2018). It is also worth noting that, in our dataset, access to banks also captures household savings, which is a very important aspect of financial inclusion that has been shown to help households finance productive investments in business and human capital, thus ensuring a lasting impact on wellbeing (Karlan, Ratan, & Zinman, 2014).

In our main results, the index of financial inclusion is based on equal weights (i.e., 1/3 each) for the three dimensions of financial inclusion. As a final check, we examine the sensitivity of our results to the use of different weights for the individual dimensions of financial inclusion. Specifically, we run alternating regressions, in which we assign higher weights to each of the three dimensions. Panel E of Table 2.5 reports

Table 2.5 Robustness checks

Variables	(1) PPI score	(2) Deprivation	(3) Poverty line
Panel A: Household head sample			
Financial inclusion	0.065***	−0.055***	−1.133***
	(0.012)	(0.015)	(0.338)
	[0.081]	[−0.046]	[−0.463]
Observations	2953	2953	2953
R-squared	0.643	0.540	−
Panel B: Effects of access to bank			
Financial inclusion	0.054***	−0.058***	−0.883***
	(0.004)	(0.006)	(0.100)
	[0.139]	[−0.102]	[−0.787]
Observations	6352	6352	6352
R-squared	0.653	0.534	−
Panel C: Effects of access to loan			
Financial inclusion	0.027***	−0.013	−0.532***
	(0.007)	(0.010)	(0.174)
	[0.032]	[−0.010]	[−0.218]
Observations	6352	6352	6352
R-squared	0.642	0.527	−
Panel D: Effects of access to insurance			
Financial inclusion	0.064***	−0.029**	−1.037***
	(0.010)	(0.014)	(0.317)
	[0.058]	[−0.018]	[−0.325]
Observations	6352	6352	6352
R-squared	0.645	0.528	−
Panel E: Weights—Bank (1/2), Loan (1/4), Insurance (1/4)			
Financial inclusion	0.061***	−0.041***	−1.153***
	(0.009)	(0.011)	(0.252)
	[0.066]	[−0.030]	[−0.429]
Observations	6352	6352	6352
R-squared	0.645	0.528	−
Panel F: Weights—Bank (1/4), Loan (1/2), Insurance (1/4)			
Financial inclusion	0.054***	−0.052***	−1.036***
	(0.011)	(0.014)	(0.277)
	[0.046]	[−0.031]	[−0.307]
Observations	6352	6352	6352
R-squared	0.644	0.528	−
Panel G: Weights—Bank (1/4), Loan (1/4), Insurance (1/2)			
Financial inclusion	0.069***	−0.024	−1.200***
	(0.012)	(0.015)	(0.413)
	[0.053]	[−0.013]	[−0.318]
Observations	6352	6352	6352
R-squared	0.644	0.527	−

Notes: All regressions include the relevant control variables. Robust standard errors in parentheses. Standardized coefficients in brackets. ***$p < 0.01$, **$p < 0.05$

results for financial inclusion, in which we assign the 'access to banks' dimension a weight of 1/2, and 1/4 each to the other two dimensions. In Panel F, we use a financial inclusion measure in which we assign the 'access to credit' dimension a weight of 1/2, and 1/4 each to the other two dimensions, while in Panel G, we use a financial inclusion measure in which we assign the 'access to insurance' dimension a weight of 1/2, and 1/4 each to the other two dimensions. We find that our results are robust to the assignment of different weight to each dimension.

5   Conclusion

The World Bank has declared universal financial inclusion by 2020 as a strategic priority. Hence, policymakers around the world have prioritized financial sector development and financial inclusion as ways to promote livelihoods and wellbeing. In Nigeria, the government has launched one of Africa's most extensive financial inclusion programs. These efforts have constituted one of the most important ways, through which Nigeria is seeking to meet its national priority of alleviating poverty. To this point, there is very little evidence on the effectiveness of specific financial inclusion programs on facilitating development around the world and no evidence on the relationship between financial inclusion and poverty in Nigeria, or Africa more broadly, despite its obvious policy significance.

Using data from a new nationally representative survey, we examine the effects of financial inclusion on poverty in Nigeria. We find that financial inclusion has contributed to lowering poverty levels. Our results, thus, confirm that well-functioning financial systems that promote access to credit, insurance and banking services, including savings, are likely to benefit poor people. This finding implies that increasing access to financial services and improving service provision and efficiency across poor and vulnerable populations is important to address poverty.

While Nigeria hosts the largest financial inclusion program in Africa, financial inclusion is still lagging behind, given the country's population. In Nigeria, only about 29% of the adult population have opened a bank account, or saved, in order to start a business (Demirguc-Kunt et al., 2018). The slow growth of financial inclusion, relative to Nigeria's population, has been attributed to the choice of pursuing a bank-led model of financial inclusion, which has been based on a weak banking system amid a slow economic recovery from a prolonged recession, caused by low oil prices (Wanga & Schueth, 2018). According to the World Bank, the Nigerian economy contracted for five consecutive quarters between 2016 and 2017 with very high and persistent inflation as well as a highly devalued currency (World Bank, 2018b). High inflation rates, coupled with a devalued currency, suggest that borrowers have to pay high interest rates on loans, while savers are paid rates below inflation. Accordingly, people are inclined to turn away from banks for their financial needs.

Insights from the FII program also suggest that the enforcement of the Bank Verification Number (BVN) system by the Central Bank of Nigeria could be an important factor working against the bank-led financial inclusion model. The BVN requires that each customer links his or her bank account to a biometric system. However, customers, especially in rural areas, have been reluctant to submit to this process and, thus, many account holders no longer use their accounts, rendering several bank accounts inactive or underused. Indeed, statistics from the Nigeria Inter-Bank Settlement System indicate that over 2 million customers ceased to use their accounts with Nigerian banks between 2016 and 2017. Further, statistics from the FII survey shows that while there is a general awareness of the location of banks, there is a lack of awareness of financial point of service (POS) locations in Nigeria and this has impeded the growth of financial inclusion.

Despite these issues, our key finding that financial inclusion alleviates poverty implies that a strengthening of the financial sector, and further emphasis on financial inclusion, will assist with Nigeria's national agenda of poverty alleviation. Our results suggest that Nigeria should adopt strategies that will (1) help strengthen financial inclusion amidst existing economic challenges, (2) promote a multi-system financial inclusion program that goes beyond a bank-led program, (3) promote the knowledge, and usage, of non-bank financial services simultaneously with the usage of banks, and (4) review existing policies that influence the efficacy of the banking sector, such as the BVN, to ensure that such policies do not have undesirable consequences. The implementation, in March 2018, of the new Shared Agent Network Expansion Facilities (SANEF) strategy, which licenses 500,000 mobile money and banking agents across Nigeria to promote financial literacy and provide digital financial services, is an important policy step, and can be developed further in the future to promote financial inclusion nationally. The SANEF program can also be adopted by African countries to expand financial inclusion and assist in fighting poverty across the continent as a whole.

Appendix

Table 2.6 Dimensions, indicators and weights for multi-dimensional poverty

Dimension (weight)	Deprived if... (weight)
Education (1/3)	Household head has less than 5 years of education (1/6)
	Any school age child is not going to school (1/6)
Health (1/3)	Household member needed a doctor but delayed or did not go because of funds in the last 6 months (1/6)
	Household has gone without enough food to eat because of funds in the last 6 months (1/6)
Standard of living (1/3)	The household does not have a refrigerator (1/18)
	The household does not have a stove/gas burner (1/18)
	The household does not have a television (1/18)
	The household does not have an electric fan (1/18)
	The household does not have a chair, stool, bench or table (1/18)
	The household does not have a motorcycle, scooter, motor car or jeep (1/18)

Table 2.7 Dimensions, indicators and weights for multi-dimensional financial inclusion

Dimension (weight)	Financially deprived if...
Bank (1/3)	Household does not have a bank account (bank account includes savings, current, fixed deposit or microfinance account)
Loan/Credit (1/3)	Household does not have access to loan/credit from bank, microfinance institution or other formal institution
Insurance (1/3)	Household does not have access to medical, life, property, unemployment/income or family insurance

Table 2.8 Description and summary statistics of variables

Variable	Description	Mean	SD
PPI score	Poverty Probability Index on a 0 to 1 scale	0.526	0.169
Deprivation	Deprivation score based on multi-dimensional poverty indicators	0.342	0.249
Poverty line	Dummy variable equals 1 if income lived on is less than $2.50 per day	0.589	0.492
Financial inclusion	Dummy variable equals 1 if household financial deprivation score is less than 0.5	0.040	0.184
Bank access	Dummy variable equals 1 if household has access to a bank	0.259	0.439
Loan access	Dummy variable equals 1 if household has access to loan/credit	0.042	0.201
Insurance access	Dummy variable equals 1 if household has access to insurance	0.024	0.154
Household size	Number of people in household	4.192	2.476
Male	Dummy variable equals 1 if household reference person is male	0.529	0.499
Age	Age of household reference person	35.606	15.613
Rural	Dummy variable equals 1 if household lives in rural area	0.719	0.449
Married	Dummy variable equals 1 if household reference person is married	0.586	0.492
Children	Number of children in household	1.775	1.851
Primary	Dummy variable equals 1 if highest level of education of household reference person is primary education	0.182	0.386
Secondary	Dummy variable equals 1 if highest level of education of household reference person is secondary education	0.389	0.487
Tertiary	Dummy variable equals 1 if highest level of education of household reference person is tertiary education	0.136	0.342
Farm land	Dummy variable equals 1 if household owns a farm land	0.343	0.479
Employed	Dummy variable equals 1 if household reference person is employed	0.160	0.367
Self-employed	Dummy variable equals 1 if household reference person is self-employed	0.392	0.488
Christian	Dummy variable equals 1 if household reference person is Christian	0.516	0.499
Muslim	Dummy variable equals 1 if household reference person is Muslim	0.476	0.499
Time to bank	Log of average time taken from residence to nearest financial institution	3.674	0.826

References

Aghion, P., & Bolton, P. (1997). A theory of trickle-down growth and development. *The Review of Economic Studies, 64*(2), 151–172. https://doi.org/10.2307/2971707

Aideyan, O. (2009). Microfinance and poverty reduction in rural Nigeria. *Savings and Development, 33*(3), 293–317.

Alkire, S., & Santos, M. E. (2010). Acute multidimensional poverty: A new index for developing countries. Retrieved March 12, 2018, from https://doi.org/10.2139/ssrn.1815243.

Ang, J. B. (2008). A survey of recent developments in the literature of finance and growth. *Journal of Economic Surveys, 22*(3), 536–576.

Awaworyi Churchill, S., & Nuhu, A. S. (2016). What has failed: Microfinance or evaluation methods? *Journal of Sustainable Finance & Investment, 6*(2), 85–94.

Beck, T., Demirgüç-Kunt, A., & Honohan, P. (2009). Access to financial services: Measurement, impact, and policies. *The World Bank Research Observer, 24*(1), 119–145.

Beck, T., Demirguc-Kunt, A., Laeven, L., & Levine, R. (2008). Finance, firm size, and growth. *Journal of Money, Credit and Banking, 40*(7), 1379–1405.

Beck, T., Demirgüç-Kunt, A., & Levine, R. (2007). Finance, inequality and the poor. *Journal of Economic Growth, 12*(1), 27–49. https://doi.org/10.1007/s10887-007-9010-6

Binswanger, H. P., & Khandker, S. R. (1995). The impact of formal finance on the rural economy of India. *The Journal of Development Studies, 32*(2), 234–262.

Brown, M., Guin, B., & Kirschenmann, K. (2016). Microfinance banks and financial inclusion. *Review of Finance, 20*(3), 907–946. https://doi.org/10.1093/rof/rfv026

Brown, T. T., Martinez-Gutierrez, M. S., & Navab, B. (2014). The impact of changes in county public health expenditures on general health in the population. *Health Economics, Policy and Law, 9*(3), 251–269.

Burgess, R., & Pande, R. (2005). Do rural banks matter? Evidence from the Indian social banking experiment. *American Economic Review, 95*(3), 780–795.

Campello, M., Graham, J. R., & Harvey, C. R. (2010). The real effects of financial constraints: Evidence from a financial crisis. *Journal of Financial Economics, 97*(3), 470–487. https://doi.org/10.1016/j.jfineco.2010.02.009

Central Bank of Nigeria. (2012). *Financial inclusion strategy*. Abuja.

Chauvet, L., & Jacolin, L. (2017). Financial inclusion, bank concentration, and firm performance. *World Development, 97*, 1–13.

Chibba, M. (2009). Financial inclusion, poverty reduction and the millennium development goals. *The European Journal of Development Research, 21*(2), 213–230.

Dang, H., & Rogers, F. (2015). The decision to invest in child quality over quantity: Household size and household investment in Vietnam. *World Bank Economic Review, 30*, 104–142.

Demirgüç-Kunt, A., & Klapper, L. (2012). *Financial inclusion in Africa*. Policy Research Working Paper. The World Bank Development Research Group Finance and Private Sector Development Team, 1–18.

Demirguc-Kunt, A., Klapper, L., & Singer, D. (2017). *Financial inclusion and inclusive growth: A review of recent empirical evidence*. Washington, DC: The World Bank.

Demirguc-Kunt, A., Klapper, L., Singer, D., Ansar, S., & Hess, J. (2018). *The Global Findex Database 2017: Measuring financial inclusion and the fintech revolution*. Washington, DC: The World Bank.

Denny, K., & Oppedisano, V. (2013). The surprising effect of larger class sizes: Evidence using two identification strategies. *Labour Economics, 23*, 57–65. https://doi.org/10.1016/j.labeco.2013.04.004

Dimova, R., & Adebowale, O. (2018). Does access to formal finance matter for welfare and inequality? Micro level evidence from Nigeria. *The Journal of Development Studies, 54*(9), 1534–1550.

Ellis, K., & Lemma, A. (2010). Financial inclusion, household investment and growth in Kenya and Tanzania. *ODI Project Briefing, 43*, 1–4.

Financial Inclusion Insights (FII). (2018). Nigeria. Retrieved from http://finclusion.org/country/africa/nigeria.html.

Frank, R., Levine, A., & Dijk, O. (2014). Expenditure cascades. *Review of Behavioral Economics, 1*(1–2), 55–73.

Galor, O., & Zeira, J. (1993). Income distribution and macroeconomics. *The Review of Economic Studies, 60*(1), 35–52. https://doi.org/10.2307/2297811

Ghosh, S., & Vinod, D. (2017). What constrains financial inclusion for women? Evidence from Indian micro data. *World Development, 92*, 60–81.

Giné, X., & Townsend, R. M. (2004). Evaluation of financial liberalization: A general equilibrium model with constrained occupation choice. *Journal of Development Economics, 74*(2), 269–307. https://doi.org/10.1016/j.jdeveco.2003.03.005

Ibrahim, M., & Alagidede, P. (2017). Nonlinearities in financial development–economic growth nexus: Evidence from sub-Saharan Africa. *Research in International Business and Finance, 46*, 95–104.

Imai, K. S., Gaiha, R., Thapa, G., & Annim, S. K. (2012). Microfinance and poverty—A macro perspective. *World Development, 40*(8), 1675–1689. Retrieved from http://www.sciencedirect.com/science/journal/0305750X/

Karlan, D., Ratan, A. L., & Zinman, J. (2014). Savings by and for the poor: A research review and agenda. *Review of Income and Wealth, 60*(1), 36–78.

Khandker, S. R. (2005). Microfinance and poverty: Evidence using panel data from Bangladesh. *World Bank Economic Review, 19*(2), 263–286.

King, R. G., & Levine, R. (1993). Finance and growth: Schumpeter might be right. *The Quarterly Journal of Economics, 108*(3), 717–737. https://doi.org/10.2307/2118406

Klein, R., & Vella, F. (2010). Estimating a class of triangular simultaneous equations models without exclusion restrictions. *Journal of Econometrics, 154*, 154–164.

Levine, R. (1998). The legal environment, banks, and long-run economic growth. *Journal of Money, Credit and Banking, 30*(3), 596–613. https://doi.org/10.2307/2601259

Levine, R. (2005). Finance and growth: Theory and evidence. In P. Aghion & S. N. Durlauf (Eds.), *Handbook of economic growth* (Vol. 1, pp. 865–934). The Netherlands: Elsevier.

Lewbel, A. (2012). Using heteroscedasticity to identify and estimate mismeasured and endogenous regressor models. *Journal of Business & Economic Statistics, 30*(1), 67–80. https://doi.org/10.1080/07350015.2012.643126

Maertens, M., & Swinnen, J. F. M. (2009). Trade, standards, and poverty: Evidence from Senegal. *World Development, 37*(1), 161–178. https://doi.org/10.1016/j.worlddev.2008.04.006

Mallick, D. (2012). The role of the elasticity of substitution in economic growth: A cross-country investigation. *Labour Economics, 19*(5), 682–694. https://doi.org/10.1016/j.labeco.2012.04.003

Mialou, A., Amidzic, G., & Massara, A. (2017). Assessing countries' financial inclusion standing—A new composite index. *Journal of Banking and Financial Economics, 2*(8), 105–126.

Mishra, V., & Smyth, R. (2015). Estimating returns to schooling in urban China using conventional and heteroskedasticity-based instruments. *Economic Modelling, 47*, 166–173.

Park, C.-Y., & Mercado, R. (2015). *Financial inclusion, poverty, and income inequality in developing Asia.* Asian Development Bank Economics Working Paper Series No. 426.

Rosenbaum, P. R., & Rubin, D. B. (1983). The central role of the propensity score in observational studies for causal effects. *Biometrika, 70*(1), 41–55. https://doi.org/10.2307/2335942

Roser, M., & Ortiz-Ospina, E. (2018). Global extreme poverty. Retrieved from https://ourworldindata.org/extreme-poverty.

Sabia, J. (2007). Early adolescent sex and diminished school attachment: Selection or spllovers? *Southern Economic Journal, 74,* 239–268.

Seck, O., Naiya, I. I., & Muhammad, A. D. (2017). *Effect of financial inclusion on household consumption in Nigeria.* IRTI Working Paper Series WP/2017/03.

Sen, G., & De, S. (2018). How much does having a bank account help the poor? *The Journal of Development Studies, 54*(9), 1551–1571.

Stock, J. H., & Yogo, M. (2005). Testing for weak instruments in linear IV regression. In D. Andrews & J. Stock (Eds.), *Identification and inference for econometric models: Essays in honor of Thomas Rothenberg* (pp. 80–105). Cambridge: Cambridge University Press.

Van Rooyen, C., Stewart, R., & De Wet, T. (2012). The impact of microfinance in sub-Saharan Africa: A systematic review of the evidence. *World Development, 40*(11), 2249–2262.

Wanga, C., & Schueth, S. (2018). In the face of economic headwinds, financial inclusion is declining in Nigeria. Retrieved October 16, 2018, from http://finclusion.org/blog/fii-updates/in-the-face-of-economic-headwinds-financial-inclusion-is-declining-in-nigeria.html.

World Bank. (2018a). Financial inclusion. Retrieved from http://www.worldbank.org/en/topic/financialinclusion/overview.

World Bank. (2018b). The World Bank in Nigeria. Retrieved from http://www.worldbank.org/en/country/nigeria/overview.

World Poverty Clock. (2018). Nigeria. Retrieved October 17, 2018, from https://worldpoverty.io/.

Xue, S. (2018). Does contact improve attitudes towards migrants in China? *Economics of Transition, 26,* 149–200.

Zhang, Q. (2017). Does microfinance reduce poverty? Some international evidence. *The BE Journal of Macroeconomics, 17*(2), 1–13.

Zhang, Q., & Posso, A. (2019). Thinking inside the box: A closer look at financial inclusion and household income. *The Journal of Development Studies, 55*(7), 1616–1631.

3

Adoption of Mobile Money for Healthcare Utilization and Spending in Rural Ghana

Chei Bukari and Isaac Koomson

1 Introduction

Healthcare utilization and spending are lower among rural households. This is largely due to the high costs associated with health expenditure and also because rural households are poorer and face higher levels of financial exclusion (Attia-Konan, Oga, Touré, & Kouadio, 2019; Demirgüç-Kunt, Klapper, Singer, Ansar, & Hess, 2018; Koomson, Annim, & Peprah, 2016;

_____

C. Bukari (✉)
Department of Applied Economics, School of Economics, University of Cape Coast, Cape Coast, Ghana

I. Koomson
UNE Business School, Faculty of Science, Agriculture, Business and Law, University of New England, Armidale, NSW, Australia

Network for Socioeconomic Research and Advancement (NESRA), Accra, Ghana
e-mail: ikoomso2@une.edu.au

© The Author(s) 2020
S. Awaworyi Churchill (ed.), *Moving from the Millennium to the Sustainable Development Goals*, https://doi.org/10.1007/978-981-15-1556-9_3

Kumar et al., 2011; Singh et al., 2018). Studies have also shown that the effects of lower health spending are more severe for rural, female-headed and uninsured households (Dhak, 2015; Mohanty et al., 2017).

Financial inclusion remains an avenue for households to obtain funds to spend on healthcare, but despite the reported improvement in financial inclusion globally, limited progress has been made in various areas across developing countries (Demirgüç-Kunt et al., 2018; Koomson, Villano, & Hadley, 2020a). For instance, there is a rural-urban gap in financial inclusion, while the gender gap in financial inclusion could be narrower (Koomson, Villano, & Hadley, 2020b). Mobile money is argued to present an opportunity to reduce the gap for rural households and for women who have lower access to formal financial services (Demirgüç-Kunt et al., 2018; Donovan, 2012). Mobile-based financial services are quickly closing the financial inclusion gap with a billion of the unbanked now having access to a mobile phone (Pénicaud & Katakam, 2019). With the progress in financial inclusion largely attributed to the surge in mobile money activities (Demirgüç-Kunt et al., 2018), the adoption of mobile money accounts by rural households is expected to enhance their healthcare utilization and spending.

Although some of the United Nations' Sustainable Development Goals (SDGs) have health-related targets, one goal, SDG 3, focuses specifically on ensuring healthy lives and promoting well-being for all at all ages. Specifically, target 3.8 of SDG 3—achieving universal health coverage (UHC), including financial risk protection, access to quality essential healthcare services, and access to safe, effective, quality and affordable essential medicines and vaccines for all—is the key to attaining the entire goal as well as the health-related targets of other SDGs (World Bank, 2017; World Health Organization, 2017). Target 3.8 has two indicators—3.8.1 on access to essential health services and 3.8.2 on the proportion of a country's population with catastrophic spending on health, defined as large household expenditure on health as a share of household total consumption or income. To obtain a clearer picture of those who are constrained in their spending and access to healthcare, it is important to simultaneously examine both healthcare utilization and spending in a single study.

Unlike, the Millennium Development Goals, the SDGs are emphatic about the role of financial services in achieving these goals. This gives credence to financial services as a powerful tool for promoting empowerment, security, opportunity and equity which accelerate households' access to good health (Asongu, 2013, 2015; Prokopenko & Holden, 2001). Of great concern is the global evidence of 2.5 billion people who are "unbanked" and lack access to formal financial services (Haas, Heymann, Riley, & Taddese, 2013). As a potential panacea to financial exclusion, mobile financial services now cover more than 60 percent of developing markets, reaching an estimated 299 million registered mobile money users, of which 103 million are estimated to be active (Pénicaud & Katakam, 2019). The value of total mobile money transactions grew by 21 percent from $26 billion in December 2016 to over $31.5 billion in December 2017. The percentage of providers who offer mobile money through a smartphone app has also increased from 56 percent in 2015 to 73 percent as of June 2017 (GSMA, 2017). Thus, there are now about 255 mobile money service platforms across 89 countries including Ghana and this has heightened competition in the financial markets leading to a corresponding piqued interest from a growing number of mobile network operators (MNOs). Along gender and location dimensions, "rural and female customers remain two of the hardest to reach groups and thus two of the most untapped commercial opportunities for mobile money providers" (GSMA, 2017, p. 12).

This chapter examines the effect of mobile money account adoption on healthcare utilization and spending in rural households. The differential effect of the expected outcome is also investigated for male- and female-headed households using sub-samples. The sub-sample analysis aligns with the aim of the SDG that seeks to "leave no one behind" and thus, advocates for indicators to be disaggregated by income, sex, age, race, ethnicity, disability, location and migratory status, wherever data allow (World Health Organization, 2016). The chapter expands the knowledge base on the link between mobile money and healthcare utilization and spending, while establishing the gender and location-specific effect of mobile money adoption to engender evidence-based policy debates.

The remaining sections of this chapter are structured as follows: Sect. 2 reviews the literature on mobile phone penetration, mobile money adoption and healthcare utilization and spending. The methodology, discussed in Sect. 3, includes data source, measurement of key variables and estimation technique. The analysis and discussion are presented in Sect. 4. Section 5 concludes with some policy recommendations.

2   Literature Review

Mobile Phone Penetration

Mobile phone usage is undoubtedly one of the fastest-spreading techno-logical innovations of the twenty-first century. From 2000 to 2018, mobile phone subscriptions increased by more than 1500 percent in low- and middle-income countries—from 4 to 72 subscriptions per 100 inhabitants. This notwithstanding, there is a 10 percent gender gap in the ownership of mobile phones (Burjorjee & Bin-Humam, 2018). In sub-Saharan Africa (SSA), there is a 14 percent and 38 percent gender gap in the ownership and use of mobile phones, respectively, with women hav-ing the lower percentage share (Burjorjee & Bin-Humam, 2018; Rowntree, 2018). As access to mobile phones multiplies in developing markets, money transfer systems based on mobile money are being lever-aged to tackle development challenges across many different sectors, including agriculture, education, finance, and most importantly, health (Pénicaud & Katakam, 2019). Mobile money consists of financial trans-actions that are conducted using a mobile phone, where value is stored virtually (e-money) in an account associated with a SIM card. Individuals can deposit cash onto a mobile account, make transactions between accounts, and withdraw funds as cash. Mobile money transactions are compatible with basic phones and do not require internet access (Pénicaud & Katakam, 2019).

Like mobile phone ownership, mobile money is growing rapidly as a substitute for cash in both developed and developing countries (Flood, West, & Wheadon, 2013). More than 70 countries have imple-mented mobile money platforms as alternatives to traditional cash payment systems or formal financial services, the majority of which are located in sub-Saharan Africa. These systems enable funds to be depos-ited, transferred and withdrawn electronically through mobile money accounts, bringing financial services to the previously under-banked (Demirgüç-Kunt et al., 2018; Kendall, Schiff, & Smadja, 2013; Rowntree, 2018)

Mobile Money Adoption and Healthcare

Notwithstanding the recent proliferation of mobile phone usage and uptake of mobile money in emerging markets, its use in the health sector remains limited and often, has not been brought to scale (Pénicaud & Katakam, 2019). While mobile money can provide a means for improving efficiency by enabling households to easily pay for healthcare fees and health insurance premiums, receive monies at low transaction cost from family, friends and co-workers to meet their health emergency needs, its adoption has been low (Haas et al., 2013). This notwithstanding, evidence from the literature depicts a bigger focus on diffusion of mobile money from the supply-side rather than household and individual adoptions (Baliamoune-Lutz, 2003; Donner, 2008; Donner & Tellez, 2008; Kshetri & Cheung, 2002).

Regarding households, mobile money is often the means of payment for services at health facilities, drugs at pharmacies, health service vouchers and insurance premiums where available, and for transport to access treatment (Asongu, 2013, 2015; Haas et al., 2013; Ky, Rugemintwari, & Sauviat, 2017; Suri, Jack, & Stoker, 2012). In response, regulators are now establishing more enabling regulatory framework for the provision of these mobile money services. Several countries including Colombia, India, Kenya and Liberia have undergone financial reforms in that regard. For instance, recently, in 47 out of 89 markets where mobile money is available, regulation allows both banks and non-banks to provide mobile money services in a sustainable way (Pénicaud & Katakam, 2019). Recognizing the potential of mobile-based financial services in bridging the financial inclusion gap and promoting good health and well-being, the SDGs are committed to accelerating the adoption and uptake of mobile money. This is due to its potential to increase financial inclusion, root out corruption, mitigate financial risk, and provide economic benefits to individuals and households (GSMA, 2014, 2017, 2018; Kendall et al., 2013; Mitręga-Niestrój, Puszer, & Szewczyk, 2018; Rowntree, 2018).

Mobile-based service providers are now expanding into neighboring markets for mobile financial services by leveraging their strengths in mobile money to provide mobile insurance, mobile savings and mobile credit to customers who were previously financially excluded. To these unbanked, mobile money provides their financial service needs and empowers them to easily pay for services at health facilities, drugs at pharmacies, transportation and insurance premiums (Ahmed & Cowan, 2019; Haas et al., 2013; Ky et al., 2017). On another note, mobile money not only allows one to easily pay for healthcare costs but also facilitates receipt of financial support from family, co-workers and friends at low transaction costs and risks in cases of health emergencies (Asongu, 2013, 2015; Haas et al., 2013). Beyond these benefits, mobile technologies are increasingly being used to enhance access to insurance, credit products and savings facilities to the underserved. This results in the deepening of the social and economic impact of mobile money in their lives (GSMA, 2014, 2017, 2018; Kendall et al., 2013). Mobile money adoption is similarly narrowing the rural-urban gap owing to its rapid increase in rural penetration and digitization along agricultural value chains. About 15 percent of rural farmers receive cash payments from the sale of agricultural products and mobile money has reduced the risks, inefficiencies and inconveniencies in these payments. Classical examples are Ghana, Kenya and Zambia where the share of farmers receiving cash payments is twice the average for developing economies and where about 40 percent receive these payments into majority mobile money registered accounts (Demirgüç-Kunt et al., 2018).

3   Data

The chapter uses data from the seventh round of the Ghana Living Standards Survey (GLSS 7). The GLSS 7 is a nationally representative survey conducted by the Ghana Statistical Service from October 2016 to October 2017, with a two-stage stratified sampling method. In the first stage, 1200 Enumeration Areas (EAs) were selected from the 10 regions in Ghana, using probability proportional to the population sizes. The second stage involved the selection of the 18,000 households from the 1200 EAs. However, 14,009 households were completely interviewed. Table 3.1 shows the distribution of sample by location and gender of the household head. Out of the total number of households interviewed,

Table 3.1 Sample composition of GLSS 7

	Total	Male	Female	Rural	Urban
Number of EAs	1200	–	–	655	545
Number of households	14,009	9643	4366	7991	6018

Note: For number of households, male and female refer to male-headed and female-headed households

6018 and 7991 are from urban and rural areas, respectively. Also, 68.83 percent of these households (9643) were headed by men with the remaining heads being women (GSS, 2018). In line with the focus of this chapter, the 7991 rural households form the target sample for this study.

The GLSS 7 used five main questionnaires namely household; non-farm household; governance, peace and security; prices of food and non-food items; and community. In this chapter, we use responses from the household questionnaire, which solicits information on demographic characteristics; education and skills training; health and fertility behavior; employment and time use of respondents; among others (GSS, 2018). The GLSS 7 also contains a section on households' access to financial services such as mobile money, credit, micro-insurance, savings and remittance, as well as their use of financial services. This makes the GLSS 7 an ideal dataset for this chapter.

Measurement of Healthcare Utilization

Consistent with the literature, we measured healthcare utilization as the number of household members that consulted a health practitioner or visited a health facility within the past two weeks before the survey (Arcury, Preisser, Gesler, & Powers, 2005; Carrasquillo, 2013). According to Carrasquillo (2013), healthcare utilization refers to the use of health-care services and can be measured as the number of health services used over a period of time divided by a population denominator (e.g. per 1000 persons). It can also be defined as the percentage of persons who use a certain service over individuals eligible for that service in a period of time (e.g. in the last three years) or an aggregate number without a denomination (Carrasquillo, 2013). Arcury et al. (2005) measured healthcare utilization as combined visits to practitioners and facilities, separately determined for chronic care and regular check-up care visits in the year prior to the interview. Evidence from the GLSS survey shows that the proportion of injured/ill that utilized healthcare had declined between 2012/2013 and 2016/2017, and this was more pronounced in the rural areas (GSS, 2018).

Health Spending

Health spending is measured as the total health expenditure of the household, which mainly covers expenses on medical products/appliances, outpatient services and hospital services. These dimensions have formed the core of total healthcare expenditure assessment in the GLSS (GSS, 2014).

Empirical Model Specification and Estimation Technique

The extant literature holds that, rural households' healthcare utilization and spending are influenced by household characteristics, including adoption of mobile money accounts, household size and location; age and educational level of household head among other factors (Adaba, Ayoung, & Abbott, 2019; Azzani, Roslani, & Su, 2019; Mojumdar, 2018; Mothobi & Grzybowski, 2017).

The empirical model to be estimated is specified as;

$$Y_i = \alpha + \beta Z_i + \gamma X_i + \varepsilon_i, \tag{3.1}$$

where Y_i is healthcare utilization or spending by household i. Healthcare utilization is a count of the number of household members that consulted a health practitioner or visited a health facility, while health spending captures total household health expenditure. Z refers to the ownership of mobile money account, defined as a binary variable which is 1 if a household head adopts mobile money account and 0 otherwise. X is a vector of household characteristics that affect household healthcare utilization and spending including the age, employment status, education and marital status of the household head, as well as the size of the household. α, β and γ are parameters to be estimated, while ε_i is a random error term. Appendix 1 presents definitions and measurement of these variables, while Appendix 2 gives their descriptive statistics.

A key methodological issue addressed in this chapter is the potential endogeneity of mobile money adoption (Abor, Amidu, & Issahaku, 2018; Munyegera & Matsumoto, 2016). Endogeneity is likely to arise for a number of reasons and, in this chapter, it is likely to emanate from reverse causality. For instance, households may adopt mobile money when they expect to electronically pay National Health Insurance Scheme (NHIS) premiums as is often the case in Ghana where households now renew their NHIS cards through mobile money. In this case, it is the nature of healthcare utilization or spending that is driving mobile money adoption. On the other hand, adoption of mobile money accounts enable households to easily save and pay for healthcare costs; and receive (send) mobile money support from (to) families, co-workers and friends at low transaction cost and risk in cases of health emergencies (Asongu, 2013, 2015; Haas et al., 2013). Measurement errors and omitted variable bias are also likely. To address this potential endogeneity, we use distance to a mobile network (Abor et al., 2018) and mobile phone penetration as instruments (Aker & Mbiti, 2010) in a two-stage least squares (2SLS) estimation. We assumed that distance to a mobile network directly affects the ownership of a mobile phone, and thus adoption of mobile money by the household, but not the household's healthcare utilization. On the other hand, we assume that mobile penetration will positively influence the ownership and adoption of mobile money by the household but not the household's healthcare utilization. We expect that the only channels through which distance to a mobile network or mobile phone penetration will influence healthcare utilization or spending is mobile money.

4 Analysis and Discussion

Figure 3.1 depicts the association between adoption of mobile money and payment of National Health Insurance Scheme (NHIS) Premiums. In general, the chi-square test indicates a statistically significant

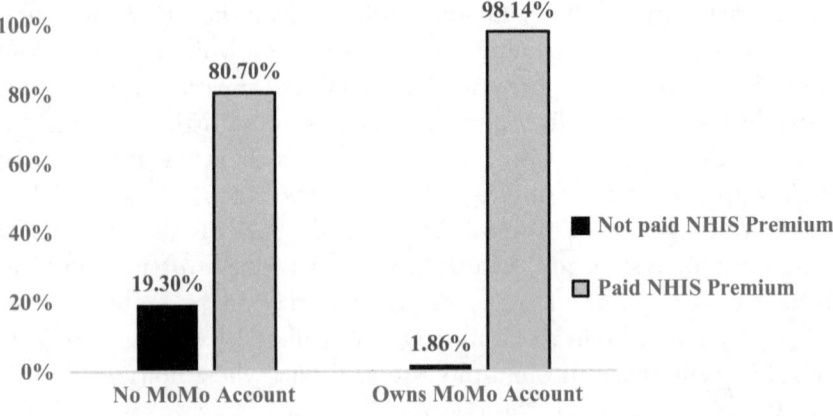

Pearson chi2(1) =   5.699   Pr = 0.017

Fig. 3.1 Chi-Square analysis of mobile money account ownership and NHIS premiums. MoMo: mobile money

association between mobile money adoption and payment of NHIS premiums (alpha level of 5 percent). We see that both adopters and non-adopters of mobile money possess some level of capacity to pay for NHIS premiums, but the proportion of adopters who have paid are about 17 percent more than non-adopters. The implication is that owning a mobile money account enables the household to honor NHIS premium payments.

The estimated link between adoption of mobile money and healthcare utilization is presented in Table 3.2. Both ordinary least squares (OLS) and 2SLS estimates are presented, but emphasis is placed on the 2SLS estimates. This is due to the endogenous nature of mobile money adoption (see results of Hausman test under the last five rows of Tables 3.2 and 3.3). The OLS estimates indicate that households that adopt mobile money are 9.6 percentage points more likely to utilize healthcare. The first stage results also show that distance to a mobile network and mobile phone penetration are strong drivers of mobile money adoption. While distance to a mobile network negatively affects the use of mobile money, mobile phone penetration promotes mobile money adoption. This finding is consistent with the existing literature (Abor et al., 2018; Aker &

Table 3.2 Effect mobile money adoption on healthcare utilization

Healthcare utilization	Full		Male		Female	
	OLS	2SLS	OLS	2SLS	OLS	2SLS
Adoption of mobile money account	0.096*	0.310***	0.106	0.289***	0.057	0.620**
	(0.058)	(0.367)	(0.074)	(0.412)	(0.094)	(0.705)
NHIS	0.266***	0.441***	0.301***	0.338***	0.224**	0.503***
	(0.057)	(0.075)	(0.076)	(0.100)	(0.089)	(0.111)
Expected benefits from NHIS	0.131**	0.068***	0.126***	0.024**	0.050*	0.079***
	(0.057)	(0.020)	(0.022)	(0.015)	(0.030)	(0.028)
Male	0.106***	−0.128**				
	(0.016)	(0.188)				
Household size	0.011	0.111**	0.036***	0.142*	0.034**	0.023**
	(0.009)	(0.055)	(0.011)	(0.102)	(0.015)	(0.037)
Marital status (base = never married)						
Married	0.143**	0.156**	0.027	0.143**	0.325**	0.240**
	(0.085)	(0.010)	(0.111)	(0.137)	(0.135)	(0.156)
Consensual	−0.176*	0.040	−0.224	0.139	−0.114	−0.079
	(0.102)	(0.127)	(0.138)	(0.181)	(0.156)	(0.175)
Separated	0.067	0.182	−0.037	0.180	0.224	0.186
	(0.120)	(0.143)	(0.215)	(0.267)	(0.154)	(0.175)
Divorced	−0.099	0.195	0.051	0.578*	−0.005	0.099
	(0.116)	(0.147)	(0.245)	(0.320)	(0.146)	(0.170)
Widowed	0.155	0.282**	−0.045	0.353	0.295**	0.255*
	(0.099)	(0.119)	(0.184)	(0.237)	(0.134)	(0.153)

(continued)

Table 3.2 (continued)

Healthcare utilization	Full		Male		Female	
	OLS	2SLS	OLS	2SLS	OLS	2SLS
Education (base = no education)						
Basic Education Certificate Examination (BECE)	-0.220***	-0.201**	-0.286***	-0.167	-0.123	-0.219*
	(0.072)	(0.084)	(0.094)	(0.117)	(0.111)	(0.131)
Middle School Leaving Certificate (MSLC)	-0.325***	-0.166**	-0.401***	-0.141	-0.149	-0.138
	(0.060)	(0.077)	(0.076)	(0.105)	(0.103)	(0.116)
SSS/Secondary	0.007	-0.089	-0.040	-0.075	0.030	-0.173
	(0.093)	(0.111)	(0.108)	(0.132)	(0.199)	(0.241)
Voc/Tech/Teacher	0.128	0.154	0.061	0.191	0.243	0.101
	(0.101)	(0.119)	(0.124)	(0.153)	(0.180)	(0.210)
Tertiary	-0.160**	-0.251**	-0.275*	-0.238***	0.562	-0.032***
	(0.135)	(0.161)	(0.151)	(0.184)	(0.408)	(0.524)
Employment (base = public employee)						
Private employee	0.007	0.109	-0.028	0.117	0.076	0.095
	(0.111)	(0.133)	(0.132)	(0.163)	(0.219)	(0.245)
Self-employed (non-agriculture)	0.001	-0.074	0.048	-0.031	-0.012	-0.141
	(0.109)	(0.129)	(0.144)	(0.176)	(0.194)	(0.224)
Self-employed (agriculture)	-0.039	0.042	-0.053	0.086	-0.026	-0.061
	(0.104)	(0.123)	(0.124)	(0.153)	(0.197)	(0.221)
Unemployed	0.260**	0.157	0.320**	0.137	0.211	0.136
	(0.120)	(0.144)	(0.154)	(0.191)	(0.209)	(0.238)
Retired	-0.097	0.084	-0.049	0.096		
	(0.331)	(0.392)	(0.345)	(0.421)		
Constant	0.739***	0.158	0.938***	-0.001	0.669***	0.452
	(0.145)	(0.202)	(0.180)	(0.281)	(0.248)	(0.294)

First stage

Distance to mobile network		−0.004**		−0.004**		−0.034**
		(0.002)		(0.002)		(0.002)
Mobile phone penetration		0.020**		0.107**		0.062**
		(0.106)		(0.100)		(0.073)
Observations	2050	2050	1193	1,187	857	857
R-squared	0.079	−0.292	0.095	−0.372	0.069	−0.191
Hausman		7.40		5.81		10.1
		(0.000)		(0.005)		(0.015)
Under identification test		6.95		4.71		4.99
		(0.030)		(0.040)		(0.036)
Weak identification test (Cragg-Donald Wald *F* statistic)		36.96		13.450		21.975
Stock-Yogo weak ID test critical values: 10% maximal IV size		19.93		19.93		19.93
Sargan statistic (over identification test of all instruments)		3.40		0.56		9.88
		(0.065)		(0.554)		(0.170)

Notes: Standard errors in parentheses. ***p < 0.01, **p < 0.05, *p < 0.1

Table 3.3 Effect of mobile money adoption on household total health expenditure

log(Health expenditure)	Full		Male		Female	
	OLS	2SLS	OLS	2SLS	OLS	2SLS
Ownership of mobile money account	0.685***	0.317***	0.465***	0.610**	0.104***	0.805***
	(0.073)	(0.998)	(0.090)	(1.314)	(0.124)	(1.465)
NHIS	−0.327***	−0.345***	−0.153*	−0.177*	−0.678***	−0.647***
	(0.065)	(0.081)	(0.080)	(0.101)	(0.112)	(0.131)
Expected benefits from NHIS	0.011	0.014**	0.029	0.035**	−0.021	0.026***
	(0.019)	(0.021)	(0.023)	(0.027)	(0.031)	(0.033)
Male (ref = female)	0.018**	0.042**				
	(0.261)	(0.070)				
Household size	−0.007	−0.004***	−0.005	−0.000***		−0.017**
	(0.001)	(0.011)	(0.011)	(0.014)		(0.021)
Marital status (base = never married)						
Married	0.208**	0.197**	0.179	0.154**	0.252	0.242**
	(0.105)	(0.109)	(0.130)	(0.146)	(0.188)	(0.190)
Consensual	0.147	0.130	0.309*	0.273	−0.146	−0.146
	(0.138)	(0.146)	(0.175)	(0.199)	(0.229)	(0.230)
Separated	0.192	0.188	0.518**	0.499*	0.032	0.013
	(0.156)	(0.156)	(0.261)	(0.266)	(0.218)	(0.223)
Divorced	0.344**	0.311*	0.364	0.296	0.346*	0.378*
	(0.149)	(0.173)	(0.278)	(0.330)	(0.209)	(0.221)
Widowed	0.216*	0.196	0.195	0.151	0.215	0.227
	(0.119)	(0.130)	(0.214)	(0.243)	(0.186)	(0.189)
Education (base = no education)						
BECE	−0.076	−0.048	−0.081	−0.049	−0.073	−0.139
	(0.095)	(0.120)	(0.116)	(0.144)	(0.164)	(0.214)
MSLC	−0.032	−0.021	−0.031	−0.019	−0.112	−0.148
	(0.078)	(0.083)	(0.092)	(0.097)	(0.152)	(0.169)

	(1)	(2)	(3)	(4)	(5)	(6)
SSS/Secondary	−0.397*** (0.116)	−0.362** (0.150)	−0.412*** (0.128)	−0.367** (0.174)	−0.298 (0.281)	−0.375** (0.325)
Voc/Tech/Teacher	−0.158 (0.128)	−0.138 (0.139)	−0.133 (0.148)	−0.113 (0.157)	−0.307 (0.254)	−0.382 (0.299)
Tertiary	−0.288** (0.176)	−0.241** (0.218)	−0.344* (0.189)	−0.291** (0.233)	0.481 (0.529)	0.292** (0.661)
Employment (base = public employee)						
Private employee	0.007 (0.141)	0.009 (0.141)	0.026 (0.159)	0.024 (0.159)	−0.117 (0.304)	−0.143 (0.310)
Self-employed (non-agriculture)	−0.029 (0.139)	−0.006 (0.152)	−0.010 (0.176)	0.023 (0.196)	−0.173 (0.268)	−0.243 (0.306)
Self-employed (agriculture)	0.068 (0.129)	0.063 (0.130)	0.127 (0.147)	0.112 (0.153)	−0.160 (0.268)	−0.188 (0.276)
Unemployed	0.001 (0.143)	0.003 (0.143)	0.115 (0.170)	0.117 (0.170)	−0.250 (0.277)	−0.275 (0.283)
Retired	0.647 (0.413)	0.634 (0.414)	0.705* (0.415)	0.688 (0.419)		
Constant	0.555*** (0.178)	0.616** (0.243)	0.364* (0.210)	0.465 (0.336)	1.079*** (0.342)	1.021*** (0.364)
First stage						
Distance to mobile network		−0.003*** (0.001)		−0.002** (0.001)		−0.004** (0.002)
Mobile phone penetration		0.139*** (0.043)		0.139** (0.054)		0.144** (0.070)
Observations	3,426	3,426	2,170	2,170	1,256	1,256
R-squared	0.439	0.434	0.418	0.409	0.491	0.478
Hausman		8.11 (0.000)		5.41 (0.030)		11.3 (0.020)

(continued)

Table 3.3 (continued)

log(Health expenditure)	Full		Male		Female	
	OLS	2SLS	OLS	2SLS	OLS	2SLS
Under identification test		18.28		10.16		9.03
		(0.000)		(0.000)		(0.010)
Weak identification test (Cragg-Donald Wald F statistic)		11.131		15.053		14.477
Stock-Yogo weak ID test critical values: 10% maximal IV size		19.93		19.93		19.93
Sargan statistic (over identification test of all instruments)		3.73		7.84		0.83
		(0.054)		(0.576)		(0.364)

Notes: Standard errors in parentheses. ***$p < 0.01$, **$p < 0.05$, *$p < 0.1$

Mbiti, 2010; Munyegera & Matsumoto, 2016). The Cragg-Donald Wald F statistics displayed in Table 3.2 are significant at the 5 percent level and imply that our instruments satisfy the relevance condition of not being weakly correlated with mobile money adoption (Stock & Yogo, 2002). The 2SLS results suggest that the endogeneity of mobile money adoption results in a downward bias in the OLS estimates because the 2SLS estimates are relatively bigger than the OLS estimates. In specific terms, households that adopt mobile money are 31 percentage points more likely to utilize healthcare. In male-headed households, adopters of mobile money accounts are about 29 percentage points more likely to utilize healthcare, while this outcome is 62 percentage points in rural-headed households. Some potential explanation offered in the literature indicate that adoption of mobile money accounts enables households to save and also receive remittance from relatives to be channeled into investments in healthcare (Haas et al., 2013; Ky et al., 2017). Unlike formal financial services, mobile money accounts are less biased against women so it gives females greater access to finance to take advantage of economic opportunities, which go a long way to increase their incomes, and, consequently, healthcare utilization. It can also be related to how adoption of mobile money expedites the receipts of monies from family members, friends, workmates or other acquaintances to help with health emergencies.

Apart from mobile money adoption, owners of NHIS policies are 44 percentage points more likely to utilize healthcare and this outcome is more pronounced in female-headed households that experience a 16.5 percentage-points higher likelihood. The implication is that the effect of NHIS on healthcare utilization is more positive among females than males. Household heads who expect to benefit from NHIS are 6.8 percentage points more likely to utilize healthcare and this outcome is about 5.5 percentage points higher among female- than male-headed households. Male-headed households' healthcare utilization is 12.8 percentage points lower than that of female-headed households, which, in other words, implies that female-headed households utilize healthcare more compared to male-headed ones. Other control variables like marital status and educational level of the household head have significant association with household healthcare utilization.

Table 3.3 presents results on the effect of mobile money on health spending. Again, the OLS estimates show that households that adopt mobile money spend 68.5 percentage points more on healthcare, while the first state regressions also indicate that the instruments are significant drivers of mobile money adoption. Since the Cragg-Donald Wald F statistics are all significant at the 10 percent level, we conclude that the instruments are not weakly correlated with mobile money adoption (Stock & Yogo, 2002). Unlike the case of healthcare utilization, the 2SLS results reveal that the endogeneity of mobile money adoption results in an upward bias in the OLS estimates in the full model while it leads to a downward bias in the male and female sub-sample estimates. Generally, household heads who adopt mobile money spend 31.7 percentage points more on healthcare. Across male-headed households, adopters of mobile money accounts spend 61 percentage points more than non-adopters while, in female-headed households, adopters spend 80.5 percentage points more. Adoption of mobile money enhances the capacity of households to spend more on utilization of healthcare services in terms of visit to clinics, consultations and medical expenses compared to non-adopters of mobile money (Ahmed & Cowan, 2019).

Beyond mobile adoption, health expenses are 34.5 percentage points lower for households that have NHIS and this healthcare expenditure-reducing effect of having NHIS is about 47 percentage points higher in female- than male-headed households. This is an indication that, in terms of healthcare spending, female-headed households benefit more from NHIS than male-headed households. Relative to those that have never been married, health expenditure for married household heads is 19.7 percentage points higher and this outcome is more pronounced for married female heads. Household health expenses are 36.2 and 24.1 percentage points lower among heads who have obtained secondary and tertiary education respectively, compared to heads who have had no formal education. This means that, having access to formal education exposes the individual to healthy life styles leading to a significant reduction in health expenditures.

5 Conclusion and Recommendation

Despite an upsurge in the ownership of mobile phone and use of mobile money services in developing countries, its health benefits remain limited and has often not been scaled up. Adoption of mobile money can provide a means for improving efficiency by enabling households to easily pay for healthcare fees, NHIS premiums and receive money with low transaction cost to meet their health needs. These benefits notwithstanding, mobile money providers identify rural households and female customers as the least beneficiaries (GSMA, 2017, p. 12). Beyond these gaps, SDG 3 focuses specifically on ensuring healthy lives and promoting well-being for all at all ages through universal health coverage (UHC). This includes financial risk protection, access to quality essential healthcare services and access to safe, effective, quality and affordable essential medicines and vaccines for all. Premised on these, this chapter examined the effect of mobile money account adoption on healthcare utilization and spending in rural households. The differential effect of the expected outcome is also investigated for male- and female-headed households using sub-sampled models. The sub-sample analysis aligns with the aim of the SDG to "leave no one behind" and thus, advocates for indicators to be disaggregated by income, sex, age, race, ethnicity, disability, location and migratory status, wherever data allow.

Addressing the potential endogeneity associated with mobile money, the findings from this chapter show that (i) mobile money adoption enhances rural household healthcare utilization and has a bigger effect in female-headed households and (ii) mobile money improves rural households' ability to spend on healthcare and this benefit is experienced more by female-headed households. Regarding policy, there is a need to strengthen the fundamentals and adopt best practices to improve the quality of mobile money services to serve a broader ecosystem of users. Providers of mobile financial services should engage with regulators and standard setting bodies to create more enabling regulatory environments to allow these services to flourish and foster sustainable investment in the services that underpin a strong digital financial ecosystem. Government policy could be aimed at regulating the mobile financial sector to optimize the sector's potential contribution to universal financial inclusion.

Appendix 1

Table 3.4 Definition and measurement of variables

Variable	Type	Definition/measurement	A priori sign
Total health expenditure	Continuous	Total household health expenditure	
Healthcare utilization	Count	Number of household members that consulted a health practitioner or visited a health facility	
Mobile money adoption	Dummy	mobile money = 1 if a household owns mobile money account and zero if otherwise	+
NHIS	Dummy	NHIS = 1 if a household members have valid NHIS cards and zero if otherwise	+
Savings (S)	Dummy	Savings = 1 if a household have savings account, susu scheme, fixed deposit account and investment account except current account and zero if otherwise	+
Age	Continuous	Age of the household head	
Dep	Continuous	Dependents (<18 + >60 years)	–
Hhsize	Continuous	Household size	–
Male	Dummy	Sex of household head	+
Urban	Dummy	Place of residence whether urban or rural	+
Expected benefits from NHIS	Dummy	1 if a household members expected benefits and zero if otherwise	+/–
HHEdL	Categorical	Level of education of the Household head	+
HHEMPL	Categorical	Employment status of the Household head	+
Marital status	Dummy	Marital status of the Household head	+
Distance to mobile network	Continuous		+
Mobile phone penetration	Continuous		

Notes: Healthcare utilization total household health expenditure is dependent variable. All other variables are independent variables

Appendix 2

Table 3.5 Descriptive statistics of the variables used

Variable	Obs	Mean	SD	Min	Max
Total health expenditure	4665	94.6702	364.0748	0	10,307.6
Access to healthcare	4665	1.282	0.960	0	6.401
Mobile money	4665	0.181	0.385	0	1
Distance to mobile network	4665	8.835	5.732	0.6	28.1
Mobile phone penetration	4665	0.827	0.117	0.419	1
NHIS	4665	0.864	0.343	0	1
Male	4665	0.574	0.495	0	1
Expected benefits from NHIS	4665	2.737	1.344	0	6
Marital status	4665	1.903	1.663	0	5
Employment status	4665	3.371	1.910	0	7
Household size	4665	3.795	2.555	1	19

References

Abor, J. Y., Amidu, M., & Issahaku, H. (2018). Mobile telephony, financial inclusion and inclusive growth. *Journal of African Business, 19*(3), 430–453.

Adaba, G. B., Ayoung, D. A., & Abbott, P. (2019). Exploring the contribution of mobile money to well-being from a capability perspective. *The Electronic Journal of Information Systems in Developing Countries, 85*(4), e12079.

Ahmed, H., & Cowan, B. W. (2019). *Mobile money and healthcare use: Evidence from East Africa.* National Bureau of Economic Research.

Aker, J. C., & Mbiti, I. M. (2010). Mobile phones and economic development in Africa. *Journal of Economic Perspectives, 24*(3), 207–232.

Arcury, T. A., Preisser, J. S., Gesler, W. M., & Powers, J. M. (2005). Access to transportation and health care utilization in a rural region. *The Journal of Rural Health, 21*(1), 31–38.

Asongu, S. (2013). *Mobile banking and mobile phone penetration: Which is more pro-poor in Africa?* African Governance and Development Institute WP/13/033.

Asongu, S. (2015). The impact of mobile phone penetration on African inequality. *International Journal of Social Economics, 42*(8), 706–716.

Attia-Konan, A. R., Oga, A. S. S., Touré, A., & Kouadio, K. L. (2019). Distribution of out of pocket health expenditures in a sub-Saharan Africa country: Evidence from the national survey of household standard of living, Côte d'Ivoire. *BMC Research Notes, 12*(1), 25.

Azzani, M., Roslani, A. C., & Su, T. T. (2019). Determinants of household catastrophic health expenditure: A systematic review. *The Malaysian Journal of Medical Sciences: MJMS, 26*(1), 15.

Baliamoune-Lutz, M. (2003). An analysis of the determinants and effects of ICT diffusion in developing countries. *Information Technology for Development, 10*(3), 151–169.

Burjorjee, D. M., & Bin-Humam, Y. (2018). *New insights on women's mobile phone ownership*. CGAP Working Paper. Retrieved from https://www.cgap.org/sites/default/files/researches/documents/Working-Paper-New-Insights-on-Womens-Mobile-Phone-Ownership-Apr-2018.pdf.

Carrasquillo, O. (2013). Health care utilization. In M. D. Gellman & J. R. Turner (Eds.), *Encyclopedia of behavioral medicine* (pp. 909–910). https://doi.org/10.1007/978-1-4419-1005-9_885

Demirgüç-Kunt, A., Klapper, L., Singer, D., Ansar, S., & Hess, J. (2018). *The Global Findex Database 2017: Measuring financial inclusion and the fintech revolution*. Retrieved from http://documents.worldbank.org/curated/en/332881525873182837/pdf/126033-PUB-PUBLIC-pubdate-4-19-2018.pdf.

Dhak, B. (2015). Demographic change and catastrophic health expenditure in India. *Social Indicators Research, 122*(3), 723–733.

Donner, J. (2008). Research approaches to mobile use in the developing world: A review of the literature. *The Information Society, 24*(3), 140–159.

Donner, J., & Tellez, C. A. (2008). Mobile banking and economic development: Linking adoption, impact, and use. *Asian Journal of Communication, 18*(4), 318–332.

Donovan, K. (2012). *Mobile money for financial inclusion*. Retrieved from http://elibrary.worldbank.org/doi/abs/10.1596/9780821389911_ch04.

Flood, D., West, T., & Wheadon, D. (2013). Trends in mobile payments in developing and advanced economies. *RBA Bulletin, 1*, 71–80.

GSMA. (2014). *State of the industry mobile financial services for the unbanked*. Retrieved from https://www.gsmaintelligence.com/research/?file=8d7e5607 1f00f28571cae54f7673181d&download.

GSMA. (2017). *State of the industry report on mobile money* (p. 33). Retrieved from https://www.gsma.com/mobilefordevelopment/wp-content/uploads/2019/02/2018-State-of-the-Industry-Report-on-Mobile-Money.pdf.

GSMA. (2018). *State of the industry report on mobile money* (p. 40). Retrieved from https://www.gsma.com/r/wp-content/uploads/2019/05/GSMA-State-of-the-Industry-Report-on-Mobile-Money-2018-1.pdf.

GSS. (2014). *Ghana living standards survey: Main report.* Retrieved from Ghana Statistical Service, Accra, website: http://www.statsghana.gov.gh/docfiles/glss6/GLSS6_Main%20Report.pdf.

GSS. (2018). *Ghana living standards survey round 7 (GLSS 7): Poverty trends in Ghana (2005–2017).* Retrieved from Ghana Statistical Service, Accra, website: http://www.statsghana.gov.gh/docfiles/publications/GLSS7/Poverty%20Profile%20Report_2005%20-%202017.pdf.

Haas, S., Heymann, M., Riley, P., & Taddese, A. (2013). *Mobile money for health.* Bethesda, MD: Health Finance and Governance Project, Abt Associates Inc.

Kendall, J., Schiff, R., & Smadja, E. (2013). Sub-Saharan Africa: A major potential revenue opportunity for digital payments. Available at SSRN 2298244.

Koomson, I., Annim, S. K., & Peprah, J. A. (2016). Loan refusal, household income and savings in Ghana: A dominance analysis approach. *African Journal of Economic and Sustainable Development, 5*(2), 172–191. https://doi.org/10.1504/AJESD.2016.076095

Koomson, I., Villano, R. A., & Hadley, D. (2020a). Effect of financial inclusion on poverty and vulnerability to poverty: Evidence using a multidimensional measure of financial inclusion. *Social Indicators Research, 25*(4), 375–387. https://doi.org/10.1007/s11205-019-02263-0

Koomson, I., Villano, R. A., & Hadley, D. (2020b). Intensifying financial inclusion through the provision of financial literacy training: A gendered perspective. *Applied Economics, 52*(4), 375–387. https://doi.org/10.1080/00036846.2019.1645943

Kshetri, N., & Cheung, M. K. (2002). What factors are driving China's mobile diffusion? *Electronic Markets, 12*(1), 22–26.

Kumar, A. S., Chen, L. C., Choudhury, M., Ganju, S., Mahajan, V., Sinha, A., & Sen, A. (2011). Financing health care for all: Challenges and opportunities. *The Lancet, 377*(9766), 668–679.

Ky, S., Rugemintwari, C., & Sauviat, A. (2017). Does mobile money affect saving behaviour? Evidence from a developing country. *Journal of African Economies, 27*(3), 285–320.

Mitręga-Niestrój, K., Puszer, B., & Szewczyk, Ł. (2018). Mobile money services development: The case of Africa. *Studia Ekonomiczne, 356,* 78–96.

Mohanty, S. K., Agrawal, N. K., Mahapatra, B., Choudhury, D., Tuladhar, S., & Holmgren, E. V. (2017). Multidimensional poverty and catastrophic health spending in the mountainous regions of Myanmar, Nepal and India. *International Journal for Equity in Health, 16*(1), 21.

Mojumdar, S. K. (2018). Determinants of health service utilization by urban households in India: A multivariate analysis of NSS case-level data. *Journal of Health Management, 20*(2), 105–121.

Mothobi, O., & Grzybowski, L. (2017). Infrastructure deficiencies and adoption of mobile money in Sub-Saharan Africa. *Information Economics and Policy, 40*, 71–79.

Munyegera, G. K., & Matsumoto, T. (2016). Mobile money, remittances, and household welfare: Panel evidence from rural Uganda. *World Development, 79*, 127–137.

Pénicaud, C., & Katakam, A. (2019). State of the industry 2013: Mobile financial services for the unbanked. *Gates Open Research, 3*.

Prokopenko, M. V., & Holden, M. P. (2001). *Financial development and poverty alleviation: Issues and policy implications for developing and transition countries*. International Monetary Fund.

Rowntree, O. (2018). The mobile gender gap report 2018. *GSMA*. Retrieved from https://www.Gsma.Com/Mobilefordevelopment/Programmes/Connected-Women/the-Mobile-Gender-Gap-Report-2018.

Singh, T., Bhatnagar, N., Singh, G., Kaur, M., Kaur, S., Thaware, P., & Kumar, R. (2018). Health-care utilization and expenditure patterns in the rural areas of Punjab, India. *Journal of Family Medicine and Primary Care, 7*(1), 39.

Stock, J. H., & Yogo, M. (2002). *Testing for weak instruments in linear IV regression*. NBER Technical Working Paper No. 284. Retrieved from https://www.nber.org/papers/t0284.

Suri, T., Jack, W., & Stoker, T. M. (2012). Documenting the birth of a financial economy. *Proceedings of the National Academy of Sciences, 109*(26), 10257–10262.

World Bank. (2017). *World Bank Annual Report* (p. 87). Retrieved from United Nations, website: http://pubdocs.worldbank.org/en/908481507403754670/Annual-Report-2017-WBG.pdf.

World Health Organization. (2016). *World health statistics 2016: Monitoring health for the SDGs sustainable development goals*. Retrieved from https://apps.who.int/iris/bitstream/handle/10665/272596/9789241565585-eng.pdf.

World Health Organization. (2017). *Tracking universal health coverage: 2017 global monitoring report*.

4

Mobile Money and Women's Decision-Making Power in India

Sefa Awaworyi Churchill, Lisa Farrell,
and Vijaya Bhaskar Marisetty

1   Introduction

The United Nations has acknowledged that the achievement of the Sustainable Development Goals (SGDs) could be difficult without women's empowerment and the narrowing of the gender gap (United Nations, 2018). Indeed, this is expected, given that the equitable contribution and participation of women is not a goal in itself, but is also relevant in achieving several development goals. Existing research has demonstrated that changes in gender relations characterised by more gender equality and female empowerment are important for economic development (see Diebolt & Perrin, 2013; Duflo, 2012; Wyndow, Li, & Mattes, 2013).

S. Awaworyi Churchill (✉) • L. Farrell
School of Economics, Finance and Marketing, RMIT University,
Melbourne, VIC, Australia
e-mail: sefa.churchill@rmit.edu.au; lisa.farrell@rmit.edu.au

V. B. Marisetty
School of Management Studies, University of Hyderabad, Hyderabad, India
e-mail: marisetty@uohyd.ac.in

© The Author(s) 2020   61
S. Awaworyi Churchill (ed.), *Moving from the Millennium to the Sustainable Development Goals*, https://doi.org/10.1007/978-981-15-1556-9_4

For instance, Hsieh, Hurst, Jones, and Klenow (2013) found that a quarter of the growth in output per capita in the US was associated with an improved allocation of human capital and talent across genders and races. At a more micro-level, decision-making at the household level is often considered a starting point for successful development. Research along these lines show that an increase in the income and decision-making power of women presents more benefits for households including better nutrition for children, lower household poverty, and higher investment in human capital among others (see, e.g., Attanasio & Lechene, 2002; Hoddinott & Haddad, 1995; Lundberg, Pollak, & Wales, 1997). Women's empowerment is therefore crucial to the development process.

In this chapter, we examine if financial inclusion, through the use of technology, can be instrumental in achieving the goal of women's empowerment, and consequently holistic development. The relevance of financial inclusion in promoting aggregate economic development has been widely discussed in the extant literature (see, e.g., Aghion & Bolton, 1997; Ang, 2008; Galor & Zeira, 1993; King & Levine, 1993). Some early theories on the finance-growth relationship suggest that financial exclusion tends to engender inequality and exacerbate issues of poverty (Aghion & Bolton, 1997; Galor & Zeira, 1993). Subsequent studies on finance and growth suggest that financial inclusion provides poor households with opportunities to access credit, make investments, build savings, and hedge against unforeseen shocks (Beck, Demirgüç-Kunt, & Honohan, 2009; Ellis & Lemma, 2010; Ghosh & Vinod, 2017). For instance, access to finance is likely to reduce transaction and information costs, which can enhance savings and investment decisions, technological innovation, and consequently economic growth in the long run (Beck et al., 2009). At the firm-level, as Melander and Bayoumi (2008) suggest, financial inclusion could help financial institutions with the diversification of loan portfolios given that it improves the penetration of credit. As discussed in the literature, lending to firms that did not previously have access could reduce the credit risk of loan portfolios and improve the ability of financial institutions to recycle funds (Ghosh & Vinod, 2017), thus stimulating aggregate economic activity (Melander & Bayoumi, 2008).

At the macro-level, evidence and reviews tend to support these arguments and have shown that economies with higher levels of financial development tend to grow faster and experience a reduction in poverty (Beck, Demirguc-Kunt, Laeven, & Levine, 2008; Beck, Demirgüç-Kunt, & Levine, 2007; Chibba, 2009; Giné & Townsend, 2004). Using cross-industry, cross-country data, Beck et al. (2008) show that the aggregate usage of financial services enhances development and reduces inequality. Giné and Townsend (2004) adopt a different approach where in a general equilibrium model of the Thai economy, they show that broader financial systems or greater access to the financial sector enhances growth rates. Based on a qualitative review of financial inclusion programs initiated by selected developing countries, Chibba (2009) also concludes that financial inclusion is an important channel for inclusive development that helps in the reduction of poverty.

Some studies, predominantly Indian based, provide evidence in the context of specific financial inclusion programs in various countries. These studies attempt to examine the impact of specific financial inclusion interventions and how this influences development outcomes (see, e.g., Binswanger & Khandker, 1995; Burgess & Pande, 2005). Binswanger and Khandker (1995) provide evidence which suggests that the Indian rural expansion program significantly increased non-agricultural employment in rural areas and thus reduced poverty. This finding is consistent with Burgess and Pande (2005), who find evidence to suggest that the state-led rural bank expansion program which started in 1969 helped reduce poverty.

Other studies have used microfinance as a proxy for financial inclusion, and examined the relationship between microfinance and outcomes such as poverty and income (e.g., Imai, Gaiha, Thapa, & Annim, 2012; Khandker, 2005; Zhang, 2017). Imai et al. (2012), for instance, use data from the Microfinance Information Exchange and the World Bank. They show that financial inclusion proxied by higher levels of gross loan portfolio per capita of microfinance institutions (MFIs) tends to lower poverty at the macro level. Similarly, Zhang (2017) uses macro-level data for a panel of 106 countries and shows that microfinance tends to lower poverty.

Our study contributes to the broader literature on the importance of finance and financial inclusion in the development process. We examine the association between mobile money and female empowerment. We use the awareness and adoption of mobile money products to proxy financial inclusion or more precisely, financial innovation aimed at promoting financial inclusion. Mobile phones and related digital devices have emerged as important technologies in providing access to financial services and products through various mobile money schemes. Mobile money schemes continue to gain traction given that financial services are increasingly becoming digital. With the increase of mobile phone ownership, policymakers are progressively pursuing the use of mobile money not only as a way to promote financial inclusion but also as a strategy with the potential to alleviate poverty (Donovan, 2012).

Financial services and products offered through mobile money schemes allow women to conveniently transact businesses from their own homes and communities. It allows for the transfer or receipt of money as part of various economic transactions without travelling or with travel over short distances. However, beyond the convenience it presents for financial transactions, does the use of mobile money influence the decision-making power of women?

We examine this research question using data from the Financial Inclusion Insights (FII) program focussing on India, which makes for an interesting case study because of its unique financial inclusion initiatives. For several decades, the government of India together with the Reserve Bank of India have made efforts to promote financial inclusion. The efforts have constituted one of the most important national goals of the country with the introduction of policies that influence the extension of commercial bank networks as well as regional and rural bank networks. These efforts, which have also led to an increase in the adoption of mobile money, have been deemed successful. According to statistics from the Global Financial Inclusion database, as of 2014, 53% of Indians had an account which represents an increase of 18% from 35% in 2011 (Demirgüç-Kunt, Klapper, Singer, & Van Oudheusden, 2015). The gender gap in financial inclusion has declined from 20% to 6%, although about 70% of financial accounts owned by women are dormant.

Thus, focussing on the sub-sample of females from the 2016 FII program, we examine how mobile money influences Women's empowerment. We focus on the decision-making power dimension of Women's empowerment. According to the United Nations, about a third of married women from developing countries do not have control over household spending on major purchases while one in ten married women are not consulted or do not participate in the decision-making process of how their own earnings are spent (United Nations, 2015). This makes many women in developing countries dependent on their husbands for basic needs, and thus understanding this dimension of empowerment is crucial.

We use three measures related to mobile money use and adoption, and measure the decision-making power of women, alternatively using variables that capture women's control or joint control over decisions relating to their own earnings, purchases of daily household needs, household assets, and the kind of financial services to use. Our results show that awareness of mobile money or mobile money use per se does not transform into increased decision-making power. Except for a marginal effect on decision-making related to one's own earning, awareness and use of mobile money does not influence the decision-making power of women. This finding is consistent with existing research that shows that microfinance, an essential approach to promote financial inclusion, has no significant association with female empowerment indicators (see Awaworyi Churchill (2015), for a review). One plausible explanation for this phenomenon can be related to discriminating social norms, where men dominate in intra household decision making. Social norms can disadvantage women in the household bargaining process, by weakening their earning possibilities in the marketplace and ideologically constructing women as dependents and men as breadwinners. This is more likely to be the base in cash-based economies such as India, and to an extent, this explains why the effects of mobile money, which is not well patronised in cash-based economies, is less effective.

This finding suggests that there are systemic barriers which still need to be addressed to ensure the optimal benefit of financial inclusion. In many developing countries, where transactions are still very much cash based, the use of mobile money or associated digital finance technologies may not necessarily translate into the control of significant finance or assets.

This calls for policies that will target the promotion of women's empowerment, especially in economies that are mostly cash based.

The remainder of the chapter is structured as follows. The next section discusses the data and empirical method. Section 3 presents the empirical results while Sect. 4 concludes.

2   Data and Empirical Method

We use data from the 2016 InterMedia's Financial Inclusion Insights (FII) program. The dataset provides information on the trends in financial inclusion, mobile money and other financial services. The survey was carried out on 45,540 individuals located in 1050 communities (towns and villages). However, given our research question, we focus on only female respondents, and thus regressions with the highest number of observations include 16,415 respondents.

To examine the relationship between mobile money (both awareness and adoption) and women's decision-making power, we specify the following model:

$$empower_i = \beta MM_i + \gamma X_i + \alpha_i + \varepsilon_i \qquad (4.1)$$

where $empower_i$ is the measure of our outcome variable, which is the decision-making power for individual i. MM_i is the measure of mobile money use or adoption, while X_i is a vector of control variables including age, marital status, household size, education, asset ownership, employment status, religion, household location (rural vs urban), and number of children in household. The variable α_i is a state-level dummy variable that controls for unobserved state-level fixed effect while ε_i is a normally distributed error term. For dependent variables (discussed below) that are binary in nature, we estimate Eq. (4.1) using probit regressions while, for the dependent variable that is based on an ordinal scale, we use the ordered logit regression approach to estimate Eq. (4.1).

Given the information in our dataset, we adopt six measures of female empowerment that reflect the decision-making power of women. The first measure is a dummy variable that captures whether respondents have a say in how the money they earn is used. It is based on the survey question: "Who usually decides how the money you earn will be used?" Our first measure of empowerment is a binary variable which takes the value one when respondents respond to the above question that they decide how the money used or take the decision jointly. The second measure of empowerment is based on the question: "Who in your household decides what purchases are made to meet daily household needs like food, clothing, and cleaning supplies?" We use a binary variable which takes the value one when respondents respond to the question that they decide what purchases are made or take the decision jointly.

The third measure of empowerment is also a binary variable which equals to one when respondents agree that they control the assets in their household or do it jointly. The fourth and fifth measures capture decisions relating to the use of financial services. The fourth is based on the question, "Who decides what kind of financial services your household uses?" while the fifth is based on the question, "Who decides what kind of financial services you can personally use?" The measures of empowerment, like the first three, are binary variables that take the value one when respondents respond to the financial services questions that they decide what kind of financial services to use or take the decision jointly. The sixth measure of empowerment is a composite scale which is based on the sum of the first five measures of empowerment.

We use three measures related to mobile money use and adoption. Our first measure captures the awareness of mobile money, and is thus a binary variable which equals one if the respondents have ever heard of mobile money, and zero if otherwise. The second measure captures the use of mobile money, and is a binary variable which equals to one if respondent has ever used a mobile money product. The last measure reflects the last time respondents used mobile money. Specifically, this measure is based on the question: "Apart from today, when was the last time you performed the following activities on your personal phone or on the phone that you borrow/rent from other people?" Responses are coded on a six-point scale in the original survey, where 1 represents "Yesterday" and 6 represents "Never". However, for ease of interpretation, we transpose the responses such that 1 = Never, 2 = More than 90 days ago, 3 = In the past 90 days, 4 = In the past 30 days, 5 = In the past 7 days, 6 = Yesterday.

3   Empirical Results

Table 4.1 reports results for the effects of mobile money awareness on various dimensions of female empowerment that reflect the decision-making power of women. Column 1 report results for effects on the composite measure of decision-making power while Columns 2 to 6 report

Table 4.1 Effects of mobile money awareness

	(1)	(2)	(3)	(4)	(5)	(6)
Mobile Money awareness	0.041	0.097*	0.010	−0.011	0.013	0.037
	(0.077)	(0.055)	(0.054)	(0.054)	(0.054)	(0.055)
Household size	−0.093***	−0.063***	−0.052***	−0.049***	−0.049***	−0.052***
	(0.011)	(0.008)	(0.008)	(0.008)	(0.008)	(0.008)
Age	0.031***	0.018***	0.018***	0.019***	0.018***	0.018***
	(0.001)	(0.001)	(0.001)	(0.001)	(0.001)	(0.001)
Rural	−0.003	0.009	−0.015	0.021	−0.014	0.008
	(0.037)	(0.026)	(0.025)	(0.025)	(0.026)	(0.026)
Married	−0.596***	−0.458***	−0.330***	−0.311***	−0.334***	−0.334***
	(0.034)	(0.023)	(0.023)	(0.023)	(0.023)	(0.023)
Children	0.093***	0.063***	0.051***	0.047***	0.044***	0.053***
	(0.016)	(0.011)	(0.011)	(0.011)	(0.011)	(0.011)
Education	−0.031	−0.042	−0.008	−0.024	−0.045	−0.024
	(0.039)	(0.027)	(0.027)	(0.027)	(0.027)	(0.027)
Farm land	0.054	0.044*	0.012	0.030	0.043*	0.020
	(0.034)	(0.024)	(0.023)	(0.023)	(0.023)	(0.023)
Employed	0.283***	0.241***	0.145***	0.134***	0.163***	0.180***
	(0.036)	(0.024)	(0.024)	(0.024)	(0.024)	(0.024)
Self-employed	0.147**	0.147***	−0.013	0.125***	0.103**	0.107**
	(0.067)	(0.045)	(0.045)	(0.045)	(0.045)	(0.045)
Christian	0.383	0.227	0.331**	0.368**	0.355**	0.165
	(0.244)	(0.169)	(0.167)	(0.166)	(0.166)	(0.166)
Islam	0.357	0.277*	0.374**	0.298*	0.290*	0.129
	(0.234)	(0.161)	(0.158)	(0.158)	(0.157)	(0.157)
Sikh	0.995***	0.582***	0.702***	0.621***	0.678***	0.508***
	(0.277)	(0.189)	(0.186)	(0.185)	(0.185)	(0.185)
Hindu	0.383*	0.258	0.369**	0.332**	0.289*	0.139
	(0.230)	(0.158)	(0.155)	(0.154)	(0.154)	(0.154)
Buddhist	0.280	0.201	0.167	0.328*	0.400**	0.132
	(0.270)	(0.185)	(0.182)	(0.181)	(0.180)	(0.180)
Observations	16,415	16,415	16,415	16,415	16,415	16,415

Notes: The dependent variable in Column 1 is the composite measure of decision-making power. The dependent variable in Columns 2 to 6 is the indicator of Empowerment 1 to Empowerment 5, respectively. Robust standard errors in parentheses. ***$p < 0.01$, **$p < 0.05$, *$p < 0.1$

results for the five individual indicators of decision-making power. Across all columns, our results show that the awareness of mobile money does not have significant effects on the dimensions of decision-making power except for Column 2, where the coefficient on mobile money awareness is positive and statistically significant. This result suggests that a shift from being unaware of mobile money to becoming aware is associated with a 9.7 percentage point increase in the probability of making decisions or being part of joint decisions on how money that is personally earned will be used. These findings suggest that awareness alone is not sufficient to change behaviours and cultural norms.

Table 4.2 reports results for the effects of mobile money use. Consistent with Table 4.1, we do not find significant effects of mobile money use on decision-making power except for Column 2, where the coefficient on mobile money use is positive and statistically significant at the 5% level. The result here suggests that the use of any mobile money product is associated with a 22.2 percentage point increase in the probability of making decisions or being part of joint decisions on how money that is personally earned will be used.

Table 4.3 reports results for the effects of temporal proximity or time pass since mobile money utilisation. Similar to Tables 4.1 and 4.2, Column 1 reports results for effects on the composite measure of decision-making power while Columns 2 to 6 report results for the five individual indicators of decision-making power. Here, we find statistically significant effects of temporal proximity in Columns 1, 3, and 4. From Column 1, we find that the more recent use of mobile money is positively associated with the composite index of decision-making power with a coefficient of 0.058 at the 10% significance level. From Column 3, we find that the more recent use of a mobile money product is associated with a 5.9 percentage point change in the probability of making decisions or being part of joint decisions on what purchases are made to meet daily household needs like food, clothing, and cleaning supplies. Findings from Column 4 show that the more recent use of a mobile money product is associated with a 3.9 percentage point change in the probability of controlling household assets.

We observe some noteworthy findings in the case of our control variables. First, larger household sizes are associated with lower

Table 4.2 Effects of mobile money use

	(1)	(2)	(3)	(4)	(5)	(6)
MM user	0.197	0.222**	−0.001	0.117	0.151	0.114
	(0.129)	(0.101)	(0.100)	(0.101)	(0.101)	(0.099)
Household size	−0.093***	−0.063***	−0.052***	−0.049***	−0.049***	−0.052***
	(0.011)	(0.008)	(0.008)	(0.008)	(0.008)	(0.008)
Age	0.031***	0.018***	0.018***	0.019***	0.018***	0.018***
	(0.001)	(0.001)	(0.001)	(0.001)	(0.001)	(0.001)
Rural	−0.002	0.008	−0.015	0.023	−0.012	0.008
	(0.036)	(0.025)	(0.025)	(0.025)	(0.025)	(0.025)
Married	−0.596***	−0.459***	−0.330***	−0.310***	−0.334***	−0.334***
	(0.034)	(0.023)	(0.023)	(0.023)	(0.023)	(0.023)
Children	0.093***	0.063***	0.051***	0.047***	0.044***	0.053***
	(0.016)	(0.011)	(0.011)	(0.011)	(0.011)	(0.011)
Education	−0.032	−0.040	−0.008	−0.026	−0.047*	−0.024
	(0.039)	(0.027)	(0.027)	(0.027)	(0.027)	(0.027)
Farm land	0.053	0.044*	0.012	0.030	0.042*	0.020
	(0.034)	(0.024)	(0.023)	(0.023)	(0.023)	(0.023)
Employed	0.284***	0.242***	0.145***	0.133***	0.163***	0.180***
	(0.036)	(0.024)	(0.024)	(0.024)	(0.024)	(0.024)
Self-employed	0.146**	0.145***	−0.013	0.124***	0.102**	0.106**
	(0.067)	(0.045)	(0.045)	(0.045)	(0.045)	(0.045)
Christian	0.380	0.224	0.331**	0.366**	0.352**	0.163
	(0.244)	(0.170)	(0.167)	(0.166)	(0.166)	(0.166)
Islam	0.355	0.275*	0.374**	0.298*	0.289*	0.128
	(0.234)	(0.161)	(0.158)	(0.158)	(0.157)	(0.157)
Sikh	0.995***	0.585***	0.702***	0.619***	0.677***	0.508***
	(0.277)	(0.189)	(0.186)	(0.185)	(0.185)	(0.185)
Hindu	0.380*	0.256	0.369**	0.331**	0.288*	0.138
	(0.229)	(0.158)	(0.155)	(0.154)	(0.154)	(0.154)
Buddhist	0.265	0.187	0.167	0.322*	0.391**	0.126
	(0.270)	(0.185)	(0.182)	(0.181)	(0.180)	(0.180)
Observations	16,415	16,415	16,415	16,415	16,415	16,415

Notes: The dependent variable in Column 1 is the composite measure of decision-making power. The dependent variable in Columns 2 to 5 is the indicator of Empowerment 1 to Empowerment 6, respectively. Robust standard errors in parentheses. ***$p < 0.01$, **$p < 0.05$, *$p < 0.1$

decision-making power for women while older females have more decision-making power. Being married is associated with lower decision-making power while having more children is associated with higher decision-making power. Being employed or self-employed is associated with higher decision-making power. Religion is also positively associated with decision-making power but with varying effect sizes depending on the religion type.

Table 4.3 Effects of time passed since mobile money use

	(1)	(2)	(3)	(4)	(5)	(6)
Time of MM use	0.058*	0.009	0.059***	0.039*	0.019	0.026
	(0.031)	(0.021)	(0.021)	(0.021)	(0.021)	(0.021)
Household size	−0.110***	−0.075***	−0.066***	−0.056***	−0.063***	−0.062***
	(0.015)	(0.010)	(0.010)	(0.010)	(0.010)	(0.010)
Age	0.032***	0.019***	0.019***	0.020***	0.019***	0.020***
	(0.002)	(0.001)	(0.001)	(0.001)	(0.001)	(0.001)
Rural	0.078*	0.040	0.041	0.065**	0.030	0.049
	(0.047)	(0.033)	(0.033)	(0.032)	(0.033)	(0.033)
Married	−0.570***	−0.444***	−0.310***	−0.271***	−0.330***	−0.342***
	(0.045)	(0.030)	(0.030)	(0.030)	(0.030)	(0.030)
Children	0.113***	0.077***	0.066***	0.060***	0.065***	0.071***
	(0.020)	(0.014)	(0.014)	(0.014)	(0.014)	(0.014)
Education	−0.101**	−0.074**	−0.027	−0.088***	−0.086***	−0.054
	(0.047)	(0.033)	(0.033)	(0.033)	(0.033)	(0.033)
Farm land	0.080*	0.097***	0.015	0.046	0.057*	0.032
	(0.044)	(0.031)	(0.030)	(0.030)	(0.031)	(0.031)
Employed	0.363***	0.304***	0.177***	0.151***	0.206***	0.227***
	(0.046)	(0.031)	(0.031)	(0.031)	(0.031)	(0.031)
Self-employed	0.146*	0.203***	−0.032	0.091	0.106*	0.075
	(0.084)	(0.058)	(0.057)	(0.058)	(0.057)	(0.057)
Christian	0.100	−0.093	0.231	0.230	0.275	0.105
	(0.383)	(0.247)	(0.239)	(0.237)	(0.234)	(0.239)
Islam	0.045	−0.049	0.225	0.126	0.170	0.059
	(0.381)	(0.241)	(0.233)	(0.231)	(0.228)	(0.232)
Sikh	0.592	0.140	0.528**	0.353	0.527**	0.432
	(0.431)	(0.272)	(0.266)	(0.263)	(0.261)	(0.265)
Hindu	0.086	−0.059	0.241	0.176	0.169	0.050
	(0.376)	(0.237)	(0.230)	(0.227)	(0.224)	(0.228)
Buddhist	0.152	−0.087	0.177	0.208	0.408	0.110
	(0.433)	(0.276)	(0.271)	(0.269)	(0.267)	(0.269)
Observations	10,009	10,009	10,009	10,009	10,009	10,009

Notes: The dependent variable in Column 1 is the composite measure of decision-making power. The dependent variable in Columns 2 to 6 is the indicator of Empowerment 1 to Empowerment 5, respectively. Robust standard errors in parentheses. ***$p < 0.01$, **$p < 0.05$, *$p < 0.1$

4   Discussion and Conclusion

In this chapter, we examine the association between mobile money and female empowerment in India. Using data from the financial inclusion insights program, the results of this study suggest that while technological diffusion is often rapid in today's global economies, cultural norms and behaviours respond slowly to these changes. Furthermore, awareness of mobile money does not automatically translate into greater female empowerment through financial decision making. It is only through the use and recent practice in the use of mobile money that we start to see differences in financial behaviours within households.

These findings have important policy lessons in that programs designed to encourage women to take up mobile money and opening online bank accounts, among others, will not be successful unless those women actively utilise these bank accounts. The pathways and mechanisms at work are complex. It might be the case that frequency of use results in greater financial capabilities and financial self-efficacy and it is these factors that then result in females demanding more financial control. Or it may be that through females practising financial skills and hence revealing their financial competency that males within the household gain trust and relinquish some of their financial control. It is not possible with our data to directly test any of these hypotheses in terms of the pathways to behaviour change. However, our study has shown that financial empowerment is a function of the usage of mobile money products.

Interestingly, financial decision making when more diversified across the male and female household members is most likely to be associated with daily household expenditures as opposed to longer term, and often larger, financial decisions. These results suggest that it may take much more for behaviours to change sufficiently to significantly financially empower women and elevate them from financial oppression and potential financial abuse.

In a world of rapid growth in technology and its diffusion, our results offer a cautionary note for policy makers. It is not sufficient just to have the technology available for behavioural change to occur. Social norms change slower than technological knowledge expands and so if the full benefits of the technology are to be realised, additional user support programs are also required to ensure both the take-up and utilisation of the technology. Even then, behaviour change may be slow and heavily dependent on cultural norms.

Appendix

Table 4.4 Description and summary statistics of variables

Variable	Description	Mean	SD
Empowerment index	Ordinal scale of female empowerment derived from the sum of the five indicators of empowerment	2.386	2.220
Empower 1	Dummy variable equals 1 if response to the following question is "self" or "joint decision": Who usually decides how the money you earn will be used?	0.460	0.498
Empower 2	Dummy variable equals 1 if response to the following question is "self" or "joint decision": Who in your household decides what purchases are made to meet daily household needs like food, clothing, and cleaning supplies?	0.466	0.499
Empower 3	Dummy variable equals 1 if response to the following question is "self" or "joint decision": Who controls assets (i.e., savings, land, and livestock) in your household?	0.434	0.496
Empower 4	Dummy variable equals 1 if response to the following question is "self" or "joint decision": Who decides what kind of financial services your household uses?	0.422	0.494
Empower 5	Dummy variable equals 1 if response to the following question is "self" or "joint decision": Who decides what kind of financial services you can personally use?	0.433	0.495
MM awareness	Dummy variable equals 1 if respondent has ever heard of mobile money	0.038	0.191
MM user	Dummy variable equals 1 if respondent has ever used a mobile money product	0.011	0.103
Time of MM use	Six-point scale (1 = Never, 2 = More than 90 days ago, 3 = In the past 90 days, 4 = In the past 30 days, 5 = In the past 7 days, 6 = Yesterday), response to the question "Apart from today, when was the last time you performed the following activities on your personal phone or on the phone that you borrow/rent from other people?"	1.129	0.668
Household size	Number of people in household	4.168	2.093

(*continued*)

Table 4.4 (continued)

Variable	Description	Mean	SD
Age	Age of respondent	37.094	14.300
Rural	Dummy variable equals 1 if respondent lives in rural area	0.691	0.462
Married	Dummy variable equals 1 if respondent is married	0.695	0.460
Children	Number of children in household	1.347	1.484
Education	Dummy variable equals 1 if highest level of education of respondent is secondary education or above	0.193	0.395
Farm land	Dummy variable equals 1 if household owns a farm land	0.374	0.484
Employed	Dummy variable equals 1 if respondent is employed	0.174	0.379
Self-employed	Dummy variable equals 1 if respondent is self-employed	0.037	0.189
Christian	Dummy variable equals 1 if respondent is Christian	0.022	0.146
Islam	Dummy variable equals 1 if respondent is Muslim	0.117	0.322
Sikh	Dummy variable equals 1 if respondent is Sikh	0.022	0.148
Hindu	Dummy variable equals 1 if respondent is Hindu	0.821	0.383
Buddhist	Dummy variable equals 1 if respondent is Buddhist	0.012	0.107

References

Aghion, P., & Bolton, P. (1997). A theory of trickle-down growth and development. *The Review of Economic Studies, 64*(2), 151–172. https://doi.org/10.2307/2971707

Ang, J. B. (2008). A survey of recent developments in the literature of finance and growth. *Journal of Economic Surveys, 22*(3), 536–576.

Attanasio, O., & Lechene, V. (2002). Tests of income pooling in household decisions. *Review of Economic Dynamics, 5*(4), 720–748.

Awaworyi Churchill, S. (2015). Impact of microfinance on female empowerment: A review of the empirical literature. In S. Moore (Ed.), *Contemporary global perspectives on gender economics* (pp. 39–54). Hershey, PA: IGI Global.

Beck, T., Demirgüç-Kunt, A., & Honohan, P. (2009). Access to financial services: Measurement, impact, and policies. *The World Bank Research Observer, 24*(1), 119–145.

Beck, T., Demirguc-Kunt, A., Laeven, L., & Levine, R. (2008). Finance, firm size, and growth. *Journal of Money, Credit and Banking, 40*(7), 1379–1405.

Beck, T., Demirgüç-Kunt, A., & Levine, R. (2007). Finance, inequality and the poor. *Journal of Economic Growth, 12*(1), 27–49. https://doi.org/10.1007/s10887-007-9010-6

Binswanger, H. P., & Khandker, S. R. (1995). The impact of formal finance on the rural economy of India. *The Journal of Development Studies, 32*(2), 234–262.

Burgess, R., & Pande, R. (2005). Do rural banks matter? Evidence from the Indian social banking experiment. *American Economic Review, 95*(3), 780–795.

Chibba, M. (2009). Financial inclusion, poverty reduction and the millennium development goals. *The European Journal of Development Research, 21*(2), 213–230.

Demirgüç-Kunt, A., Klapper, L. F., Singer, D., & Van Oudheusden, P. (2015). *The global findex database 2014: Measuring financial inclusion around the world.* World Bank Policy Research Working Paper No. 7255.

Diebolt, C., & Perrin, F. (2013). From stagnation to sustained growth: The role of female empowerment. *American Economic Review, 103*(3), 545–549.

Donovan, K. (2012). Mobile money for financial inclusion. *Information and Communications for Development, 61*(1), 61–73.

Duflo, E. (2012). Women empowerment and economic development. *Journal of Economic Literature, 50*(4), 1051–1079.

Ellis, K., & Lemma, A. (2010). Financial inclusion, household investment and growth in Kenya and Tanzania. *ODI Project Briefing, 43*, 1–4.

Galor, O., & Zeira, J. (1993). Income distribution and macroeconomics. *The Review of Economic Studies, 60*(1), 35–52. https://doi.org/10.2307/2297811

Ghosh, S., & Vinod, D. (2017). What constrains financial inclusion for women? Evidence from Indian micro data. *World Development, 92*, 60–81.

Giné, X., & Townsend, R. M. (2004). Evaluation of financial liberalization: A general equilibrium model with constrained occupation choice. *Journal of Development Economics, 74*(2), 269–307. https://doi.org/10.1016/j.jdeveco.2003.03.005

Hoddinott, J., & Haddad, L. (1995). Does female income share influence household expenditures? Evidence from Côte d'Ivoire. *Oxford Bulletin of Economics and Statistics, 57*(1), 77–96.

Hsieh, C.-T., Hurst, E., Jones, C. I., & Klenow, P. J. (2013). *The allocation of talent and us economic growth.* NBER Working Paper No. 18693.

Imai, K. S., Gaiha, R., Thapa, G., & Annim, S. K. (2012). Microfinance and poverty—A macro perspective. *World Development, 40*(8), 1675–1689. http://www.sciencedirect.com/science/journal/0305750X/

Khandker, S. R. (2005). Microfinance and poverty: Evidence using panel data from Bangladesh. *World Bank Economic Review, 19*(2), 263–286. Retrieved from http://wber.oxfordjournals.org/

King, R. G., & Levine, R. (1993). Finance and growth: Schumpeter might be right. *The Quarterly Journal of Economics, 108*(3), 717–737. https://doi.org/10.2307/2118406

Lundberg, S. J., Pollak, R. A., & Wales, T. J. (1997). Do husbands and wives pool their resources? Evidence from the United Kingdom child benefit. *Journal of Human Resources, 32*(3), 463–480.

Melander, O., & Bayoumi, T. (2008). *Credit matters: Empirical evidence on US macro-financial linkages.* Washington, DC: International Monetary Fund.

United Nations. (2015). *The World's Women 2015: Trends and statistics.* New York: United Nations, Department of Economic and Social Affairs, Statistics Division.

United Nations. (2018). *Turning promises into action: Gender equality in the 2030 Agenda for Sustainable Development.* New York: UN Women Headquarters.

Wyndow, P., Li, J., & Mattes, E. (2013). Female empowerment as a core driver of democratic development: A dynamic panel model from 1980 to 2005. *World Development, 52*, 34–54. https://doi.org/10.1016/j.worlddev.2013.06.004

Zhang, Q. (2017). Does microfinance reduce poverty? Some international evidence. *The BE Journal of Macroeconomics, 17*(2), 1–13.

5

Fertility Gap and Child Nutrition: Evidence from India

Ankita Mishra and Sefa Awaworyi Churchill

1 Introduction

Fertility decisions have long been associated with human capital accumulation, which is a main driver of economic growth (Barro & Becker, 1989; Becker, Murphy, & Tamura, 1990). Consequently, economic development has been accompanied by significant declines in fertility, a phenomenon referred to as the demographic transition (Doepke & Tertilt, 2018). Beyond studies that examine the role of fertility in economic growth (see, e.g., Ashraf, Weil, & Wilde, 2013; Brander & Dowrick, 1994; Wang, Yip, & Scotese, 1994), a large body of literature examines various aspects of fertility given that fertility is considered an important factor in the development process. Along these lines, economists and demographers have expressed interest in understanding the determinants and effects of fertility rates. This interest has led to a large

A. Mishra (✉) • S. Awaworyi Churchill
School of Economics, Finance and Marketing, RMIT University,
Melbourne, VIC, Australia
e-mail: ankita.mishra@rmit.edu.au; sefa.churchill@rmit.edu.au

© The Author(s) 2020   77
S. Awaworyi Churchill (ed.), *Moving from the Millennium to the Sustainable Development Goals*, https://doi.org/10.1007/978-981-15-1556-9_5

body of literature that examines such factors as education (e.g., Kravdal, 2002; Rindfuss, Morgan, & Offutt, 1996), urbanization (e.g., Gries & Grundmann, 2018; Guo, Wu, Schimmele, & Li, 2012), culture, religion and peer effect (e.g., Khan & Raeside, 1997; McQuillan, 2004; Mishra & Parasnis, 2017), income (e.g., Herzer, Strulik, & Vollmer, 2012; Klawon & Tiefenthaler, 2001) and labor market choices (e.g., Hondroyiannis, 2010), among others as determinants of fertility.

Another strand of literature examines the effects fertility on such development outcomes as education (e.g., Becker, Cinnirella, & Woessmann, 2010; Lloyd & Gage-Brandon, 1994), wellbeing (e.g., Cáceres-Delpiano & Simonsen, 2012; Kohler, Behrman, & Skytthe, 2005; Schultz, 2005) and labor force participation (e.g., Chun & Oh, 2002), among others. This chapter contributes to this body of literature by examining the impact of fertility gap on child nutrition in India. We examine the relationship between two important variables that are relevant for development and consequential in the development process. Fertility gap is the difference between a woman's preferred number of children and her actual number of children. The decisions on how many children to have are among the most consequential in developing countries, and, in this study, we hypothesize the potential effects of these decisions on child nutrition. Child nutrition represents an important development agenda and has been identified as a major global priority over the past two decades. Child nutrition first formed part of the recently ended millennium development goals (MDGs) and has continued to remain a global priority on the post-2015 development agenda. Thus, understanding factors that influence this development goal is important.

India makes for an important case study to examine the impact of the fertility gap on child nutrition for several reasons. First, India introduced a national family planning program in the 1950s, making it one of the first countries in the world to introduce such a program on a national scale. The initiation of this program, coupled with several other fertility-related changes across Indian states over the years, has led to persistent demographic transitions characterized by declining fertility and mortality rates (Drèze & Murthi, 2001). Since the 1980s, India's fertility rate has halved with the current rate recorded at 2.3 per woman. This figure of 2.3 represents a decline of more than 50% in the fertility rate of approximately 5 recorded in the late 1970s to early 1980s. This fertility trend has been argued to defy prevailing trends of developing countries especially given that such low fertility rates are only achieved at higher levels of income and economic growth in other parts of the world (UNPF, 2018).

Second, evidence suggests that the fertility gap in India has been persistent. In an analysis based on the National Family Health Survey (NFHS), Mishra and Parasnis (2018) show that for the period 2005–2006, there is evidence of a fertility gap in India and this gap has remained persistent for over a decade for most women.

Third, the incidence of malnutrition in India is very high. According to statistics from the United Nations Children's Fund (UNICEF), one in five children (approximately 20%) of children under the age of five in India suffer from acute undernutrition and 48% of them suffer from chronic undernutrition. More than 40% of children in India under the age of the five are underweight and over 30% of the world's children who suffer from acute undernutrition or are wasted live in India. Similarly, India accounts for more than 30% of stunted children in the world.

Using data from the fourth wave of the National Family Health Survey (NFHS-4) of India, we measure the fertility gap as a dummy variable taking the value 1 if a woman exceeds her fertility target and 0 otherwise. The outcome variable, child nutrition, also takes the form of binary variable taking the value 1 if a woman has at least one child who is stunted/wasted/anemic and 0 otherwise. By focusing on these three measures, and particularly on stunted and wasted children, our study captures chronic and acute cases of malnutrition, respectively. Our results suggest that the odds of having malnourished children who are stunted, wasted or anemic are higher for women who exceed their fertility target compared to those who have achieved or underachieved it. These results are consistent with the literature that has emphasized the importance of lower fertility rate on development outcomes, and thus lends support to the need for policies that promote lower fertility rates.

While our empirical evidence is for India, similar fertility trends across developing countries suggest that our findings have relevance for other developing countries as well. Across both developed and developing countries, children have been used as instruments to secure support of parents in old age. This phenomenon, referred to in the literature as the old-age security hypothesis (Caldwell, 1976; Neher, 1971), proposes that an important reason behind fertility decision or parents' choice of having many children is the transfer from children to parents. Since Neher (1971) and Caldwell (1976), several authors have theoretically and empirically explored and validated the old-age security hypothesis and its role in shaping fertility decisions (Bental, 1989; Nugent, 1985; Zhang & Nishimura, 1993). Despite the benefits of fertility as proposed by the old-age security hypothesis, it is important to also bring into purview the potential negative effects on outcomes such as child nutrition. Fertility thus may generate costs or benefits for society, and this may either be captured through direct impacts within a family or significant externality that influence the welfare of society in general (Schultz, 2005). Our findings thus prompt policymakers on the need to take a more holistic perspective on the effects of fertility when devising policy.

2   Related Literature

Very limited literature exists on the fertility gap, especially on developing countries because of data availability issues. Several studies, however, examine lifetime fertility intentions, completed fertility and the estimated gap between them using European and North American data. Studies on the United Kingdom (e.g., Berrington & Pattaro, 2014; Smallwood & Jefferies, 2003), the United States (e.g., Freedman, Freedman, & Thornton, 1980; Morgan & Rackin, 2010) and Norway (e.g., Noack & Østby, 2002) have found evidence suggesting that couples tend to have fewer children than planned with a persisting gap.

In the United Kingdom, Smallwood and Jefferies (2003) show a gap of 0.2–0.3 birth per woman for birth intentions between ages 21 and 23 and actual birth, for birth cohorts 1957 to 1959. In the United States, an earlier study by Freedman et al. (1980) showed that the gap was one child per woman for women who were first interviewed in early adulthood in 1962, while Morgan and Rackin (2010), on the other hand, show that the gap between birth intentions at the age of 24 and actual birth was 0.25 per woman for birth cohorts 1957–1964. In Norway, Noack and Østby (2002) demonstrated a fertility gap of 0.3 identifying that women aged between 20 and 24 (birth cohorts 1953–1957) intended to have an average of 2.4 children, but ended up with an average of 2.1 actual births by their 40s.

In a more recent study, Beaujouan and Berghammer (2019) examine the aggregate fertility gap between intended and actual fertility in 19 European countries and the United States. They focus on women aged between 20 and 24 who were born in the early 1970s. They find that the fertility gap is widest in German-speaking countries and Southern European countries, but smallest in Central and Eastern European countries. Further analysis which takes into account educational level suggests that in most countries, the fertility gap is largest among highly educated women. This finding is consistent with previous studies that examine how fertility intentions and their realization differ by education attainment. This body of literature suggest that the fertility gap widens with education (Berrington & Pattaro, 2014), and compared to their less educated counterparts, highly educated women tend to reach smaller completed family sizes. This pattern is more apparent in Central and Eastern European countries and states such as Austria, Germany, Spain and Italy, where families receive little institutional support to take for their citizens (Beaujouan & Berghammer, 2019; Neyer & Hoem, 2008).

The only study on fertility gap that focuses on a developing country, of which we are aware, is Mishra and Parasnis (2018). They examine the fertility gap distribution in India and factors that could explain trends in this gap. Their results suggest that the preference for sons as influenced by Indian culture plays an important role in influencing the actual number of family, and by extension contributes to the trends in fertility gap.

This chapter contributes to the discourse on fertility gap in India but deviates from Mishra and Parasnis (2018) in that we do not seek to understand factors influencing the fertility gap in India, but we examine the role of fertility gap in shaping development outcomes, specifically child nutrition. In this regard, we contribute to the rather limited literature on the impact of fertility gap, and more narrowly the literature on the interplay between fertility, fertility choices and child nutrition (e.g., Blau, 1984, 1986; Horton, 1986).

3   Data and Estimation Strategy

Data and Variables

We use data from the National Family Health Survey (NFHS) conducted by the International Institute for Population Sciences (IIPS) under the Ministry of Health and Family Welfare (MOHFW), Government of India. This large-scale, multi-round survey is conducted in a representative sample of households throughout India. We employ the latest round: NFHS 4, conducted in 2015–2016. While the survey covers all 29 states of India, we include 17 states in this present analysis.[1] The survey provides detailed information on fertility for women aged 15–49. We restrict our sample to those women who have at least one child below the age of 5 years as information on nutritional parameters of children used in this study is only available for children below 5 years of age. Using this restricted sample and removing other outliers, we are left with a working sample of 138,009 women nationally, out of which 29,972 (21.7%) reported negative fertility gap (exceeding the desired number of children) and the remaining 108,037 (78.3%) reported 'no to positive fertility gap' (achieving or underachieving the desired number of children).

Our outcome variable captures the nutritional status of children who are in the age group of 0 to 5 years. The nutritional status is measured by one long term (i.e., stunted or not) and two short term (wasted or not, and anemic or not) health parameters. A child is considered 'stunted' if his/her 'height for age' z-score is below 2 standard deviations from the reference median as prescribed by World Health Organization (WHO hereafter); 'wasted' if his/her 'weight for age' z-score is below 2 standard deviations from the reference median as prescribed by WHO; and 'anemic' if a child suffers from 'severe' to 'moderate' anemia. Information on these variables is directly available in NFHS-4.

---

[1] The 17 major states included in our analysis account for roughly 90% of India's population and make up around 87% of India's GDP. The remaining 11 states, not included in the analysis, were small with missing or unreliable data points. The states not included are Chhattisgarh, Jharkhand, Uttrakhand, Goa, Mizoram, Sikkim, Arunachal Pradesh, Meghalaya Jammu, Kashmir and Nagaland.

The main explanatory variable is fertility gap, defined as the difference between a woman's ideal number of children and her actual number of children. A woman is said to have a (1) negative fertility gap if she exceeds her ideal family size, (2) positive, if she does not achieve her desired number of children and (3) zero fertility gap if the actual number of children is equal to her stated ideal. We work with the underlying hypothesis that women who have more children than desired may face greater constraints on their time as well as material and health resources, thus, resulting in poorer health outcomes for the children. To test this hypothesis, our measure of fertility gap takes the form of a dummy variable that takes the value 0 for women with no (i.e., achieved the ideal number of children) or positive fertility gap (i.e., has fewer children than ideal), and 1 for women with negative fertility gap (i.e., have more children than desired).

We control for potential factors that are likely to influence child nutrition outcomes. These control variables include mother's age and years of education, religion (i.e., dummy variable equals to one if respondent is Hindu and zero if otherwise), economic status, location (rural vs. urban), and health status (i.e., Body Mass Index (BMI) and anemic status).

Empirical Strategy

We estimate an empirical equation of the form:

$$Y_i = \alpha_i + \gamma F_i + \beta_i X_i + e_i$$

Here, outcome variable $\left(Y_i\right)$ is a binary variable, which takes the value 0 if a woman has no stunted/wasted/anemic children below the age of 5 years and 1 if woman has at least one child who is stunted/wasted/anaemic. F_i is the main explanatory variable, representing the fertility gap outcome for woman i as explained above. X_i is a set of control variables capturing individual characteristics. We also control for geographical (or regional) fixed effects. e_i is an error term.

Given that our outcome variable is binary in nature, we use logistic regression to estimate the equation above.

Table 5.2 Child's nutritional status by fertility gap

	% of women									
	Number of children alive		Children below 5 years		Stunted children		Wasted children		Anemic children	
Number of children	No/ Pos. gap	Neg. gap	No/ Pos. gap	Neg. gap	No/Pos. fertility gap	Neg. gap	No/ Pos. gap	Neg. gap	No/ Pos. gap	Neg. gap
0	0	0	0	0	20.88	14.65	23.44	18.27	68.68	62.77
1	43.07	3.06	72.97	58.8	61.57	56.72	60.66	55.7	28.17	31.09
2	42.03	9.08	25.55	33.18	16.71	24.25	15.19	22.26	3.09	5.75
3	10.75	39.18	1.45	7.72	0.83	4.26	0.7	3.68	0.06	0.39
4 & more	4.14	48.68	0.03	0.28	0.01	0.12	0.01	0.08	0	0

those with no or positive fertility gap. More than 87% of the women in the sample with negative fertility gap have three or more children, while for the women with no or positive fertility gap, this proportion is only about 15%. We also observe that women with no or positive fertility gap are younger, and thus a relatively large proportion (approximately 98%) of them have one or two children below the age of 5 years. Similarly, majority of the women without stunted or anemic children are those with no or positive fertility gap.

This preliminary data investigation points to some notable differences in child health status between the women who are exceeding their desired fertility compared to the women achieving/underachieving it. In the next section, we will present the results from formal empirical investigation of this relationship.

Multi-variate Regression Results

Table 5.3 reports logistic regression results (coefficients/odds ratios) for the relationship between child nutritional status and mother's outcome for fertility gap.

The results suggest that the odds of having stunted children are 1.3 times higher for women with a negative fertility gap over women with a no to positive fertility gap with an estimated coefficient of 0.255. This indicates that women with more than desired children are more likely to

Table 5.3 Logit results: effect of fertility gap on child nutritional outcomes

	Stunted children (0/1)		Wasted children (0/1)		Anemic children (0/1)	
	Coef	OR	Coef	OR	Coef	OR
Fertility gap	0.2553***	1.2908***	0.1981***	1.2190***	0.1891***	1.2082***
	(0.0198)	(0.0256)	(0.0183)	(0.0224)	(0.0155)	(0.0187)
Mother: Education (yrs)	−0.0421***	0.9588***	−0.0284***	0.9720***	−0.0407***	0.9601***
	(0.0016)	(0.0016)	(0.0015)	(0.0015)	(0.0014)	(0.0013)
Woman: Age (yrs)	0.0010	1.0010	−0.0049***	0.9952***	−0.0221***	0.9781***
	(0.0015)	(0.0015)	(0.0014)	(0.0014)	(0.0013)	(0.0013)
Hindu	0.0335*	1.0340*	0.0314*	1.0319*	−0.0553***	0.9462***
	(0.0187)	(0.0193)	(0.0175)	(0.0181)	(0.0162)	(0.0153)
Economic status	−0.1605***	0.8517***	−0.1429***	0.8668***	−0.1333***	0.8752***
	(0.0181)	(0.0154)	(0.0171)	(0.0148)	(0.0152)	(0.0133)
Rural	0.0838***	1.0874***	0.0753***	1.0782***	−0.0158	0.9843
	(0.0172)	(0.0187)	(0.0164)	(0.0177)	(0.0155)	(0.0152)
State fixed effects	Included	Included	Included	Included	Included	Included
Observations	138,009	138,009	138,009	138,009	138,009	138,009
Pseudo-R-squared	0.0318	0.0318	0.0210	0.0210	0.0426	0.0426

Notes: Standard errors in parentheses. ***$p < 0.01$, **$p < 0.05$, *$p < 0.1$

have children with poor long-term health outcomes. Likewise, looking at the short-term health parameters, children from the women 'overshooting' their desired fertility are more likely to be 'wasted' and 'anemic'. The corresponding odds are approximately 1.2 times higher for women with a negative fertility gap compared to those with a no to positive fertility gap. Here, the estimated coefficients, which are positive and statistically significant at the 1% significance level, are 0.198 for 'wasted children' and 0.189 for 'anemic' children.

Coefficients on control variables suggest that mother's education and economic status are important and relevant factors for improving the odds of poor health outcomes for children both in the short term and in the longer term. These results, therefore, support conclusions from existing studies which suggest that an increase in mother's years of education lowers the odds of having stunted/wasted/anemic children (see, e.g., Smith & Haddad, 2015). Likewise, the women from relatively affluent sections of the society have lower odds of having stunted/wasted/anemic children compared to the women who belong to the poorer strata.

Other findings suggest that age of a mother affects the nutritional outcomes for children only in the short term but not in the long term. Specifically, the coefficient of age is statistically insignificant in the model examining stunted growth but an increase in age of the mother, marginally lowers the odds of having 'wasted' and 'anemic' children. This finding is consistent with the literature which has shown that childbirth at relatively younger ages is associated with poorer nutritional outcomes for children (see, e.g., Martorell & Young, 2012).[2]

The odds of stunting and wasting in children are 1.8 times higher for women residing in rural areas compared to those residing in urban areas. This may be explained by the lack of quality and sufficient diets as well as good sanitation often associated with individuals living in poor rural areas, which have been found to contribute to stunted and wasted growth

---

[2] These results must be contextualized in an Indian setting where most of the women start their fertility rather early in life. The median age of first marriage is still very low in India. As per NFHS 4 survey report, the median age at first marriage is 19 years among women aged 20–49 and 40% of women aged 20–49 marry before the legal minimum age for marriage of 18 years (Indian National Family Health Survey NFHS 4, 2015–16, Chapter 6, page number 157).

(Smith & Haddad, 2015; Martorell & Young, 2012). However, location does not seem to affect the odds of anemia in children.

In addition to the various control variables discussed above, mother's health has also been hypothesized to influence children nutritional outcomes. The existing literature shows that undernutrition and vitamin deficiencies in mothers can lead to fetal growth restriction and sub-optimal breast feeding, which consequently contributes to stunting and wasting in children (Black et al., 2013). We take into account these findings, and thus extend our model to include indicators that capture the health of mothers. We adopt two indicators to capture mother's health: BMI and anemic status of mothers. BMI associated with poor health of a mother is defined by the range <18.5 kg/meter^2 or > 30 kg/meter^2. Anemic status of a mother is measured by hemoglobin levels and levels below 10 grams/deciliter (g/dl) are taken as poor health parameters. In the sample used, approximately 29% of women are considered unhealthy per the BMI standard and 15% are considered anemic.

Table 5.4 presents the results in which we include mother's health status as additional covariates. We find that the inclusion of information on mother's health only slightly improved the overall explanatory power of the model and does not alter the effect of the fertility gap on the nutritional status of children. We do find that mothers' anemic status positively influences the odds of a child having poor nutritional outcomes, with the strongest association observed in the case of children being anemic. Mother's BMI status does not significantly affect the odds of being stunted but influences the odds of being wasted and anemic. Given that being wasted and anemic are associated with short-term health factors, this finding suggests that BMI of a mother tends to affect the nutritional status of children only in the short term but not over the longer term.

We also investigate the effect of the interaction between a mother's health condition and fertility gap on her child's nutritional outcomes. Specifically, we attempt to understand if mothers with poor health and negative fertility gap are likely to have children with poorer nutritional status. We achieve this by including two interaction terms between (1) mother's BMI and fertility gap and (2) mother's anemic status and fertility gap. These interaction terms are statistically insignificant.

Table 5.4 Logit results: effect of fertility gap and mother's health on child nutritional outcomes

	Stunted children (0/1)		Wasted children (0/1)		Anemic children (0/1)	
	Coef	OR	Coef	OR	Coef	OR
Fertility gap	0.2557***	1.2914***	0.1988***	1.2199***	0.1947***	1.2150***
	(0.0198)	(0.0256)	(0.0183)	(0.0224)	(0.0156)	(0.0189)
Mother: BMI	−0.0032	0.9968	0.0862***	1.0900***	0.1061***	1.1120***
	(0.0156)	(0.0155)	(0.0149)	(0.0163)	(0.0131)	(0.0146)
Mother: Anemic	0.2081***	1.2313***	0.1601***	1.1737***	0.6262***	1.8705***
	(0.0208)	(0.0256)	(0.0193)	(0.0227)	(0.0157)	(0.0294)
Mother: Education (yrs)	−0.0412***	0.9596***	−0.0273***	0.9731***	−0.0378***	0.9629***
	(0.0016)	(0.0016)	(0.0015)	(0.0015)	(0.0014)	(0.0013)
Woman: Age (yrs)	0.0011	1.0011	−0.0044***	0.9956***	−0.0212***	0.9791***
	(0.0015)	(0.0015)	(0.0014)	(0.0014)	(0.0013)	(0.0013)
Hindu	0.0315*	1.0320*	0.0293*	1.0297*	−0.0623***	0.9396***
	(0.0187)	(0.0193)	(0.0175)	(0.0181)	(0.0163)	(0.0153)
Economic status	−0.1573***	0.8544***	−0.1342***	0.8744***	−0.1165***	0.8900***
	(0.0181)	(0.0155)	(0.0171)	(0.0150)	(0.0153)	(0.0137)
Rural	0.0824***	1.0858***	0.0729***	1.0757***	−0.0214	0.9788
	(0.0172)	(0.0186)	(0.0165)	(0.0177)	(0.0156)	(0.0153)
State fixed effects	Included	Included	Included	Included	Included	Included
Observations	138,009	138,009	138,009	138,009	138,009	138,009
Pseudo-R-squared	0.0326	0.0326	0.0217	0.0217	0.0520	0.0520

Notes: Standard errors in parentheses. ***$p < 0.01$, **$p < 0.05$, *$p < 0.1$

5   Conclusion

This chapter examines the effects of the fertility gap on child nutrition in India. Child nutrition is one of the key indicators of development and one of the most important millennium and sustainable development goal. The importance of child nutrition is reflected in the fact that it is not just an independent development outcome, but it is instrumental in achieving the goals of poverty, poor health and inadequate social conditions. Specifically, good nutrition plays an important role in achieving the development goals of health, education and economic growth because of the importance of human capital in the development process. Child nutrition is crucial for the human capital components of economic development and good health. Good nutrition enables children benefit from education, it reduces mortality among children and mothers, and, more importantly, it contributes to the development of resilient communities. Accordingly, malnourishment can be linked with poor development and productivity.

Using a nationally representative data from India, we examine the association between fertility gaps and child nutrition with a specific focus on stunted growth, wasted growth and anemia. Fertility gap, defined as the difference between a woman's ideal number of children and her actual number of children, is measured using a dummy variable. The dummy variable that takes the value 0 for women with no (i.e., achieved the ideal number of children) or positive fertility gap (i.e., has fewer children than ideal), and the value 1 for women with negative fertility gap (i.e., have more children than desired). Our results show that the odds of having malnourished children that are stunted, wasted or anemic are higher for women who exceed their fertility target compared to those who have achieved or underachieved it.

The findings from this research emphasize the importance of policies that promote low fertility. In the Indian context, where fertility period begins relatively early in life for most women, making it more likely for them to exceed their fertility targets, it is important to promote the awareness of family planning programs and contraception methods. This will ensure that the early onset of fertility cycle observed in India does not lead to more children than desired. Policies promoting the education of women are also important given the finding that education is associated with better fertility decisions.

References

Ashraf, Q. H., Weil, D. N., & Wilde, J. (2013). The effect of fertility reduction on economic growth. *Population and Development Review, 39*(1), 97–130.

Barro, R. J., & Becker, G. S. (1989). Fertility choice in a model of economic growth. *Econometrica, 57*(2), 481–501. https://doi.org/10.2307/1912563

Beaujouan, E., & Berghammer, C. (2019). The gap between lifetime fertility intentions and completed fertility in Europe and the United States: A cohort approach. *Population Research and Policy Review*. https://doi.org/10.1007/s11113-019-09516-3

Becker, G. S., Murphy, K. M., & Tamura, R. (1990). Human capital, fertility, and economic growth. *Journal of Political Economy, 98*(5, Part 2), S12–S37.

Becker, S. O., Cinnirella, F., & Woessmann, L. (2010). The trade-off between fertility and education: Evidence from before the demographic transition. *Journal of Economic Growth, 15*, 177–204.

Bental, B. (1989). The old age security hypothesis and optimal population growth. *Journal of Population Economics, 1*(4), 285–301.

Berrington, A., & Pattaro, S. (2014). Educational differences in fertility desires, intentions and behaviour: A life course perspective. *Advances in Life Course Research, 21*, 10–27. https://doi.org/10.1016/j.alcr.2013.12.003

Black, R. E., Victora, C. G., Walker, S. P., Bhutta, Z., Christian, P., de Onis, M., … Webb, P. (2013). Maternal and child undernutrition and overweight in low-income and middle-income countries. *Lancet, 382*, 427–477.

Blau, D. M. (1984). A model of child nutrition, fertility, and women's time allocation: The case of Nicaragua. *Research in Population Economics, 5*, 113–135.

Blau, D. M. (1986). Fertility, child nutrition, and child mortality in Nicaragua: An economic analysis of interrelationships. *The Journal of Developing Areas, 20*(2), 185–202.

Brander, J. A., & Dowrick, S. (1994). The role of fertility and population in economic growth. *Journal of Population Economics, 7*(1), 1–25.

Cáceres-Delpiano, J., & Simonsen, M. (2012). The toll of fertility on mothers' wellbeing. *Journal of Health Economics, 31*(5), 752–766. https://doi.org/10.1016/j.jhealeco.2012.05.006

Caldwell, J. C. (1976). Toward a restatement of demographic transition theory. *Population and Development Review, 2*(3/4), 321–366. https://doi.org/10.2307/1971615

Chun, H., & Oh, J. (2002). An instrumental variable estimate of the effect of fertility on the labour force participation of married women. *Applied Economics Letters, 9*(10), 631–634.

Doepke, M., & Tertilt, M. (2018). *Women's empowerment, the gender gap in desired fertility, and fertility outcomes in developing countries*. Paper presented at the AEA Papers and Proceedings.

Drèze, J., & Murthi, M. (2001). Fertility, education, and development: Evidence from India. *Population and Development Review, 27*(1), 33–63.

Freedman, R., Freedman, D. S., & Thornton, A. D. (1980). Changes in fertility expectations and preferences between 1962 and 1977: Their relation to final parity. *Demography, 17*(4), 365–378.

Gries, T., & Grundmann, R. (2018). Fertility and modernization: The role of urbanization in developing countries. *Journal of International Development, 30*(3), 493–506.

Guo, Z., Wu, Z., Schimmele, C. M., & Li, S. (2012). The effect of urbanization on China's fertility. *Population Research and Policy Review, 31*(3), 417–434. https://doi.org/10.1007/s11113-012-9230-0

Herzer, D., Strulik, H., & Vollmer, S. (2012). The long-run determinants of fertility: One century of demographic change 1900–1999. *Journal of Economic Growth, 17*(4), 357–385. https://doi.org/10.1007/s10887-012-9085-6

Hondroyiannis, G. (2010). Fertility determinants and economic uncertainty: An assessment using European panel data. *Journal of Family and Economic Issues, 31*(1), 33–50. https://doi.org/10.1007/s10834-009-9178-3

Horton, S. (1986). Child nutrition and family size in the Philippines. *Journal of Development Economics, 23*(1), 161–176. https://doi.org/10.1016/0304-3878(86)90086-6

International Institute for Population Sciences (IIPS) & ICF. (2017). National family health survey (NFHS-4), 2015–16. Mumbai: IIPS.

Khan, H. T. A., & Raeside, R. (1997). Factors affecting the most recent fertility rates in urban-rural Bangladesh. *Social Science & Medicine, 44*(3), 279–289. https://doi.org/10.1016/S0277-9536(96)00076-7

Klawon, E., & Tiefenthaler, J. (2001). Bargaining over family size: The determinants of fertility in Brazil. *Population Research and Policy Review, 20*(5), 423–440. https://doi.org/10.1023/A:1013337201896

Kohler, H. P., Behrman, J. R., & Skytthe, A. (2005). Partner+ children= happiness? The effects of partnerships and fertility on well-being. *Population and Development Review, 31*(3), 407–445.

Kravdal, Ø. (2002). Education and fertility in sub-Saharan Africa: Individual and community effects. *Demography, 39*(2), 233–250. https://doi.org/10.1353/dem.2002.0017

Lloyd, C. B., & Gage-Brandon, A. J. (1994). High fertility and children's schooling in Ghana: Sex differences in parental contributions and educational outcomes. *Population studies, 48*(2), 293–306.

Martorell, R., & Young, M. F. (2012). Patterns of stunting and wasting: Potential explanatory factors. *Advances in Nutrition, 3*, 227–233.

McQuillan, K. (2004). When does religion influence fertility? *Population and Development Review, 30*(1), 25–56.

Mishra, A., & Parasnis, J. (2017). Peers and fertility preferences: An empirical investigation of the role of neighbours, religion and education. *Social Indicators Research, 134*(1), 339–357.

Mishra, A., & Parasnis, J. (2018). *Husband, sons and fertility gap: Evidence from India*. Monash University Department of Economics Working Paper Series, 17/18, 1–37.

Morgan, S. P., & Rackin, H. (2010). The correspondence between fertility intentions and behavior in the United States. *Population and Development Review, 36*(1), 91–118.

Neher, P. A. (1971). Peasants, procreation, and pensions. *The American Economic Review, 61*(3), 380–389.

Neyer, G., & Hoem, J. M. (2008). Education and permanent childlessness: Austria vs. Sweden. A research note. In J. Surkyn, P. Deboosere, & J. Van Bavel (Eds.), *Demographic challenges for the 21st century: A state of the art in demography* (pp. 91–112). Brussels: Brussels University Press.

Noack, T., & Østby, L. (2002). Free to choose–but unable to stick to it? Norwegian fertility expectations and subsequent behaviour in the following 20 years. In E. Klijzing & M. Corijn (Eds.), *Dynamics of fertility and partnership in Europe: Insights and lessons from comparative research* (pp. 103–116). New York: United Nations.

Nugent, J. B. (1985). The old-age security motive for fertility. *Population and Development Review, 11*(1), 75–97. https://doi.org/10.2307/1973379

Rindfuss, R. R., Morgan, S. P., & Offutt, K. (1996). Education and the changing age pattern of American fertility: 1963–1989. *Demography, 33*(3), 277–290. https://doi.org/10.2307/2061761

Schultz, T. P. (2005). *Effects of fertility decline on family well-being: Opportunities for evaluating population programs*. New Haven: Yale University.

Smallwood, S., & Jefferies, J. (2003). Family building intentions in England and Wales: Trends, outcomes and interpretations. *Population Trends, 112,* 15–28.

Smith, L. C., & Haddad, L. (2015). Reducing child undernutrition: Past drivers and priorities for the post-MDG era. *World Development, 68,* 180–204.

UNPF. (2018). *The state of world population 2018.* New York: United Nations Population Fund.

Wang, P., Yip, C. K., & Scotese, C. A. (1994). Fertility choice and economic growth: Theory and evidence. *The Review of Economics and Statistics, 76*(2), 255–266. https://doi.org/10.2307/2109880

Zhang, J., & Nishimura, K. (1993). The old-age security hypothesis revisited. *Journal of Development Economics, 41*(1), 191–202. https://doi.org/10.1016/0304-3878(93)90047-Q

6

Sexual Orientation and Sexually Transmissible Infections (STIs)

Sefa Awaworyi Churchill, Lisa Farrell, and Janet Exornam Ocloo

1 Introduction and Background

A steady rise in the prevalence of HIV and other sexually transmissible infections (STIs) has been well documented across the literature over the past few decades (see, e.g., Ma et al., 2007; Maulsby et al., 2014; Musyoki et al., 2015; Oster et al., 2014; Satterwhite et al., 2013; Welz et al., 2007; Zhang et al., 2014). This is of concern, both in developing and developed countries, and thus the health targets in both the millennium and sustainable development goals emphasise the need to address the prevalence of HIV and other health epidemics.

STIs are defined as infections that can be transferred from one sexual partner to another through sexual contact. STIs are most commonly

S. Awaworyi Churchill (✉) • L. Farrell
School of Economics, Finance and Marketing, RMIT University, Melbourne, VIC, Australia
e-mail: sefa.churchill@rmit.edu.au; lisa.farrell@rmit.edu.au

J. E. Ocloo
Korle-bu Teaching Hospital, Accra, Ghana

© The Author(s) 2020
S. Awaworyi Churchill (ed.), *Moving from the Millennium to the Sustainable Development Goals*, https://doi.org/10.1007/978-981-15-1556-9_6

95

spread via oral, vaginal, or anal contact, and can also be transmitted by skin-to-skin contact. The increased prevalence and risk of acquiring STIs are not attributable to a single or distinct cause, but a combination of several factors. One strand of the literature highlights factors such as sexual orientation, or identity and sexual behaviour (see, e.g., Everett, 2013; Friedman et al., 2014; Wu et al., 2013), and statistics from various countries support this hypothesis. For instance, statistics from the United States Department of Health and Human Services suggests that since 2000, rates of STIs among men who have sex with men (MSM) have increased dramatically, with about 47% of all HIV/AIDS cases diagnosed in 2004 associated with MSM. Further, the joint United Nations Program on HIV/AIDS (UNAIDS) 2004 report suggests that in many developed countries and regions, such as North America, Australia, and Western Europe, about 70% of HIV/AIDS infections have occurred among homosexuals.

A number of studies (e.g., Dougan, Evans, & Elford, 2007; Liu et al., 2006; Wade et al., 2005) have cited risky sexual behaviour as the principal cause of the high prevalence rates of STIs. Although there appears to be a growing literature on the subject, much of this literature focuses on the United States, with relatively very few studies examining other geographic areas. Consequently, the generalizability of existing conclusions related to the association between sexual orientation, sexual behaviour, and the prevalence of STIs may be questioned. We present new evidence examining the relationship between sexual orientation, sexual behaviour, and STIs using new data from Britain, which has not received the same level of attention as data from the United States. In Britain, the rapid increase in STIs has become a significant public health threat due to the comorbidities associated with such infections and the amount of resources spent in managing them. The increasing prevalence of STIs in Britain increases the risk to the entire population; consequently, understanding the factors of influence is of significant interest to public health policymakers and health practitioners.

Reducing the prevalence of HIV/AIDS formed part of the millennium development goals (MDGs) and have continued to be part of the sustainable development goals (SDGs). Unfortunately, in most cases, the development goals are only examined in the context of developing countries. However, development targets relating to health and gender equality are very relevant for developed countries as well, and thus there is need to also examine these goals in the context of developed countries. In this chapter, we seek to contribute to the literature by focusing on the health dimension of the development target by examining individual level evidence from Britain. Our focus on Britain is particularly relevant given the increasing prevalence of STIs which also includes HIV, a key focus of the SDGs. We present individual level evidence on how sexual behaviour influences sexual health.

Since the 1990s, trends in sexual behaviour have evolved significantly alongside public health improvements in preventative care and medical treatment options for STIs. This could affect attitudes towards sexual activity and risky sexual behaviour. For instance, since the introduction of efficient antiretroviral therapies, there has been a significant reduction in HIV-related mortalities. The availability of current treatment options for STIs may influence sexual behaviour; thus, there is a need to understand this relationship to ensure safe and informed sexual practices, which could have tremendous impact on the achievement of the health-related SDGs.

Additionally, much remains to be understood about the association between sexual orientation, sexual behaviour, and the prevalence of STIs. Our study responds to the several calls for researchers to examine sexual identity or orientation in conjunction with sexual behaviour to further understand the prevalence of STIs (see, e.g., Malebranche, Arriola, Jenkins, Dauria, & Patel, 2010; Moradi, Mohr, Worthington, & Fassinger, 2009; Young & Meyer, 2005). Specifically, although sexual behaviours are closely associated with sexual identities, they are distinct and observing them as such could help us to better understand the prevalence of STIs. Previous studies (e.g., Everett, 2013; Nakamura, Semple, Strathdee, & Patterson, 2011; Wells, McGee, & Beautrais, 2011) have established that sexual behaviour and identity do not always align, and thus the risk of STIs could vary by both sexual behaviour and sexual identity. For instance, Xu, Sternberg, and Markowitz (2010) using the National Health and Nutritional Survey (2001–2006), showed that only 18% of women who indicated they had agreed to have had same-sex sexual relationships identify as gay or lesbian, whereas about 50% reported a heterosexual identity.

Using data from the British National Surveys of Sexual Attitudes and Lifestyles (Natsal), we contribute to the growing literature by exploring sexual orientation and sexual behaviour as potential factors that can explain the prevalence of STIs. We find that both sexual behaviour and orientation are factors that explain the prevalence of STIs. Further, sexual orientation appears to be a stronger factor of influence compared to all measures of sexual behaviour, except the effects of having anal sex.

The remainder of the chapter is structured as follows: the next section presents an overview of the data and variables. Section 3 presents the empirical methods, and Sect. 4 reports and discusses the results. Section 5 concludes the study.

2   Data

Natsal is one of the largest surveys of sexual behaviour in the world, and has produced several publications (see, e.g., Erens et al., 2014; Jones et al., 2014; Macdowall et al., 2015; Mercer et al., 2013; Tanton et al., 2015). Three Natsal surveys have taken place: Natsal-1 in 1990–1991, Natsal-2 in 1999–2001, and Natsal-3 in 2010–2012. For the purpose of our study, the latest wave of the survey, Natsal-3, provides the most current, complete, and comprehensive information required. The survey used stratified probability sampling to select households from which one eligible individual was selected at random and invited to participate. The overall response rate was 57.7%. Further details of the methodology have been published previously (see, e.g., Erens et al., 2013). Overall, Natsal-3 interviewed 15,162 men and women aged 16–74 years, residents in Britain. However, accounting for missing observations, our largest estimation sample for the regression analysis includes data on 12,222 respondents.

Given the objectives of this study, our dependent variables focus on Natsal-3 survey questions that attempt to capture a person's STI exposure and experience. We focus on three main dependent variables: (1) a dummy variable that equals 1 if the respondent has ever been diagnosed with an STI; (2) a four-point scale for self-assessed HIV/AIDS risk. This is based on the Natsal-3 question "given your personal sexual lifestyle, what do you think about the HIV risks to you personally? Where an answer of 1 means 'not at all at risk', 2 means 'not very much', 3 means 'quite a lot', 4 means 'greatly at risk'"; and (3) an additive index that represents a count of the number of STIs with which a respondent has been diagnosed. Our study focuses on five types of STIs, namely chlamydia, gonorrhoea, genital warts, syphilis, and herpes. For robustness, we also examine the effects of our explanatory variables on the prevalence of each of the five STIs. These include (1) a dummy variable that equals to 1 if the respondent has ever been diagnosed with chlamydia; (2) a dummy variable that equals to 1 if the respondent has ever been diagnosed with gonorrhoea; (3) a dummy variable that equals to 1 if the respondent has ever been diagnosed with genital warts; (4) a dummy variable that equals to 1 if the respondent has ever been diagnosed with syphilis; and (5) a dummy variable that equals to 1 if the respondent has ever been diagnosed with herpes. These are the most prevalent STIs to be captured by the survey.

Our key explanatory variables focus on sexual orientation and various aspects of sexual behaviour, especially same-sex sexual engagement. The first explanatory variable captures sexual identity or orientation and is a dummy variable that equals to 1 if the respondent identifies as gay/lesbian. Other explanatory variables capture sexual behaviour. Specifically, the second variable captures the number of same-sex partners a respondent has had in the past year. The third and fourth variables are dummy variables that are equal to 1 if the respondent ever had a same-sex experience with genital contact and same-sex anal sex, respectively. The fifth variable focuses on the frequency of same-sex intercourse in the past seven days. The last variable focuses on a social dimension of behaviour and is based on the question "how often, if at all, do you usually go to gay pubs, bars, and clubs? Where 0 means 'never or not applicable', 1 means 'less often than once a year', 2 means 'less often but at least once a year', 3 means 'less often but at least twice a year', 4 means 'less often but at least once a month', and 5 means 'at least once a week'". Our data also allows us to control for whether the respondent has ever been raped. Evidence shows that rape victims are at high risk of contracting STIs from their attackers (see, e.g., Carole et al., 1990; Kawsar, Anfield, Walters, McCabe, & Forster, 2004).

Control variables included in our regressions are the respondents' gender, age, educational and marital status, income, employment status, and ethnicity. We also include regional dummies to account for regional fixed effects. Specifically, we include dummies for North, South, and East England, as well as London, Wales, and Scotland. We exclude the West as the base category. Description and summary statistics of variables are reported in Appendix Table 6.4. The raw data shows that 29% of the British population have experienced an STI at some point in their life and yet perceptions of HIV risk across the population is relatively low at a mean of 1.27 on the four-point scale ranging from low risk to high risk. Untangling these interesting patterns in the data requires a multivariate framework, as detailed in the next section.

3   Empirical Specification and Methods

To examine the association between sexual orientation and STIs, we estimate the following equation:

$$STI_i = \alpha + \beta_1 SOB_i + \sum_n \beta_n X_{n,i} + \varepsilon_i \tag{6.1}$$

where i indexes the individuals, STI is the measure of sexually transmissible infection, SOB_i is the set of variables that capture sexual orientation and sexual behaviours, X_n is a set of control variables described earlier, β_1 and β_n are parameters to be estimated, and ε is the random error term. Given the binary nature of our first dependent variable, we estimate Eq. (6.1) using logit estimation techniques. Regressions for our second and third dependent variables (i.e., HIV/AIDS risk and prevalence index, respectively) are estimated using ordered logit estimation. The regressions for the separate STIs are estimated via logit techniques. All regressions are estimated using heteroscedasticity robust standard errors.

4   Results and Discussions

Panel A of Table 6.1 presents results for the effects of sexual orientation and sexual behaviour on the likelihood of being diagnosed with an STI. Panel B presents results for the effects on self-assessed risk of getting HIV/AIDS. Panel C presents effects on our prevalence index of the count of STIs experienced by the respondent. In each panel, Columns 1 to 6 include our main sexual orientation and behaviour variables, one at a time in each regression, while Column 7 includes all six explanatory variables at the same time in a single regression model. Looking at Panel A of Table 6.1, we consistently find that both sexual orientation and sexual behaviours increase the odds of having an STI. From Column 1, given the estimated coefficients, the results suggest that being gay or lesbian significantly increases the odds of being diagnosed with an STI. Results from Column 2 show that an increase in the number of same-sex partners increases the odds of being diagnosed with an STI and the self-assessed risk levels of respondents regarding HIV/AIDS. From Columns 3 and 4, we observe that respondents who have had a same-sex sexual experience with genital contact and those who have had same-sex anal sex, respectively, have higher odds of being diagnosed with STIs as well as higher self-assessed risk of getting HIV/AIDS. Similar results are also observed in Columns 5 and 6, with an increase in the frequency of same-sex sex and visitations to gay clubs, respectively, increasing the odds of being diagnosed with STIs.

However, from Column 7, the inclusion of all explanatory variables in our model shows that having a same-sex experience with genital contact and having anal sex appear to be the most important factors that influence the prevalence of STIs. This set of results suggest that being gay or lesbian increases the odds of contracting an STI through same-sex sexual behaviour involving genital contact. It is also important to note that anal sex is a risk factor associated with the entire population (this sexual behaviour is not restricted to same-sex experiences).

Panels B and C also show similar trends, where sexual orientation appears to be a stronger factor as captured by same-sex experience with genital contact, and anal sex is also a high-risk factor (except in relation to the number of STIs experienced). Our results also show that rape victims are at higher risk of STIs—this finding is consistent across all specifications.

Table 6.1 The impact of sexual orientation and sexual behaviour

	(1)	(2)	(3)	(4)	(5)	(6)	(7)
Panel A: Sexual orientation, sexual behaviour and STI (logit regression)							
Gay/lesbian	0.870***						−0.570
	(0.180)						(0.389)
Partners		0.120**					−0.104
		(0.050)					(0.115)
Experience			0.773***				0.770***
			(0.082)				(0.194)
Anal sex				1.767***			1.049*
				(0.205)			(0.552)
Occasions					0.230**		0.010
					(0.092)		(0.093)
Gay clubs						0.428***	0.169
						(0.058)	(0.149)
Rape	0.596***	0.601***	0.506***	0.583***	0.526***	0.586***	0.495***
	(0.079)	(0.079)	(0.080)	(0.078)	(0.085)	(0.078)	(0.085)
Observations	12,222	12,222	12,222	12,222	11,576	12,216	11,576
Panel B: Sexual orientation, sexual behaviour, and HIV/AIDS risk (ordered logit regression)							
Gay/lesbian	0.919***						−0.540
	(0.145)						(0.363)
Partners		0.277***					0.130
		(0.047)					(0.107)
Experience			0.747***				0.556***
			(0.074)				(0.173)
Anal sex				1.744***			1.109**
				(0.192)			(0.485)
Occasions					0.268***		−0.013
					(0.080)		(0.096)

Gay clubs						0.390*** (0.053)	0.073 (0.142)
Rape	0.446*** (0.090)	0.440*** (0.090)	0.338*** (0.091)	0.431*** (0.090)	0.434*** (0.100)	0.441*** (0.089)	0.400*** (0.100)
Observations	12,179	12,179	12,179	12,179	11,536	12,173	11,536

Panel C: Sexual orientation, sexual behaviour, and STI index (ordered logit regression)

Gay/lesbian	0.835*** (0.176)						−0.044 (0.442)
Partners		0.175*** (0.044)					−0.052 (0.134)
Experience			0.787*** (0.091)				0.546** (0.237)
Anal sex				1.572*** (0.222)			0.735 (0.589)
Occasions					0.229*** (0.068)		0.058 (0.109)
Gay clubs						0.348*** (0.061)	0.022 (0.160)
Rape	0.714*** (0.096)	0.717*** (0.096)	0.604*** (0.098)	0.699*** (0.096)	0.682*** (0.107)	0.706*** (0.096)	0.652*** (0.107)
Observations	12,222	12,222	12,222	12,222	11,576	12,216	11,576

Notes: All regressions include relevant control variables and regional fixed effects (Full tables with all covariates are in Tables 6.5, 6.6, and 6.7 of the Appendix). In Panel A, the dependent variable is a dummy variable equals to 1 if respondent has ever been diagnosed with an STI. In Panel B, the dependent variable is a four-point scale for self-assessed HIV/AIDS risk. In Panel C, the dependent variable is an additive index. That is, a count of five types of STIs. Robust standard errors in parentheses. ***$p < 0.01$, **$p < 0.05$, *$p < 0.1$

Robustness and Sensitivity Checks

We conduct two major set of analyses to examine the robustness and sensitivity of our results. First, we examine the robustness of our results if we use the individual indicators that were combined to generate the additive index. As indicated earlier, one of our measures of STIs is an additive index that represents a count of the number of STIs with which respondents have been diagnosed. We run regressions with each of the five indicators (STIs) that were added to form the composite index. Table 6.2 presents results for this exercise, which are consistent with our existing conclusion that both sexual orientation and sexual behaviour increase the odds of having an STI.

Table 6.2 Robustness checks (logit regression)

	(1)	(2)	(3)	(4)	(5)	(6)
	Gay/lesbian	Partners	Experience	Anal sex	Occasions	Gay clubs
Dependent variable: Dummy if diagnosed with chlamydia						
Explanatory	0.627***	0.141***	0.786***	1.481***	0.134	0.373***
variable	(0.236)	(0.054)	(0.114)	(0.269)	(0.082)	(0.070)
Observations	12,222	12,222	12,222	12,222	11,576	12,216
Dependent variable: Dummy if diagnosed with gonorrhoea						
Explanatory	2.021***	0.311***	1.425***	2.790***	0.319***	0.641***
variable	(0.267)	(0.055)	(0.209)	(0.295)	(0.094)	(0.081)
Observations	12,222	12,222	12,222	12,222	11,576	12,216
Dependent variable: Dummy if diagnosed with warts						
Explanatory	1.174***	0.218***	0.688***	1.598***	0.227**	0.302***
variable	(0.236)	(0.053)	(0.143)	(0.296)	(0.088)	(0.091)
Observations	12,222	12,222	12,222	12,222	11,576	12,216
Dependent variable: Dummy if diagnosed with syphilis						
Explanatory	3.350***	0.493***	2.762***	3.729***	0.469***	0.936***
variable	(0.444)	(0.076)	(0.427)	(0.554)	(0.128)	(0.132)
Observations	10,654	10,654	10,654	10,654	10,104	10,648
Dependent variable: Dummy if diagnosed with herpes						
Explanatory	0.650	0.153**	1.013***	1.057**	0.278***	0.184
variable	(0.422)	(0.076)	(0.211)	(0.536)	(0.083)	(0.146)
Observations	12,222	12,222	12,222	12,222	11,576	12,216

Notes: Explanatory variables are indicated on top of each column. All regressions include relevant control variables and regional fixed effects. Robust standard errors in parentheses. ***$p < 0.01$, **$p < 0.05$

Second, the existing literature provides some indication of different levels of vulnerability to STIs depending on age. For instance, it has been argued that young adults and adolescents, for both behavioural and biological reasons, are more vulnerable to STIs than older people (Heise, 1994). Specifically, sexual activity begins for most individuals during adolescence and sexual intercourse at a young age is a strong risk factor for STIs. Further, young people, especially adolescent girls, are less able to refuse sex and/or insist on the use of adequate protection putting them at greater risk (Heise, 1994; Noble, Cover, & Yanagishita, 1996; Weiss, Shelan, & Gupta, 1996). We split our sample into three age groups to examine the sensitivity of our results. Consistent with the UN age classification of youth, which is 15 to 24 years, our first age group captures respondents up to 24 years. Our sample includes respondents from ages 16 to 74 years. Thus, regressions for the first age sample include respondents from 16 to 24 years. The second and third age groups include respondents aged 25 to 44 years and 45 years and above, respectively.

Results for this exercise are reported in Table 6.3. Quite robustly, we find that both sexual orientation and sexual behaviour increase the odds of having an STI. However, we note that, in most cases, comparing the magnitude of coefficients, the effects of sexual orientation and sexual behaviour are relatively stronger for respondents in the 16 to 24 years age group compared to those in the 25 to 44 years age group. However, the effects reported for the third age group (45–74 years) appear to be the strongest. These results suggest the presence of strong cohort or life-course effects. In particular, we find as expected that adolescence is associated with high risk sexual behaviours. The oldest cohorts are those who are likely to have been exposed to the least sexual health education during their youth, when sexual activity is most likely to begin. Alternatively, later life might be associated with more sexual confidence that leads to a broader range of sexual practices. Unfortunately, given that our data is cross-sectional, we are unable to distinguish between life-cycle effects and cohort effects.

Table 6.3 Robustness checks (different age group)

Variables	(1) Gay/lesbian	(2) Partners	(3) Experience	(4) Anal sex	(5) Occasions	(6) Gay clubs
Panel A: 16–24 years age group						
Dependent variable: Dummy if respondent has ever been diagnosed with an STI						
Explanatory	1.136***	0.173	0.725***	1.735***	0.364*	0.422***
variable	(0.395)	(0.119)	(0.183)	(0.494)	(0.210)	(0.143)
Observations	2388	2388	2388	2388	2251	2388
Dependent variable: Four-point scale for self-assessed HIV/AIDS risk						
Explanatory	1.373***	0.496***	0.906***	1.537***	0.233	0.374***
variable	(0.320)	(0.084)	(0.159)	(0.439)	(0.169)	(0.118)
Observations	2382	2382	2382	2382	2245	2382
Dependent variable: An additive index. That is, a count of five types of STIs						
Explanatory	0.976**	0.030	0.558***	1.540***	0.306	0.386**
variable	(0.440)	(0.130)	(0.216)	(0.544)	(0.224)	(0.155)
Observations	2388	2388	2388	2388	2251	2388
Panel B: 25–44 years age group						
Dependent variable: Dummy if respondent has ever been diagnosed with an STI						
Explanatory	0.532**	0.093	0.619***	1.348***	0.216**	0.329***
variable	(0.243)	(0.082)	(0.114)	(0.284)	(0.106)	(0.073)
Observations	5348	5348	5348	5348	5037	5347
Dependent variable: Four-point scale for self-assessed HIV/AIDS risk						
Explanatory	0.990***	0.295***	0.688***	1.921***	0.237*	0.441***
variable	(0.210)	(0.078)	(0.106)	(0.274)	(0.143)	(0.076)
Observations	5330	5330	5330	5330	5020	5329
Dependent variable: An additive index. That is, a count of five types of STIs						
Explanatory	0.547**	0.173**	0.627***	1.123***	0.246***	0.273***
variable	(0.235)	(0.070)	(0.123)	(0.294)	(0.087)	(0.076)
Observations	5348	5348	5348	5348	5037	5347
Panel C: 45 years and above age group						
Dependent variable: Dummy if respondent has ever been diagnosed with an STI						
Explanatory	1.035***	0.119*	0.952***	2.557***	−0.007	0.570***
variable	(0.359)	(0.068)	(0.163)	(0.461)	(0.183)	(0.153)
Observations	4302	4302	4302	4302	4118	4297
Dependent variable: Four-point scale for self-assessed HIV/AIDS risk						
Explanatory	0.414	0.174***	0.686***	1.575***	0.320***	0.336***
variable	(0.328)	(0.063)	(0.152)	(0.349)	(0.055)	(0.091)
Observations	4284	4284	4284	4284	4102	4279
Dependent variable: An additive index. That is, a count of five types of STIs						
Explanatory	1.160***	0.199***	1.063***	2.522***	−0.008	0.419***
variable	(0.352)	(0.063)	(0.192)	(0.458)	(0.150)	(0.149)
Observations	4302	4302	4302	4302	4118	4297

Notes: All regressions include relevant control variables and regional fixed effects. Robust standard errors in parentheses. ***$p < 0.01$, **$p < 0.05$, *$p < 0.1$

5   Conclusion

This study examines the effects of sexual orientation and sexual behaviours on sexually transmissible infections (STIs). Despite a high prevalence of STIs in the United Kingdom, much of the literature that attempts to examine the factors influencing STIs focus on other countries, especially the United States. Given existing public health concerns that have emerged because of the rapid increase in STIs in the United Kingdom, it is important to examine potential factors contributing to this increase. Thus, we examine the relationship between sexual orientation, sexual behaviour, and STIs using data from the Natsal-3.

We find evidence that both sexual behaviour and sexual orientation are important factors that influence the prevalence of STIs. Additionally, except for the effects of having anal sex, evidence suggests that sexual orientation is a stronger factor of influence on STIs compared to all other measures of sexual behaviour. Our results also show that rape victims are a high-risk subpopulation. Important variations are also observed across age groups.

There are clear policy and practice implications of this study. It appears that despite increasing awareness of sexual health through health promotion activities, certain groups in the British population have higher risk factors. Importantly, these risk factors are not confined to same-sex sexual practices and differ across age groups. However, it is especially important to note that individuals within same-sex relationships have an elevated risk relative to the rest of the population. Thus, to continually meet the health targets associated with the SDGs, there is clearly a need for targeted sexual health promotion activities. Finally, the results regarding rape victims suggest that careful health screening and support for this exceptionally vulnerable group is required.

Some recommendations arise for future research. Despite the contributions of this study, much remains to be understood about factors that influence STIs. Without a clear understanding of factors that influence the prevalence of STIs, especially HIV, policy formulation and implementation relevant for achieving the health targets of the SDGs may be hindered. Future research can thus explore further to understand factors influencing the prevalence of STIs. The role of sexual identity and sexual networks in explaining the high prevalence of STIs is an important area that needs attention as well. Additionally, the high prevalence of STIs cut across various geographic locations, and thus it is worthwhile for future studies to examine, more holistically, the impact of sexual orientation and sexual behaviours on STIs by exploring data emerging from other countries, both developed and developing.

Appendix

Table 6.4 Description and summary statistics of variables

Variable	Descriptions	Mean	SD	Min	Max
STI	Dummy variable equals to 1 if respondent has ever been diagnosed with an STI	0.29	0.45	0	1
HIV	Four-point scale for self-assessed HIV/AIDS risk. Given your personal sexual lifestyle, what do you think about the HIV risks to you personally? 1 means "not at all at risk", 2 means "not very much", 3 means "quite a lot", 4 means "greatly at risk".	1.27	0.54	1	4
STI index	An additive index. That is, a count of five types of STIs	0.12	0.38	0	5
Chlamydia	Dummy variable equals to 1 if respondent has ever been diagnosed with chlamydia	0.06	0.24	0	1
Gonorrhoea	Dummy variable equals to 1 if respondent has ever been diagnosed with gonorrhoea	0.01	0.11	0	1
Warts	Dummy variable equals to 1 if respondent has ever been diagnosed with warts	0.03	0.18	0	1
Syphilis	Dummy variable equals to 1 if respondent has ever been diagnosed with syphilis	0.002	0.04	0	1
Herpes	Dummy variable equals to 1 if respondent has ever been diagnosed with herpes	0.01	0.12	0	1
Gay/lesbian	Dummy variable equals to 1 if respondent identifies as gay/lesbian	0.02	0.12	0	1
Partners	Number of same-sex partners in the last year. Groups as 0, 1, 2, 3–4, 5+	0.06	0.49	0	9
Experience	Dummy variable equals to 1 if respondent ever had same-sex experience with genital contact	0.07	0.26	0	1

(continued)

Table 6.4 (continued)

Variable	Descriptions	Mean	SD	Min	Max
Anal sex	Dummy variable equals to 1 if respondent ever had same-sex anal sex	0.01	0.12	0	1
Occasions	Number of occasions of same-sex sex in the last seven days	0.02	0.31	0	1
Gay clubs	How often, if at all, do you usually go to gay pubs, bars, and clubs? 0 means "never or not applicable", 1 means "less often than once a year", 2 means "less often but at least once a year", 3 means "less often but at least twice a year", 4 means "less often but at least once a month", 5 means "at least once a week".	0.03	0.33	0	1
Rape	Dummy variable equals to 1 if anyone had sex with respondent against their will	0.07	0.25	0	1
Female	Dummy variable equals to 1 if respondent is female	0.59	0.49	0	1
Age	Age of respondent	39.74	16.20	16	74
Degree	Dummy variable equals to 1 if respondent has a degree	0.24	0.43	0	1
Below degree	Dummy variable equals to 1 if respondent has a tertiary qualification below degree-level	0.27	0.45	0	1
O level	Dummy variable equals to 1 if respondent has an O-level qualification	0.35	0.48	0	1
Married	Dummy variable equals to 1 if respondent is married	0.38	0.48	0	1
Single	Dummy variable equals to 1 if respondent is single (never married)	0.33	0.47	0	1
Unemployed	Dummy variable equals to 1 if respondent is unemployed	0.20	0.40	0	1
Income	Eight-point income scale. <2500, 2500–4999, 5000–9999, 10,000–19,999, 20,000–29,999, 30,000–39,999, 40,000–49,999, 50,000+	5.20	1.97	1	8
Black	Dummy variable equals to 1 if respondent is of African ethnic origin	0.05	0.22	0	1
Asian	Dummy variable equals to 1 if respondent is of Asian ethnic origin	0.03	0.16	0	1
Other/mixed race	Dummy variable equals to 1 if respondent is of other ethnic origin or Mixed race (not Black, Asian, White)	0.03	0.16	0	1

Table 6.5 Sexual orientation, sexual behaviour, and STI (logit regression)

	(1)	(2)	(3)	(4)	(5)	(6)	(7)
Gay/lesbian	0.870*** (0.180)						-0.570 (0.389)
Partners		0.120** (0.050)					-0.104 (0.115)
Experience			0.773*** (0.082)				0.770*** (0.194)
Anal sex				1.767*** (0.205)			1.049* (0.552)
Occasions					0.230** (0.092)		0.010 (0.093)
Gay clubs						0.428*** (0.058)	0.169 (0.149)
Rape	0.596*** (0.079)	0.601*** (0.079)	0.506*** (0.080)	0.583*** (0.078)	0.526*** (0.085)	0.586*** (0.078)	0.495*** (0.085)
Female	1.491*** (0.050)	1.481*** (0.050)	1.489*** (0.050)	1.541*** (0.051)	1.517*** (0.052)	1.529*** (0.051)	1.551*** (0.053)
Age	-0.004** (0.002)	-0.004** (0.002)	-0.004** (0.002)	-0.004** (0.002)	-0.004** (0.002)	-0.004** (0.002)	-0.004** (0.002)
Degree	0.997*** (0.087)	1.012*** (0.087)	0.977*** (0.087)	1.002*** (0.087)	0.986*** (0.090)	1.000*** (0.087)	0.978*** (0.090)
Below degree	0.694*** (0.085)	0.706*** (0.085)	0.681*** (0.085)	0.701*** (0.085)	0.692*** (0.088)	0.699*** (0.085)	0.686*** (0.088)
O level	0.695*** (0.080)	0.706*** (0.080)	0.687*** (0.080)	0.705*** (0.080)	0.699*** (0.082)	0.703*** (0.080)	0.695*** (0.083)
Married	-0.237*** (0.054)	-0.240*** (0.054)	-0.223*** (0.054)	-0.236*** (0.054)	-0.222*** (0.056)	-0.235*** (0.054)	-0.220*** (0.056)

Single	-0.414***	-0.403***	-0.417***	-0.421***	-0.394***	-0.418***
	(0.061)	(0.061)	(0.061)	(0.061)	(0.064)	(0.061)
Unemployed	0.181***	0.180***	0.167***	0.181***	0.182***	0.181***
	(0.057)	(0.057)	(0.057)	(0.057)	(0.059)	(0.057)
Income	0.039***	0.040***	0.040***	0.038***	0.041***	0.039***
	(0.013)	(0.013)	(0.013)	(0.013)	(0.014)	(0.013)
Asian	-1.330***	-1.348***	-1.305***	-1.329***	-1.326***	-1.328***
	(0.141)	(0.141)	(0.140)	(0.141)	(0.144)	(0.141)
Black	0.147	0.131	0.180	0.152	0.168	0.151
	(0.133)	(0.133)	(0.133)	(0.133)	(0.136)	(0.133)
Other/mixed race	0.063	0.054	0.058	0.069	0.025	0.068
	(0.131)	(0.131)	(0.131)	(0.131)	(0.138)	(0.131)
Constant	-2.469***	-2.471***	-2.512***	-2.507***	-2.541***	-2.506***
	(0.151)	(0.151)	(0.152)	(0.152)	(0.157)	(0.152)
Regional dummies	Yes	Yes	Yes	Yes	Yes	Yes
Observations	12,222	12,222	12,222	12,222	11,576	12,216

-0.403***
(0.064)
0.178***
(0.059)
0.040***
(0.014)
-1.319***
(0.144)
0.180
(0.137)
0.037
(0.139)
-2.563***
(0.157)
Yes
11,576

Notes: Dependent variable: Dummy variable equals to 1 if respondent has ever been diagnosed with an STI. Robust standard errors in parentheses. ***$p < 0.01$, **$p < 0.05$, *$p < 0.1$

Table 6.6 Sexual orientation, sexual behaviour, and HIV/AIDS risk (ordered logit regression)

	(1)	(2)	(3)	(4)	(5)	(6)	(7)
Gay/lesbian	0.919*** (0.145)						-0.540 (0.363)
Partners		0.277*** (0.047)					0.130 (0.107)
Experience			0.747*** (0.074)				0.556*** (0.173)
Anal sex				1.744*** (0.192)			1.109** (0.485)
Occasions					0.268*** (0.080)		-0.013 (0.096)
Gay clubs						0.390*** (0.053)	0.073 (0.142)
Rape	0.446*** (0.090)	0.440*** (0.090)	0.338*** (0.091)	0.431*** (0.090)	0.434*** (0.100)	0.441*** (0.089)	0.400*** (0.100)
Female	-0.480*** (0.047)	-0.481*** (0.047)	-0.499*** (0.047)	-0.439*** (0.047)	-0.495*** (0.048)	-0.447*** (0.047)	-0.471*** (0.049)
Age	-0.016*** (0.002)	-0.017*** (0.002)	-0.016*** (0.002)	-0.016*** (0.002)	-0.017*** (0.002)	-0.016*** (0.002)	-0.017*** (0.002)
Degree	0.258*** (0.092)	0.273*** (0.092)	0.228** (0.092)	0.256*** (0.092)	0.230** (0.095)	0.251*** (0.092)	0.213** (0.095)
Below degree	0.166* (0.091)	0.184** (0.091)	0.149 (0.091)	0.170* (0.091)	0.175* (0.093)	0.166* (0.091)	0.166* (0.093)
O level	0.141 (0.087)	0.158* (0.087)	0.131 (0.087)	0.151* (0.087)	0.140 (0.089)	0.145* (0.087)	0.135 (0.089)
Married	-0.515*** (0.065)	-0.512*** (0.065)	-0.502*** (0.065)	-0.515*** (0.065)	-0.511*** (0.067)	-0.510*** (0.065)	-0.511*** (0.067)
Single	0.612*** (0.060)	0.618*** (0.060)	0.617*** (0.060)	0.610*** (0.060)	0.591*** (0.063)	0.613*** (0.060)	0.584*** (0.062)

Unemployed	−0.005	−0.011	−0.017	−0.004	0.008	−0.008	0.001
	(0.062)	(0.062)	(0.062)	(0.062)	(0.064)	(0.062)	(0.064)
Income	−0.000	−0.000	0.001	−0.001	−0.000	−0.000	−0.001
	(0.013)	(0.013)	(0.013)	(0.013)	(0.014)	(0.013)	(0.014)
Asian	0.196*	0.177	0.219*	0.205*	0.185	0.197*	0.197*
	(0.116)	(0.117)	(0.116)	(0.116)	(0.118)	(0.117)	(0.118)
Black	0.664***	0.660***	0.706***	0.673***	0.668***	0.669***	0.686***
	(0.133)	(0.134)	(0.133)	(0.133)	(0.135)	(0.133)	(0.134)
Other/mixed race	0.129	0.126	0.121	0.135	0.070	0.133	0.085
	(0.129)	(0.128)	(0.128)	(0.128)	(0.138)	(0.128)	(0.138)
Regional dummies	Yes	Yes	Yes	Yes	Yes	Yes	Yes
Observations	12,179	12,179	12,179	12,179	11,536	12,173	11,536

Notes: Dependent variable: Four-point scale for self-assessed HIV/AIDS risk. Given your personal sexual lifestyle, what do you think about the HIV risks to you personally? 1 means "not at all at risk", 2 means "not very much", 3 means "quite a lot", 4 means "greatly at risk". Robust standard errors in parentheses. ***p < 0.01, **p < 0.05, *p < 0.1

Table 6.7 Sexual orientation, sexual behaviour, and STI index (ordered logit regression)

	(1)	(2)	(3)	(4)	(5)	(6)	(7)
Gay/lesbian	0.835***						−0.044
	(0.176)						(0.442)
Partners		0.175***					−0.052
		(0.044)					(0.134)
Experience			0.787***				0.546**
			(0.091)				(0.237)
Anal sex				1.572***			0.735
				(0.222)			(0.589)
Occasions					0.229***		0.058
					(0.068)		(0.109)
Gay clubs						0.348***	0.022
						(0.061)	(0.160)
Rape	0.714***	0.717***	0.604***	0.699***	0.682***	0.706***	0.652***
	(0.096)	(0.096)	(0.098)	(0.096)	(0.107)	(0.096)	(0.107)
Female	0.186***	0.178***	0.166***	0.240***	0.180***	0.222***	0.205***
	(0.064)	(0.064)	(0.064)	(0.066)	(0.067)	(0.065)	(0.068)
Age	−0.023***	−0.023***	−0.022***	−0.023***	−0.023***	−0.023***	−0.023***
	(0.002)	(0.002)	(0.002)	(0.002)	(0.003)	(0.002)	(0.003)
Degree	0.632***	0.649***	0.604***	0.633***	0.642***	0.633***	0.628***
	(0.127)	(0.127)	(0.127)	(0.127)	(0.133)	(0.127)	(0.134)
Below degree	0.377***	0.393***	0.357***	0.381***	0.396***	0.382***	0.386***
	(0.126)	(0.126)	(0.126)	(0.126)	(0.132)	(0.126)	(0.132)
O level	0.444***	0.460***	0.432***	0.454***	0.462***	0.452***	0.456***
	(0.119)	(0.119)	(0.119)	(0.119)	(0.125)	(0.119)	(0.126)
Married	−0.515***	−0.516***	−0.499***	−0.512***	−0.449***	−0.512***	−0.449***
	(0.081)	(0.081)	(0.081)	(0.081)	(0.085)	(0.081)	(0.085)

Single	−0.256***	−0.247***	−0.258***	−0.265***	−0.213**	−0.259***	−0.222***
	(0.080)	(0.080)	(0.080)	(0.080)	(0.085)	(0.080)	(0.085)
Unemployed	0.219***	0.214***	0.205***	0.219***	0.215***	0.219***	0.212***
	(0.075)	(0.075)	(0.075)	(0.075)	(0.079)	(0.075)	(0.079)
Income	0.005	0.005	0.007	0.004	−0.000	0.005	−0.001
	(0.018)	(0.018)	(0.018)	(0.018)	(0.019)	(0.018)	(0.019)
Asian	−1.711***	−1.742***	−1.682***	−1.703***	−1.738***	−1.706***	−1.726***
	(0.288)	(0.290)	(0.289)	(0.288)	(0.300)	(0.288)	(0.300)
Black	0.451***	0.436***	0.501***	0.461***	0.470***	0.456***	0.485***
	(0.157)	(0.157)	(0.157)	(0.157)	(0.161)	(0.157)	(0.161)
Other/mixed race	0.145	0.136	0.145	0.152	0.100	0.149	0.114
	(0.166)	(0.166)	(0.167)	(0.166)	(0.177)	(0.166)	(0.176)
Constant	−1.781***	−1.789***	−1.814***	−1.813***	−1.828***	−1.812***	−1.837***
	(0.212)	(0.212)	(0.212)	(0.212)	(0.224)	(0.212)	(0.224)
Regional dummies	Yes	Yes	Yes	Yes	Yes	Yes	Yes
Observations	12,222	12,222	12,222	12,222	11,576	12,216	11,576

Notes: Dependent variable: An additive index. That is, a count of five types of STIs. Robust standard errors in parentheses.
***$p < 0.01$, **$p < 0.05$

References

Carole, J., Hooton, T. M., Bowers, A., Copass, M. K., Krieger, J. N., Hillier, S. L., ... Holmes, K. K. (1990). Sexually transmitted diseases in victims of rape. *The New England Journal of Medicine, 322*(11), 713–716.

Dougan, S., Evans, B. G., & Elford, J. (2007). Sexually transmitted infections in Western Europe among HIV-positive men who have sex with men. *Sexually Transmitted Diseases, 34*(10), 783–790.

Erens, B., Burkill, S., Couper, M. P., Conrad, F., Clifton, S., Tanton, C., ... Copas, A. J. (2014). Nonprobability web surveys to measure sexual behaviors and attitudes in the general population: A comparison with a probability sample interview survey. *Journal of Medical Internet Research, 16*(12), e276. https://doi.org/10.2196/jmir.3382

Erens, B., Phelps, A., Clifton, S., Mercer, C. H., Tanton, C., Hussey, D., ... Johnson, A. M. (2013). Methodology of the third British National Survey of Sexual Attitudes and Lifestyles (Natsal-3). *Sexually Transmitted Infections.* https://doi.org/10.1136/sextrans-2013-051359

Everett, B. G. (2013). Sexual orientation disparities in sexually transmitted infections: Examining the intersection between sexual identity and sexual behavior. *Archives of Sexual Behavior, 42*(2), 225–236.

Friedman, M. R., Wei, C., Klem, M. L., Silvestre, A. J., Markovic, N., & Stall, R. (2014). HIV infection and sexual risk among men who have sex with men and women (MSMW): A systematic review and meta-analysis. *PLoS ONE, 9*(1), e87139.

Heise, L. L. (1994). Gender-based violence and women's reproductive health. *International Journal of Gynecology & Obstetrics, 46*(2), 221–229.

Jones, K. G., Johnson, A. M., Wellings, K., Sonnenberg, P., Field, N., Tanton, C., ... Mercer, C. H. (2014). The prevalence of, and factors associated with, paying for sex among men resident in Britain: Findings from the third National Survey of Sexual Attitudes and Lifestyles (Natsal-3). *Sexually Transmitted Infections.* https://doi.org/10.1136/sextrans-2014-051683

Kawsar, M., Anfield, A., Walters, E., McCabe, S., & Forster, G. E. (2004). Prevalence of sexually transmitted infections and mental health needs of female child and adolescent survivors of rape and sexual assault attending a specialist clinic. *Sexually Transmitted Infections, 80*(2), 138–141.

Liu, H., Yang, H., Li, X., Wang, N., Liu, H., Wang, B., ... Stanton, B. (2006). Men who have sex with men and human immunodeficiency virus/sexually transmitted disease control in China. *Sexually Transmitted Diseases, 33*(2), 68–76.

Ma, X., Zhang, Q., He, X., Sun, W., Yue, H., Chen, S., ... Du, H. (2007). Trends in prevalence of HIV, syphilis, hepatitis C, hepatitis B, and sexual risk behavior among men who have sex with men: Results of 3 consecutive respondent-driven sampling surveys in Beijing, 2004 through 2006. *JAIDS Journal of Acquired Immune Deficiency Syndromes, 45*(5), 581–587.

Macdowall, W., Jones, K. G., Tanton, C., Clifton, S., Copas, A. J., Mercer, C. H., ... Wellings, K. (2015). Associations between source of information about sex and sexual health outcomes in Britain: Findings from the third National Survey of Sexual Attitudes and Lifestyles (Natsal-3). *BMJ Open, 5*(3). https://doi.org/10.1136/bmjopen-2015-007837

Malebranche, D. J., Arriola, K. J., Jenkins, T. R., Dauria, E., & Patel, S. N. (2010). Exploring the "bisexual bridge": A qualitative study of risk behavior and disclosure of same-sex behavior among Black bisexual men. *American Journal of Public Health, 100*(1), 159–164.

Maulsby, C., Millett, G., Lindsey, K., Kelley, R., Johnson, K., Montoya, D., & Holtgrave, D. (2014). HIV among black men who have sex with men (MSM) in the United States: A review of the literature. *AIDS and Behavior, 18*(1), 10–25.

Mercer, C. H., Tanton, C., Prah, P., Erens, B., Sonnenberg, P., Clifton, S., ... Johnson, A. M. (2013). Changes in sexual attitudes and lifestyles in Britain through the life course and over time: Findings from the National Surveys of Sexual Attitudes and Lifestyles (Natsal). *The Lancet, 382*(9907), 1781–1794. https://doi.org/10.1016/S0140-6736(13)62035-8

Moradi, B., Mohr, J. J., Worthington, R. L., & Fassinger, R. E. (2009). Counseling psychology research on sexual (orientation) minority issues: Conceptual and methodological challenges and opportunities. *Journal of Counseling Psychology, 56*(1), 5.

Musyoki, H., Kellogg, T. A., Geibel, S., Muraguri, N., Okal, J., Tun, W., ... Kim, A. A. (2015). Prevalence of HIV, sexually transmitted infections, and risk behaviours among female sex workers in Nairobi, Kenya: Results of a respondent driven sampling study. *AIDS and Behavior, 19*(1), 46–58.

Nakamura, N., Semple, S. J., Strathdee, S. A., & Patterson, T. L. (2011). HIV risk profiles among HIV-positive, methamphetamine-using men who have sex with both men and women. *Archives of Sexual Behavior, 40*(4), 793–801.

Noble, J., Cover, J., & Yanagishita, M. (1996). *The world's youth 1996*. Population Reference Bureau.

Oster, A. M., Sternberg, M., Nebenzahl, S., Broz, D., Xu, F., Hariri, S., ... Paz-Bailey, G. (2014). Prevalence of HIV, sexually transmitted infections, and viral hepatitis by urbanicity, among men who have sex with men, injection drug users, and heterosexuals in the United States. *Sexually Transmitted Diseases, 41*(4), 272–279.

Satterwhite, C. L., Torrone, E., Meites, E., Dunne, E. F., Mahajan, R., Ocfemia, M. C. B., ... Weinstock, H. (2013). Sexually transmitted infections among US women and men: Prevalence and incidence estimates, 2008. *Sexually Transmitted Diseases, 40*(3), 187–193.

Tanton, C., Jones, K. G., Macdowall, W., Clifton, S., Mitchell, K. R., Datta, J., ... Mercer, C. H. (2015). Patterns and trends in sources of information about sex among young people in Britain: Evidence from three National Surveys of Sexual Attitudes and Lifestyles. *BMJ Open, 5*(3). https://doi.org/10.1136/bmjopen-2015-007834

Wade, A. S., Kane, C. T., Diallo, P. A. N., Diop, A. K., Gueye, K., Mboup, S., ... Lagarde, E. (2005). HIV infection and sexually transmitted infections among men who have sex with men in Senegal. *AIDS, 19*(18), 2133–2140.

Weiss, E., Shelan, D., & Gupta, G. R. (1996). *Vulnerability and opportunity: Adolescents and HIV/AIDS in the developing world; findings from the women and AIDS Research Program.* International Center for Research on Women. ICRW Reports and Publications, 1.

Wells, J. E., McGee, M. A., & Beautrais, A. L. (2011). Multiple aspects of sexual orientation: Prevalence and sociodemographic correlates in a New Zealand national survey. *Archives of Sexual Behavior, 40*(1), 155–168.

Welz, T., Hosegood, V., Jaffar, S., Bätzing-Feigenbaum, J., Herbst, K., & Newell, M.-L. (2007). Continued very high prevalence of HIV infection in rural KwaZulu-Natal, South Africa: A population-based longitudinal study. *AIDS, 21*(11), 1467–1472.

Wu, Z., Xu, J., Liu, E., Mao, Y., Xiao, Y., Sun, X., ... Dou, Z. (2013). HIV and syphilis prevalence among men who have sex with men: A cross-sectional survey of 61 cities in China. *Clinical Infectious Diseases, 57*(2), 298–309.

Xu, F., Sternberg, M. R., & Markowitz, L. E. (2010). Women who have sex with women in the United States: Prevalence, sexual behavior and prevalence of herpes simplex virus type 2 infection—Results from National Health and Nutrition Examination Survey 2001–2006. *Sexually Transmitted Diseases, 37*(7), 407–413.

Young, R. M., & Meyer, I. H. (2005). The trouble with "MSM" and "WSW": Erasure of the sexual-minority person in public health discourse. *American Journal of Public Health, 95*(7), 1144–1149.

Zhang, C., Li, X., Su, S., Zhang, L., Zhou, Y., Shen, Z., & Tang, Z. (2014). Prevalence of HIV, syphilis, and HCV infection and associated risk factors among male clients of low-paying female sex workers in a rural county of Guangxi, China: A cross-sectional study. *Sexually Transmitted Infections, 90*(3), 230–236.

7

Trade-led Growth: A Path to Sustainable Development in Sub-Saharan Africa

Shanaz Broermann

1   Introduction

Ending multifaceted poverty is central to both the millennium development goals (Mdgs) and the sustainable development goals (Sdgs). Sustainable and inclusive economic growth has been acknowledged as the single most effective means to foster economic development and reduce poverty. Thus, achieving economic growth is not just an independent sustainable development goal but also important in achieving other goals such as poverty alleviation.

This chapter applies an open economy demand-led growth model to determine the main constraints to growth in sub-Saharan Africa. We empirically test the balance of payments constrained growth model which accounts for sustainable debt accumulation, interest payments and the

S. Broermann (✉)
Collaborative Africa Budget Reform Initiative (CABRI),
Centurion, South Africa
e-mail: s.broermann.fs@odi.org.uk

© The Author(s) 2020   **119**
S. Awaworyi Churchill (ed.), *Moving from the Millennium to the Sustainable Development Goals*, https://doi.org/10.1007/978-981-15-1556-9_7

terms of trade movements. The model is export driven as the latter is considered as an important component of autonomous demand.

The balance of payments constrained growth model was first developed by Thirlwall (1979) using Harrod's (1933) foreign trade multiplier. Thirlwall (2013) argues that for most countries demand constraints operate long before supply constraints take effect. In the original Thirlwall (1979) model, the balance of payments constrained growth, $*y_B$, is equal to the income elasticity of demand for exports multiplied by the growth in world income, divided by the income elasticity of demand for imports. This is described as the strong version of Thirlwall's law as both the import and export demand functions need to be estimated (Perraton, 2003).

Based on the same assumption of constant relative prices, the balance of payments constrained growth rate is equal to the growth in exports, divided by the income elasticity of demand for imports. This is recognised as the weak version, as only the import demand function is needed to derive the balance of payments constrained growth rate. It can also be interpreted as the dynamic Harrod (1933) trade multiplier result.[1]

The original model described above was extended to include capital flows and terms of trade (Thirlwall & Hussain, 1982). The extension was particularly relevant for developing countries, where capital flows, changes in the terms of trade and the real exchange rate have been very important.

The extended model with capital flows and the terms of trade was first empirically tested by Thirlwall and Hussain (1982) for 20 developing countries covering the 1951–1969 period. Just three sub-Saharan African countries were included in the study: Kenya, Sudan and Zaire.[2] Their results showed that countries in the sample had a "very mixed" experience, however, on balance, changes in the terms of trade constrained growth by 0.6% per annum, while capital inflows relaxed the balance of payments constraint and allowed countries to grow faster by about 0.05% per annum.

---

[1] The static Harrod trade multiplier result, $Y = X / m$, where Y is the level of income, X is the level of exports and m is the marginal propensity to import and $1/m$ is the foreign trade multiplier. The weak version of the balance of payments constrained growth can be seen as the dynamic Harrod trade multiplier result, x/π (Thirlwall, 2011).

[2] Zaire is now known as the Democratic Republic of Congo.

Hussain (1999), applied the Thirlwall and Hussain (1982) model to 29 African and 11 Asian economies covering the 1970–1990 period, providing evidence in support of the model. However, although acceptable at the time, the study did not make use of adequate time series estimation techniques therefore casting doubt on the estimated results.[3]

The Thirlwall and Hussain (1982) model had a tendency to over predict the rate of growth. The model was therefore extended by Elliott and Rhodd (1999, p. 1146) to include interest rate payments for "demand financed by capital flows generally carries with it debt accumulation and servicing." Drawing from the sample of countries employed in the Thirlwall and Hussain (1982) study and extending the model to include external debt financing, Elliott and Rhodd (1999) were able to reduce the degree of over prediction, concluding that economic growth is additionally constrained by debt service payments which drain on the limited financial resources needed for economic growth.

The Elliott and Rhodd (1999) model was further criticised by Moreno-Brid (1999) as it did not set a limit to the amount of capital flows into a country and therefore assumed that a country can forever increase its level of indebtedness relative to Gross Domestic Product (GDP). In practice, a developing country's creditworthiness, and therefore access to global financial markets, is influenced by its debt accumulation as perceived by the creditors as the current account to GDP ratio and the foreign debt to GDP ratio. As these ratios increase and reach critical levels, developing countries may experience difficulties in attracting foreign capital. This was seen in the 1980s debt crisis which affected many developing countries including Latin America and sub-Saharan Africa (Devlin & Ffrench-Davis, 1995).

Sustainable debt accumulation is incorporated into the model by imposing a long run constraint taken as a constant ratio of the current account deficit to income (Moreno-Brid, 2003).

This version of the model which accounts for sustainable debt accumulation, interest rate payments and the terms of trade has not been tested for the sub-Saharan African region.

---

[3] This was the last comprehensive study on the balance of payments constrained growth model for sub-Saharan Africa.

An empirical study on the latter is necessary, as 33 of the 39 countries described as Heavily Indebted Poor Countries (HIPC) are in sub-Saharan Africa (World Bank, 2015). More recently, debt levels have been increasing across the continent raising concerns over debt sustainability (IMF, 2018). In addition, majority of the countries depend on production of primary products in international markets making the terms of trade effects more pronounced. A study that uses the above extended version of the model, applying recent data and more appropriate econometric techniques is therefore warranted. Understanding the main constraints to growth will facilitate the achievement of the sustainable development goals, especially the target of sustained economic growth related to goal 8.

2   Data and Methodology

There have been several extensions to the original balance of payments constrained growth model. The chosen model for the sub-Sahara African region is the one modified by Moreno-Brid (2003) which allows for sustainable debt accumulation, interest rate payments and the terms of trade. As far as we are aware, there are no current papers which test this version of the model for the region. Below is an outline of the data, model and the methodology used to estimate and test the balance of payments constrained growth model.

Data

Data covering the 1960–2014 period is used in the analysis. The time period used differs for individual countries due to data availability. The variables used are exports of goods and services, imports of goods and services, Gross Domestic Product (GDP), world income, import price index, export price index, interest payments on external debt and the real effective exchange rate. Please see Appendix 1 for a full description of the data and sources used.

The Model

In line with Thirlwall and Hussain (1982), Moreno-Brid (2003) and Thirlwall (2012), the starting point of the extended model of the balance of payments constrained growth model is the balance of payments accounting identity in disequilibrium which we modify accordingly to accommodate for sustainable debt accumulation, interest rate payments and the terms of trade. Details of the model are discussed in Appendix 2.

Estimation Methodology

The estimation methodology is outlined below, and this includes the unit root tests used to test the stationarity of the data, the Autoregressive Distributed Lag (ARDL) model and the bounds testing procedure used to test for cointegration.

Unit Root Tests and Structural Breaks

The sub-Saharan African countries have experienced several shocks over the last five decades. It is therefore necessary to account for structural breaks when testing the stationarity of the data. Our preferred unit root test is the Clemente, Montanes and Reyes (CMR) test,[4] which allows for two endogenously determined structural breaks (Clemente et al., 1998). It is a modification of the Perron and Vogelsang (1992a, b) unit root test which accounts for one break in the series. If evidence of only one structural break is found in the series, then the Perron and Vogelsang test will be used. If there is no evidence of any structural break in the series then the traditional Augmented Dickey Fuller (ADF) and Phillips Perron (PP) unit root tests will be used.

Structural breaks in the data will be addressed during estimation through the use of dummy variables. Including dummy variables to

---

[4] The Clemente, Montanes and Reyes unit root test allows for two different types of structural breaks. Sudden changes in the series are captured by the Additive Outliers (AO) model while a gradual shift in the mean of the series is detected by the Innovational Outliers (IO) model (Baum, 2005). Both forms of structural change will be tested.

account for structural breaks is more efficient than splitting the sample, particularly when the sample size is relatively small (McCombie, 1997). Only significant dummy variables will be retained in the model.

Autoregressive Distributed Lag (ARDL) Model

The presence of structural breaks in the data creates uncertainty as to the stationarity of the variables. An ARDL model will therefore be used to estimate the import and export demand functions needed to calculate the balance of payments constrained growth rate. One advantage of the ARDL model is that it provides consistent estimates irrespective of whether the variables are integrated of order one (I(1)), or zero I(0) (Pesaran & Shin, 1998). The purpose of the unit root tests are to ensure that none of the series included are I(2), as this would invalidate the methodology.

In addition, it is possible to test for cointegration using the bounds testing procedure. Other cointegration tests such as the Johansen system-based reduced rank regression approach or the Engle-Granger two step residual-based procedure are restricted to only I(1) variables. Pesaran and Shin (1998) further show that the bounds cointegration test is superior to the Johansen cointegration test in small samples.

When using the ARDL model, selecting the right lag order is important for valid inferences. The appropriate lag order will be selected using the Schwarz Bayesian Criterion (SBC). The usual normality tests will be carried out to ensure appropriate model selection. This includes the Breusch-Pagan/Cook-Weisberg test for heteroscedasticity and the Breusch-Godfrey test for serial correlation. The stability of the model over time is tested by calculating and graphing the cumulative sums (CUSUM) as well as the CUSUM squared of the recursive residuals from the variables defined in the model and their respective 95% confidence bands.

Following the selection of the appropriate ARDL model, the long run parameters and valid standard errors need to be obtained.[5] The

---

[5] The ARDL long run variance is defined as $\sigma_\eta^2 \big/ \big[\phi(1)\big]^2$.

latter will be estimated using the Ordinary Least Squares (OLS) delta method (Δ-method).[6]

In the absence of cointegration, we take the first difference of the variables and estimate the import and export demand function using OLS.

Testing the Balance of Payments Constrained Growth Model

Several procedures have been proposed for testing the equivalence of the balance of payments constrained growth rate to the actual growth rate of a country.[7] We make use of two formal approaches. The first approach allows us to formally test the balance of payments constrained growth model for an individual country while the second approach allows us to test the model for a group of countries. For the first approach, we make use of the method proposed by McCombie (1989) which is to calculate the hypothetical income elasticity of demand which exactly equates the actual rate of growth using the balance of payments constrained model. We then test if it is equal to the estimated income elasticity of demand from the import demand function using the Wald test. Failing to reject the null hypothesis for the equivalence between the two elasticities of demand would provide evidence in favour of the balance of payments constrained growth rate.

Due to variations in the export to import ratio, θ, and the interest payment to import ratio, θ_1, we calculate the hypothetical growth rate using both the start value at the beginning of the period concerned and the average value for the period (Britto & McCombie, 2009). The hypothetical income elasticities that would equate the actual rate of growth given by the balance of payments constrained growth model are shown in Table 7.1.

Our second approach, first proposed by McGregor and Swales (1985) and later modified by McCombie (1997), makes use of pooled data for all the countries. McGregor and Swales (1985) regress the actual rate of growth on the balance of payments constrained growth and test the hypothesis that

---

[6] The Bewley's (1979) regression approach is an alternative method for estimating the long run parameters from the selected ARDL model. It provides identical results to the OLS delta method (Pesaran & Shin, 1998). Preference is based on computational convenience.

[7] For a full outline of all the different methods proposed, see McCombie (1997).

Table 7.1 Hypothetical income elasticity of demand for imports, π_H (Moreno-Brid, 2003)

Balance of payments constrained growth model	Solving for the income elasticity of demand
*$y_{BSDART} = \dfrac{\theta \epsilon z - \theta_1 r + (\theta \eta + \psi + 1)\left(p_d - p_f - e\right)}{\pi - (1 - \theta + \theta_1)}$	*$\pi_{HBSDART} = (1 - \theta + \theta_1) + \dfrac{\theta \epsilon z - \theta_1 r + (\theta \eta + \psi + 1)\left(p_d - p_f - e\right)}{y}$
$y_{BSDRT} = \dfrac{\theta x - \theta_1 r + (\psi + 1)\left(p_d - p_f - e\right)}{\pi - (1 - \theta + \theta_1)}$	$\pi_{HBSDRT} = (1 - \theta + \theta_1) + \dfrac{\theta x - \theta_1 r + (\psi + 1)\left(p_d - p_f - e\right)}{y}$
$y_{BSDAR} = \dfrac{\theta x - \theta_1 r}{\pi - (1 - \theta + \theta_1)}$	$\pi_{HBSDAR} = (1 - \theta + \theta_1) + \dfrac{\theta x - \theta_1 r}{y}$
$y_{BSDA} = \dfrac{\theta x}{\pi - (1 - \theta)}$	$\pi_{HBSDA} = (1 - \theta) + \dfrac{\theta x}{y}$
$y_B = \dfrac{x}{\pi}$	$\pi_{HB} = \dfrac{x}{y}$

Notes: *y_{BSDART} is the balance of payments constrained growth with sustainable debt accumulation, interest payments abroad and the terms of trade interacted with the price elasticities of demand for imports and exports

y_{BSDART} is the balance of payments constrained growth with sustainable debt accumulation, interest payments and the terms of trade (only the income and price elasticities from the import demand function are included)

y_{BSDAR} is the balance of payments constrained growth with sustainable debt accumulation and interest payments abroad

y_{BSDA} is the balance of payments constrained growth with sustainable debt accumulation

y_B is the 'weak' original version of the balance of payments constrained growth model

the intercept and slope coefficient are not statistically different from 0 and 1, respectively. As pointed out by McCombie (1997, p. 347), the above regression suffers from a, "misspecification analogous to an error in variables problem," as the balance of payments constrained growth rates are stochastic as they were derived from prior estimation coefficients which have associated standard errors. A simple way to overcome this is to regress the balance of payments constrained growth rate on the actual growth rate.[8] The modified method proposed by McCombie (1997) will be applied. One of the limitations of this approach is that countries that persistently run a balance of payments surplus must be excluded from the regression. According to McCombie (1997), this does not invalidate the balance of payments constrained model as not all countries can be balance of payments constrained. In this case, we are testing that the sub-Saharan African countries are balance of payments constrained.

3   Results

A summary of the results obtained from the unit root tests, the estimated import and export demand functions using the ARDL model and the estimates for the balance of payments constrained growth model are presented in this section.[9]

Unit Root Tests

All the variables were either I(0) or I(1) as determined by the Augmented Dickey Fuller (ADF) test, the Phillips Perron (PP) test, the Perron and Vogelsang test and the Clemente, Montanes and Reyes (CMR) test. The appropriate unit root test was chosen based on the presence of no structural break, one structural break or two structural breaks, respectively. As all the variables are either I(0) or I(1), we proceed with the ARDL model to estimate the import and export demand functions.

---

[8] The decision to regress the balance of payments constrained growth on the actual rate of growth does not indicate causality (McCombie, 1997).

[9] More detailed results are available on request.

Import Demand Function

The import demand function is estimated for 22 sub-Saharan African countries. The summary of results derived using the ARDL model can be seen in Table 7.2. Only the long run estimates for the income elasticity of demand and the price elasticity of demand for imports along with some of the diagnostic tests are reported.

For 13 countries, the price elasticity of demand for imports was small and insignificant, ranging from −1.494 for Kenya to −0.121 for Uganda, highlighting the small role relative prices have played in the region. The income elasticity of demand for imports was significant for 20 countries. For Zambia, the income elasticity of demand for imports was 4.562, which is relatively high as the income elasticity of demand for imports for the rest of the 19 countries ranged from 0.475 for Gambia to 2.310 for Sierra Leone. This provides evidence in favour of the balance of payments constrained growth rate as it shows that relative prices play a very small or no role in the import demand function. What is of importance is the income elasticity of demand for imports which is determined by a country's economic structure.

For Gabon, Democratic Republic of Congo, Mali, Sierra Leone, Sudan and Uganda we do not find any evidence against the null hypothesis of no cointegration between the variables using the bounds testing procedure. We therefore take the first difference of the variables and re-estimate the import demand function using OLS. We follow the same procedure for Togo as we could not estimate a stable import demand function using the ARDL model. A summary of the results can be seen in Table 7.3.

The income elasticity of demand using OLS for the Democratic Republic of Congo, Gabon, Uganda and Sudan were close to that estimated using the ARDL model as there was less than a 0.5 point difference. We therefore proceed to estimate the balance of payments constrained growth using both the estimates obtained from the ARDL model as well as OLS for the above mentioned countries.

The income elasticity of demand for imports using OLS ranged from 0.963 for Sudan to 2.372 for the Democratic Republic of Congo. The price elasticity of demand for imports ranged from −0.834 for Togo to −0.05 for the Democratic Republic of Congo.

Table 7.2 Summary of the long run estimates from the import demand function estimated using the ARDL model

	The income elasticity of demand for imports, π		The price elasticity of demand for imports, ψ		ARDL	SBC	R²	Bounds F test	Breusch-Pagan/ Cook-Weisberg test for heteroscedasticity (P value)	Breusch-Godfrey test for serial correlation (P value)
Benin	1.142***	(0.109)	−1.08***	(0.242)	(1 1 1)	−74.481	0.795	10.289***	0.997	0.508
Botswana	0.896***	(0.023)	−0.53***	(0.168)	(3 1 0)	−67.41	0.756	10.200***	0.471	0.744
Cameroon	1.379***	(0.087)	0.657***	(0.177)	(1 0 0)	−63.204	0.403	5.775**	0.639	0.664
Chad	0.659***	(0.157)	−0.278*	(0.152)	(2 0 0)	−21.17	0.852	20.472***	0.163	0.681
Congo, Dem. Rep.[a]	2.179*	(1.266)	−0.278	(0.546)	(2 1 1)	−12.424^AIC	0.568	3.754	0.772	0.193
Congo, Rep.	1.483***	(0.291)	−1.036	(0.627)	(3 3 3)	−57.642	0.968	4.221*	0.493	0.293
Gabon	1.275***	(0.155)	−0.85***	(0.226)	(1 1 0)	−57.804	0.659	3.182	0.257	0.751
Gambia	0.475***	(0.193)	−0.25	(0.243)	(2 1 1)	−63.965^AIC	0.44	4.212*	0.67	0.346
Kenya	0.986***	(0.212)	−1.494***	(0.354)	(1 0 0)	−58.354	0.272	3.892*	0.119	0.644
Mali	2.195**	(1.07)	−0.64	(2.089)	(1 1 1)	−35.912	0.179	0.716	0.136	0.156
Mauritius	1.183***	(0.165)	−1.131	(1.537)	(1 2 4)	−83.903	0.86	5.404**	0.893	0.095*
Mozambique	1.877***	(0.451)	−0.168**	(0.064)	(1 2 1)	−50.439	0.696	9.674***	0.535	0.562
Namibia	1.946***	(0.184)	−0.148	(0.615)	(1 2 2)	−64.769	0.786	5.280**	0.829	0.817
Nigeria	0.941***	(0.299)	−0.148	(0.109)	(1 3 1)	−6.661	0.872	9.114***	0.238	0.135
Senegal	1.107***	(0.081)	−0.126	(0.126)	(1 0 0)	−97.159	0.491	6.911***	0.515	0.452
Sierra Leone	2.310**	(0.977)	0.68	(0.802)	(1 1 1)	−3.750^AIC	0.363	2.87	0.039**	0.843
South Africa[b]	0.819	(0.59)	−1.064	(0.399)	(1 1 0)	−131.366	0.803	10.590***	0.776	0.263
Sudan	0.957***	(0.197)	0.177	(0.309)	(1 0 0)	−1.585	0.147	2.657	0.743	0.802
Uganda	1.553***	(0.236)	−0.121	(0.157)	(4 4 3)	−83.982	0.953	2.751	0.435	0.886
Zambia	4.562*	(2.169)	−0.267	(0.199)	(1 4 5)	−18.215	0.841	4.912**	0.364	0.953
Zimbabwe	1.167***	(0.237)	−0.281*	(0.146)	(1 0 1)	−19.28	0.695	9.487***	0.008***	0.938

Notes: ^AIC indicates that the model was selected using the AIC criterion due to the persistence of autocorrelation when using the model selected by SBC. Standard errors are in parenthesis. *** Indicates significance at the 99% level. **Indicates significance at the 90% level

[a] For the Democratic Republic of Congo we control for the ongoing civil war which started in 1997 till present

[b] A trend is added for South Africa. We control for apartheid which made very little difference to the outcome

Table 7.3 Summary of results for the import demand function estimated using OLS

Country	The income elasticity of demand for imports, π	The price elasticity of demand for imports, ψ	R^2	Breusch-Pagan/Cook-Weisberg test for heteroscedas-ticity (P value)	Breusch-Godfrey test for serial correlation (P value)
Congo, Dem. Rep.	2.372***	−0.053 (0.127)	0.247	0.805	0.524
	(0.605)				
Gabon[robust]	0.979***	−0.178 (0.221)	0.579		
	(0.284)				
Mali	0.049	−0.099 (0.169)	0.352	0.314	0.197
	(0.374)				
Togo[robust]	1.608***	−0.834*** (0.203)	0.217		
	(0.495)				
Uganda[robust]	2.061***	−0.225*** (0.059)	0.557		
	(0.613)				
Sierra Leone	0.775	0.416* (0.216)	0.173	0.323	0.675
	(0.501)				
Sudan	0.963	−0.095 (0.094)	0.070	0.172	0.392
	(0.562)				

Notes: Standard errors are in parenthesis. [robust] are heteroscedasticity consistent standard errors. *** Indicates significance at the 99% level. * Indicates significance at the 90% level

It was not possible to estimate reasonable import demand functions using OLS for Mali and Sierra Leone as the income elasticity of demand for imports was insignificant at the 10% level. The price elasticity of demand for imports for Mali was insignificant and had the wrong sign for Sierra Leone. We therefore proceed with the results obtained from the ARDL model for these two countries although caution is needed when making inferences.

Comparing the Estimated Income Elasticity of Demand with Those from Other Studies

Due to the importance of the income elasticity of demand for calculating the balance of payments constrained growth rate, we compare our estimates with those from other studies. According to McCombie (1997), the income elasticity of demand for imports is stable over time as it represents non price based competition which changes very slowly. It is therefore still informative to compare our results with those from other studies in the region despite the time frame covered being different. The comparison can be seen in Table 7.4. Our estimates appear reasonable as they are close to those estimated in other studies. The income elasticity of demand ranged from 0.34 to 5.0 in other studies (Senhadji, 1998; Hussain, 1999; Perraton, 2003) while it ranged from 0.475 to 4.562 in our analysis.

Export Demand Function

A summary of the results for the export demand function can be seen in Table 7.5. Only the long run estimates and the results from the diagnostic tests are shown.

We were able to estimate the export demand function for 19 countries using the ARDL model. The income elasticity of demand for exports ranged from 0.606 for Senegal to 3.446 for Uganda; however, it was much higher for Mozambique at 4.786, Zambia at 8.041 and Zimbabwe at 14.607. The price elasticity of demand for exports was less than zero in absolute terms for 12 countries. It was insignificant for 14 countries. For the five countries where the price elasticity of demand for exports was

Table 7.4 Comparison of the estimated income elasticity of demand with other studies

Country	Our estimates	Senhadji (1998)	Hussain (1999)	Perraton (2003)
Benin	1.142	4.91	1.97	
Botswana	0.896			
Cameroon	1.379	1.01	0.84	0.88
Chad	0.656			
Congo Dem. Rep.	2.179			
Congo Rep.	1.483	0.87	1.44	
Gabon	1.275		1.37	
Gabon (OLS)	0.979			
Kenya	1.06	1.14	0.98	1.84
Gambia	0.475	1.51		
Mali	2.195			0.87
Mauritius	1.183	2.25	1.23	1.17
Mozambique	1.877			
Namibia	1.946			
Nigeria	0.941	1.81	2.70	
Senegal	1.107		2.26	0.98
Sierra Leone	2.310		1.54	
South Africa	0.955	0.67	1.38	
Sudan	0.957		1.57	
Togo	1.608		1.93	5.00
Uganda	1.553			
Uganda (OLS)	2.061			
Zambia	4.562	0.34	1.11	
Zimbabwe	1.167		1.64	

Note: OLS indicates the income elasticity of demand from the import demand function using OLS

significant at the 5% level, it stood at -1.577 for Botswana, -0.605 for the Republic of Congo, -0.860 for Mali, -6.865 for Sudan and -1.390 for Zimbabwe. These results provide further support for the balance of payments constrained growth model.

For Kenya, Benin, Cameroon, Democratic Republic of Congo, Chad and Mauritius, we fail to find any evidence of cointegration using the bounds testing procedure. For Gabon, we could not estimate a stable export demand function with the ARDL model and therefore proceeded with OLS, making the necessary adjustments to account for the non-stationarity of the variables (Table 7.6).

Table 7.5 Summary of results for the export demand function estimated using the ARDL model

	The income elasticity of demand for exports, ε		The price elasticity of demand for exports, η		ARDL	SBC	R^2	Bounds F test	Breusch-Pagan/ Cook-Weisberg test for heteroscedasticity (P value)	Breusch-Godfrey test for serial correlation (P value)
Benin[a]	2.673***	(0.54)	0.058	(0.455)	(6 7 6)	13.046	0.591	1.927	0.811	0.223
Botswana	1.937***	(0.188)	−1.577**	(0.689)	(1 1 0)	−48.83	0.621	3.465	0.225	0.212
Cameroon	1.348***	(0.379)	−0.496	(0.749)	(1 1 0)	−51.295	0.574	2.555	0.373	0.75
Chad	2.469**	(0.968)	1.261	(0.896)	(1 2 0)	22.52	0.483	2.26	0.045**	0.181
Congo, Dem. Rep.	2.83	(1.098)	0.74	(0.648)	(1 1 1)	−9.155	0.407	3.724	0.424	0.278
Congo, Rep.	1.018***	(0.113)	−0.605***	(0.125)	(1 2 0)	−98.318	0.65	6.615***	0.892	0.158
Gambia	1.198***	(0.247)	0.873	(0.259)	(2 1 1)	−63.188[AIC]	0.658	7.447***	0.282	0.249
Kenya	1.218***	(0.372)	−0.425	(1.123)	(1 0 1)	−103.528	0.197	0.622	0.662	0.162
Mali	1.851***	(0.248)	−0.860***	(0.279)	(1 0 4)	−62.539	0.745	8.413***	0.852	0.57
Mauritius	1.581***	(0.418)	−0.816	(1.652)	(1 1 1)	−81.53	0.489	0.575	0.034**	0.203
Mozambique	4.786***	(0.44)	−0.45	(0.423)	(1 0 0)	−50.477	0.665	9.997***	0.239	0.283
Namibia	1.299***	(0.052)	0.187	(0.136)	(2 2 2)	−68.298	0.753	13.251***	0.975	0.274
Nigeria	1.668***	(0.263)	0.035	(0.119)	(1 0 0)	1.534	0.389	4.366*	0.456	0.347
Senegal	0.606***	(0.089)	−0.099	(0.128)	(1 3 0)	−61.174	0.717	16.575***	0.040**	0.515
South Africa	1.637**	(0.629)	0.268	(0.839)	(1 1 1)	−175.118	0.598	6.253**	0.095*	0.234
Sudan	0.719	(0.503)	−6.865**	(2.868)	(2 0 3)	−22.575	0.565	13.214***	0.018**	0.598
Uganda	3.466***	(0.586)	−0.011	(0.287)	(1 1 1)	−16.188	0.43	4.599*	0.95	0.201
Zambia	8.041**	(3.557)	−10.155	(7.02)	(2 2 2)	−25.404	0.809	11.132***	0.152	0.599
Zimbabwe	14.607***	(3.615)	−1.390***	(0.278)	(4 1 4)	−36.537	0.806	8.502***	0.074*	0.331

Notes: [AIC] indicates that the model was selected using the AIC criterion due to the persistence of autocorrelation when using the model selected by SBC. Standard errors are in parenthesis. *** Indicates significance at the 99% level. ** Indicates significance at the 95% level. * Indicates significance at the 90% level

[a]The export demand function for Benin is from 1974 to 2015 due to data availability

Table 7.6 Summary of results for the export demand function estimated using OLS

Country	The income elasticity of demand for imports, π		The price elasticity of demand for imports, ψ		R^2	Breusch-Pagan/ Cook-Weisberg test for heteroscedasticity (P value)	Breusch-Godfrey test for serial correlation (P value)
Congo, Dem. Rep.	3.972**	(1.793)	−0.066	(0.111)	0.135	0.389	0.522
Gabon	1.781	(0.988)	−0.071	(0.201)	0.145	0.838	0.908

Notes: Standard errors are in parenthesis. ** Indicates significance at the 95% level

The Balance of Payments Constrained Growth

The estimates for the income and price elasticities of demand from the import and export demand functions are applied to calculate the balance of payments constrained growth rates given in Eqs. (7.4), (7.5), (7.6), (7.7) and (7.8). These can be seen in Table 7.7 and include the original weak version of Thirlwall's law, y_B, the strong version of Thirlwall's law, $*y_B$, the balance of payments constrained growth rate with sustainable debt accumulation, y_{BSDA}, the balance of payments constrained growth with sustainable debt accumulation and interest rate payments abroad, y_{BSDAR}, and finally the two versions of the balance of payments constrained growth with sustainable debt accumulation, interest rate payments and the terms of trade. In the former version, the terms of trade are interacted with the price elasticities of demand for exports and imports, $*y_{BSDART}$, and, in the latter, the terms of trade are only interacted with the price elasticity of demand for imports, y_{BSDART}.

The different balance of payments constrained growth rates are estimated for the entire sample period which ranges from around the 1960s to the 2014 period. This can be seen in Table 7.7 where the estimated balance of payments constrained growth rates are compared with the actual growth rate for the period concerned.

The balance of payments constrained growth model does a very good job at predicting the actual growth rate for the region. The absolute difference between the actual growth rate and the balance of payments constrained growth rate was less than 0.5 for 17 out of 22 countries and less than one for 19 countries. The simple model best explained the growth process for South Africa, Mali, Uganda and Zimbabwe as the absolute difference between the balance of payments constrained growth rate and the actual growth rate was 0.18, 0.04, 0.84 and 0.06, respectively. The strong version of the model best explained the growth process for Kenya where the difference was 0.42 while the model which allows for sustainable debt accumulation best predicted the growth rate for Cameroon with an absolute error of 0.11.

The model with the most predictive power was the balance of payments constrained growth with sustainable debt accumulation and interest payments abroad. The model closely predicted the growth rates of the Democratic Republic of Congo, Sudan, Mauritius, Senegal, Sierra Leone and Togo with an absolute error of 0.02, 0.15, 0.04, 0.17, 0.01 and 0.17, respectively. This

Table 7.7 The balance of payments constrained growth rate estimated for the 1960–2014 period

Period	Country	Actual	Start^N						Average^N			
			y_B	$*y_B$	y_{BSDA}	y_{BSDAR}	$*y_{BSDART}$	y_{BSDART}	y_{BSDA}	y_{BSDAR}	$*y_{BSDART}$	y_{BSDART}
1975–2014	Benin	3.680	7.197	8.281	6.453	5.830	7.0800	6.066	5.880	5.788	6.981	6.090
1975–2014	Botswana	7.535	9.284	6.552	9.101	9.095	6.158	9.166	9.654	9.657	6.555	9.780
1960–2014	Cameroon	3.647	3.530		3.535	3.371	−0.461	3.314	3.514	3.405	−0.184	3.405
1960–2005	Chad	3.617	14.524		80.780	85.006	−27.788	58.628	67.030	67.866	−20.615	47.611
1960–2014	Congo, Dem. Rep.	1.348	3.030	4.597	3.472	1.438	3.255	1.357	4.523	4.035	6.356	3.983
1960–2014	Congo Dem. Rep.[a] (OLS)	1.348	2.783	5.927	3.222	1.329	5.085	1.254	4.302	3.834	8.709	3.785
1960–2014	Congo, Rep.	4.501	5.082	2.428	5.953	5.326	2.128	4.867	3.418	3.001	0.287	1.831
1960–2014	Gabon	4.47	4.087		4.607	4.162		4.116	4.624	4.460		4.416
1960–2014	Gabon (OLS)[b]	4.47	5.322	6.436	5.263	4.776	5.572	4.430	5.261	5.083	5.871	4.755
1966–2013	Gambia	3.977	8.770	8.330	66.656	107.126	−127.012	−44.516	−13.443	−13.358	10.352	3.707
1960–2014	Kenya	4.789	4.161	4.369	4.167	3.969	3.906	3.621	4.180	4.137	4.034	3.807
1967–2007	Mali	3.731	3.683	2.953	2.271	2.099	1.674	2.152	1.699	1.639	1.343	1.697
1976–2014	Mauritius	4.581	4.872	3.975	4.809	4.617	3.924	4.831	4.558	4.512	3.934	4.778
1980–2014	Mozambique	5.044	4.907	7.399	3.035	2.644	5.021	3.452	1.668	1.625	3.444	2.595
1980–2014	Namibia	3.531	1.626	1.937	1.558		1.551	1.254	1.676		1.687	1.370
1980–2013	Nigeria	4.279	5.566	5.211	5.378	3.489	4.409	4.786	5.747	4.626	8.760	9.149
1960–2014	Senegal	2.829	3.107	1.936	2.996	2.543	0.446	1.630	3.027	2.975	1.014	2.161
1967–2014	Sierra Leone	3.137	3.811		3.150	2.240		2.650	3.382	3.242		3.624
1960–2014	South Africa	3.239	3.058	6.068	3.035	2.851	6.002	2.914	3.014	2.888	5.974	2.939
1960–2014	Sudan	3.934	5.900	2.658	5.901	3.813	−31.232	9.220	5.874	3.346	−32.290	8.212
1960–2014	Sudan (OLS)	3.934	5.864		5.864	3.789		9.161	5.841	3.324		8.164
1960–2014	Togo	3.934	5.243		4.201	3.761		3.692	3.279	3.142		3.058
1982–2014	Uganda	6.089	6.960	6.717	4.826	4.912	1.067	1.240	4.055	4.191	−0.251	−0.099
1982–2014	Uganda (OLS)	6.089	5.245		3.199	3.222		1.356	2.576	2.599		0.536
1960–2013	Zambia	3.389	2.007	6.271	1.607	−0.634	3.965	0.05	1.369	0.865	4.507	1.506
1976–2014	Zimbabwe	1.586	1.528	37.24	1.469	0.319	35.494	1.390	1.502	1.476	35.947	2.396

Notes: Start refers to the start of period value for the share of exports in import ratio and the share of interest payments in imports ratio. Average refers to the average value for these two ratios for the period considered

y_B is the 'weak' original version of the balance of payments constrained growth model

y_B is the 'strong' original version of the balance of payments constrained growth model

y_{BSDA} is the balance of payments constrained growth with sustainable debt accumulation

y_{BSDAR} is the balance of payments constrained growth with sustainable debt accumulation and interest payments abroad

*y_{BSDART} is the balance of payments constrained growth with sustainable debt accumulation, interest payments abroad and the terms of trade interacted with the price elasticities of demand for imports and exports

y_{BSDART} is the balance of payments constrained growth with sustainable debt accumulation, interest payments and the terms of trade (only the income and price elasticities from the import demand function are included)

OLS indicates the growth rates that have been estimated using the import and export demand functions derived from OLS

[a]For the Democratic Republic of Congo both the import and export demand functions use OLS

[b]For Gabon both the import and export demand functions use OLS

was closely followed by the balance of payments constrained growth which includes the terms of trade interacted with the price elasticities of demand for imports and exports, which closely predicted the growth rates of Nigeria, Botswana, Republic of Congo, Gabon, Mozambique and Zambia with an error of 0.13, 0.98, 0.37, 0.04, 0.02 and 0.58, respectively.

Finally, the balance of payments constrained growth rate which included the terms of trade and only the price elasticity of demand for imports best predicted the growth rate of Gambia with a difference of 0.27.

The model failed to make a reasonable prediction for the actual growth rate for three countries. These are Namibia, Benin and Chad where the absolute difference between the actual and predicted growth rate was 1.59, 2.11 and 10.91, respectively.

Formally Testing the Balance of Payments Constrained Growth Model

We were able to estimate the balance of payments constrained growth rate for 22 countries. We begin by formally testing the model for each individual country. A summary of the results can be seen in Table 7.8. For 18 countries, which is almost 82% of the countries included in the analysis, we could not reject the null hypothesis for the equality between the estimated income elasticity of demand for imports and the hypothetical income elasticity of demand for imports that would exactly equate the actual growth rate of the country concerned for at least one of the balance of payments constrained growth models using the Wald test. This provides strong evidence that these 18 African countries were indeed balance of payments constrained during the 1960–2014 period. These results are consistent with Hussain (1999) who found evidence in favour of the model for 26 out of 29 African countries.[10]

The balance of payments constrained growth with sustainable debt accumulation and interest rate payments abroad best explained the growth process of the region as we found evidence of the equality of the estimated income elasticity of demand and the hypothetical income elasticity of demand for 17 of the 18 countries. This highlights the important role of capital flows

---

[10] Hussain (1999) study included North Africa, which is excluded here.

Table 7.8 Wald test results for the equality of the estimated income elasticity of demand, $\hat{\pi}$, and the hypothetical income elasticity of demand, π_H, 1960–2014

Period	Country	$\hat{\pi}$	Average						Start			
			π_{HB}	$*\pi_{HB}$	π_{HBSDA}	π_{HBSDAR}	$*\pi_{HBSDART}$	$\pi_{HBSDART}$	π_{HBSDA}	π_{HBSDAR}	$*\pi_{HBSDART}$	$\pi_{HBSDART}$
1960–2013	Benin	1.142	2.233	2.569	1.640	1.512	1.727	1.553	1.440	1.426	1.586	1.466
	F statistic		118.00***	170.28***	20.71***	11.42***	28.58***	14.10***	7.40**	6.72**	16.46***	7.70***
	P value		0.000	0.000	0.000	0.002	0.000	0.000	0.010	0.014	0.000	0.009
1975–2014	Botswana	0.896	1.104	0.779	1.125	1.121	0.697	1.131	1.078	1.073	0.813	1.084
	F statistic		77.66***	24.59***	94.14***	90.88***	71.13***	99.13***	59.46***	56.23***	12.38***	63.44***
	P value		0.000	0.000	0.000	0.000	0.000	0.000	0.000	0.000	0.001	0.000
1960–2014	Cameroon	1.379	1.335		1.336	1.281		1.260	1.329	1.311		1.290
	F statistic				0.25	1.26		1.86	0.33	0.61		1.04
	P value				0.621	0.268		0.180	0.567	0.438		0.313
1960–2005	Chad	0.656	2.634		1.637	1.623	0.282	1.309	1.655	1.650	0.280	1.337
	F statistic		104.46***		38.90***	37.79***	5.69**	17.22***	40.34***	39.93***	5.75**	18.73***
	P value		0.000		0.000	0.000	0.024	0.000	0.000	0.000	0.024	0.000
1960–2014	Congo, Dem. Rep.	2.179	4.898	7.431	6.099	2.336	5.508	2.195	10.999	9.539	15.896	9.397
	F statistic		4.61**	17.19***	9.58***	0.02	6.91**	0.00	48.49***	33.77***	117.28***	32.48***
	P value		0.038	0.000	0.003	0.902	0.012	0.990	0.000	0.000	0.000	0.000
1960–2014	Congo, Dem. Rep. (OLS)	2.372	4.898	10.431	6.099	2.336	5.508	2.195	10.999	9.539	23.588	9.397
	F statistic		17.41***		37.90***	0.00	135.99***	0.09	203.12***	140.18***	1228.56***	134.68***
	P value		0.000		0.000	0.952	0.000	0.770	0.000	0.000	0.000	0.000
1960–2012	Congo, Rep.	1.483	1.674	0.800	2.224	1.886	0.321	1.662	1.270	1.195	0.675	0.971
	F statistic		0.43	5.49**	6.73**	1.91	15.89***	0.38	0.54	0.98	7.69**	3.09*
	P value		0.522	0.032	0.019	0.186	0.001	0.548	0.474	0.337	0.013	0.098
1960–2014	Gabon	1.275	1.165		1.348	1.116		1.093	1.359	1.269		1.246
	F statistic		0.51		0.22	1.06		1.39	0.29	0.00		0.04
	P value		0.479		0.643	0.308		0.245	0.594	0.965		0.848

(continued)

Table 7.8 (continued)

Period	Country	$\hat{\pi}$	π_{HB}	$*\pi_{HB}$	Average				Start			
					π_{HBSDA}	π_{HBSDAR}	$*\pi_{HBSDART}$	$\pi_{HBSDART}$	π_{HBSDA}	π_{HBSDAR}	$*\pi_{HBSDART}$	$\pi_{HBSDART}$
1960–2014	Gabon[a] (OLS)	0.979	1.165	1.409	1.348	1.116	1.473	0.961	1.359	1.269	1.642	1.114
	F statistic		0.43	2.28	1.68	0.23	3.01*	0.00	1.78	1.04	5.43**	0.22
	P value		0.517	0.137	0.201	0.633	0.089	0.948	0.188	0.313	0.024	0.638
1966–2013	Gambia	0.475	1.048	0.994	1.027	0.838	0.014	0.304	1.019	1.017	0.276	0.483
	F statistic		8.74***	7.17**	8.11***	3.51*	5.66**	0.78	7.88***	7.82***	1.05	0.00
	P value		0.005	0.011	0.007	0.069	0.022	0.383	0.008	0.008	0.311	0.967
1960–2014	Kenya	0.986	0.857	0.900	0.871	0.875	0.867	0.828	0.892	0.893	0.878	0.846
	F statistic		0.37	0.16	0.29	0.27	0.31	0.55	0.20	0.19	0.26	0.43
	P value		0.547	0.687	0.591	0.604	0.578	0.461	0.660	0.663	0.613	0.513
1967–2007	Mali[b]	2.195	2.166	1.737	1.544	1.478	1.291	1.501	1.371	1.350	1.231	1.374
	F statistic		0.00	0.18	0.37	0.45	0.71	0.42	0.59	0.62	0.18	0.59
	P value		0.978	0.671	0.547	0.508	0.405	0.521	0.447	0.436	0.374	0.449
1976–2014	Mauritius	1.183	1.258	1.026	1.238	1.191	1.028	1.241	1.178	1.170	1.060	1.220
	F statistic		0.20	0.90	0.11	0.00	0.88	0.12	0.00	0.01	0.56	0.05
	P value		0.653	0.354	0.744	0.962	0.360	0.730	0.975	0.937	0.465	0.826
1980–2014	Mozambique	1.877	1.826	2.753	1.356	1.265	1.871	1.471	1.160	1.152	1.538	1.358
	F statistic		0.01	3.75*	1.33	1.84	0.00	0.81	2.52	2.57	0.56	1.32
	P value		0.910	0.066	0.261	0.189	0.989	0.378	0.127	0.123	0.461	0.263
1980–2014	Namibia[c]	1.946	0.896	1.067	0.904		0.901	0.743	0.892		0.909	0.731
	F statistic		32.35***	22.68***	31.86***		32.05***	42.46***	32.60***		31.56***	43.31***
	P value		0.000	0.000	0.000		0.000	0.000	0.000		0.000	0.000
1985–2013	Nigeria	0.941	1.224	1.146	1.504	0.572	1.001	1.177	1.149	0.987	1.504	1.592
	F statistic		0.89	0.47	3.53*	1.52	0.04	0.62	0.48	0.02	3.53*	4.72**
	P value		0.359	0.504	0.078	0.235	0.845	0.443	0.498	0.881	0.078	0.045
1960–2014	Senegal	1.107	1.215	0.757	1.156	1.027	0.440	0.771	1.169	1.153	0.538	0.897
	F statistic		1.75	18.64***	0.36	0.98	67.61***	17.18***	0.57	0.31	49.21***	7.72**
	P value		0.193	0.000	0.553	0.328	0.000	0.000	0.453	0.578	0.000	0.013

Period		C1	C2	C3	C4	C5	C6	C7	C8	C9	C10	C11
1967–2014	Sierra Leone[d]	2.310	2.806		2.318	1.747		2.004	2.476	2.380		2.638
	F statistic		0.26		0.00	0.33		0.10	0.03	0.01		0.11
	P value		0.615		0.994	0.567		0.755	0.866	0.944		0.739
1960–2014	South Africa	0.955	0.901	1.789	0.882	0.821	1.905	0.843	0.857	0.805	2.119	0.827
	F statistic		0.01	2.31	0.02	0.06	2.99*	0.04	0.03	0.07	4.50**	0.02
	P value		0.922	0.136	0.894	0.808	0.09	0.839	0.859	0.785	0.039	0.880
1964–2013	Sudan[e]	0.957	1.435	0.646	1.435	0.978	−7.365	2.208	1.484	0.802	−8.564	2.081
	F statistic		5.87**	2.50	5.87**	0.01	1784***	40.26***	7.14***	0.62	2333***	32.50***
	P value		0.019	0.121	0.019	0.917	0.000	0.000	0.010	0.434	0.000	0.000
1964–2013	Sudan (OLS)	0.963	1.435		1.435	0.978		2.208	1.484	0.802		2.081
	F statistic		0.76		0.70	0.00		4.89**	0.86	0.08		3.95*
	P value		0.388		0.406	0.980		0.031	0.359	0.774		0.052
1960–2014	Togo (OLS)	1.608	2.143		1.690	1.555		1.534	1.442	1.408		1.387
	F statistic		1.16		0.03	0.01		0.02	0.11	0.16		0.17
	P value		0.286		0.870	0.914		0.888	0.738	0.687		0.678
1982–2014	Uganda[f]	1.553	1.775	1.713	1.345	1.365	0.753	0.781	1.257	1.294	0.689	0.710
	F statistic		0.87	0.45	0.78	0.64	11.43***	10.64***	1.57	1.20	13.33***	12.69***
	P value		0.369	0.514	0.395	0.440	0.005	0.006	0.233	0.294	0.003	0.003
1982–2014	Uganda (OLS)	2.061	1.775		1.345	1.365		0.912	1.257	1.294		0.841
	F statistic		0.22		1.37	1.29		3.52*	1.72	1.57		3.96*
	P value		0.644		0.252	0.265		0.071	0.200	0.221		0.056
1960–2014	Zambia	4.562	2.702	8.441	2.290	0.085	5.203	0.853	2.065	1.540	5.901	2.308
	F statistic		0.74	3.20*	1.10	4.26*	0.09	2.92	1.32	1.94	0.38	1.08
	P value		0.406	0.097	0.314	0.059	0.772	0.111	0.270	0.187	0.547	0.317
1976–2014	Zimbabwe	1.167	1.124	27.399	1.097	0.440	20.622	1.054	1.111	1.093	24.110	1.708
	F statistic		0.03	12,190***	0.09	9.37***	6705***	0.23	0.06	0.10	9324***	5.18**
	P value		0.857	0.000	0.770	0.005	0.000	0.638	0.815	0.758	0.000	0.032

Table 7.8 (continued)

Notes: Start refers to the start of period value for the share of exports in import ratio and the share of interest payments in imports ratio. Average refers to the average value for these two ratios for the period considered. *** Indicates significance at the 99% level. ** Indicates significance at the 95% level. * Indicates significance at the 90% level

π_{HB} is the hypothetical income elasticity of demand from the original 'weak' version of the balance of payments constrained growth model

*π_{HB} is the hypothetical income elasticity of demand from the original 'strong' version of the balance of payments constrained growth model

π_{HBSDA} is the hypothetical income elasticity of demand from the balance of payments constrained growth model with sustainable debt accumulation

π_{HBSDAR} is the hypothetical income elasticity of demand from the balance of payments constrained growth model with sustainable debt accumulation and interest payments abroad

*$\pi_{HBSDART}$ is the hypothetical income elasticity of demand from the balance of payments constrained growth model with sustainable debt accumulation, interest payments abroad and the terms of trade interacted with the price elasticities of demand for imports and exports

$\pi_{HBSDART}$ is the hypothetical income elasticity of demand from the balance of payments constrained growth model with sustainable debt accumulation, interest payments and the terms of trade (only the income and price elasticities from the import demand function are included)

[a]For Gabon, both the import and export demand functions are estimated with OLS

[b]For Mali, the ARDL estimates for the import and export demand function are used

[c]For Namibia, there is no data on interest payments abroad

[d]Sierra Leone uses the ARDL model

[e]Sudan uses the ARDL estimate for both the export and import demand function

[f]For Uganda, both import and export demand functions are estimated with the ARDL model

to the region as well as the significance of interest rate payments abroad. The results are similar to those obtained by Moreno-Brid (2003) for Mexico.

This was followed closely by the original version of the model which was able to explain the growth experience of 16 countries. This is not surprising as a study by Hussain (1999) found that the basic and extended model which allows for capital flows, were good predictors for the actual growth rate in Africa and Asia. Perraton (2003) for a group of developing countries, additionally found that the original version of the model slightly outperformed the extended model with the terms of trade as it held for the majority of the countries included in the analysis.

Using the individual country test, we could not find evidence for any of the balance of payments constrained growth models for Benin, Botswana, Chad and Namibia. This result is not surprising for Benin and Chad as the estimated balance of payments constrained growth rate given in Table 7.7 had little predictive power for the actual growth rate. For Namibia, this may be due to the lack of data on interest payments abroad.

Caution is needed when rejecting the balance of payments constrained growth model for Botswana based on the Wald test as the estimated income elasticity is 0.896 while the hypothetical income elasticity for the model with sustainable debt accumulation, interest payments abroad and the terms of trade is 0.81; a difference of 0.08. No other studies have been done for Botswana, Chad and Namibia; however, a study by Perraton (2003) included Benin, found evidence in favour of the original and extended model which includes the terms of trade effects.

There is very little difference in the results from the Wald test when testing the balance of payments constrained growth rate estimated using the average ratios and the start of period ratios for the share of exports in imports and the share of interest payments abroad in imports. For the latter, the result is in line with the literature as we expect the share of interest payments abroad to have a limited effect on the balance of payments constrained growth rate (Thirlwall, 2012).

Our second formal test for the balance of payments constrained model can be seen in Table 7.9. We regressed each of our calculated balance of payments constrained growth rates on the actual growth rate for all 22 countries. We use two different specifications; with and without a trend. When we exclude the trend, we find strong evidence in support of the balance of payments constrained model as the coefficient on the actual

Table 7.9 Regression results of the balance of payments constrained growth, y_B, on the actual growth rate (logarithmic form)

Dependent variable	Constant, α	Coefficient on the actual growth rate, β	R^2	F statistic	Wald test (β = 1) P value	Wald test (α = 0) P value
y_B	0.382 (0.366)	0.834*** (0.268)	0.325	9.65***	0.544	0.308
y_B		1.104*** (0.072)	0.918	234.95***	0.161	
*y_B	2.371*** (0.578)	−0.539 (0.427)	0.102	1.59	0.002***	0.001***
*y_B		1.132*** (0.184)	0.715	37.75***	0.482	
Average[N] y_{BSDA}	0.617 (0.791)	0.712 (0.579	0.070	1.51	0.625	0.443
y_{BSDA}		1.148*** (0.153)	0.726	55.86***	0.344	
y_{BSDAR}	−0.396 (0.932)	1.403** (0.678)	0.192	4.28**	0.559	0.676
y_{BSDAR}		1.126*** (0.184)	0.663	37.36***	0.499	
*y_{BSDART}	1.960** (0.798)	−0.457 (0.591)	0.044	0.60	0.028**	0.029**
*y_{BSDART}	0.921*** (0.213)		0.570	18.56***	0.720	
y_{BSDART}	−0.230 (0.997)	1.008 (0.731)	0.091	1.90	0.990	0.819
y_{BSDART}		0.846*** (0.195)	0.483	18.71***	0.441	

	Start^N					
y_{BSDA}	0.793 (0.671)	0.417 (0.492)	0.036	0.72	0.251	0.252
y_{BSDA}		0.977*** (0.136)	0.719	51.36***	0.869	
y_{BSDAR}	0.433 (0.513)	0.723 (0.701)	0.038	0.71	0.284	0.316
y_{BSDAR}		0.941*** (0.143)	0.692	42.86	0.685	
*y_{BSDART}	2.522** (0.906)	−0.854 (0.670)	0.103	1.62	0.015**	0.014**
*y_{BSDART}		0.924*** (0.242)	0.491	14.50***	0.759	
y_{BSDART}	1.113 (0.724)	0.118 (0.531)	0.002	0.05	0.112	0.140
y_{BSDART}		0.904*** (0.146)	0.644	38.0***	0.522	

Notes: Start refers to the start of period value for the share of exports in import ratio and the share of interest payments in imports ratio. Average refers to the average value for these two ratios for the period considered. Standard errors are in parenthesis. *** Indicates significance at the 99% level. ** Indicates significance at the 95% level

y_B is the 'weak' original version of the balance of payments constrained growth model
*y_B is the 'strong' original version of the balance of payments constrained growth model
y_{BSDA} is the balance of payments constrained growth with sustainable debt accumulation
y_{BSDAR} is the balance of payments constrained growth with sustainable debt accumulation and interest payments abroad
*y_{BSDART} is the balance of payments constrained growth with sustainable debt accumulation, interest payments abroad and the terms of trade interacted with the price elasticities of demand for imports and exports
y_{BSDART} is the balance of payments constrained growth with sustainable debt accumulation, interest payments and the terms of trade (only the income and price elasticities from the import demand function are included)

rate of growth ranged from 0.846 to 1.14. In addition, using the Wald test, we accept the hypothesis that the coefficient is equal to one. These results confirm and strengthen the results obtained from the single country tests. As Benin, Botswana, Chad and Namibia were included in the regressions in Table 7.9, it would be erroneous to dismiss the balance of payments constrained growth as being irrelevant for these countries.

4   Concluding Remarks

The balance of payments constrained growth rate was estimated for 22 sub-Saharan African countries. The model proved to have strong predictive power as it was able to closely predict the growth rate of 17 countries with an absolute error of less than 0.5. This figure increased to 19 at an absolute error below 1.

When formally testing the model for each individual country, by testing the equality between the estimated income elasticity of demand for imports and the hypothetical income elasticity of demand for imports that would exactly equate the actual rate of growth, again we find strong evidence in support of the balance of payments constrained growth model. For 18 countries, we found evidence in support of at least one of the balance of payments constrained growth models.

The model which accounts for sustainable debt accumulation and interest rate payments abroad outperformed all the other models both in its predictive power and when testing the equality of the estimated and hypothetical income elasticities of demand. It was able to explain the growth experience of 77.3% of the countries included in the study. This highlights the importance of capital flows and interest rate payments in the region.

Unsurprisingly, the same countries where the balance of payments constrained growth model had poor predictive power, failed the formal test. These are Benin, Botswana, Chad and Namibia. Caution however is needed when rejecting the balance of payments constrained growth rate for Namibia as data on interest payments abroad was not available. By applying only the simple balance of payments constrained growth model, we could erroneously reject the model when it actually does apply. This would have been the case for the Democratic Republic of Congo and Gambia. It is therefore important to account for capital flows and interest payments abroad.

When pooling the results from the 22 countries, we find strong evidence in favour of all six models for the balance of payments constrained growth for the full sample of countries, including Benin, Botswana, Chad and Namibia. These results strengthen those obtained from the single country tests.

Our results provide strong evidence that the demand-led, export driven, long run growth model developed by Thirlwall (1979) is relevant for the sub-Saharan African region. This provides important insight into policy reform necessary for achieving the sustainable development goals. One of the implications of the balance of payments constrained growth model is that the structure of production and exports determines the income elasticity of demand for exports which therefore determines the rate of growth of one country relative to another. What a country exports has to do with how its economic activity is structured. Changing the structure of the economy is therefore imperative in order to bring about long term economic growth and development in the region.

Appendix 1

Table 7.10 Data and sources for calculating the balance of payments constrained growth rate

Variable	Source
Exports of goods and services (constant 2005 USD)	World Development Indicators (World Bank)
Imports of goods and services (constant 2005 USD)	World Development Indicators (World Bank)
GDP (constant 2005 USD)	World Development Indicators (World Bank)
GDP deflator (base year 2005)	World Development Indicators (World Bank)
Consumer price index (CPI)	World Development Indicators (World Bank)
World Income, less own country income (constant 2005 USD)	World Development Indicators (World Bank)
Export price index (unit value of exports, f.o.b) (Base year 2005)	International Financial Statistics (IMF)
Import price index (unit value of imports, f.o.b) (Base year 2005)	International Financial Statistics (IMF)
Interest payment on external debt (constant 2005 USD)	World Development Indicators (World Bank)
REER (Real effective exchange rate, CPI-based)	REER database (Bruegel)

REER measures the development of the real value of a country's currency against the basket of the trading partners of the country. It therefore can be expressed as P_d / P_f or P_d / P_m which is domestic to foreign prices.

We use REER to estimate the import and export demand functions. In the export demand function, we make use of the domestic to foreign price ratio P_d / P_m. REER is therefore used in the export demand function. For the import demand function, we make use of the foreign to domestic price ratio P_f / P_d, 1/REER is therefore used in the import demand function.

Other price indices were also used when REER was not available. We use the price index recommended by Tharnpanich and McCombie (2013).

$$RPM2 = \frac{\text{Import price index}}{GDP \text{ deflator}}$$

$$RPM3 = \frac{\text{Import price index}}{CPI}$$

$$RPM4 = \frac{\text{Import price index}}{\text{Export price index}}$$

$$RPX4 = \frac{\text{Export price index}}{\text{Import price index}}$$

Appendix 2: Details of the Model

$$P_d X + FP_d = P_f ME \tag{7.1}$$

where P_d is the price of exports in the domestic currency, X, is the volume of exports, F is the current account deficit in real terms, so that FP_d, is nominal capital flows to finance the deficit, P_f, is the price of imports in foreign currency, M, is the volume of imports and E, is the exchange rate measured as the domestic price of foreign currency.[11]

Taking the first difference of the variables in logarithmic form yields,

$$\theta\left(p_d + x\right) + \left(1 - \theta\right)\left(f + P_d\right) = p_f + m + e \qquad (7.2)$$

where θ and $\left(1 - \theta\right)$, represent the share of exports and capital flows as a proportion of total receipts respectively. Therefore $\theta = P_d X / R$ and $\left(1 - \theta\right) = FP_d / R$, where R is total receipts which can also be expressed as the import bill financed by export earnings and capital flows. Lower case letters denote growth rates.

Equation (7.2) is modified to include sustainable debt accumulation and interest rate payments abroad (Moreno-Brid, 2003). We account for interest payments abroad by subtracting interest payments from capital flows,

$$\theta\left(p_d + x\right) - \theta_1\left(p_d + r\right) + \left(1 - \theta + \theta_1\right)\left(f + P_d\right) = p_f + m + e \quad (7.3)$$

where r is the growth rate of real net interest payments abroad and, θ_1, is the share of foreign exchange used for interest payments abroad. Corresponding to sustainable debt accumulation in the long run, we assume that the current account deficit to GDP ratio is constant, hence we set $f = y$.[12] Substituting the growth of imports and exports, setting $f = y$ and solving for the growth of income,[13]

$$y_{BSDART} = \frac{\theta\varepsilon z - \theta_1 r + \left(\theta\eta + \psi + 1\right)\left(p_d - p_f - e\right)}{\pi - \left(1 - \theta + \theta_1\right)} \qquad (7.4)$$

---

[11] For simplicity, the nominal exchange rate is assumed to be fixed and equal to one (Moreno-Brid, 2003).

[12] Following Moreno-Brid (2003), we set the growth in capital flows equal to the growth in income $\frac{df}{f} = \frac{dy}{y}$.

[13] Substituting the import and export demand functions in Eq. (7.3) yields

$\theta\left(p_d + \left(\eta\left(p_{d-e-p_f}\right) + \varepsilon z\right)\right) - \theta_1\left(p_d + r\right) + \left(1 - \theta + \theta_1\right)\left(f + P_d\right) = p_f + \left(\psi\left(p_f + e - p_d\right) + \pi y\right) + e.$

where y_{BSDART} is the balance of payments constrained growth rate with sustainable debt accumulation, interest rate payments abroad and the terms of trade.

Under the assumption of constant relative prices,[14] Eq. (7.4) reduces to,

$$*y_{BSDART} = \frac{\theta x - \theta_1 r + (\psi + 1)(p_d - p_f - e)}{\pi - (1 - \theta + \theta_1)} \tag{7.5}$$

If the terms of trade are neutral and the Marshall Lerner condition is met, that is, $\psi = -1$ then Eq. (7.5) reduces to,

$$y_{BSDAR} = \frac{\theta x - \theta_1 r}{\pi - (1 - \theta + \theta_1)} \tag{7.6}$$

where y_{BSDAR} is the balance of payments constrained growth rate with sustainable debt accumulation and interest payments abroad. If there are no interest payments, hence, $\theta_1 = 0$, then Eq. (7.6) becomes,

$$y_{BSDA} = \frac{\theta x}{\pi - (1 - \theta)} \tag{7.7}$$

where y_{BSDA} is the balance of payments constrained growth rate with sustainable debt accumulation. If a country does not have a deficit then, $\theta_1 = 1$, and Eq. (7.7) reduces to the weak form of Thirlwall's original law,

$$y_B = x / \pi \tag{7.8}$$

---

[14] This specification $*y_{BSDART} = \dfrac{\theta x - \theta_1 r + (\psi + 1)(p_d - p_f - e)}{\pi - (1 - \theta + \theta_1)}$, does not include estimates from the export demand function, that is, the income elasticity of demand or the price elasticity of demand for exports.

When comparing the different models of the balance of payments constraint growth rate we expect,

- the balance of payments constrained growth rate with capital flows to be higher than the original model as we assume the countries under consideration to be net borrowers and hence capital inflows relax the balance of payments constraint.
- the terms of trade effect to be either negative or positive depending on the experience of the country in question.
- the balance of payments constraint growth model with sustainable debt accumulation and interest rate payments to be lower than the model that does not set a limit to capital inflows or account for interest rate payments abroad.[15]

Economic Propositions

The higher the income elasticity of demand for imports $\neq$, the lower the balance of payments constrained growth rate. A faster growth rate of world income z, will raise the balance of payments constrained growth rate.

Furthermore, the Marshall–Lerner condition is assumed to be true. That is, devaluations or a currency depreciation measured by the increase in the domestic price of foreign currency ($e > 0$), will improve the balance of payments constrained growth rate provided that the absolute value of the sum of the price elasticity of demand for exports weighted by the proportion of the total import bill financed by export earnings and the price elasticity of demand for imports is greater than unity, that is, $|\theta\eta + \psi| > 1$. However, even if the condition ($|\theta\eta + \psi| > 1$) is satisfied, a once off devaluation will not raise the balance of payments constrained growth rate permanently. After an initial devaluation, e will fall back to zero and the growth rate will backslide to its former level (Thirlwall & Hussain, 1982).

---

[15] We do not estimate the balance of payments constrained growth model with unlimited capital flows as it is not necessary to include this specification of the model in order to obtain the balance of payments constrained growth rate with sustainable debt accumulation. In addition, there is a lack of comparable data across countries on capital flows.

References

Baum, C. F. (2005). Stata: The language of choice for time-series analysis? *The Stata Journal, 5*(1), 46–63.

Bewley, R. (1979). The direct estimation of the equlillibrium response in a linear dynamic model. *Economics Letters, 3*, 357–361.

Britto, G., & McCombie, J. S. L. (2009). Thirlwall's law and the long-run equilibrium growth rate: An application to Brazil. *Journal of Post-Keynesian Economics, 35*(4), 695–696.

Clemente, J., Montanes, A., & Reyes, M. (1998). Testing for a unit root in variables with a double change in the mean. *Economics Letters, 59*, 175–182.

Devlin, R., & Ffrench-Davis, R. (1995). The great Latin American debt crisis: A decade of asymmetric adjustment. *Revista de Economia Politica, 15*(3), 117–142.

Elliott, D. R., & Rhodd, R. (1999). Explaining growth rate differences in highly indebted countries: An extension to Thirlwall and Hussain. *Applied Economics, 31*(9), 1145–1148.

Harrod, R. (1933). *International economics.* Cambridge: Cambridge University Press.

Hussain, M. N. (1999). The balance of payments constraint and growth rate differences among African and East Asian economies. *African Development Review, 11*(1), 103–137.

International Monetary Fund. (2018). *Regional economic outlook: Sub-Saharan Africa.* Washington, DC: International Monetary Fund.

McCombie, J. S. L. (1989). Thirlwall's law and balance of payments constrained growth: A comment on the debate. *Applied Economics, 21*, 611–629.

McCombie, J. S. L. (1997). On the empirics of balance-of-payments-constrained growth. *Journal of Post Keynesian Economics, 19*(3), 345–375.

McGregor, P. G., & Swales, J. K. (1985). Professor Thirlwall and balance of payments constrained growth. *Applied Economics, 17*, 17–32.

Moreno-Brid, J. C., (1999). On Capital Flows and the Balance of Payments Constrained Growth Model. *Journal of Post Keynesian Economics, 21*(2), 283–298.

Moreno-Brid, J. C. (2003). Capital flows, interest payments and the balance of payments constrained growth model: A theoretical and empirical analysis. *Metroeconomica, 54*(2 and 3), 346–365.

Perraton, J. (2003). Balance of payments constrained growth and developing countries: An examination of Thirwall's hypothesis. *International Review of Applied Economics, 17*(1), 1–22.

Perron, P., & Vogelsang, T. (1992a). Nonstationarity and level shifts with an application to purchasing parity. *Journal of Business and Economic Statistics, 10*, 301–320.

Perron, P., & Vogelsang, T. J. (1992b). Testing for a unit root in a time series with a changing mean: Corrections and extensions. *Journal of Business and Economic Statistics, 10*(4), 467–470.

Pesaran, M. H., & Shin, Y. (1998). An autoregressive distributed lag modelling approach to cointegration analysis. *Econometric Society Monographs, 31*, 371–413.

Senhadji, A. (1998). Time-Series Estimation of Structural Import Demand Equations: A Cross-Country Analysis. *IMF Staff Papers, 45*(2), 236.

Tharnpanich, N. & McCombie, J. S. L., (2013). Balance of Payments Constrained Growth, Structural Change, and the Thai Economy. *Journal of Post Keynesian Economics, 35*(4), 569–598.

Thirlwall, A. P., (1979). The Balance of Payments Constraint as an Explanation of International Growth Rate Differences. *BNL Quarterly Review, 32*(128), 45–53.

Thirlwall, A. P. (2011). *Economics of development* (9th ed.). London: Palgrave Macmillan.

Thirlwall, A. P. (2012). Balance of Payments Constrained Growth Models: History and Overview. In E., Soukiazis, & P. A. Cerqueira (Eds). *Models of Balance of Payments Constrained Growth: History, Theory and Empirical Evidence* (pp. 11–49). Basingstoke: Palgrave Macmillan.

Thirlwall, A. P. (2013). *Economic growth in an open developing economy: The role of structure and demand*. Cheltenham: Edward Elgar.

Thirlwall, A. P., & Hussain, M. N. (1982). The balance of payments constraint, capital flows and growth rate differences between developing countries. *Oxford Economic Papers, 34*, 498–510.

World Bank. (2015). *Heavily indebted poor countries (HIPC)*. [Online]. Retrieved September 9, 2015, from http://data.worldbank.org/income-level/HPC

8

Ethnic Diversity and Progress Towards the Millennium Development Goals

Sefa Awaworyi Churchill, Meg Elkins, and Simon Feeny

1   Introduction

Following the signing of the Millennium Declaration in September 2000, all United Nation (UN) member states committed themselves to the achievement of the Millennium Development Goals (MDGs). The eight MDGs were designed to alleviate poverty in its many forms by 2015, using 1990 as a baseline. As recently reported by the UN (2015), "the MDGs helped to lift more than one billion people out of extreme poverty, to make inroads against hunger, to enable more girls to attend school than ever before and to protect our planet". At the same time, it is undeniable that the progress made has been uneven across countries. For instance, statistics reveal that in 2011, about 60 per cent of the world's billion people living in extreme poverty lived in five countries

S. Awaworyi Churchill (✉) • M. Elkins • S. Feeny
School of Economics, Finance and Marketing, RMIT University,
Melbourne, VIC, Australia
e-mail: sefa.churchill@rmit.edu.au; meg.elkins@rmit.edu.au;
simon.feeny@rmit.edu.au

© The Author(s) 2020
S. Awaworyi Churchill (ed.), *Moving from the Millennium to the Sustainable
Development Goals*, https://doi.org/10.1007/978-981-15-1556-9_8

4   Empirical Results

Summary Statistics

Table 5.1 reports the mean values for the control variables by fertility gap status. These summary statistics reveal that there are significant differences in mothers' characteristics between the two sub-groups. Compared to women with negative fertility gaps, women with positive or no fertility gap are approximately 4 years younger, and have, on average, 3 more years of education. We also observe some significant economic and locational differences between the two sub-groups of women. We find that more women with negative fertility gaps belong to poorer economic status and reside in rural areas. On the health front, women with positive to no fertility gap are marginally healthier using the BMI and anemic status as indicators of health.

Table 5.2 presents an overview of the share of women associated with various nutritional statuses for children. We find that women with a negative fertility gap have a higher number of children alive compared to

Table 5.1 Mother's characteristics by fertility gap (mean values)

Variables	Entire sample	Having more children than desired (negative fertility gap)	Having equal or fewer children than desired (positive fertility gap)	Difference
Mother's age (years)	27.00	30.71	25.97	−4.733∗∗∗
Mother's education (years)	6.429	4.121	7.071	3.019∗∗∗
Hindu (0/1: 1 if 'Hindu')	0.807	0.791	0.811	0.012∗∗
Economic Status (0/1: 1 if 'not poor')	0.528	0.414	0.560	0.169∗∗∗
Rural (0/1: 1 if 'rural')	0.751	0.781	0.742	−0.037∗∗∗
Mother's health				
Mother's BMI (0/1: 1 if BMI 'not healthy')	0.288	0.292	0.287	−0.015∗∗∗
Mother's anemic status (0/1: 1 if 'anemic')	0.150	0.156	0.148	−0.014∗∗∗
Observations	138,009	29,972	108,037	

poverty is higher in such settings (Perera & Lee, 2013). With respect to education, Miguel and Gugerty (2005) demonstrate that ethnic diversity is associated with lower school funding and worse school facilities, which is likely to affect the achievement of the second MDG of achieving universal primary education. Further, gender differences are deeply rooted in cultural and social norms, which reflect the societal and institutional disposition towards gender equality (Hiller, 2014). Thus, as argued by Awaworyi Churchill, Nuhu, and Lopez (2019), ethnic diversity influences gender equality through its role in strengthening cultural and social norms that preserve existing gender gaps, impacting on the achievement of the third MDG.

Similar arguments can be made for how ethnic diversity impacts on the achievement of other MDGs including the health and mortality related goals. For instance, evidence suggests that social networks and information flows significantly foster healthcare utilization. Individuals that increase social participation and build informal or formal social networks have the opportunity to casually share information about relevant health issues such as communicable diseases and nutrition (Awaworyi Churchill, Ocloo, & Siawor-Robertson, 2016a; DeLoach & Lamanna, 2011; Devillanova, 2008). However, trust and social networks are lower in fractionalized or ethnically diverse communities (Awaworyi Churchill, 2017; Leigh, 2006). Additionally, higher levels of ethnic diversity have also been associated with a higher probability of conflict (Blimes, 2006), and therefore higher mortality rates.

Potentially counteracting these negative impacts of ethnic diversity on development are a number of positive influences. For instance, higher levels of ethnic heterogeneity can be associated with more skilled workers (Fafchamps, 2000), and this could improve the quality of health workers in a community. The underlying logic behind this argument is that various ethnic groups can be associated with different skills which promote innovation and creativity, leading to higher levels of productivity, growth and development (Lee, 2014; McLeod, Lobel, & Cox, 1996; Nathan, 2014).

This study, therefore, examines the hypothesis that cross-country differences in ethnic diversity can explain differences in MDG levels and progress across countries. We examine the impact of ethnic diversity on a number of targets for the MDGs. Our main measure of ethnic diversity is sourced from Alesina and Zhuravskaya (2011), who present indices of fractionalization for a cross-section of countries, capturing the probability that two randomly selected individuals in a country belong to different ethnic groups. Our results show that ethnic fractionalization hinders development and MDG progress, and this is consistent across the MDG targets employed in the study. These findings suggest that ethnic diversity is important in understanding MDG progress and thus it should be a factor of interest when strategizing and implementing development projects across countries. Further, the results from this study can further inform appropriate strategies to adopt to assist with the achievement of the Sustainable Development Goals.

The remainder of this chapter is structured as follows. Section 2 describes the data used to examine the relationship between ethnic diversity and progress towards the MDGs. Section 3 presents the methodology used to analyse the data and Sect. 4 provides the results from the model estimations. Finally, Sect. 5 concludes with some policy recommendations.

2   Data

Data used in this study are drawn from two sources. Data on ethnic diversity are drawn from Alesina, Devleeschauwer, Easterly, Kurlat, and Wacziarg (2003) while measures of MDG progress and control variables (discussed below) are from the World Bank's *World Development Indicators* (WDI) and *World Governance Indicators* (WGI) databases. The MDG progress variables that are considered in this chapter are based on data availability. Specifically, they relate to the poverty headcount ratio at $1.90 a day (a measure of extreme poverty), the prevalence of undernourishment (as a measure of hunger), enrolment in primary school education, the gender parity index (at school), infant and maternal mortality rates, the prevalence of HIV-AIDS and access to an improved water source.[2]

The measure of ethnic diversity is an index of ethnic fractionalization which captures the probability that two randomly selected individuals from a given country are from different ethnic groups (Alesina et al., 2003). This index is based on the Herfindhal index and higher values of the index represent higher levels of ethnic diversity. Thus, where s_{ej} is the share of ethnic group e in country j;

$$\text{FRACTIONALIZATION}_J = 1 - \sum_{e=1}^{N} S_{eJ}^2 \qquad (8.1)$$

Indices of fractionalization are computed for a cross-section of countries. Consistent with the existing literature (see, e.g., Alesina et al., 2003; Alesina & Zhuravskaya, 2011; Awaworyi Churchill, 2017; Awaworyi Churchill, Okai, & Posso, 2016b; Easterly & Levine, 1997), for MDG indicators, we take the average for each country for the decade 2004 to 2013, and merged this with the fractionalization data. Ethnic composition of a population does not change over short periods of time and is effectively a time invariant variable employed in the empirical model. Alesina et al. (2003) argue that indices of diversity are stable for periods of about 30 years.

The data include 119 developing countries, although some countries are not included in some versions of the model due to an absence of requisite data.[3] A list of countries included in our analysis is presented in Table 8.6 in the Appendix. Table 8.1 presents summary statistics and a description of the variables used.

---

[2] Access to improved drinking water includes piped water on premises, and other improved drinking water sources (public taps or standpipes, tube wells or boreholes, protected dug wells, protected springs and rainwater collection).

[3] Our classifications are based on the World Bank income groupings. Besides high-income countries, we consider all other countries as developing.

Table 8.1 Description and summary of variables

Variable	Description	Mean	SD
Ethnic diversity	Index of Ethnic Fractionalization from Alesina et al. (2003)	0.480	0.244
Diversity (*Ethnologue*)	Index of Ethnic Fractionalization from *Ethnologue*	0.472	0.323
Diversity (Fearon)	Index of Ethnic Fractionalization from Fearon (2003)	0.519	0.242
Diversity (Desmet)	Index of Ethnic Fractionalization Desmet et al. (2009)	0.493	0.317
Poverty	Percentage of the population living on less than $1.90 a day (proxy for extreme poverty)	1.796	2.042
Hunger	Percentage of a population whose food intake is insufficient to meet dietary energy requirements continuously (proxy for extreme hunger)	2.561	0.724
Education	Ratio of total enrolment in primary, regardless of age, to the population of the age group that officially corresponds to the level of education (proxy for the achievement of universal primary education)	4.628	0.161
Gender	Gender parity index that is, the ratio of girls to boys enrolled in public and private schools (proxy for gender equality)	−0.094	0.189
Child mortality	Number of infants dying before reaching one year of age, per 1000 live births in a given year	3.289	0.846
Maternal mortality	number of women who die from pregnancy-related causes while pregnant or within 42 days of pregnancy termination per 100,000 live births	4.743	1.416
HIV	Percentage of people ages 15–49 who are infected with HIV	−0.114	1.549
Water	Percentage of the population using an improved drinking water source	4.385	0.230
GDP per capita	Real GDP Per Capita in constant dollars	7.851	1.148
Institution	Average of World Bank Governance Indicators	−0.400	0.619
Growth	GDP per capita growth	1.165	0.609
Urbanization	Urban Population (Percentage)	3.776	0.495
Duration of human settlement	Duration of human settlement from Ahlerup and Olsson (2012)	6.268	5.258
Distance to coast or river	Mean distance to nearest river or coast from Alesina, Michalopoulos, and Papaioannou (2016)	0.394	0.449

Notes: Variables logged except for indices of fractionalization

3   Methodology

For our main set of results, the study estimates a model with the following form using cross-sectional data:

$$MDG_i = \alpha + \beta F_i + \sigma' X_i + \varepsilon_i \qquad (8.2)$$

where MDG_i represents the various MDG targets; F represents the index of ethnic fractionalization and X is a vector of control variables. These variables are expected to be important for progress towards the MDGs and include institutional quality, economic growth, income and levels of urbanization. ε is the heteroskedastic error term. Control variables are drawn from the WDI database, and include GDP per capita (a proxy for income), GDP per capita growth (a proxy for economic growth) and percentage of urban population (a proxy for urbanization). We also include a proxy for institutional quality. Our measure of institutional quality is consistent with the existing literature (Easterly, 2007), and is captured by the average of the size indicators of institutional quality reported in the World Bank's World Governance Indicators (WGI) database.[4] We also introduce regional dummies to control for region fixed effects.[5]

For the baseline regressions, the model is estimated using Ordinary Least Squares (OLS) with standard errors adjusted for heteroskedasticity. To control for potential endogeneity (discussed below), the model is also estimated using two-stage least squares (2SLS). In addition to the cross-sectional model in (2), the analysis uses and exploits the panel nature of the data, by using annual data. The model is then estimated using mixed effects. The mixed effect model allows for the inclusion of both time variant and invariant variables which makes it possible to examine the impact of ethnic diversity on changes in the MDG progress indicators.

---

[4] The WGI measures of institutional quality include government effectiveness, control of corruption, political stability, voice and accountability, rule of law and regulatory quality.

[5] Countries are classified into the following geographical regions: Africa, Asia and Oceania, Latin America, Europe, North America and the Middle East.

Endogeneity

It is likely that there are several unobservable factors that are correlated with both ethnic diversity and MDG outcomes that are not included in the model leading to the problem of endogeneity. In an attempt to control for endogeneity, the study adopts a 2SLS instrumental variable (IV) technique. Consistent with the existing literature, the duration of human settlement and distance to a coast or river are used as instruments for ethnic fractionalization (see, e.g., Ahlerup, 2009; Ahlerup & Olsson, 2012; Awaworyi Churchill & Smyth, 2017; Casey & Owen, 2014).[6]

Ahlerup and Olsson (2012) argue that the duration of a human settlement determines the formation of ethnolinguistic diversity around the globe. The formation of ethnic groups takes considerable time and accordingly, longer durations of human settlement correspond with more time for ethnic group formation. The historical duration of uninterrupted human settlements is calculated based on archaeological research. They further argue that populations that are closer to the coast or waterways are less isolated than those that are not, and thus will be less fractionalized.

For increased predictive power, we proceed to instrument ethnic fractionalization with duration of human settlement and the mean distance to coast or river. The exclusion restriction for these instruments is likely to hold since they are unlikely to impact directly on country-level progress towards the MDGs, but they should be highly correlated with ethnic fractionalization. Diagnostic tests reported at the bottom of Table 8.2 support the validity of these instruments.

To further ensure robustness, we also employ the Lewbel (2012) method, which relies on the existence of heteroskedasticity in the data to establish causality.

The relevant model is:

$$MDG = X'\beta_1 + F\Upsilon_1 + \xi_1 \quad \xi_1 = \alpha_1 U + V_1 \tag{8.3}$$

---

[6] Data on duration of human settlement are taken directly from Ahlerup and Olsson (2012) while distance from coast is taken from Alesina et al. (2016). Ahlerup and Olsson (2012) provide further discussion on the exogeneity of these variables and how they correlate with ethnic fractionalization.

Table 8.2 Effects of ethnic fractionalization on MDG indicators (2SLS results)

Variables	(1) Poverty	(2) Hunger	(3) Education	(4) Gender	(5) Child mortality	(6) Maternal mortality	(7) HIV	(8) Water
Panel A—2SLS results without controls								
Ethnic diversity	6.519***	2.751***	−0.539***	−0.856***	4.821***	6.930***	7.510***	−1.175***
	(1.459)	(0.868)	(0.184)	(0.229)	(0.988)	(1.513)	(2.256)	(0.240)
	[0.801]	[0.937]	[−0.813]	[−0.722]	[0.892]	[0.791]	[0.849]	[−0.746]
Observations	104	95	118	97	119	119	90	119
R-squared	0.192	0.256	0.252	0.048	0.617	0.121	0.625	0.491
First stage								
F-statistic	13.91	12.83	11.93	12.29	13.06	26.39	9.95	14.36
J-statistic	1.967	0.487	2.036	1.161	1.919	1.602	2.191	1.830
J-statistic (*P*-value)	0.3740	0.7838	0.3613	0.5595	0.3831	0.4488	0.1863	0.4005
Panel B—2SLS results with controls								
Ethnic diversity	2.180**	0.500	−0.576**	−0.454**	2.761***	3.690***	8.198**	−0.574***
	(1.100)	(0.756)	(0.256)	(0.218)	(0.851)	(1.090)	(3.236)	(0.221)
	[0.268]	[0.170]	[−0.869]	[−0.595]	[0.797]	[0.634]	[0.855]	[−0.609]
Institution	−0.051	−0.234	0.021	−0.006	−0.374***	−0.348**	0.528	0.088**
	(0.217)	(0.155)	(0.035)	(0.036)	(0.142)	(0.171)	(0.540)	(0.043)
	[−0.015]	[−0.178]	[0.079]	[−0.018]	[−0.274]	[−0.151]	[0.189]	[0.236]
Growth	0.195	0.347***	0.015	0.007	0.032	0.003	0.120	−0.065**
	(0.151)	(0.113)	(0.026)	(0.029)	(0.125)	(0.164)	(0.488)	(0.026)
	[0.058]	[0.285]	[0.057]	[0.020]	[0.023]	[0.001]	[0.045]	[−0.172]
GDP per capita	−0.744***	−0.313***	−0.057	0.078**	−0.036	−0.195	0.626	0.003
	(0.238)	(0.100)	(0.043)	(0.035)	(0.144)	(0.194)	(0.482)	(0.047)
	[−0.415]	[−0.466]	[−0.406]	[0.481]	[−0.048]	[−0.157]	[0.441]	[0.014]
Urbanization	−0.394	−0.047	0.123	−0.029	−0.481*	−0.657*	−1.564*	0.176**
	(0.425)	(0.181)	(0.076)	(0.063)	(0.273)	(0.351)	(0.906)	(0.078)

(continued)

Table 8.2 (continued)

Variables	(1) Poverty	(2) Hunger	(3) Education	(4) Gender	(5) Child mortality	(6) Maternal mortality	(7) HIV	(8) Water
	[−0.096]	[−0.031]	[0.381]	[−0.077]	[−0.282]	[−0.231]	[−0.509]	[0.378]
Observations	104	95	118	97	119	119	90	119
R-squared	0.702	0.583	0.239	0.401	0.393	0.643	0.635	0.417
First stage								
F-statistic	13.54	5.803	10.15	11.91	9.08	19.73	12.91	13.14
J-statistic	3.038	0.766	2.013	1.529	1.305	2.668	1.560	2.157
J-statistic (P-value)	0.2189	0.6816	0.3655	0.4656	0.5208	0.2635	0.476	0.3401

Notes: All regressions include regional dummies. Robust standard errors, adjusted for heteroskedasticity in parentheses. Standardized coefficients in brackets. ***$p < 0.01$, **$p < 0.05$, *$p < 0.1$

$$F = X'\beta_2\xi_2 \quad \xi_2 = \alpha_2 U + V_2 \qquad (8.4)$$

MDG represents the *MDG* progress indicators and F is ethnic fractionalization. U denotes unobserved characteristics, which affects both ethnic fractionalization and *MDG* progress. V_1 and V_2 are idiosyncratic errors. The Lewbel (2012) approach uses the heteroskedasticity in the data to estimate the 2SLS regression. The Lewbel (2012) approach involves taking a vector Z of observed exogenous variables and utilizing $\left[Z - E(Z)\right]\xi_2$ as an instrument, provided that:

$$E(X\xi_1) = 0, E(X\xi_2), \quad \text{cov}(Z, \xi_1, \xi_2) = 0 \qquad (8.5)$$

and there is heteroskedasticity in ξ_j. The vector Z could be a subset of X or equal to X. As ξ_2 is a population parameter, and it cannot be directly observed, we use its sample estimate $\widehat{\xi_2}$, obtained from the first stage regression and consequently use the vector $\left[Z - E(Z)\right]\widehat{\xi_2}$ as instruments.

This approach is often used in the literature to deal with endogeneity where external instruments are either unavailable or weak, and also as a robustness check on findings with external instruments (see, e.g., Awaworyi Churchill & Mishra, 2017; Awaworyi Churchill, Valenzuela, & Sablah, 2016d; Belfield & Kelly, 2012; Mishra & Smyth, 2015). We use the Lewbel 2SLS method combining both internal and external instruments to increase the predictive power of our instruments.

4 Results

Figures 8.1, 8.2, 8.3, 8.4, 8.5, 8.6, 8.7 and 8.8 in the Appendix provide bivariate relationships between ethnic fractionalization and our measures of MDG progress. The scatterplots suggest a detrimental impact of ethnic fractionalization on the various MDG progress indicators. Specifically, the plots show that fractionalization increases poverty headcount, hunger, child and infant mortality as well as the prevalence of HIV. Further, fractionalization hinders the attainment of universal education, gender equality and access to clean water sources. However, these graphs only provide suggestive evidence, and it is important to control for relevant covariates, which allow us to isolate the effects of fractionalization. Thus, we estimate the models presented above.

Table 8.3 presents the results from OLS estimations while Table 8.2 presents the results from 2SLS. In each table, Panel A presents results for regressions in which our explanatory variable includes only the index of fractionalization. Panel B presents the results from when the additional control variables are included. Indices of fractionalization are significantly associated with progress towards the MDG variables. The discussion focuses on the findings from the regressions with the control variables. From Panel B of Table 8.3, results show that a one standard deviation increase in fractionalization is associated with an increase of 0.116 in the poverty headcount ratio at $1.90 a day, and 0.116 and 0.123 increases in child and maternal mortality rates, respectively. There is also a positive association between ethnic diversity and prevalence of HIV-AIDS, characterized by a standardized coefficient of 0.242. Results also suggest that a one standard deviation increase in ethnic fractionalization is associated with a decline of 0.186 standard deviations in the rate of primary school enrolment, 0.301 standard deviations in the ratio of girls to boys enrolled in schools, and 0.188 standard deviations in access to improved water source. However, the inclusion of control variables renders the coefficients on the ethnic fractionalization variables statistically insignificant in the regression for extreme hunger.

Consistent across the model specifications, we find that GDP per capita has a desirable effect on MDG progress. Specifically, an increase in income is associated with lower levels of extreme poverty, hunger, child and maternal mortality rates. Increased income is also associated with gender equality. When statistically significant, results suggest that better institutions promote progress towards the MDGs. Specifically, the measure of institutional quality is negatively associated with child mortality and maternal mortality rates, and positively associated with improved water source. The coefficients on urbanization are statistically insignificant and the same is mostly true for the coefficients on the growth variable.

Table 8.2 presents the 2SLS results which are consistent with OLS, although relatively stronger in terms of magnitude. Comparing standardized coefficients, we find that the effect of fractionalization on MDG progress is larger in 2SLS than in the OLS estimations. Specifically, 2SLS results show that a standard deviation increase in fractionalization is

Table 8.3 Effects of ethnic fractionalization on MDG indicators (OLS results)

Variables	(1) Poverty	(2) Hunger	(3) Education	(4) Gender	(5) Child mortality	(6) Maternal mortality	(7) HIV	(8) Water
Panel A—OLS results without controls								
Ethnic diversity	1.472**	0.572*	−0.140**	−0.358***	1.045***	1.526***	1.512**	−0.302***
	(0.652)	(0.312)	(0.057)	(0.068)	(0.289)	(0.437)	(0.747)	(0.078)
	[0.181]	[0.195]	[−0.211]	[−0.469]	[0.302]	[0.262]	[0.231]	[−0.320]
Observations	104	95	118	97	119	119	90	119
R-squared	0.515	0.197	0.043	0.280	0.375	0.583	0.144	0.224
Panel B—OLS results with controls								
Ethnic diversity	0.948*	0.332	−0.123**	−0.230***	0.402**	0.716***	1.584**	−0.177***
	(0.564)	(0.272)	(0.056)	(0.065)	(0.172)	(0.248)	(0.716)	(0.064)
	[0.116]	[0.113]	[−0.186]	[−0.301]	[0.116]	[0.123]	[0.242]	[−0.188]
Institution	0.080	−0.110	0.036	−0.002	−0.427***	−0.392***	0.521	0.097**
	(0.317)	(0.152)	(0.033)	(0.036)	(0.113)	(0.142)	(0.402)	(0.043)
	[0.023]	[−0.084]	[0.136]	[−0.006]	[−0.312]	[−0.170]	[0.187]	[0.260]
Growth	−0.113	0.209**	0.018	0.011	0.037	0.014	−0.404	−0.066***
	(0.149)	(0.100)	(0.020)	(0.031)	(0.063)	(0.089)	(0.275)	(0.024)
	[−0.034]	[0.172]	[0.067]	[0.033]	[0.027]	[0.006]	[−0.153]	[−0.174]
GDP per capita	−1.306***	−0.403***	−0.010	0.099***	−0.260***	−0.467***	0.148	0.041
	(0.242)	(0.095)	(0.029)	(0.026)	(0.091)	(0.126)	(0.289)	(0.038)
	[−0.728]	[−0.602]	[−0.072]	[0.609]	[−0.353]	[−0.378]	[0.104]	[0.202]
Urbanization	0.008	−0.026	0.049	−0.056	−0.164	−0.261	−1.248**	0.123*
	(0.409)	(0.176)	(0.064)	(0.051)	(0.162)	(0.212)	(0.528)	(0.067)
	[0.002]	[−0.017]	[0.152]	[−0.148]	[−0.096]	[−0.092]	[−0.406]	[0.264]
Observations	104	95	118	97	119	119	90	119
R-squared	0.595	0.504	0.078	0.460	0.730	0.832	0.231	0.546

Notes: All regressions include regional dummies. Robust standard errors, adjusted for heteroskedasticity in parentheses. Standardized coefficients in brackets. ***$p < 0.01$, **$p < 0.05$, *$p < 0.1$

associated with a decline of 0.869 (vs 0.186 in OLS) standard deviations in the rate of primary school enrolment, and 0.609 (vs 0.188 in OLS) standard deviations in access to improved water source. Similarly, a standard deviation increase in ethnic fractionalization is associated with an increase of 0.268 (vs 0.116 in OLS) in poverty headcount ratio, 0.797 (vs 0.116 in OLS) in child mortality rate, 0.0.634 (vs 0.123 in OLS) in maternal mortality rate and 0.855 (vs 0.242 in OLS) in the prevalence of HIV. Effect on hunger remains statistically insignificant with the introduction of control variables. The 2SLS results therefore strengthen the emerging conclusions from the OLS analysis.[7] In summary, the results consistently show that higher levels of ethnic fractionalization have hindered development as measured by the MDGs.

Further Analysis

In this section, we examine the sensitivity of our results to alternative measures of fractionalization and other estimation methods.

Firstly, we examine the sensitivity of our results to alternative measures of diversity by employing indices of diversity reported by Fearon (2003) and the *Ethnologue* diversity index. The *Ethnologue* index, compiled by anthropologists, linguists and geologists, is argued to be a comprehensive index that takes into account the different languages spoken in the world. Both Fearon (2003) and Alesina et al. (2003) use information from *Encyclopedia Britannica*, the *CIA World Factbook* and the *Ethnologue* project as a baseline. However, Fearon (2003) categorizes ethno-linguistic groups according to linguistic-cultural distance. Table 8.4 Panels 1 and 2 present the results for effects using the *Ethnologue* index and Fearon's index, respectively, and these results demonstrate that the chapter's findings are not sensitive to this alternative measure of ethnic diversity.

Secondly, estimation of the Lewbel (2012) model to control for endogeneity also provides similar results. Table 8.5 Panel 1 presents the results for the Lewbel estimations. Thirdly, findings are also broadly consistent with

---

[7] First stage statistics and over-identifying restriction tests support the validity of our instrumental variables. We fail to reject the null hypothesis for the over-identifying restriction tests. Therefore the instruments used were not over-identified in the first-stage regressions. Furthermore, F-statistics also show that the three instruments used in our 2SLS regressions are jointly significant.

Table 8.4 Sensitivity check (alternative measures of fractionalization)

Variables	(1) Poverty	(2) Hunger	(3) Education	(4) Gender	(5) Child mortality	(6) Maternal mortality	(7) HIV	(8) Water
Panel 1: Alternative measure of fractionalization—Ethnologue index								
Diversity (Ethnologue)	1.822**	0.301	−0.387***	−0.260**	1.790***	2.459***	5.836***	−0.385**
	(0.766)	(0.454)	(0.147)	(0.112)	(0.409)	(0.568)	(1.492)	(0.151)
	[0.295]	[0.133]	[−0.769]	[−0.451]	[0.685]	[0.558]	[0.804]	[−0.542]
Controls?	Yes	Yes	Yes	Yes	Yes	Yes	Yes	Yes
Observations	104	95	118	97	119	119	90	119
R-squared	0.738	0.592	0.123	0.450	0.604	0.719	0.280	0.433
Panel 2: Alternative measure of fractionalization—Fearon (2003)								
Diversity (Fearon)	3.189**	0.291	−0.681*	−0.491**	3.365***	4.490***	8.829***	−0.514*
	(1.517)	(0.772)	(0.395)	(0.214)	(1.068)	(1.368)	(3.182)	(0.269)
	[0.392]	[0.097]	[−0.981]	[−0.632]	[0.952]	[0.762]	[0.898]	[−0.540]
Controls?	Yes	Yes	Yes	Yes	Yes	Yes	Yes	Yes
Observations	97	90	106	92	109	109	87	109
R-squared	0.697	0.575	0.430	0.328	0.237	0.541	0.974	0.504

Notes: All regressions include regional dummies. Robust standard errors, adjusted for heteroskedasticity in parentheses. Standardized coefficients in brackets. ***$p < 0.01$, **$p < 0.05$, *$p < 0.1$

Table 8.5 Sensitivity check (alternative estimation methods)

Variables	(1) Poverty	(2) Hunger	(3) Education	(4) Gender	(5) Child mortality	(6) Maternal mortality	(7) HIV	(8) Water
Panel 1: Lewbel 2SLS with external and internal instruments								
Ethnic diversity	2.060**	0.074	−0.450**	−0.367*	1.923***	2.233***	5.793***	−0.472***
	(0.921)	(0.606)	(0.201)	(0.189)	(0.690)	(0.756)	(2.115)	(0.173)
	[0.253]	[0.025]	[−0.679]	[−0.481]	[0.555]	[0.384]	[0.887]	[−0.501]
Controls?	Yes	Yes	Yes	Yes	Yes	Yes	Yes	Yes
Observations	104	95	118	97	119	119	90	119
R-squared	0.581	0.594	0.087	0.438	0.590	0.783	0.106	0.475
First stage								
J-statistic	14.908	4.932	13.232	16.464	9.632	15.495	7.811	10.043
J-statistic (*P*-value)	0.0610	0.8402	0.1485	0.0578	0.3811	0.0782	0.1894	0.3470
Panel 2: Mixed effect regression								
Ethnic diversity	0.870***	0.062	−0.143***	−0.179***	0.443***	0.832***	1.180***	−0.176***
	(0.288)	(0.079)	(0.021)	(0.036)	(0.062)	(0.085)	(0.242)	(0.022)
Controls?	Yes	Yes	Yes	Yes	Yes	Yes	Yes	Yes
Observations	373	789	867	211	983	973	747	983

Notes: All regressions include regional dummies. Robust standard errors, adjusted for heteroskedasticity in parentheses. Standardized coefficients in brackets. ***$p < 0.01$, **$p < 0.05$, *$p < 0.1$

the use of panel data and a mixed effects estimator. Mixed effects regression results are reported in Panel 2 of Table 8.5. Thus, overall, the finding that ethnic diversity hinders MDGs progress is valid and consistent across alternative measures of fractionalization and estimation methods.

5 Conclusion

Using cross-country data for developing countries, this chapter has found strong support for the notion that ethnic diversity impeded country level progress towards the MDGs. This finding applies to a number of MDG targets and is robust to different estimation techniques. Clearly, countries with high levels of fractionalisation have faced an additional challenge in achieving the international development targets. There are two broad explanations for this finding with differing implications for policy. Future research should examine which of these explanations dominates.

The first is that some ethnic minorities in ethnically diverse countries have faced discrimination with respect to basic services such as education, health, water and sanitation. Where this is the case, governments and donors should better direct resources to these minorities to improve their well-being. Higher levels of inequality can lead to social unrest and hamper development in the long term.

The second is that the negative impacts of high rates of ethnic diversity, such as increased tensions and lower levels of trust are outweighing the potentially positive impacts of greater creativity and productivity. Here, policymakers need to be more creative, finding examples of successful interventions that have improved cohesion and strengthened diverse communities from both within and outside of their own countries. Insights are more likely to come from in-depth single country case studies rather than cross-country analysis.

The findings have important implications for the achievement of the latest round of international development targets: the Sustainable Development Goals (SDGs). The SDGs comprise 17 goals and 169 targets providing an additional layer of complexity for countries with ethnically diverse populations. Measures such as building state capacity and inclusive institutions, social and economic resilience, human security, peace, justice, and violence prevention were not included in the MDGs, but are explicit within goal 16 of the SDGs. Goal 16 of the current development goals specifically calls to *"Promote peaceful and inclusive societies for sustainable development, provide access to justice for all and build effective, accountable and inclusive institutions at all levels"* (United Nations, 2014). Unless the benefits of diversity can be properly harnessed by the leaders of ethnically diverse and fractionalised countries, the achievement of the SDGs by 2030 is likely to prove elusive.

Appendix

Table 8.6 List of countries

Afghanistan	Czech Republic	Lebanon	Senegal
Albania	Djibouti	Lesotho	Seychelles
Algeria	Dominica	Liberia	Sierra Leone
Angola	Dominican Republic	Lithuania	Slovak Republic
Argentina	Ecuador	Madagascar	Solomon Islands
Armenia	El Salvador	Malawi	South Africa
Azerbaijan	Equatorial Guinea	Malaysia	Sri Lanka
Bangladesh	Eritrea	Mali	Sudan
Belarus	Estonia	Mauritania	Suriname
Belize	Ethiopia	Mauritius	Swaziland
Benin	Fiji	Mexico	Tajikistan
Bhutan	Gabon	Mongolia	Tanzania
Bolivia	Georgia	Morocco	Thailand
Bosnia and Herzegovina	Ghana	Mozambique	Togo
Botswana	Grenada	Namibia	Tonga
Brazil	Guatemala	Nepal	Tunisia
Bulgaria	Guinea	Nicaragua	Turkey
Burkina Faso	Guyana	Niger	Turkmenistan
Burundi	Haiti	Nigeria	Uganda
Cambodia	Honduras	Oman	Ukraine
Cameroon	Hungary	Pakistan	Uruguay
Central African Republic	India	Panama	Uzbekistan
Chad	Indonesia	Papua New Guinea	Vanuatu
Chile	Iraq	Paraguay	Vietnam
China	Jamaica	Peru	Zambia
Colombia	Jordan	Philippines	Zimbabwe
Comoros	Kazakhstan	Poland	
Costa Rica	Kenya	Russia	
Cote d'Ivoire	Kyrgyzstan	Rwanda	
Croatia	Laos	Samoa	
Cuba	Latvia	Saudi Arabia	

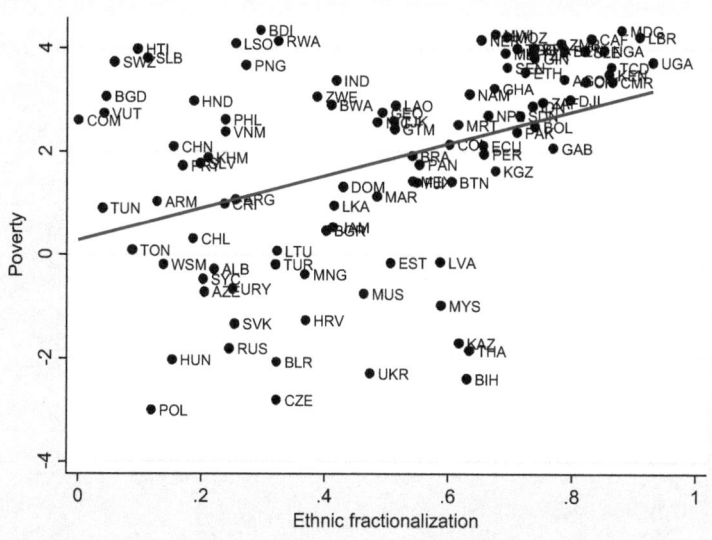

Fig. 8.1 Fractionalization and poverty

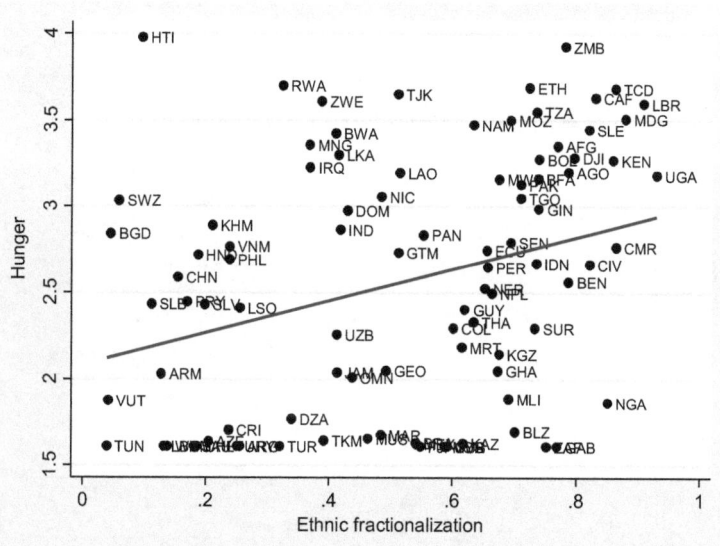

Fig. 8.2 Fractionalization and hunger

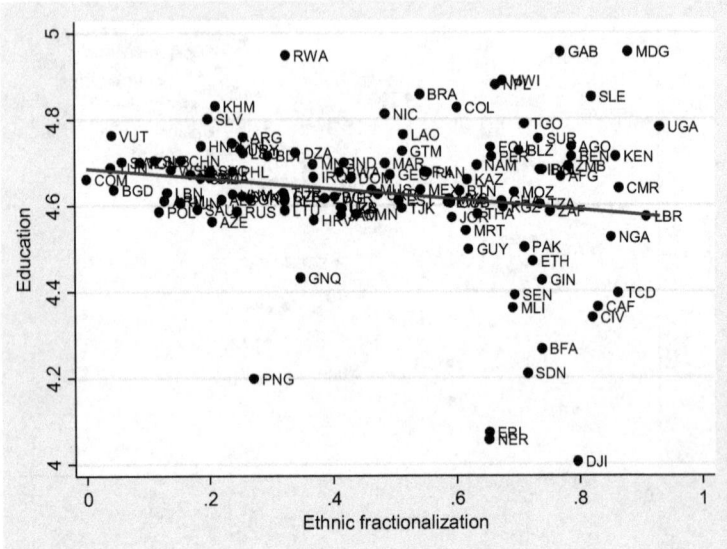

Fig. 8.3 Fractionalization and education

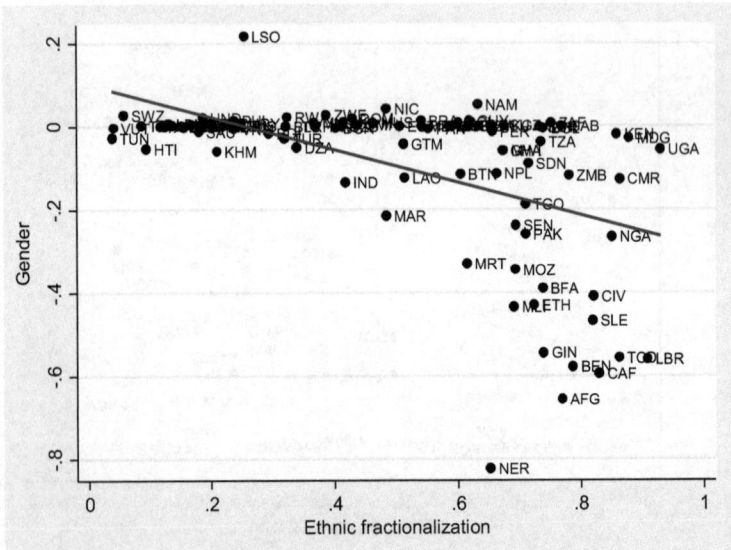

Fig. 8.4 Fractionalization and gender

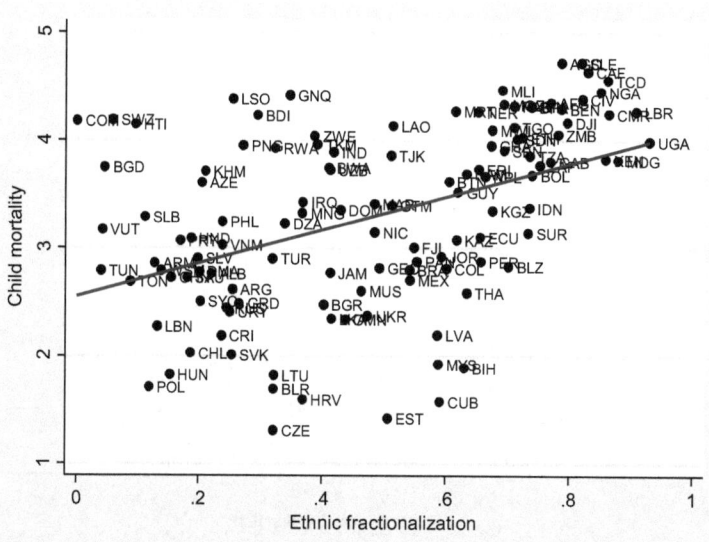

Fig. 8.5 Fractionalization and child mortality

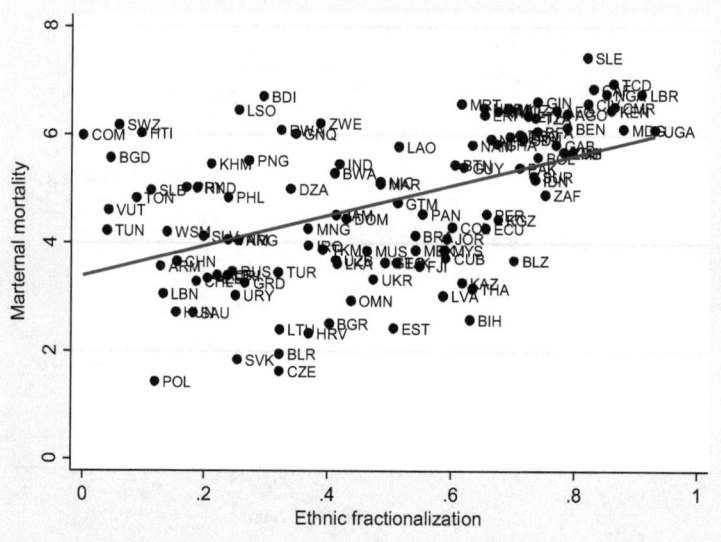

Fig. 8.6 Fractionalization and maternal mortality

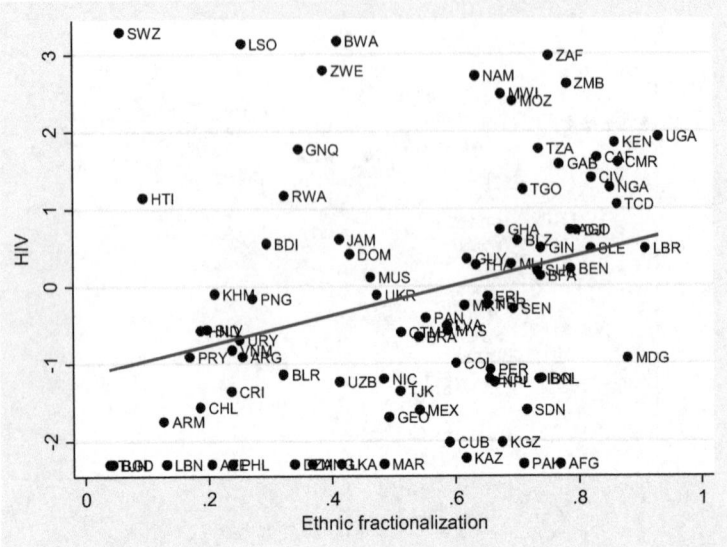

Fig. 8.7 Fractionalization and HIV

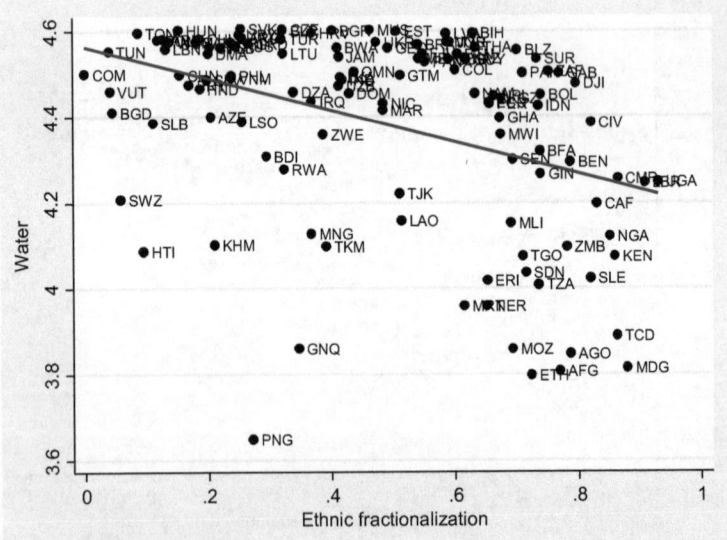

Fig. 8.8 Fractionalization and water

References

Ahlerup, P. (2009). *The causal effects of ethnic diversity: An instrumental variables approach.* Working Papers in Economics 386, University of Gothenburg, Department of Economics.

Ahlerup, P., & Olsson, O. (2012). The roots of ethnic diversity. *Journal of Economic Growth, 17*(2), 71–102.

Alesina, A., Devleeschauwer, A., Easterly, W., Kurlat, S., & Wacziarg, R. (2003). Fractionalization. *Journal of Economic Growth, 8*(2), 155–194.

Alesina, A., Michalopoulos, S., & Papaioannou, E. (2016). Ethnic inequality. *Journal of Political Economy, 124*(2), 428–488.

Alesina, A., & Zhuravskaya, E. (2011). Segregation and the quality of government in a cross section of countries. *The American Economic Review, 101*(5), 1872–1911. https://doi.org/10.2307/23045625

Awaworyi Churchill, S. (2017). Fractionalization, entrepreneurship, and the institutional environment for entrepreneurship. *Small Business Economics, 48*(3), 577–597. https://doi.org/10.1007/s11187-016-9796-8

Awaworyi Churchill, S., & Mishra, V. (2017). Trust, social networks and subjective wellbeing in China. *Social Indicators Research, 132*(1), 313–339.

Awaworyi Churchill, S., Nuhu, A. S., & Lopez, K. (2019). Persistence of gender inequality: the role of ethnic divisions. *Applied Economics, 51*(8), 781–796.

Awaworyi Churchill, S., Ocloo, J. E., & Siawor-Robertson, D. (2016a). Ethnic diversity and health outcomes. *Social Indicators Research,* 1–36. https://doi.org/10.1007/s11205-016-1454-7

Awaworyi Churchill, S., Okai, D., & Posso, A. (2016b). Internet use and ethnic heterogeneity in a cross-section of countries. Economic Papers: *A Journal of Applied Economics and Policy, 35*(1), 59–72. https://doi.org/10.1111/1759-3441.12125

Awaworyi Churchill, S., & Smyth, R. (2017). Ethnic diversity and poverty. *World Development, 95,* 285–302. https://doi.org/10.1016/j.worlddev.2017.02.032

Awaworyi Churchill, S., Valenzuela, M. R., & Sablah, W. (2016d). Ethnic diversity and firm performance: Evidence from China's materials and industrial sectors. *Empirical Economics,* 1–21. https://doi.org/10.1007/s00181-016-1174-5

Barros, F. C., Matijasevich, A., Requejo, J. H., Giugliani, E., Maranhao, A. G., Monteiro, C. A., ... Victora, C. G. (2010). Recent trends in maternal, newborn, and child health in Brazil: Progress toward Millennium Development Goals 4 and 5. *American Journal of Public Health, 100*(10), 1877–1889.

Belfield, C. R., & Kelly, I. R. (2012). The benefits of breast feeding across the early years of childhood. *Journal of Human Capital, 6*(3), 251–277. https://doi.org/10.1086/667415

Blimes, R. J. (2006). The indirect effect of ethnic heterogeneity on the likelihood of civil war onset. *Journal of Conflict Resolution, 50*(4), 536–547.

Camacho, A. V., Castro, M., & Kaufman, R. (2006). Cultural aspects related to the health of Andean women in Latin America: A key issue for progress toward the attainment of the Millennium Development Goals. *International Journal of Gynecology & Obstetrics, 94*(3), 357–363.

Casey, G. P., & Owen, A. L. (2014). Inequality and fractionalization. *World Development, 56*, 32–50.

DeLoach, S. B., & Lamanna, E. (2011). Measuring the impact of microfinance on child health outcomes in Indonesia. *World Development, 39*(10), 1808–1819. Retrieved from http://www.elsevier.com/wps/find/journaldescription.cws_home/386/description#description

Desmet, K., Weber, S., & Ortuño-Ortín, I. (2009). Linguistic diversity and redistribution. *Journal of the European Economic Association, 7*(6), 1291–1318.

Devillanova, C. (2008). Social networks, information and health care utilization: Evidence from undocumented immigrants in Milan. *Journal of Health Economics, 27*(2), 265–286.

Easterly, W. (2007). Inequality does cause underdevelopment: Insights from a new instrument. *Journal of Development Economics, 84*(2), 755–776.

Easterly, W., & Levine, R. (1997). Africa's growth tragedy: Policies and ethnic divisions. *The Quarterly Journal of Economics, 112*(4), 1203–1250.

Fafchamps, M. (2000). Ethnicity and credit in African manufacturing. *Journal of Development Economics, 61*(1), 205–235.

Fay, M., Leipziger, D., Wodon, Q., & Yepes, T. (2005). Achieving child-health-related Millennium Development Goals: The role of infrastructure. *World Development, 33*(8), 1267–1284.

Fearon, J. D. (2003). Ethnic and cultural diversity by country. *Journal of Economic Growth, 8*(2), 195–222.

Hazarika, I. (2011). Factors that determine the use of skilled care during delivery in India: Implications for achievement of MDG-5 targets. *Maternal and Child Health Journal, 15*(8), 1381–1388.

Hiller, V. (2014). Gender inequality, endogenous cultural norms, and economic development. *The Scandinavian Journal of Economics, 116*(2), 455–481.

Jowitt, P. W. (2009). Water infrastructure, the UN MDGs and sustainable development. *Desalination, 248*(1), 510–516.

Lee, N. (2014). Migrant and ethnic diversity, cities and innovation: Firm effects or city effects? *Journal of Economic Geography*. https://doi.org/10.1093/jeg/lbu032

Leigh, A. (2006). Trust, inequality and ethnic heterogeneity. *Economic Record, 82*(258), 268–280.

Leipziger, D., Fay, M., Wodon, Q. T., & Yepes, T. (2003). *Achieving the millennium development goals: The role of infrastructure.* World Bank Policy Research Working Paper(3163).

Lewbel, A. (2012). Using heteroscedasticity to identify and estimate mismeasured and endogenous regressor models. *Journal of Business & Economic Statistics, 30*(1), 67–80.

Mahmoudi, H., Liaghati, H., & Zohari, M. (2007). *The role of organic agriculture in achieving the millennium development goals: Challenge and prospects in Iran.* Paper presented at the Conference of Tropentag.

McLeod, P. L., Lobel, S. A., & Cox, T. H. (1996). Ethnic diversity and creativity in small groups. *Small Group Research, 27*(2), 248–264. https://doi.org/10.1177/1046496496272003

Miguel, E., & Gugerty, M. K. (2005). Ethnic diversity, social sanctions, and public goods in Kenya. *Journal of Public Economics, 89*(11–12), 2325–2368. https://doi.org/10.1016/j.jpubeco.2004.09.004

Mishra, V., & Smyth, R. (2015). Estimating returns to schooling in urban China using conventional and heteroskedasticity-based instruments. *Economic Modelling, 47*, 166–173. https://doi.org/10.1016/j.econmod.2015.02.002

Mpembeni, R. N., Killewo, J. Z., Leshabari, M. T., Massawe, S. N., Jahn, A., Mushi, D., & Mwakipa, H. (2007). Use pattern of maternal health services and determinants of skilled care during delivery in Southern Tanzania: Implications for achievement of MDG-5 targets. *BMC Pregnancy and Childbirth, 7*(1), 1.

Nathan, M. (2014). Same difference? Minority ethnic inventors, diversity and innovation in the UK. *Journal of Economic Geography*. https://doi.org/10.1093/jeg/lbu006

Onda, K., LoBuglio, J., & Bartram, J. (2012). Global access to safe water: Accounting for water quality and the resulting impact on MDG progress. *International Journal of Environmental Research and Public Health, 9*(3), 880–894.

Perera, L. D. H., & Lee, G. H. Y. (2013). Have economic growth and institutional quality contributed to poverty and inequality reduction in Asia? *Journal of Asian Economics, 27*, 71–86. https://doi.org/10.1016/j.asieco.2013.06.002

United Nations. (2014). *The road to dignity by 2030: Ending poverty, transforming all lives and protecting the planet. Synthesis report of the secretary-general on the post-2015 agenda*. New York, NY.

United Nations. (2015). *Millennium Development Goals Report 2015*. New York: United Nations.

9

Foreign Aid and Development Goals: Revisiting the Evidence

Musharavati Ephraim Munyanyi,
Sefa Awaworyi Churchill, and Ahmed Skali

1 Introduction

The lack of adequate domestic resources to alleviate poverty in most, if not all, developing countries has led to a reliance on foreign aid for most of these countries. The effectiveness of foreign aid, especially in reducing poverty has however been the subject of a long history of research (see, e.g., Boone, 1996; Bourguignon & Platteau, 2017; Chong, Gradstein, & Calderon, 2009; Leeson, 2008; Mosley, Hudson, & Horrell, 1987). On the one hand, some studies have argued that the effects of aid tend to be negative, by creating what is referred to as the aid dependency syndrome, which is characterised by misallocation of resources and distortion of systems in aid-receiving countries. On the other hand, other studies have argued in favour of development-enhancing effects of aid, with evidence

M. E. Munyanyi • S. Awaworyi Churchill (✉) • A. Skali
School of Economics, Finance and Marketing, RMIT University,
Melbourne, VIC, Australia
e-mail: ephraim.munyanyi@rmit.edu.au; sefa.churchill@rmit.edu.au;
ahmed.skali@rmit.edu.au

© The Author(s) 2020
S. Awaworyi Churchill (ed.), *Moving from the Millennium to the Sustainable Development Goals*, https://doi.org/10.1007/978-981-15-1556-9_9

to suggest that aid tends to reduce poverty in aid-receiving countries (see, e.g., Alvi & Senbeta, 2012; Arndt, Jones, & Tarp, 2015; Hirano & Otsubo, 2014; Kaya, Kaya, & Gunter, 2013; Minasyan, Nunnenkamp, & Richert, 2017).

Despite the uncertainty about its effectiveness as a development tool, foreign aid is still considered one of the largest modes of development interventions in the world with billions transferred from various sources to developing countries each year. As part of the 2030 Agenda for Sustainable Development (United Nations, 2015), increased investment in "smarter" foreign aid is being advanced as an important approach to achieve the sustainable development goals (SDGs). However, within the framework of the recently ended millennium development goals (MDGs), an important question that has emerged is: have decades of foreign aid to developing countries been beneficial to development?

We examine the impact of foreign aid on eight development targets capturing poverty, education, extreme hunger, gender equality, child mortality, maternal mortality, prevalence of HIV and access to portable water. Our main measure of foreign aid is net Official Development Assistance (ODA) received. This measure of foreign aid, which is consistent with the literature (see e.g., Alvi & Senbeta, 2012; Hirano & Otsubo, 2014; Kaya et al., 2013), includes all disbursements of development aid to recipient countries. We also examine the impact of aid availed to eight sectors, including agriculture, education, government and civil society, health, industry, production, water supply and sanitation, and social infrastructure and services.

Our results are encouraging. We show that an increase in net ODA is associated with a decline in the prevalence of HIV and child mortality, which suggests that aid money may be most effectively spent on programmes targeting these two key issues in developing countries. Further, our analysis of sectoral aid revealed that more targeted aid is likely to be more beneficial for development. However, we do not find statistically significant evidence of net ODA's effect on poverty, hunger, education, gender equality, access to clean water and maternal mortality. The associations we find between ODA and each of these latter outcomes are all of the expected signs, but are not significantly different from zero. Further research is necessary in order to understand why this is the case.

This study contributes to the literature by examining the effect of aid on several development outcomes. Specifically, we study the effect of total and sectoral-targeted aid on a wide range of development targets. Understanding the impact of sectoral-targeted aid is essential, as it adds to our understanding of the effect of aid allocated to a specific sector on development outcomes.

The results have the following policy implications. There is a need to practice good governance and establish quality institutions in order to promote aid effectiveness in aid-recipient countries. Further, donor coordination should be improved to ensure aid reaches the right projects. Lastly, a combination of social (e.g., education, health, water supply and sanitation) and economic (e.g., agriculture) aid would be an advantageous policy mix to improve aid effectiveness.

The rest of the chapter is organised as follows. The next section reviews the related literature. Section 3 describes the data and methods used. Section 4 discusses the results, and Sect. 5 concludes.

2   Brief Overview of Related Literature

The empirical literature on the impact of foreign aid is voluminous and provides mixed results. In this section, we do not provide an exhaustive review of the literature but an overview of selected findings from different strands of the extant literature.

Findings from one strand of literature confirm the effectiveness of aid. This literature also speaks to the importance of specific components of aid or aid directed towards specific sectors (see, e.g., Alvi & Senbeta, 2012; Arndt et al., 2015; Kaya et al., 2013). For instance, Alvi and Senbeta (2012) disaggregate aid by source and type to examine the impact of aid on poverty using measures of poverty such as the headcount index, poverty gap and poverty gap index. Using dynamic panel techniques on a sample of 79 developing nations, they found evidence that aid eliminates poverty. Similarly, in a sample of 46 countries, Kaya et al. (2013) find that aid allocated to the agricultural sector directly and indirectly (through growth) reduces poverty. Arndt et al. (2015) show that aid promotes social welfare and is associated with higher life expectancy, reduced mortality rates and lower poverty rates.

Within the broader literature that has established the effectiveness of aid, some studies have argued that aid is only effective if some conditions are met. For instance, economic environments characterised by good public policy and quality institutions are often said to benefit the most from foreign aid (Burnside & Dollar, 1998, 2000; Hirano & Otsubo, 2014). These papers argue that quality institutions and good public policy not only ensure development-enhancing effects of aid but also prevent potential undesirable effects. The chain of logic here suggests that when institutions are poor, foreign aid leads to misallocation of resources, hinders economic development and continues the cycle of poverty. A poor institutional environment also creates the aid dependency syndrome where aid recipients become over-reliant on aid without visible development (Doucouliagos & Paldam, 2006; Griffin, 1970; Hansen & Tarp, 2000; Weisskopf, 1972).

Some studies argue that good institutions need to be accompanied by good economic policies. For instance, bad policies that lead to the misallocation of resources in aid-receiving countries are likely to hinder development even with good institutions (Chong et al., 2009; Easterly, 2003; Easterly, Levine, & Roodman, 2004). The optimal use of resources is vital to development. Thus, in some cases, investing in national security over poverty reduction schemes may not be beneficial for development. Put differently, the effectiveness of aid is dependent on aid being used for the most productive and relevant activities. In addition, aid availed to countries with poor institutions has also been associated with rent-seeking behaviour and corruption. In such situations, aid is likely to be misappropriated and redirected to other purposes that have nothing to do with poverty alleviation and sustainable development (Boone, 1996; Mosley et al., 1987). For instance, in the absence of strong institutions characterised by accountability, governments have been known to divert funds intended for development activities to maximise the welfare of the rich (Boone, 1996).

Leeson (2008) argues that aid has disastrous effects on recipient countries. He notes that aid leads to corruption, fraud and misallocation of aid through embezzlement by political leaders, which will then lead to poverty. This argument supports the finding of a negative effect from the extant literature (see, e.g., Arvin & Barillas, 2002; Fielding, McGillivray,

& Torres, 2007; Maiga, 2014; Mallik, 2008; Mitra, Hossain, & Hossain, 2015; Mitra & Hossain, 2013; Thomson, Kentikelenis, & Stubbs, 2017). Some studies also report no significant association between aid and development (see, e.g., Chong et al., 2009; Mishra & Newhouse, 2009; Wilson, 2011). Chong et al. (2009) show that aid fails to improve income distribution and reduce poverty while Mishra and Newhouse (2009) and Wilson (2011) show that aid fails to reduce mortality.

3   Data and Methods

Development outcome variables are from the World Bank's World Development Indicators (WDI) database. The development outcomes used include the poverty headcount ratio at $1.90 a day, extreme hunger, enrolment in primary school education, the gender parity index at school, infant and maternal mortality rates, the prevalence of HIV-AIDS and access to an improved water source.

The poverty headcount ratio at $1.90 a day is the percentage of the population living on less than $1.90 a day, and is used as a proxy for extreme poverty (Awaworyi Churchill & Smyth, 2017; Kaya et al., 2013; Yontcheva & Masud, 2005). We capture extreme hunger using the prevalence of undernourishment defined as the percentage of a population whose food intake is insufficient to meet dietary energy requirements. Enrolment in primary education captures the total number of pupils enrolled at primary level in public and private schools. This variable is a proxy for the achievement of universal primary education. The gender parity index is our measure of gender equality and captures the ratio of girls to boys enrolled in public and private schools. Infant mortality rate is the number of infants dying before reaching one year of age, per 1,000 live births in a given year, while maternal mortality ratio is the number of women who die from pregnancy-related causes while pregnant or within 42 days of pregnancy termination per 100,000 live births. Prevalence of HIV refers to the percentage of people aged 15–49 who are infected with HIV. Lastly, improved water source refers to the percentage of the population using an improved drinking water source. The improved drinking water source includes piped water on premises, and other improved drinking water sources (public taps or standpipes, tube wells or bore-holes, protected dug wells, protected springs, and rainwater collection).

Data on foreign aid is collected from the Organisation for Economic Co-operation and Development (OECD)'s Creditor Reporting System (CRS). The CRS database provides detailed and readily available data on aid allocations as well as data on aid projects and programmes. This makes it possible to analyse aid by sector and geographical location. Data from this database is often used by studies that examine foreign aid (see e.g., Alvi & Senbeta, 2012; Hirano & Otsubo, 2014; Kaya et al., 2013). Consistent with the literature, Official Development Assistance (ODA) in US dollars is used as a proxy for foreign aid (see e.g., Arndt et al., 2015; Chong et al., 2009; Kaya et al., 2013). In order to examine the effectiveness of various types of aid, in addition to ODA, we also examine the impact of 8 subcat-egories of aid availed to different sectors. These include agriculture, educa-tion, government and civil society, health, industry, production, water supply and sanitation, and social infrastructure and services.

To control for the level of growth and development among the sample countries, GDP per capita is used as a proxy for national income. We also control for institutional quality by taking the average of the six World Bank's Word Governance Indicators (political stability, rule of law, con-trol of corruption, regulatory quality, government effectiveness, and voice and accountability). This measure of institutional quality is commonly used in the literature (see, e.g., Easterly, 2007).

For regressions with the most observations, we have an unbalanced panel data covering 154 countries over a 58-year period (1960–2017), while for regressions with the least number of observations, we have data covering 45 countries over the period 2000–2015. Table 9.5 in Appendix presents summary statistics and description of the variables.

We estimate panel fixed effects model that control for time and coun-try fixed effects in addition to the relevant control variables. To address the potential endogenous relationship between aid and the development outcomes, in robustness checks, we adopt the Lewbel (2012) two stage least square (2SLS) approach, which relies on heteroskedasticity in the data to establish causality.[1]

---

[1] See Lewbel (2012) for details.

4   Results

We start by presenting results for bivariate regressions that examine the relationship between total aid and our measures of development. The results for this exercise are presented in Table 9.1. Columns (4) and (7), respectively, show strong and statistically significant negative effects of aid on the prevalence of HIV and child mortality. In the other columns, we do not find statistically significant effects of foreign aid on development outcomes, but the coefficients we estimate are of the expected sign. Aid has a positive coefficient when explaining hunger, education, gender quality, and access to clean water, and a negative coefficient when explaining poverty and maternal mortality (refer to Table 9.5 for variable definitions).

Although results from Table 9.1 provide useful suggestive evidence on the relationship between foreign aid and individual development outcomes, they do not control for the economic and institutional environments within which aid-receiving countries operate. As discussed in the literature, it might be that the effects of aid on development are influenced by, or operating through, channels such as the economic and institutional environment of the aid-receiving countries. Thus, in Table 9.2, we present results for regressions which add measures of institutional quality and economic development. We find that with the inclusion of measures of economic development and institutional quality in our model, the effects of foreign aid remain robust. We again find strong evidence that aid reduces HIV prevalence and child mortality. However, the inclusion of the economic development and institutional quality variables reduces the size of the coefficient on the foreign aid variable in regressions examining the prevalence of HIV and child mortality. This suggests that the economic and institutional environment of aid-receiving countries are likely channels through which aid operates to influence development outcomes, in this case, the prevalence of HIV and child mortality.

In Table 9.3, we examine the robustness of our results to endogeneity using the Lewbel (2012) approach. The Breusch and Pagan (1979) test shows that our data satisfies the heteroskedasticity assumption. Across all columns, except for column 3, the first stage F statistics are greater than 10 indicating that, at the 10% significance level, our instruments are

Table 9.1 Bivariate model results

Variables	(1) Poverty	(2) Hunger	(3) Education	(4) HIV	(5) Gender	(6) Water	(7) Child mortality	(8) Maternal mortality
Net ODA	−0.098	0.480	0.880	−0.232***	0.008	0.401	−1.648**	−0.032
	(0.756)	(0.408)	(0.536)	(0.077)	(0.005)	(0.564)	(0.680)	(0.037)
Observations	907	1,903	2,890	2,842	3,656	646	7,038	587
R-squared	0.398	0.288	0.438	0.083	0.394	0.391	0.771	0.208

Notes: All regressions include year and country fixed effects. Robust standard errors in parentheses. ***$p < 0.01$, **$p < 0.05$

Table 9.2 Multivariate model results

Variables	(1) Poverty	(2) Hunger	(3) Education	(4) HIV	(5) Gender	(6) Water	(7) Child mortality	(8) Maternal mortality
Net ODA	0.048	0.325	0.627	−0.140**	0.006	0.752	−1.113**	−0.005
	(0.627)	(0.351)	(0.458)	(0.063)	(0.009)	(0.581)	(0.484)	(0.037)
Income	−6.752	−10.630***	−1.180	−1.345**	0.006	9.355**	−6.453**	−0.426*
	(4.716)	(2.606)	(4.202)	(0.643)	(0.029)	(3.776)	(2.706)	(0.237)
Institution	0.344	−1.050	2.035	−0.285	−0.020	−3.767	−3.869	−0.179
	(3.158)	(1.440)	(2.211)	(0.267)	(0.013)	(4.100)	(2.973)	(0.156)
Observations	656	1,771	1,463	1,873	1,506	604	2,495	486
R-squared	0.459	0.385	0.243	0.087	0.248	0.427	0.633	0.192

Notes: All regressions include year and country fixed effects. Robust standard errors in parentheses. ***$p < 0.01$, **$p < 0.05$, *$p < 0.1$

Table 9.3 Lewbel 2SLS estimates

Variables	(1) Poverty	(2) Hunger	(3) Education	(4) HIV	(5) Gender	(6) Water	(7) Child mortality	(8) Maternal mortality
Net ODA	0.244	0.768	2.245	−1.048**	0.003	0.550	−5.719***	0.022
	(0.614)	(1.468)	(1.377)	(0.421)	(0.007)	(0.770)	(1.421)	(0.043)
Income	−14.275***	−7.883***	7.836***	−1.418***	0.038***	11.183***	−17.676***	−0.850***
	(0.851)	(0.789)	(0.736)	(0.271)	(0.004)	(2.336)	(0.875)	(0.054)
Institution	1.768	−5.811***	3.116***	1.659***	0.048***	0.581	−12.638***	−0.049
	(1.346)	(0.856)	(1.177)	(0.303)	(0.007)	(1.672)	(1.224)	(0.115)
Observations	656	1,771	1,463	1,873	1,506	604	2,495	486
R-squared	0.555	0.228	0.311	0.009	0.362	0.449	0.560	0.470
First stage								
F-statistics	12.49	1.44	9.40	19.75	22.41	13.36	33.56	18.71
Partial R2	0.322	0.1078	0.1124	0.372	0.207	0.296	0.382	0.346
J P-value	0.3875	0.2866	0.4635	0.4987	0.0731	0.2335	0.1799	0.0919

Notes: Robust standard errors in parentheses. ***$p < 0.01$, **$p < 0.05$

strongly correlated with foreign aid (Stock & Yogo, 2005). Further, we do not reject the null hypothesis for the overidentifying restriction test, which suggests that the instruments from the first-stage are not overidentified. We find that, consistent with our baseline estimates, only coefficients in column 4 (on the prevalence of HIV) and column 7 (on child mortality) are statistically significant. The results show that foreign aid is associated with a decline in the prevalence of HIV and child mortality. However, given the magnitude of the coefficients, compared to those from the fixed effect model in Table 9.2, we find that endogeneity causes a considerable downward bias in our baseline (fixed effect) results.

In Table 9.4, we examine the effects of sectoral aid on development outcomes. Each coefficient comes from a separate regression of a given development outcome on a given sectoral aid amount. Columns 1 and 2 report results for the effects of total aid availed to the agriculture and education sectors, respectively, while Column 3 reports effects on aid availed to the government and civil society sector of aid-receiving countries. Columns 4, 5 and 6 present results for the effects of aid availed to the health, industrial and production sectors, respectively. Results for the effects of aid availed to the water supply and sanitation sector are reported in Column 7, while results for aid to the social infrastructure and services sector are reported in Column 8.

The results from Table 9.4 indicate no statistically significant association between aid across the eight sectors and poverty. However, we find that aid availed to the health sector has a negative effect on our indicator of malnourishment (i.e., Hunger). Thus, aid availed to the health sector is associated with a decline in the percentage of the population whose food intake is insufficient to meet dietary energy requirements.

For education, results show a positive effect of aid availed to the agriculture, industrial and production, water supply and sanitation, and social infrastructure and services sectors. Thus, aid availed to these are associated with an increase in the ratio of total enrolment in primary education. Our results also show a negative association between the prevalence of HIV and aid availed to the agriculture, health, industrial, production, and water supply and sanitation sectors. An increase in aid availed to these sectors is therefore associated with a decline in the prevalence of HIV.

Aid availed to the agriculture, health, and production sectors tend to increase the ratio of girls to boys enrolled at primary and secondary levels in public and private schools. With regard to access to water, we find no

Table 9.4 Further analysis using sectoral aid

Variables	(1) Agric aid	(2) Educ. aid	(3) Govt. aid	(4) Health aid	(5) Ind. aid	(6) Prod. aid	(7) Water aid	(8) Social aid
Poverty	0.180	−0.311	0.917	−0.319	−0.060	0.075	−0.043	−0.266
	(0.278)	(0.887)	(0.564)	(0.324)	(0.156)	(0.392)	(0.153)	(0.733)
Hunger	−0.111	0.011	0.097	−0.225**	−0.044	−0.144	−0.063	0.023
	(0.121)	(0.279)	(0.203)	(0.113)	(0.084)	(0.139)	(0.064)	(0.342)
Education	0.512**	−0.003	0.462	0.332	0.280	0.561**	0.275***	1.232**
	(0.210)	(0.456)	(0.296)	(0.237)	(0.192)	(0.273)	(0.104)	(0.473)
HIV	−0.063**	−0.034	−0.046	−0.067***	−0.035*	−0.092**	−0.048***	−0.073
	(0.029)	(0.063)	(0.046)	(0.025)	(0.019)	(0.036)	(0.018)	(0.073)
Gender	0.005***	0.002	0.002	0.004**	0.002	0.004***	0.001	0.003
	(0.001)	(0.003)	(0.002)	(0.001)	(0.001)	(0.001)	(0.001)	(0.003)
Water	−0.172	−0.041	0.510	−0.551	−0.240	−0.577	−0.075	−0.248
	(0.156)	(0.679)	(0.864)	(0.691)	(0.199)	(0.940)	(0.131)	(0.608)
Child mortality	−0.533**	−0.250	−0.044	−0.804***	−0.236*	−0.644**	−0.354***	−1.416***
	(0.210)	(0.388)	(0.271)	(0.214)	(0.140)	(0.248)	(0.119)	(0.478)
Maternal mortality	0.002	−0.088	−0.052	−0.019	−0.019	−0.005	0.001	−0.114**
	(0.019)	(0.061)	(0.040)	(0.018)	(0.016)	(0.024)	(0.011)	(0.057)

Notes: The measure of sectoral aid used in regressions are reported at the top of each column. Coefficients represent the effects of sectoral aid (indicated at the top of the column) on the corresponding development outcome in each row. Robust standard errors in parentheses. ***$p < 0.01$, **$p < 0.05$, *$p < 0.1$

Agric aid is aid to the agricultural sector
Educ. aid is aid to the education sector
Govt. aid is aid to the government and civil society sector
Health aid is aid to the health sector
Ind. aid is aid to the industrial sector
Prod. aid is aid to the production sector
Water aid is aid to the water supply and sanitation sector
Social aid is aid to the social infrastructure and services sector

statistically significant association between aid across the eight sectors and access to improved water source. However, except for aid availed to the education and government sectors, aid across all sectors is associated with a decline in child mortality. Lastly, besides aid availed to social infrastructure and services sector, which is associated with a decline in maternal mortality, aid across other sectors do not have a significant association with maternal mortality.

5   Conclusion

The consideration of foreign aid as a viable development tool as part of the sustainable development goals (SDGs) has provided further scope for understanding the effectiveness of aid. We re-examine the impact of foreign aid on eight development outcomes consistent with the SDGs. In addition to the effects of overall aid, we also examine the effects of aid availed to eight different sectors. We find that that more targeted aid is likely to be more beneficial for development. Our results also confirm the relevance of good institutions and economic development as enabling factors that promote the effectiveness of foreign aid.

The effectiveness of sectoral aid on selected development outcomes suggests that an optimal mix of aid targeted towards economic interventions on the one hand, and social interventions on the other, is likely to maximise the benefits of foreign aid. Aid targeted towards economic interventions in specific sectors is likely to promote growth while those targeted towards social dimensions are likely to contribute towards the welfare of the poor.

Given the poor level of institutional quality characterised by high levels of corruption in many developing countries, donor coordination might be an important consideration to ensure the effectiveness of aid. Donor coordination and oversight aid in the development process by efficiently allocating foreign aid across relevant sectors in developing countries, and ensuring that funds are channelled towards the right projects (Bigsten & Tengstam, 2015). Higher levels of corruption, as in many developing countries, need to be accompanied by better aid governance to ensure effectiveness.

Appendix

Table 9.5 Summary statistics

Variable	Description	Mean	Std. Dev.
Poverty	Percentage of the population living on less than $1.90 a day	12.107	18.821
Hunger	Percentage of the population whose food intake is insufficient to meet dietary energy requirements continuously	12.568	12.220
Education	Ratio of total enrolment in primary school, regardless of age, to the population of the age group that officially corresponds to the level of education	85.418	18.132
Gender	Gender parity index—the ratio of girls to boys enrolled at primary and secondary levels in public and private schools	0.925	0.161
HIV	Percentage of people aged 15–49 who are infected with HIV	1.965	4.354
Water	Percentage of the population using an improved drinking water source	76.784	26.115
Child mortality	The number of infants dying before reaching one year of age, per 1,000 live births in a given year	52.578	46.208
Maternal mortality	The number of women who die from pregnancy-related causes while pregnant or within 42 days of pregnancy termination per 100,000 live births	177.152	275.919
Income	Log of GDP per capita	8.217	1.519
Institution	Average of World Bank Governance Indicators	−0.034	0.914
Net ODA received	Net official development assistance received (in millions of US$)	442	839
ODA agriculture sector	Total official development assistance (in millions of US$) availed to the agriculture sector of recipient countries	20.608	45.156
ODA education sector	Total official development assistance (in millions of US$) availed to the education sector of recipient countries	37.080	67.280
ODA government & civil society	Total official development assistance (in millions of US$) availed to the government & civil society sector of recipient countries	48.237	161.481
ODA health sector	Total official development assistance (in millions of US$) availed to the health sector of recipient countries	21.312	39.848

(continued)

Table 9.5 (continued)

Variable	Description	Mean	Std. Dev.
ODA industry sector	Total official development assistance (in millions of US$) availed to the industry sector of recipient countries	6.156	30.255
ODA production sectors	Total official development assistance (in millions of US$) availed to the production sectors (agriculture, & industry) of recipient countries	32.189	76.019
ODA water supply & sanitation sector	Total official development assistance (in millions of US$) availed to the water supply & sanitation sector of recipient countries	29.433	76.812
ODA social infrastructure sector	Total official development assistance (in millions of US$) availed to the social infrastructure and services sector	164.302	297.232

References

Alvi, E., & Senbeta, A. (2012). Does foreign aid reduce poverty? *Journal of International Development, 24*(8), 955–976.

Arndt, C., Jones, S., & Tarp, F. (2015). Assessing foreign aid's long-run contribution to growth and development. *World Development, 69*(C), 6–18.

Arvin, B. M., & Barillas, F. (2002). Foreign aid, poverty reduction, and democracy. *Applied Economics, 34*(17), 2151–2156.

Awaworyi Churchill, S., & Smyth, R. (2017). Ethnic diversity and poverty. *World Development, 95*, 285–302.

Bigsten, A., & Tengstam, S. (2015). International coordination and the effectiveness of aid. *World Development, 69*(C), 75–85.

Boone, P. (1996). Politics and the effectiveness of foreign aid. *European Economic Review, 40*(2), 289–329.

Bourguignon, F., & Platteau, J.-P. (2017). Does aid availability affect effectiveness in reducing poverty? A review article. *World Development, 90*, 6–16.

Breusch, T., & Pagan, A. (1979). A simple test for heteroscedasticity and random coefficient variation. *Econometrica, 47*(5), 1287–1294.

Burnside, C., & Dollar, D. (1998). *Aid, the incentive regime, and poverty reduction*. Policy Research Working Papers. World Bank.

Burnside, C., & Dollar, D. (2000). Aid, policies, and growth. *The American Economic Review, 90*(4), 847–868.

Chong, A., Gradstein, M., & Calderon, C. (2009). Can foreign aid reduce income inequality and poverty? *Public Choice, 140*(1), 59–84.

Doucouliagos, H., & Paldam, M. (2006). Aid effectiveness on accumulation: A meta study. *Kyklos, 59*(2), 227–254.

Easterly, W. (2003). Can foreign aid buy growth? *Journal of Economic Perspectives, 17*(3), 23–48.

Easterly, W. (2007). Inequality does cause underdevelopment: Insights from a new instrument. *Journal of Development Economics, 84*(2), 755–776.

Easterly, W., Levine, R., & Roodman, D. (2004). Aid, policies, and growth: Comment. *The American Economic Review, 94*(3), 774–780.

Fielding, D., McGillivray, M., & Torres, S. (2007). A wider approach to aid effectiveness: Correlated impacts on health, wealth, fertility and education. In G. Mavrotas & A. Shorrocks (Eds.), *Advancing development: Core themes in global economics* (pp. 183–196). London: Palgrave Macmillan UK.

Griffin, K. (1970). Foreign capital, domestic savings and economic development. *Oxford Bulletin of Economics & Statistics, 32*(2), 99–112.

Hansen, H., & Tarp, F. (2000). Aid effectiveness disputed. *Journal of International Development, 12*(3), 375–398.

Hirano, Y., & Otsubo, S. (2014). *Aid is good for the poor.* Washington, DC: World Bank Group.

Kaya, O., Kaya, I., & Gunter, L. (2013). Foreign aid and the quest for poverty reduction: Is aid to agriculture effective? *Journal of Agricultural Economics, 64*(3), 583–596.

Leeson, P. (2008). Escaping poverty: Foreign aid, private property, and economic development. *Journal of Private Enterprise, 23*(2), 39–64.

Lewbel, A. (2012). Using heteroscedasticity to identify and estimate mismeasured and endogenous regressor models. *Journal of Business & Economic Statistics, 30*(1), 67–80.

Maiga, E. (2014). *Does foreign aid in education foster gender equality in developing countries?* WIDER Working Paper Series 048. Helsinki, Finland: UNU-WIDER.

Mallik, G. (2008). Foreign aid and economic growth: A cointegration analysis of the six poorest African countries. *Economic Analysis and Policy, 38*(2), 251–260.

Minasyan, A., Nunnenkamp, P., & Richert, K. (2017). Does aid effectiveness depend on the quality of donors? *World Development, 100*, 16–30.

Mishra, P., & Newhouse, D. (2009). Does health aid matter? *Journal of Health Economics, 28*(4), 855–872.

Mitra, R., Hossain, M. S., & Hossain, M. I. (2015). Aid and per-capita economic growth in Asia: A panel cointegration test. *Economics Bulletin, 35*(3), 1693–1699.

Mitra, R., & Hossain, S. (2013). The determinants of economic growth in Africa: A dynamic causality and panel cointegration analysis. *Economic Analysis and Policy, 43*(2), 217–226.

Mosley, P., Hudson, J., & Horrell, S. (1987). Aid, the public sector and the market in less developed countries. *The Economic Journal, 97*(387), 616–641.

Stock, J. H., & Yogo, M. (2005). Testing for weak instruments in linear IV regression. In D. Andrews & J. Stock (Eds.), *Identification and inference for econometric models: Essays in honor of Thomas Rothenberg* (pp. 80–105). Cambridge: Cambridge University Press.

Thomson, M., Kentikelenis, A., & Stubbs, T. (2017). Structural adjustment programmes adversely affect vulnerable populations: A systematic-narrative review of their effect on child and maternal health. *Public Health Reviews, 38*, 13.

United Nations. (2015). *Transforming our world: The 2030 agenda for sustainable development*. New York: United Nations.

Weisskopf, T. E. (1972). The impact of foreign capital inflow on domestic savings in underdeveloped countries. *Journal of International Economics, 2*(1), 25–38.

Wilson, S. E. (2011). Chasing success: Health sector aid and mortality. *World Development, 39*(11), 2032–2043.

Yontcheva, B., & Masud, N. (2005). *Does foreign aid reduce poverty? Empirical evidence from nongovernmental and bilateral aid*. Washington, DC: International Monetary Fund.

10

Towards a Sustainable Development: The Role of Energy and Institutions in Combating CO_2 Emissions for the ASEAN-8

Khalid Ahmed and Mita Bhattacharya

1 Introduction

The role of infrastructure and quality institutions in achieving sustainable development is crucial. However, existing literature exploring the relationship between institutional quality and sustainable development in emerging markets remains limited. The Millennium Development Goals (MDGs) and current Sustainable Development Goals (SDGs) have constituted the most effective global initiatives to achieve the common goal of sustainable development. The implementation of policies associated with these goals takes place at the national, regional and local levels, which require strong institutions.

K. Ahmed
Sukkur IBA University, Sukkur, Pakistan
e-mail: khalid.ahmed@iba-suk.edu.pk

M. Bhattacharya (✉)
Department of Economics, Monash University, Melbourne, VIC, Australia
e-mail: mita.bhattacharya@monash.au

© The Author(s) 2020
S. Awaworyi Churchill (ed.), *Moving from the Millennium to the Sustainable Development Goals*, https://doi.org/10.1007/978-981-15-1556-9_10

Strong institutions are expected to play significant roles in achieving several of the development goals, if not all. This includes development goals related to environmental quality. Across the globe, deteriorating environmental conditions and its implications for socio-economic well-being remain a challenging issue. Developing countries, in particular, are struggling to control environmental degradation and its negative impact. Combating CO_2 emissions and its potential problems are high on the agenda for the SDG program.[1] The concentration of atmospheric CO_2 emissions has rapidly increased by around 45% within the last 130 years (Carbon Footprint, 2018).

A growing body of literature discusses the issue of climate change (Agrawal, 2001; Bäckstrand, 2006; Gupta, 2002; Jordan, 2008; Lehtonen, 2004; Loorbach, 2010; Young, 1997; Zelli, Gupta, & Van Asselt, 2013). Recently, Biermann, Kanie, and Kim (2017) examined 'governance through goals', a unique strategy adopted by the United Nations (UN) for the SDGs. The findings conclude that there are significant ambiguities and operational challenges that need to be identified to ensure progress on the goals. Lehtonen (2004) concludes that the environmental–social interface of sustainable development requires a three-dimensional approach—capability, social capital and institutions. Over the last two decades, the literature on this front mainly consists of studies on developed countries. Most developed countries are now economically and environmentally sustainable than a decade ago and it is anticipated that there will be continuous improvement in coming years. However, the conditions in developing and emerging countries are a stark contrast. Production in developing and emerging countries is highly polluting and energy intensive, while some of these countries are highly vulnerable with high risk from changes to the overall environment.

In this chapter, we consider major elements of institutional quality as the driving forces in mitigating emissions and achieving the SDGs for a selected panel of countries from the Association of South East Asian Nations (ASEAN). Analyzing the emissions, energy use and GDP growth profile for these countries, the chapter attempts to disseminate important

---

[1] https://unstats.un.org/sdgs/report/2018

messages for improving institutional quality for future sustainable development. In particular, our empirical analysis establishes some research-based policy recommendations for governments, policy analysts and relevant stakeholders for devising effective tools to achieve SDGs.

We focus on the ASEAN region for a number of reasons. First, countries like Brunei Darussalam, Indonesia, Malaysia, Myanmar, Philippines, Singapore, Thailand and Vietnam are within this fast-growing region. The ASEAN countries comprise 3.3% of the total land area of the world including around 8.7% of the total world population. GDP growth in this region is the fastest growing in the world—on average, around 1.4% per annum. Second, ASEAN is a hub for the global energy field in terms of energy consumption and economic growth, which ultimately raises the CO_2 emissions in the region. Investors and policy advisers of ASEAN countries have revealed a great interest in the area of energy consumption because it plays a vital role in economic growth.

According to the ASEAN Center for Energy, demand for energy consumption in ASEAN is expected to increase up to 583 million tons (oil equivalent) in 2020 from 280 million tons (oil equivalent) in 2000. To sustain its economic growth, the ASEAN would need as much as 461 billion US dollars in investments in the energy sector between 2001 and 2020 (Yoo, 2006). In the twelfth Meeting of the Conference of the Parties (COP-12) to the ASEAN Agreement on Transboundary Haze Pollution (AATHP), a road map was established with various strategies to enhance sustainable development, pollution and institutional quality.[2] Our research is timely, offering some guidance on these aspects based on recent data.

To our knowledge, there is no research in the context of ASEAN-8 countries that links factors affecting sustainable development (i.e. emissions inventory and energy demand) to the governance–growth nexus. Previous studies have mostly focused on analyzing the causal relationships between the energy consumption and economic growth of developed economies, ignoring the effect of governance variables.

---

[2] Held in Kuala Lumpur, Malaysia on 11 August 2016. See https://asean.org/wp-content/uploads/2018/02/50.-December-2017-ASEAN-Cooperation-on-Environment-At-A-Glance.pdf

We aim to fill the gap in the empirical literature and address the impact of institutional quality (considering bureaucratic quality, corruption and democratic accountability) on CO_2 emissions and energy consumption by controlling for economic growth (measured in GDP) and trade openness (export and import) in the case of these emerging ASEAN-8 countries.

2   An Overview of the Literature

This section provides an overview of related literature that has examined at least one dimension of the association among economic growth, institutions and environmental quality in isolation.

The existing literature linking environmental deprivation and economic development has become prominent since the Club of Rome (1975) report. Meadows, Meadows, and Randers (1992) report that economic growth is essential to sustain development, despite being a risk to environment quality in the long term. Kolstad and Krautkraemer (1993) show that there is a dynamic link between economic activity, resource consumption and the environment. They argue that, while energy resource use produces economic benefits, it has long-term negative effects on the environment and overall ecosystem. Diwan and Shafik (1992) and Birdsall and Wheeler (1993) suggest that the process involved in promoting economic development tend to produce hazardous waste products, which have harmful implications for both human health and the environment.

Industrial growth is therefore seen as a major cause of rapid increase in CO_2 emissions, particularly in the developing world (Maslin, 2008; Shahbaz, Ozturk, Afza, & Ali, 2013). According to the carbon dioxide information analysis center, per capita CO_2 emissions have increased almost two-fold since 1950, following the same trend as global energy consumption. Examining selected South Asian countries, Ahmed, Bhattacharya, Shaikh, Ramzan, and Ozturk (2017) established that energy consumption and population are contributing factors to increasing emissions.

A related strand of literature examines the role of institutions in promoting environmental quality (see e.g., Bhattacharya, Churchill, & Paramati, 2017; Povitkina, 2015; Zhang, Jin, Chevallier, & Shen, 2016).

Panayotou (1997) establishes that the improved quality of institutions and policies in a country can considerably lessen environmental degradation. Countries with a strong institutional background are usually better-off in terms of regulation of their emissions (Tamazian & Rao, 2010).

Another strand of literature explores the role of institutions in economic development focusing on various development outcomes (see e.g., Kyriacou, 2016; Dijkstra, Bitondo, Nooteboom, Post, & Boven, 2017). This literature has examined the impact of institutions and corruption on economic growth, community investment and foreign direct investment, among others. Some studies show a negative relationship between corruption and economic performance (Mauro, 1995; Burki & Perry, 1998; Kaufmann & Kraay, 2002). According to Bai and Wei (2000), corruption restricts the formulation of effective policies and their implementation for development. Considering other development indications, corruption and child mortality have been shown to be related, as countries with a high level of corruption have high infant mortality rates (Verhoeven, Gupta, & Tiongson, 1999).

Corruption has also been argued to encourage economic growth (Leff, 1964; Huntington, 2006). For example, money generated through corruption may be helpful to prevent deferrals due to bureaucratic red tape. Corruption may create an incentive for corrupt workers (as they receive bribes) to work efficiently and quickly in some sections of the economy. On the other hand, some evidence shows that corruption works against economic growth. Murphy, Shleifer, and Vishny (1991) established that a high rent-seeking division is linked with a much lower growth rate. The institutional quality, such as the degree of corruption, has great impact on investment and economic growth similar to the other political indicators (Knack & Keefer, 1995).

The literature has focused on various governance indicators including property rights, political stability and violence, rule of law, voice and accountability, government effectiveness, and regulatory burden (Kaufmann, Kraay, & Zoido-Lobatón, 1999; Kaufman, 2004; Rajkumar & Swaroop, 2008). Some studies emphasize the subtle differences among the various measures of institutions. For instance, Adsera, Boix, and Payne (2003) show that bureaucracy is slightly distinct from political pressure in low-risk countries. Joseph (1998) suggests that democratic accountability reduces corruption. Held (2002) explains that democratic accountability might be theorized as a proposed structure where actions of representatives make a significant influence on the lives of common citizens.

The literature on the impact of institutional quality on environmental quality has focused on a wide range of proxies for environmental quality. For instance, Li and Reuveny (2006) show that democracy has an impact on oxides of nitrogen, carbon dioxide, deforestation, organic pollution in water and land degradation. They conclude that improvements in democracy result in better environmental performance. Farzin and Bond (2006) find that freedom in democracy leads to reduced absorptions or emissions of pollutant. Bernauer and Koubi (2009) also show that presidential systems and democracies have a constructive influence on air quality.

3   Model, Data and Estimations

In this section, we describe the empirical model and data for the analysis.

The Model and Data

Grossman and Krueger (1991, 1995) in their seminal research, describe the Environmental Kuznets Curve (EKC), where economic growth has scale-up effects at the initial stage and scale-down at later stages for CO_2 emissions. We consider CO_2 emissions (metric tons per capita) as our dependent variable. Following López-Menéndez, Pérez, and Moreno (2014), we consider a cubic function with economic growth for estimation purposes. We consider GDP per capita (in constant 2010 USD) as a proxy for economic growth (denoted by Y in Eq. (10.1) below).

Total energy consumption (EN, measured in kg of oil equivalent per capita) increases CO_2 emissions in the absence of energy transition towards renewable energy and investment in energy technology. For institutional quality, we consider three proxies: bureaucratic quality (BQ), democratic accountability (DA) and corruption (C), measured as country risk rating.[3]

---

[3] For details follow ICRG https://epub.prsgroup.com/list-of-all-variable-definitions

In addition, we consider both imports (IM) and exports (EX, in constant 2010 USD) to capture openness. In earlier research, Ahmed, Shahbaz, Qasim, and Long (2015) and Ahmed, Rehman, and Ozturk (2017) emphasised that emission-intensive trade will increase overall energy demand and CO_2 emissions for most of the countries in our panel. Our model is as follows:

$$CO_{2it} = f\left(Y_{it} / Y_{it}^2 / Y_{it}^3, EN_{it}, BQ_{it}, DA_{it}, C_{it}, IM_{it}, EX_{it}\right) \quad (10.1)$$

The data for all the variables span between 1984 and 2014. The period of our study has been selected subject to data availability.

The data for CO_2 emissions, GDP per capita, energy consumption, imports and exports are from the World Development Indicators data series maintained by the World Bank. The data for institutional quality is extracted from the International Country Risk Guide (ICRG) data (ICRG, 2018).

The log-linear form of the model is considered here, where estimated parameters represent the value of elasticities with respect to CO_2 emissions:

$$\ln CO_{2it} = \beta_0 + \beta_1\left(Y_{it} / Y_{it}^2 / Y_{it}^3\right) + \beta_2 \ln EN_{it} + \beta_3 \ln BQ_{it}$$
$$+ \beta_4 \ln DA_{it} + \beta_5 \ln C_{it} + \beta_6 \ln IM_{it} + \beta_7 \ln EX_{it} + \mu_{it} \quad (10.2)$$

where i is the number of countries $(1,...,n)$, t is time and $\propto$ is a stochastic disturbance term.

Cross-Sectional Dependence Tests

In applied energy economics research, it is well established that heterogeneity exists across countries within the panel and they are cross-sectionally interdependent. Being part of the global economic system, such cross-sectional interdependence potentially possesses unobserved common shocks which later cause inconsistent residual values (for details see;

De Hoyos & Sarafidis, 2006; Driscoll & Kraay, 1998). We follow the test developed by Friedman (1937) and Pesaran (2007) to check cross-sectional dependence. The specification is as follows:

Freidman's statistics compute:

$$R = \frac{2}{N(N-1)} \sum_{i=1}^{N-1} \sum_{j=i+1}^{N} \hat{r}_{ij} \qquad (10.3)$$

where $\hat{r}$ is the Spearman's rank correlation coefficient of the residuals;

$$r_{ij} = r_{ji} = \frac{\sum_{t=1}^{T} (r_{it} - (T+1/2))(r_{jt} - (T+1/2))}{\sum_{t=1}^{T} (r_{it} - (T+1/2))^2} \qquad (10.4)$$

Pesaran's statistics compute:

$$CD = \sqrt{\frac{2T}{N(N-1)}} \left(\sum_{i=1}^{N-1} \sum_{j=i+1}^{N} \hat{\rho}_{ij} \right) \qquad (10.5)$$

where $\hat{\rho}_{ij}$ is the estimate of;

$$\rho_{ij} = \rho_{ji} = \frac{\sum_{t=1}^{T} \varepsilon_{it} \varepsilon_{jt}}{\left(\sum_{t=1}^{T} \varepsilon_{it}^2 \right)^{1/2} \left(\sum_{t=1}^{T} \varepsilon_{jt}^2 \right)^{1/2}} \qquad (10.6)$$

The null hypothesis to be tested is $\rho_{ij} = \rho_{ji} = \mathrm{corr}(\varepsilon_{it}, \varepsilon_{jt}) = 0$ for $i \uparrow j$ and the alternative hypothesis to be tested is $\rho_{ij} = \rho_{ji} \neq 0$ for some $i \uparrow j$.

Panel Unit Root Tests

We try to establish the long-term relationships between economic growth, energy use and the CO_2 emissions and institutions. Data must be stationary and should not possess a unit root to conduct further analysis. In the first step, we apply the unit root test to verify the stationarity property of the data. There are a number of panel unit root tests proposed by researchers (Levin & Lin, 1993; Hansen, 2005; Im, Pesaran, & Shin, 2003; Maddala & Wu, 1999; Levin, Lin, & Chu, 2002). We apply the three-panel unit root tests proposed by Levin, Lin, Chu (LLC) (2002), Im, Pesaran, Shin (IPS) (2003) and Hadri (2000) to ensure the data is free from the unit root in order to obtain robust and reliable empirical results.

The LLC test is built on pooled data, allowing heterogeneity in the constant term, and the IPS test is obtained as an average of ADF statistics. This test allows heterogeneity both in constant and trend. Both tests have the null hypothesis that each cross-section panel contains a unit root while Hadri (2000) has the null hypothesis that all the panels are stationary at trend. The LLC test and IPS test show that most of the series have significant results, allowing rejection of the null hypothesis. On the other hand, the Hadri (2000) test indicates rejection of the null hypothesis and each series is (trend) nonstationary.[4]

Panel ARDL Test

Following Pesaran, Shin, and Smith (2001), we select the panel ARDL model for long-term estimation and apply an error-correction representation of the ARDL model for short-term analysis. This approach has two key advantages over other panel estimation techniques. First, this approach uses pooled estimators, which are useful even when the parameters differ across groups and the regressors are serially correlated. Second, owing to cross-sectional dependence, the pooled regressions can measure different parameters than the averages of the corresponding parameters in time-series regressions, but this problem is overcome using this technique.

---

[4] Hadri test often rejects the null hypothesis despite having highly stationary panels and rejection of null hypothesis does not lead to the acceptance of alternative hypothesis.

Following Pesaran, Shin, and Smith (1999, 2001) we estimate an ARDL model:

$$y_{it} = \sum_{j=1}^{p} \lambda_{ij} y_{i,t-j} + \sum_{j=0}^{q} \delta'_{ij} x_{i,t-j} + \gamma'_i d_t + \varepsilon_{it}, \qquad (10.7)$$

where $i = 1,2,\ldots,n$ stands for the country; $t = 1,2,\ldots,n$ for the time period; $x_{it} = (k \times 1)$ and $d_t (s \times 1)$ for the vectors of explanatory variables.

Re-parameterizing (10.7) we obtain an error correction model of the form:

$$\Delta y_{it} = \phi_i y_{i,t-1} + \beta'_i x_{it} + \sum_{j=1}^{p-1} \lambda^*_{ij} \Delta y_{i,t-j} + \sum_{j=0}^{q-1} \delta^{*'}_{ij} \Delta x_{i,t-j} + \gamma'_i d_t + \varepsilon_{it} \qquad (10.8)$$

where

$$\phi_i = -\left(1 - \sum_{j=1}^{p} \lambda_{ij}\right), \beta_i = \sum_{j=0}^{q} \delta_{ij}, \lambda^*_{ij} = -\sum_{m=j+1}^{p} \lambda_{im}, j = 1,\ldots,p-1 \qquad (10.9)$$

and

$$\delta^*_{ij} = -\sum_{m=j+1}^{q} \delta_{im}, j = 1,\ldots,q-1, i = 1,\ldots,N \qquad (10.10)$$

Following Pedroni (1999, 2001) we estimate the long-run relationship as follows:

$$y_{i,t} = \alpha_i + \delta_i t + \beta_{1i} x_{1i,t} + \beta_{2i} x_{2i,t} + \cdots + \beta_{Mi} x_{Mi,t} + e_{i,t} \qquad (10.11)$$

for $t = 1,\ldots,T$; $i = 1,\ldots,N$; $m = 1,\ldots,M$ with T being the number of observations (time), N the number of individual countries in the panel and M the number of regression variables. After estimating (10.7) and identifying the long-term relationships, we estimate a panel VECM model:

$$\Delta y_{it} = \theta_{1i} + \lambda_{1i}EC_{i,t-1} + \sum_{k=1}^{m}\theta_{11ik}\Delta y_{i,t-k} + \sum_{k=1}^{m}\theta_{12ik}\Delta p_{i,t-k} + \sum_{k=1}^{m}\theta_{13ik}\Delta e_{i,t-k} + u_{1it}$$

$$(10.12)$$

In order to examine the long-term relationship between exogenous and endogenous variables, we test $H_0: \lambda_{1i}, \lambda_{2i}, \lambda_{3i} = 0$ for all i and k in (10.12) (i.e., no long-term stable relationship between independent and dependent variables in the model).

Panel Cointegration Estimates

We established the variables are cointegrated so, in the next phase, we estimate the long-term association of variables. The fixed effect, random effect and GMM method could steer to inappropriate and miscalculated coefficients when used for panel data that are cointegrated. Thus, based on the applied macro-econometrics literature, this study incorporates a fully modified OLS (FMOLS) method to estimate the models. Pedroni (2001) explains that the FMOLS technique evaluates consistent estimates even if the sample is small and does not experience large size distortions in cases of endogeneity and of heterogeneous nature. The panel FMOLS estimator for the coefficient β is defined as:

$$\hat{\beta} = N^{-1}\sum_{i=1}^{N}\left(\sum_{t=1}^{T}(y_{it}-\overline{y})^2\right)^{-1}\left(\sum_{t=1}^{T}(y_{it}-\overline{y})\right)z_{it}^{*} - T\hat{\eta}_i \quad (10.13)$$

where $z_{it}^{*} = \left(z_{it}-\overline{z}\right) - \dfrac{\hat{L}_{21i}}{\hat{L}_{22i}}\Delta y_{it}$, $\hat{\eta}_i \equiv \hat{\Gamma}_{21i} + \hat{\Omega}_{21i}^{0} - \dfrac{\hat{L}_{21i}}{\hat{L}_{22i}}\left(\hat{\Gamma}_{22i} + \hat{\Omega}_{22i}^{0}\right)$ and $\hat{L}_i$ is a lower triangular decomposition of $\hat{\Omega}_i$. The associated t-statistics gives:

$$t_{\hat{\beta}^{*}} = N^{-1/2}\sum_{i=1}^{N}t_{\hat{\beta}^{*},i}, \quad \text{where} \quad t_{\hat{\beta}^{*},i} = \left(\hat{\beta}_i^{*} - \beta_0\right)\left[\hat{\Omega}_{11i}^{-1}\sum_{t=1}^{T}(y_{it}-\overline{y})^2\right]^{1/2} \quad (10.14)$$

4   Findings and Discussions

In this section, we first consider the basic properties of the data using descriptive statistics that include the mean, the standard deviation and the variation of coefficients, as presented in Table 10.1. The table shows the real values (without logarithm) of each variable used for empirical purposes. It is observed that the data are normally distributed and appropriate for further analyses. Table 10.2 depicts the correlation-matrix reflecting no high correlations among variables. Table 10.3 presents the findings with cross-section dependence test and signifies no cross-sectional dependence among variables.

Panel Unit Root Tests

We apply three unit root tests, viz. Levin, Lin, and Chu (LLC, 2002), Im, Pesaran, and Shin (IPS, 2003), and Hadri (2000); the results are reported in Table 10.3. The results show that all the variables are stationary at the first difference and confirm that the data are suitable for cointegration analysis (Table 10.4).

Panel Cointegration Test

Once we checked the stationarity of the series, the next step is the cointegration analysis. The existing literature proposes a number of panel cointegration tests developed by Pedroni (1999); Kao (1999); the Johansen-Fisher cointegration test (Fisher, 1932; Maddala & Wu, 1999) and others. We conduct the Johansen-Fisher cointegration test for a dynamic panel data set derived by Maddala and Wu (1999). The Johansen-Fisher cointegration test is an extension of the individual Johansen (1988) cointegration test in which the Fisher effect is added to transform into the panel form. The null-hypothesis for the Johansen-Fisher panel cointegration test is that there is no cointegration. The results of Johansen-Fisher cointegration are shown in Table 10.5. The results show that all the variables are cointegrated and possess a long-term

Table 10.1 Descriptive statistics

	$\ln Y_{it}$	$\ln EN_{it}$	$\ln CO_{2it}$	$\ln BQ_{it}$	$\ln DA_{it}$	$\ln C_{it}$	$\ln M_{it}$	$\ln EX_{it}$
Mean	10.522	7.010	2.816	2.221	2.265	2.266	21.162	22.097
Median	10.516	6.677	2.786	2.197	2.303	2.251	21.163	21.888
Maximum	10.703	9.193	3.228	2.398	2.565	2.565	22.012	23.288
Minimum	10.414	5.539	2.173	1.946	1.946	1.946	20.237	21.259
Std. Dev.	0.057	1.143	0.284	0.131	0.173	0.126	0.532	0.654
Skewness	1.259	0.449	−0.268	−0.660	−0.345	−0.010	−0.144	0.501
Kurtosis	5.172	1.813	2.167	2.513	1.982	2.848	2.156	1.797
Jarque-Bera	114.274	22.900	10.135	20.435	15.637	0.244	8.229	25.334
Probability	0.000	0.000	0.006	0.000	0.000	0.885	0.016	0.000
Sum	2609.452	1738.506	698.330	550.796	561.756	562.082	5248.092	5479.979
Sum Sq. Dev.	0.809	322.483	19.869	4.208	7.406	3.925	69.925	105.577
Observations	248	248	248	248	248	248	248	248

Note: $Y \rightarrow$ GDP, $EN \rightarrow$ energy consumption, $CO_2 \rightarrow CO_2$ emissions, $BQ \rightarrow$ bureaucratic quality, $DA \rightarrow$ democratic accountability, $C \rightarrow$ corruption, $IM \rightarrow$ imports, $EX \rightarrow$ exports

Table 10.2 Correlation matrix

	Y_{it}	EN_{it}	CO_{2it}	BQ_{it}	DA_{it}	C_{it}	IM_{it}	EX_{it}
Y_{it}	1.00							
EN_{it}	0.938	1.00						
CO_{2it}	0.85	0.929	1.00					
BQ_{it}	0.673	0.649	0.642	1.00				
DA_{it}	−0.344	−0.35	−0.282	0.059	1.00			
C_{it}	0.593	0.505	0.528	0.639	0.068	1.00		
IM_{it}	0.308	0.152	0.09	0.391	0.253	0.245	1.00	
EX_{it}	0.33	0.175	0.106	0.392	0.237	0.236	0.992	1.00

Note: Variables notation are same as Table 10.1

Table 10.3 Cross-section dependence test

	Breusch-Pagan LM	Pesaran scaled LM	Bias-corrected scaled LM	Pesaran CD
$\ln Y_{it}$	704.835***	90.446***	90.313***	15.929***
$\ln EN_{it}$	308.375***	37.467***	37.333***	13.618***
$\ln CO_{2it}$	394.287***	48.947***	48.814***	10.835***
$\ln BQ_{it}$	461.837***	57.973***	57.840***	4.693***
$\ln DA_{it}$	236.598***	27.875***	27.742***	1.816*
$\ln C_{it}$	191.924***	21.905***	21.772***	6.053***
$\ln IM_{it}$	737.634***	94.829***	94.695***	27.109***
$\ln EX_{it}$	779.903***	100.477***	100.344***	27.896***

Notes: Variables notation are same as Table 10.1. *** and * denote significance at the 1% and 10% level, respectively

equilibrium relationship. The Johansen Fisher panel cointegration approach is applied to inspect whether there is cointegration present among the variables or not. The findings are reported in Table 10.4. Both the trace test and max-eigen test confirm that there is cointegration for all models. This notion infers that the variables of institutional quality (i.e., bureaucracy quality, democratic accountability and corruption), carbon dioxide emissions, economic growth, energy use, imports and exports have a long-term association in our panel. This result indicates institutional quality has a significant influence on CO_2 emissions in the long-run for the ASEAN-8.

Table 10.4 Unit root tests

Variables	LLC test statistics		IPS test statistics		Hadri test statistics	
	Constant	Constant and trend	Constant	Constant and trend	Constant	Constant and trend
lnY_{it}	−1.954**	−2.243**	−2.024**	−4.687***	8.613***	5.258***
ΔlnY_{it}	−10.880***	−10.582***	−11.596***	−9.271***	1.380*	6.029***
$lnEN_{it}$	−2.378**	−1.036	−0.239	0.613	9.312***	6.394***
$\Delta lnEN_{it}$	−3.391***	−2.632***	−5.529***	−4.824***	1.962**	2.465**
$lnCO_{2it}$	−0.647	1.118	−2.293**	−0.316	0.883	1.804**
$\Delta lnCO_{2it}$	−8.493***	−8.310***	−7.779***	−6.059***	−0.793	2.801***
$lnBQ_{it}$	−0.893	1.382	0.154	1.358	6.969***	4.943***
$\Delta lnBQ_{it}$	−3.206***	−6.080***	−6.535***	−4.909***	−0.583	2.337**
$lnDA_{it}$	−0.894	0.875	−0.813	0.225	4.978***	4.730***
$\Delta lnDA_{it}$	−7.813***	−6.543***	−8.738***	−7.210***	0.13	2.964***
lnC_{it}	−2.134**	−0.343	−2.179**	−0.292	4.998***	3.084***
ΔlnC_{it}	−8.628***	−7.948***	−8.774***	−7.177***	−0.553	1.658*
$lnIM_{it}$	−1.360*	0.223	0.296	0.284	7.410***	1.419*
$\Delta lnIM_{it}$	−1.925**	0.085	−4.894***	−2.867***	−1.377	1.748**
$lnEX_{it}$	2.149	−5.609***	4.154	−5.009***	8.874***	7.581***
$\Delta lnEX_{it}$	−12.504***	−10.748***	−10.654***	−8.437***	2.560**	6.004***

Notes: Variables notation are same as Table 10.1. ***, ** and * show significance at 1%, 5% and 10% level, respectively

Table 10.5 Johansen Fisher panel cointegration test

Hypothesis	Trace test	Max-eigen test
$R = 0$	410.300***	207.700***
$R \leq 1$	235.200***	137.800***
$R \leq 2$	123.700***	46.330***
$R \leq 3$	81.950***	44.820***
$R \leq 4$	46.770***	26.260*
$R \leq 5$	29.560**	17.390
$R \leq 6$	23.910*	25.320*
$R \leq 7$	12.360	12.360

Note: ***, **, * shows rejection of null-hypothesis at 1%, 5% and 10% of significance level, respectively

Panel ARDL Results

The autoregressive distributed lag (ARDL) model is considered in finding the long- and short-run dynamics among the underlying variables, following Pesaran, Shin, and Smith (1997). The long- and short-run estimates are presented in Table 10.6.

In the long-run, economic growth has a positive influence on CO_2 emissions, although at a decreasing rate (in column 1), while the effect is negative in the short-run. We could not establish any pattern in the CO_2 emissions path both in the long- and short-run for the full panel. On the other hand, BQ variable has a reducing effect on CO_2 emissions in the long run. Corruption reduces CO_2 emissions in the short run, although no significant effect in the long run is observed. Both exports and imports are positive and have a significant influence on CO_2 emissions in the short run; imports have CO_2-increasing effects in the long run. ECT_{t-1} shows that the speed of adjustment from short run to long run, which is 42.7% annually, is significant at 1%.[5]

The FMOLS country-specific long-term estimates are reported in Table 10.7. Economic growth reduces CO_2 emissions in Brunei Darussalam and increases emissions in the Philippines and Thailand. Energy consumption exacerbates CO_2 emissions in Malaysia, Myanmar, Philippines, Thailand and Vietnam.

---

[5] The long-run dynamics are validated by the FMOLS estimation for the full panel. The results are similar to the ARDL estimates in the long run and not reported here due to space constraints.

Table 10.6 Long- and short-run analysis

Independent variables	Dependent variables		
	1	1′	1″
	$\ln CO_{2it}$	$\ln CO_{2it}$	$\ln CO_{2it}$
Long-run estimates			
$\ln Y_{it}$	−0.055	2.508**	2.465**
	(−0.054)	(2.817)	(2.324)
$\ln Y_{it}^2$	0.008	−0.144***	0.090*
	(0.188)	(−4.801)	(1.899)
$\ln Y_{it}^3$	0.005	−0.096***	0.060*
	0.188	(−4.801)	(1.899)
$\ln EN_{it}$	−0.286*	−0.045	−0.014
	(−1.916)	(−0.505)	(−0.128)
$\ln BQ_{it}$	−0.901**	–	–
	(−2.175)		
$\ln DA_{it}$	–	–	0.040
			(0.141)
$\ln C_{it}$	–	0.139	–
		(0.595)	
$\ln IM_{it}$	0.176*	0.165**	0.146**
	(1.816)	(2.803)	(2.160)
$\ln EX_{it}$	0.100	0.162***	0.171***
	(1.522)	(3.402)	(3.027)
Short-run estimates			
$\ln Y_{it}$	−2.585***	−6.409***	−6.652***
	(−13.696)	(−8.404)	(−16.300)
$\ln Y_{it}^2$	0.788	−0.202	0.179
	(0.123)	(−0.579)	(0.792)
$\ln Y_{it}^3$	0.525	−0.135	0.119
	(0.123)	(0.563)	(0.263)
$\ln EN_{it}$	−0.003	0.113	0.287
	(−0.011)	(0.336)	(0.829)
$\ln BQ_{it}$	−0.181	–	–
	(−0.555)		
$\ln DA_{it}$	–	–	0.435
			(0.895)
$\ln C_{it}$	–	−0.915**	–
		(−2.442)	
$\ln IM_{it}$	0.339***	0.293***	0.310***
	(19.942)	(8.134)	(8.572)
$\ln EX_{it}$	0.249***	0.119***	0.108**
	(11.168)	(2.895)	(2.433)
Constant	0.604***	−17.703***	−15.750***
	(9.643)	(−14.197)	(−12.995)
ECT_{t-1}	−0.427***	−0.576***	−0.310***
	(−34.148)	(−14.302)	(−13.067)

Notes: Variables notation are same as Table 10.1. ***, ** and * show significance at 1%, 5% and 10% level, respectively

(UN, 2015).[1] The date for the achievement of the MDGs has now passed and the Sustainable Development Goals (SDGs) have replaced them in the post-2015 development agenda. It is necessary to have a clear understanding of factors that influenced the success and failure of MDGs across countries in order to provide insights for the policies that can best contribute to SDG achievement.

Since their inception, many studies have sought to identify the factors that influence progress towards the MDGs. Existing studies have examined *inter alia* the role of innovations in healthcare delivery (see, e.g., Barros et al., 2010; Camacho, Castro, & Kaufman, 2006; Hazarika, 2011; Mpembeni et al., 2007), infrastructure (see, e.g., Fay, Leipziger, Wodon, & Yepes, 2005; Jowitt, 2009; Leipziger, Fay, Wodon, & Yepes, 2003; Onda, LoBuglio, & Bartram, 2012) and agriculture (see, e.g., Mahmoudi, Liaghati, & Zohari, 2007). Yet one specific factor which has yet to receive sufficient attention is whether progress towards the MDGs was dependent on ethnic diversity. Specifically, whether differences in MDG progress observed across countries can be explained by their differences in ethnic fractionalisation.

The role of ethnic diversity in the MDG achievement and development is not apparent *prima facie*. Of the five countries with the largest numbers of people living in poverty, three are very ethnically diverse. According to the ethnolinguistic dataset of Fearon (2003), Nigeria, the Democratic Republic of Congo and India have fractionalisation index values of 0.805, 0.933 and 0.811, respectively. However, large numbers also live in poverty in China and Bangladesh which are relatively homogenous, although significant progress has been made by these countries towards other MDGs.

Ethnic diversity is associated with poorer economic performance and institutional quality (see Alesina & Zhuravskaya, 2011; Awaworyi Churchill, 2017; Easterly & Levine, 1997), and the prevalence of income

---

[1] It should not be surprising that progress towards the MDGs varied greatly across countries given their different initial levels of development as well as important differences in their institutions, geography, history and resources. It should also be noted that the MDGs were designed to be achieved at a global level rather than at the individual country level.

Table 10.7 Fully modified OLS (FMOLS) for individual country

Independent variables	Dependent variables
	M1
	$\ln CO_{2it}$
Brunei Darussalam	
$\ln Y_{it}$	−4.438***
	(−4.366)
$\ln Y_{it}^2$	−2.269***
	−4.394***
$\ln Y_{it}^3$	−1.512
	−4.394
$\ln EN_{it}$	−0.093
	(−3.629)
$\ln BQ_{it}$	2.428
	(0.830)
$\ln DA_{it}$	1.621
	(1.415)
$\ln C_{it}$	0.399
	(0.357)
$\ln IM_{it}$	$\ln IM_{it}$
$\ln EX_{it}$	0.042
	(0.306)
Constant	36.781***
	(3.202)
Indonesia	
$\ln Y_{it}$	0.293
	(0.859)
$\ln Y_{it}^2$	0.234
	0.777
$\ln Y_{it}^3$	0.089
	0.777
$\ln EN_{it}$	0.242
	(1.112)
$\ln BQ_{it}$	0.200
	(0.830)
$\ln DA_{it}$	0.218
	(1.428)
$\ln C_{it}$	0.070
	(0.503)
$\ln IM_{it}$	0.010
	(0.062)
$\ln EX_{it}$	0.211
	(1.456)
Constant	−10.178***
	(−19.336)

(continued)

Table 10.7 (continued)

Independent variables	Dependent variables
	M1
	$\ln CO_{2it}$
Malaysia	
$\ln Y_{it}$	−0.318
	(−0.610)
$\ln Y_{it}^2$	−0.155
	−0.592
$\ln Y_{it}^3$	−0.103
	−0.592
$\ln EN_{it}$	0.816***
	(3.412)
$\ln BQ_{it}$	−0.167
	(−0.425)
$\ln DA_{it}$	−0.205*
	(−1.811)
$\ln C_{it}$	0.841*
	(2.061)
$\ln IM_{it}$	0.248
	(1.574)
$\ln EX_{it}$	0.053
	(0.264)
Constant	−10.321***
	(−6.353)
Myanmar	
$\ln Y_{it}$	0.157
	(0.901)
$\ln Y_{it}^2$	0.069
	0.612
$\ln Y_{it}^3$	0.046
	0.546
$\ln EN_{it}$	2.012***
	(4.935)
$\ln BQ_{it}$	1.207
	(1.565)
$\ln DA_{it}$	−0.036
	(−0.134)
$\ln C_{it}$	−1.175*
	(−1.873)
$\ln IM_{it}$	0.006
	(0.095)
$\ln EX_{it}$	−0.017
	(−0.171)
Constant	−13.656***
	(−4.231)

(*continued*)

Table 10.7 (continued)

| Independent variables | Dependent variables |
| | M1 |
	$\ln CO_{2it}$
Philippines	
$\ln Y_{it}$	0.317***
	(1.358)
$\ln Y_{it}^2$	0.159***
	3.569
$\ln Y_{it}^3$	0.106***
	3.569
$\ln EN_{it}$	1.358***
	(8.652)
$\ln BQ_{it}$	0.208
	(1.272)
$\ln DA_{it}$	−0.103
	(−0.719)
$\ln C_{it}$	0.161
	(1.791)
$\ln IM_{it}$	0.225***
	(4.903)
$\ln EX_{it}$	−0.110*
	(−1.915)
Constant	−14.250***
	(−12.840)
Singapore	
$\ln Y_{it}$	2.183
	(1.584)
$\ln Y_{it}^2$	1.231
	1.391
$\ln Y_{it}^3$	0.820
	1.391
$\ln EN_{it}$	0.095
	(0.493)
$\ln BQ_{it}$	3.619
	(1.074)
$\ln DA_{it}$	1.601
	(1.074)
$\ln C_{it}$	−1.698*
	(−2.063)
$\ln IM_{it}$	2.862***
	(3.313)
$\ln EX_{it}$	−3.650***
	(−3.867)
Constant	−8.914
	(−0.866)

(*continued*)

Table 10.7 (continued)

| Independent variables | Dependent variables |
| | M1 |
	$\ln CO_{2it}$
Thailand	
$\ln Y_{it}$	1.058**
	(2.174)
$\ln Y_{it}^2$	0.626*
	1.998
$\ln Y_{it}^3$	0.417*
	1.998
$\ln EN_{it}$	1.001**
	(2.680)
$\ln BQ_{it}$	0.850*
	(1.927)
$\ln DA_{it}$	0.610***
	(3.872)
$\ln C_{it}$	−0.240
	(−1.134)
$\ln IM_{it}$	−0.382***
	(−4.199)
$\ln EX_{it}$	0.030
	(0.270)
Constant	−8.740***
	(−10.220)
Vietnam	
$\ln Y_{it}$	0.253
	(0.681)
$\ln Y_{it}^2$	0.106
	0.346
$\ln Y_{it}^3$	0.080
	0.641
$\ln EN_{it}$	1.003***
	(3.894)
$\ln BQ_{it}$	−0.611
	(−1.172)
$\ln DA_{it}$	−0.630***
	(−5.678)
$\ln C_{it}$	−0.683***
	(−4.501)
$\ln IM_{it}$	0.342***
	(4.291)
$\ln EX_{it}$	−0.216***
	(−3.102)
Constant	−6.843***
	(−6.107)

Notes: Variables notation are same as Table 10.1. ***, ** and * show significance at 1%, 5% and 10% level, respectively

Our findings reflect that bureaucratic quality reduces emissions in Vietnam and democratic accountability reduces emissions in Malaysia and Vietnam. Control of corruption increases emissions in Malaysia and Vietnam and reduces emissions in Myanmar and Singapore. Heterogeneity across countries is noticeable for institutional quality in reducing CO_2 emissions.

5   Concluding Remarks

The chapter investigates the relationship between economic growth, energy consumption, CO_2 emissions and institutional quality for ASEAN-8 (Brunei Darussalam, Indonesia, Malaysia, Myanmar, Philippines, Singapore, Thailand and Vietnam) over the period of 1984 to 2014. Fisher panel cointegration and the panel autoregressive distributed lag (ARDL) model are applied for cointegration and long- and short-term dynamics, respectively. The findings are validated by the FMOLS full panel and country-specific estimates as robustness checks.

In summary, our findings suggest that economic growth (measured in GDP per capita), energy consumption and institutional quality have long-term effects on environmental degradation (measured by CO_2 emissions). In addition, economic growth does not follow the EKC pattern strictly in the long run.

Energy consumption is emission-intensive for Malaysia, Myanmar, Philippines, Thailand and Vietnam. Bureaucratic quality, democratic accountability and control of corruption are the significant factors affecting emissions intensity in the region for selected countries. Our findings reflect that bureaucratic quality reduces emissions in Vietnam and democratic accountability reduces emissions in Malaysia and Vietnam. Control of corruption increases emissions in Malaysia and Vietnam and reduces emissions in Myanmar and Singapore. Heterogeneity across countries is noticeable for institutional quality in reducing CO_2 emissions. Both exports and imports are emission-intensive.

Based on these results, we suggest that adopting growth strategies with low emissions, aligned with socio-economic development objectives is an important way to achieve sustainable development. It is important to ensure an institutional framework with good governance towards green growth and low-carbon economy within the region. Findings relating to the effects of trade suggest the need to promote sustainable trade and provide incentives to agri-business and other low carbon industries and extend inter-regional cooperation to achieve sustainable development.

References

Adsera, A., Boix, C., & Payne, M. (2003). Are you being served? Political accountability and quality of government. *The Journal of Law, Economics, and Organization, 19*(2), 445–490.

Agrawal, A. (2001). Common property institutions and sustainable governance of resources. *World Development, 29*(10), 1649–1672.

Ahmed, K., Bhattacharya, M., Shaikh, Z., Ramzan, M., & Ozturk, I. (2017). Emission intensive growth and trade in the era of the Association of Southeast Asian Nations (ASEAN) integration: An empirical investigation from ASEAN-8. *Journal of Cleaner Production, 154*, 530–540.

Ahmed, K., Rehman, M. U., & Ozturk, I. (2017). What drives carbon dioxide emissions in the long-run? Evidence from selected South Asian Countries. *Renewable and Sustainable Energy Reviews, 70*, 1142–1153.

Ahmed, K., Shahbaz, M., Qasim, A., & Long, W. (2015). The linkages between deforestation, energy and growth for environmental degradation in Pakistan. *Ecological Indicators, 49*, 95–103.

Bäckstrand, K. (2006). Multi-stakeholder partnerships for sustainable development: Rethinking legitimacy, accountability and effectiveness. *European Environment, 16*(5), 290–306.

Bai, C. E., & Wei, S. J. (2000). *Quality of bureaucracy and open-economy macro policies.* NBER Working Paper No. 7766. Cambridge, MA.

Bernauer, T., & Koubi, V. (2009). Effects of political institutions on air quality. *Ecological Economics, 68*(5), 1355–1365.

Bhattacharya, M., Churchill, S. A., & Paramati, S. R. (2017). The dynamic impact of renewable energy and institutions on economic output and CO_2 emissions across regions. *Renewable Energy, 111*, 157–167.

Biermann, F., Kanie, N., & Kim, R. E. (2017). Global governance by goal-setting: The novel approach of the UN Sustainable Development Goals. *Current Opinion in Environmental Sustainability, 26*, 26–31.

Birdsall, N., & Wheeler, D. (1993). Trade policy and industrial pollution in Latin America: Where are the pollution havens? *The Journal of Environment & Development, 2*(1), 137–149.

Burki, S., & Perry, G. (1998). *Beyond the Washington consensus: Institutions matter*. Washington, DC: World Bank.

Carbon Footprint Network. (2018). Retrieved from https://www.footprintnetwork.org/our-work/climate-change/

Club, D. R., Mesarovic, M., & Pestel, E. C. (1975). *Mankind at the turning point. The second report to the Club of Rome*. Hutchinson.

De Hoyos, R. E., & Sarafidis, V. (2006). Testing for cross-sectional dependence in panel-data models. *The Stata Journal, 6*(4), 482–496.

Dijkstra, G., Bitondo, D., Nooteboom, S., Post, R., & Boven, G. V. (2017). Supporting governance of economic development: The PAANEEAC experience in Central Africa. *Journal of Developing Societies, 33*(1), 51–74.

Diwan, I., & Shafik, N. (1992). *Investment, technology and the global environment: Towards international agreement in a world of disparities*. World Bank Discussion Papers.

Driscoll, J. C., & Kraay, A. C. (1998). Consistent covariance matrix estimation with spatially dependent panel data. *Review of Economics and Statistics, 80*(4), 549–560.

Farzin, Y. H., & Bond, C. A. (2006). Democracy and environmental quality. *Journal of Development Economics, 81*(1), 213–235.

Fisher, R. A. (1932). *Statistical methods for research workers* (4th ed.). Edinburgh: Oliver & Boyd.

Friedman, M. (1937). The use of ranks to avoid the assumption of normality implicit in the analysis of variance. *Journal of the American Statistical Association, 32*(200), 675–701.

Grossman, G., & Krueger, A. (1995). Economic growth and the environment. *Quarterly Journal of Economics, 110*, 353–377.

Grossman, G. M., & Krueger, A. B. (1991). *Environmental impacts of a North American free trade agreement*. National Bureau of Economic Research, No. w3914.

Gupta, J. (2002). Global sustainable development governance: Institutional challenges from a theoretical perspective. *International Environmental Agreements, 2*(4), 361–388.

Hadri, K. (2000). Testing for stationarity in heterogeneous panel data. *The Econometrics Journal, 3*(2), 148–161.

Hansen, B. E. (2005). Challenges for econometric model selection. *Econometric Theory, 21*(1), 60–68.

Held, D. (2002). Law of states, law of peoples: Three Models of Sovereignty. *Legal Theory, 8*(1), 1–44.

Huntington, S. P. (2006). *Political order in changing societies.* Yale University Press.

Im, K. S., Pesaran, M. H., & Shin, Y. (2003). Testing for unit roots in heterogeneous panels. *Journal of Econometrics, 115*, 53–74.

International Country Risk Guide (ICRG). (2018). Retrieved from https://epub.prsgroup.com/products/international-country-risk-guide-icrg

Johansen, S. (1988). Statistical analysis of cointegration vectors. *Journal of Economic Dynamics and Control, 12*(2–3), 231–254.

Jordan, A. (2008). The governance of sustainable development: Taking stock and looking forwards. *Environment and Planning C: Government and Policy, 26*(1), 17–33.

Joseph, R. (1998). Africa, 1990–1997: From abertura to closure. *Journal of Democracy, 9*(2), 3–18.

Kao, C. (1999). Spurious regression and residual-based tests for cointegration in panel data. *Journal of Econometrics, 90*(1), 1–44.

Kaufman, G. (2004). *The psychology of shame: Theory and treatment of shame-based syndromes.* Springer Publishing Company.

Kaufmann, D., & Kraay, A. (2002). Growth without governance. *Economia, 3*, 169–230.

Kaufmann, D., Kraay, A., & Zoido-Lobatón, P. (1999). *Aggregating governance indicators* (Vol. 2195). World Bank Publications.

Knack, S., & Keefer, P. (1995). Institutions and economic performance: Cross-country tests using alternative institutional measures. *Economics and Politics, 7*(3), 207–227.

Kolstad, C. D., & Krautkraemer, J. A. (1993). Natural resource use and the environment. *Handbook of Natural Resource and Energy Economics, 3*, 1219–1265.

Kyriacou, A. P. (2016). Individualism–collectivism, governance and economic development. *European Journal of Political Economy, 42*, 91–104.

Leff, N. H. (1964). Economic development through bureaucratic corruption. *American Behavioral Scientist, 8*(3), 8–14.

Lehtonen, M. (2004). The environmental–social interface of sustainable development: Capabilities, social capital, institutions. *Ecological Economics, 49*(2), 199–214.

Levin, A., & Lin, C. F. (1993). *Unit root tests in panel data: New results.* Economics Working Paper Series. University of California San Diego.

Levin, A., Lin, C. F., & Chu, C. S. (2002). Unit root tests in panel data: Asymptotic and finite sample properties. *Journal of Econometrics, 108*, 1–24.

Li, Q., & Reuveny, R. (2006). Democracy and environmental degradation. *International Studies Quarterly, 50*(4), 935–956.

Loorbach, D. (2010). Transition management for sustainable development: A prescriptive, complexity-based governance framework. *Governance, 23*(1), 161–183.

López-Menéndez, A. J., Pérez, R., & Moreno, B. (2014). Environmental costs and renewable energy: Re-visiting the environmental Kuznets curve. *Journal of Environmental Management, 145*, 368–373.

Maddala, G. S., & Wu, S. (1999). A comparative study of unit root tests with panel data and a new simple test. *Oxford Bulletin of Economics and Statistics, 61*(S1), 631–652.

Maslin, M. (2008). *Global warming: A very short introduction.* Oxford: Oxford University Press.

Mauro, P. (1995). Corruption and growth. *Quarterly Journal of Economics, 110*, 681–712.

Meadows, D. H., Meadows, D. L., & Randers, J. (1992). *Beyond the limits: Confronting global collapse, envisioning a sustainable future.* Post Mills, VT: Chelsea Green Publishing Co.

Murphy, K., Shleifer, A., & Vishny, R. (1991). The allocation of talent: Implication for growth. *Quarterly Journal of Economics, 106*(2), 503.

Panayotou, T. (1997). Demystifying the environmental Kuznets curve: Turning a black box into a policy tool. *Environment and Development Economics, 2*(4), 465–484.

Pedroni, P. (1999). Critical values for cointegration tests in heterogeneous panels with multiple regressors. *Oxford Bulletin of Economics and statistics, 61*(S1), 653–670.

Pedroni, P. (2001). Purchasing power parity tests in cointegrated panels. *Review of Economics and Statistics, 83*(4), 727–731.

Pesaran, M. H. (2007). A simple panel unit root test in the presence of cross-section dependence. *Journal of Applied Econometrics, 22*(2), 265–312.

Pesaran, M. H., Shin, Y., & Smith, R. P. (1997). *Pooled estimation of long-run relationships in dynamic heterogeneous panels.* Cambridge Working Papers in Economics, 9721.

Pesaran, M. H., Shin, Y., & Smith, R. P. (1999). Pooled mean group estimation of dynamic heterogeneous panels. *Journal of the American Statistical Association, 94*(446), 621–634.

Pesaran, M. H., Shin, Y., & Smith, R. J. (2001). Bounds testing approaches to the analysis of level relationships. *Journal of Applied Econometrics, 16*(3), 289–326.

Povitkina, M. (2015). *Democracy, bureaucratic capacity and environmental quality.* Working Paper Series, July 2015: At the QOG the Quality of Government Institute, Department of Political Science, University of Gothenburg, Sweden.

Rajkumar, A. S., & Swaroop, V. (2008). Public spending and outcomes: Does governance matter? *Journal of Development Economics, 86*(1), 96–111.

Shahbaz, M., Ozturk, I., Afza, T., & Ali, A. (2013). Revisiting the environmental Kuznets curve in a global economy. *Renewable and Sustainable Energy Reviews, 25,* 494–502.

Tamazian, A., & Rao, B. B. (2010). Do economic, financial and institutional developments matter for environmental degradation? Evidence from transitional economies. *Energy Economics, 32*(1), 137–145.

Verhoeven, M., Gupta, M. S., & Tiongson, M. E. (1999). *Does higher government spending buy better results in education and health care?* International Monetary Fund.

Yoo, S. H. (2006). The causal relationship between electricity consumption and economic growth in the ASEAN countries. *Energy Policy, 34*(18), 3573–3582.

Young, O. R. (Ed.). (1997). *Global governance: Drawing insights from the environmental experience.* Cambridge, MA: MIT Press.

Zelli, F., Gupta, A., & Van Asselt, H. (2013). Institutional interactions at the crossroads of trade and environment: The dominance of liberal environmentalism? *Global Governance, 19,* 105–118.

Zhang, Y. J., Jin, Y. L., Chevallier, J., & Shen, B. (2016). The effect of corruption on carbon dioxide emissions in APEC countries: A panel quantile regression analysis. *Technological Forecasting and Social Change, 112,* 220–227.

11

Did Social Protection Assist with Progress Towards the Millennium Development Goals?

Meg Elkins, Simon Feeny,
and Sefa Awaworyi Churchill

1   Introduction

In 2011, the International Labour Organisation (ILO) nominated social protection policies as basic human rights, calling on countries to strengthen their social protection programs. The latest set of United Nations development goals, the Sustainable Development Goals (SDGs), have two explicit targets for social protection under one goal of reducing poverty and another in reducing inequality. Similarly, social protection often plays an important role in the World Bank's Poverty Reduction Strategy Papers. Collectively, international development organisations therefore recognise the potential role social protection plays in achieving better wellbeing outcomes. As of 2014, about

M. Elkins (✉) • S. Feeny • S. Awaworyi Churchill
School of Economics, Finance and Marketing, RMIT University,
Melbourne, VIC, Australia
e-mail: meg.elkins@rmit.edu.au; simon.feeny@rmit.edu.au;
sefa.churchill@rmit.edu

© The Author(s) 2020
S. Awaworyi Churchill (ed.), *Moving from the Millennium to the Sustainable Development Goals*, https://doi.org/10.1007/978-981-15-1556-9_11

80 per cent of developing nations were in the process of strengthening their social protection systems (Fiszbein, Kanbur, & Yemtsov, 2014).

This chapter examines whether higher levels of social protection were associated with greater progress towards the Millennium Development Goals (MDGs). Social protection schemes have been argued to assist the vulnerable and poor in managing risk and preventing them from sliding into deeper poverty. According to Fiszbein et al. (2014), social protection has effectively prevented 150 million people from falling into income poverty. Such schemes are also likely to raise human capital and improve livelihoods. However, social protection schemes rarely cover the entire population. There are questions over whether they are able to reach the poorest members of society and whether they are sufficient to prevent people from experiencing poverty. By using eligibility thresholds to determine inclusion, social protection schemes are also said to be divisive (Ellis, 2012). Further, while it has been shown that social assistance policies are more effective at reducing poverty than social insurance policies (Barrientos, 2011), the different types of social protection which have the greatest impact on development are not well known.

Assessing whether social protection policies were important in spurring progress towards the MDGs is therefore important. The MDGs recognised the multidimensional nature of poverty and expanded development priorities beyond traditional income poverty. The MDGs were eight time-bound goals aimed at *inter alia* halving income poverty, achieving universal primary school enrolment, reducing gender inequality, reducing infant mortality by three-quarters and maternal mortality by two-thirds, reducing the prevalence of infectious diseases, increasing environmental goals such as access to safe water and sanitation and connecting the developed world to the developing world through stronger institutions.

There has been much conjecture about inequality and social protection being missing elements of the original MDGs (Elkins, 2014; Fukuda-Parr, 2010). The recognition of the role that social protection can play in development has not been explicit until the post-2015 development agenda. The new round of goals: the Sustainable Development Goals (SDGs) expand the focus of the MDGs to include goals for environmental sustainability and equity. More specifically, SDG 1 calls for reduced poverty and 1.3 sets out a target for the implementation of "nationally appropriate social protection systems and measures for all, including floors, and by 2030 to achieve substantial coverage of the poor and the vulnerable". SDG 10 calls for reduced inequality and target 10.4 calls for the global community to adopt policies, especially fiscal, wage and social protection policies to progressively achieve greater equality. By examining whether social protection played a role in progress towards the MDGs, policymakers can be better informed about whether and how it can be harnessed to achieve progress towards the current SDGs.

This study uses cross-sectional data for 101 developing countries (Appendix Table 11.6). We examine the relationship between social protection and the MDGs using composite and disaggregated measures of both social protection and MDG progress. Specifically, this chapter seeks to address the following questions: (i) Do higher levels of social protection coverage result in better progress towards the MDGs? and (ii) what components of social protection are effective at spurring specific MDG targets? The findings show a significant association between the composite MDG progress indicator and social protection. Specifically, social assistance and social insurance are found to be positively associated with MDG progress. We find no evidence of labour standards contributing towards the progress of the MDGs.

The remainder of this chapter is organised as follows: the next section provides a brief overview of the literature on MDG progress and evidence of social protection's impact on poverty. The third section outlines the data and methodology used. The fourth section presents and interprets the results from estimating the empirical model. The final section concludes with some policy recommendations.

2 Background and Review of the Literature

Social protection represents a set of actions and policies designed to reduce levels of vulnerability, risk and deprivation, and improve resilience. It is widely believed to be an important mechanism in directly addressing inequality (Barrientos, 2011; Barrientos & Hulme, 2009; Guillaumont & Chauvet, 2001). Social protection is designed not only to respond to risks facing the entire population such as unemployment, disability and old age, but also to structural problems such as poverty and inequality (Cecchini, Filgueira, Martínez, & Rossel, 2015). There are three distinct components of social protection: social insurance, social assistance and labour market standards.

Social insurance includes the contributory and non-contributory schemes designed to protect workers and their households against life-course and work-related contingencies such as maternity, old age, unemployment, sickness and accidents. Social assistance includes programs and policies supporting those vulnerable and in poverty. Examples of social assistance include cash transfers, humanitarian and disaster relief programs, food stamps, school feeding programs, public works, in-kind transfers, housing subsidies and fee waivers. Labour market standards are legal frameworks aimed at ensuring minimum standards for employment and work and safeguarding of workers' rights. Social insurance and labour market standards tend to benefit the middle and upper quintiles income groups and have a longer-term focus, while social assistance is temporary in its nature, and tends to be targeted towards the more vulnerable in the lower income quintiles (Cecchini, 2014).

The specific objectives of social protection programs vary across developing countries and the scale of programs is generally increasing. Latin American countries have gradually adopted a rights-based, systematic and comprehensive approach (Cecchini et al., 2015). In 2003, 12 Latin American countries adopted structural reforms to their pension systems. Mongolia, Romania, Thailand, and Chile have programs that now cover the majority of the population (Mesa-Lago, 2012). Generally, countries across Eastern Europe are more generous in their coverage while the least generous in coverage are those countries in South Asia as well as Middle-East and North Africa. Social insurance schemes and labour regulation are less prevalent in Sub-Saharan Africa. The focus of this region is on social assistance programs (Niño-Zarazúa, Barrientos, Hickey, & Hulme, 2012). Peng and Wong (2010) find that Asian countries sacrificed the welfare state in favour of rapid industrialisation and economic growth, mostly due to the role of family-based social protection. The growth of conditional cash transfers has increased rapidly across the developing world. These short-term income transfer programs tend to improve the living conditions for vulnerable families and serve as a mechanism to improve the human capital of children (Cecchini, 2014).

Over the last 20 years there has been an expansion in non-contributory pensions in Latin America (Mesa-Lago, 2012), while social insurance in Eastern Europe is more institutionalised. Most literature from Latin America focuses on the innovations and effectiveness of the conditional cash transfer programs. But alongside these programs, there has also been an increase in the spread of social insurance policies. In Brazil, reforms and conditional cash transfers in the form of Bolsa Familia have accounted for a 25 per cent fall in inequality in the 2000s (Soares, Soares, Medeiros, & Osório, 2006). Social insurance is more effective in Middle Income Countries (MIC) and social assistance is more effective in Low Income Countries (LIC) (Niño-Zarazúa et al., 2012). However, social protection has not received unanimous support. For example, Ellis (2012) finds that social assistance programs targeted to the chronically deprived tend to be divisive as the beneficiaries eligible infer others on the margin are excluded.

The objective of the chapter is to determine whether social protection has contributed to progress towards the achievement of the MDGs. It builds on the work of Ortiz, Fajth, Yablonski, and Rabi (2012) which examine the effectiveness of social protection programs in delivering outcomes to achieve selected MDGs and equity, but the research only examines country-specific cases rather than empirically examining the relationship for all developing countries.

3   Methods and Data

The social protection data for this research comes from the Atlas of Social Protection Indicators of Resilience and Equity (ASPIRE) database which covers 108 developing countries for the period 2000 to 2013. An MDG progress index variable is drawn from the Centre for Global Development and used as the dependent variable in the empirical model. The variable is an aggregated score of the eight core targets, and if countries are on the required trajectory to meet the goals, their performance is assessed as a 1. This index was only available for the period 2010 to 2013. We also use eight commonly used MDG targets drawn from the World Bank databases as additional dependent variables. These include headcount poverty, hunger, primary school completion, gender equality, infant mortality, maternal mortality, HIV/AIDS prevalence, and access to safe water. These indicators are commonly used in the development literature due to data availability and their capacity to explain progress on the original tenets of the Millennium Declaration (Leo & Barmeier, 2010). There are additional indicators from the World Development Indicators database (discussed below) which we use as control variables. We take the average over the data period to give us a cross-sectional dataset. This allows us to effectively deal with missing values across some countries for selected years.

The following empirical model is specified and estimated:

$$y_i = \alpha + \beta' S_i + \sigma' X_i + \varepsilon_i$$

where y_i denotes country-specific MDG progress variables, including a composite MDG progress variable.

S_i is a vector of social protection variables including the percentage of the population covered by social assistance, social insurance and labour standards. X_i represents a vector of control variables which includes other variables expected to impact on MDG progress. Following the existing literature this vector will include governance, capital formation, GDP per capita, government expenditure on health and education, conflict and initial values of MDG indicators. We also include a set of regional dummies to account for regional fixed effects. ε_i represents the error term and would be estimated using heteroskedasticity robust standard errors. We estimate regressions using ordinary least squares (OLS) adjusted for heteroskedasticity.

4   Results

Table 11.1 presents results for the association between social protection variables and the MDG progress index. We report results for the effects of an average social protection measure, which is derived as the mean of the individual indicators of social protection including labour market regulations, social assistance, social insurance, cash transfers and conditional cash transfers. We also report results for the effects of these individual indicators. These results are based on averaged observations over the period 2010 to 2013 given that the MDGs progress index data covers

Table 11.1 Social protection and MDGs progress index

Variables	(1) MDG progress index	(2) MDG progress index	(3) MDG progress index	(4) MDG progress index	(5) MDG progress index	(6) MDG progress index
Social protection average	0.02**					
	(0.01)					
Labour market regulations		0.01				
		(0.02)				
Social assistance			0.01***			
			(0.01)			
Social insurance				0.01		
				(0.01)		
Cash transfer					0.01	
					(0.01)	
Conditional cash transfer						−0.05
						(0.13)
Governance	0.64*	−0.31	0.53	0.47	0.90**	−0.83*
	(0.33)	(0.40)	(0.34)	(0.36)	(0.40)	(0.45)
GDP growth	0.07*	0.08	0.06	0.08**	0.05	0.08
	(0.03)	(0.05)	(0.04)	(0.04)	(0.04)	(0.06)
GD per capita	−0.00**	−0.00	−0.00	−0.00	−0.00*	0.00
	(0.00)	(0.00)	(0.00)	(0.00)	(0.00)	(0.00)
Health expenditure	−0.11	0.02	−0.12	−0.03	−0.10	0.06
	(0.08)	(0.11)	(0.08)	(0.08)	(0.09)	(0.15)
Education expenditure	−0.25***	−0.52***	−0.22***	−0.24***	−0.28***	−0.97***
	(0.07)	(0.13)	(0.08)	(0.09)	(0.09)	(0.14)
Capital formation	−0.01	−0.02	0.00	−0.01	0.04	0.03
	(0.02)	(0.04)	(0.02)	(0.02)	(0.04)	(0.07)
						(0.03)
Constant	6.17***	7.08***	5.77***	6.00***	5.48***	8.46***
	(0.80)	(1.53)	(0.91)	(0.90)	(1.12)	(1.80)
Observations	95	46	90	84	56	14
R-squared	0.16	0.23	0.16	0.10	0.19	0.73

Notes: Robust standard errors in parentheses. ***$p < 0.01$, **$p < 0.05$, *$p < 0.1$

only this period. Of all the indicators of social protection used, we find that only the coefficients on the overall (averaged) measure of social protection and the sub-components of social assistance are statistically significant. Specifically, results show that social protection and social assistance are associated with greater MDGs progress.

Table 11.2 examines the association between the overall measure of social protection and the individual MDGs indicators drawn from the World Bank databases. We examine effects on the following MDGs: headcount poverty, hunger, primary school enrolment, gender parity ratio, infant mortality, maternal mortality, HIV prevalence and access to water. We find that social protection is negatively associated with poverty, child mortality and maternal mortality. This suggests that a stronger social protection system tends to reduce poverty as well as child and maternal mortality. We also find that social protection is positively associated with primary school enrolment and gender parity ratio. These suggest that stronger social protection is associated with higher primary school enrolment rates and an increase in the ratio of girls to boys enrolled in public and private schools. We do not find evidence of a statistically significant association between social protection and the other indicators including hunger, HIV and access to water.

In Tables 11.3, 11.4, and 11.5, we examine the effects of the social insurance, social assistance and labour market standards sub-components of social protection. Table 11.3 presents results for the effects of social insurance on the various MDG indicators. We find that social insurance is negatively associated with poverty, hunger, child mortality, maternal mortality and the prevalence of HIV. Results also suggest a positive association between social insurance and access to water. These finding indicate that strong social insurance systems tend to reduce poverty, hunger, child and maternal mortality, and the prevalence of HIV. Such systems also tend to improve access to portable water. From Table 11.4, we find that the effect of social assistance is only statistically significant in three of our models. Specifically, results show that social assistance is negatively associated with poverty, maternal mortality and the prevalence of HIV. Thus, strong social assistance systems tend to reduce the prevalence of poverty, maternal mortality and HIV.

Table 11.5 presents results for the effects of labour market regulations. Except for the poverty and hunger models, the coefficient on the labour

Table 11.2 Social protection and MDGs indicators

Variables	(1) Poverty	(2) Hunger	(3) Education	(4) Gender	(5) Child mortality	(6) Maternal mortality	(7) HIV	(8) Water
Social protection average	-0.44***	0.01	0.27***	0.00**	-0.46***	-4.07**	-0.02	-0.00
	(0.11)	(0.06)	(0.10)	(0.00)	(0.12)	(1.93)	(0.03)	(0.09)
Governance	-1.19	-3.65*	1.40	0.02	-7.64**	64.91	0.14	2.46
	(3.86)	(1.92)	(2.19)	(0.01)	(3.32)	(55.35)	(0.96)	(2.16)
GDP growth	-0.87**	-0.04	0.32	0.00**	-0.38	-16.38***	-0.16**	0.36
	(0.36)	(0.20)	(0.28)	(0.00)	(0.67)	(5.98)	(0.07)	(0.31)
GDP per capita	-0.00***	-0.00***	0.00***	0.00	-0.00***	-0.03***	-0.00**	0.00***
	(0.00)	(0.00)	(0.00)	(0.00)	(0.00)	(0.01)	(0.00)	(0.00)
Health expenditure	-1.97*	0.43	0.66	0.00	-0.71	-28.81*	0.29	-0.07
	(1.14)	(0.49)	(0.72)	(0.00)	(1.41)	(16.26)	(0.23)	(0.62)
Education expenditure	1.09	0.16	-0.11	0.00	1.04	43.77	1.33***	0.80
	(1.06)	(0.53)	(0.66)	(0.00)	(1.13)	(31.00)	(0.40)	(0.55)
Capital formation	-0.03	0.10	-0.23	0.00	-0.23	8.12*	-0.02	0.11
	(0.15)	(0.16)	(0.20)	(0.00)	(0.26)	(4.52)	(0.08)	(0.16)
Constant	41.40***	15.47***	78.39***	0.85***	60.06***	231.22	-2.86	70.58***
	(11.58)	(5.74)	(8.04)	(0.05)	(11.08)	(143.02)	(2.08)	(6.37)
Observations	95	82	96	99	101	99	82	101
R-squared	0.47	0.45	0.28	0.26	0.49	0.49	0.32	0.42

Notes: Robust standard errors in parentheses. ***$p < 0.01$, **$p < 0.05$, *$p < 0.1$

Table 11.3 Social insurance and MDGs indicators

Variables	(1) Poverty	(2) Hunger	(3) Education	(4) Gender	(5) Child mortality	(6) Maternal mortality	(7) HIV	(8) Water
Social insurance	−0.40***	−0.20**	−0.01	0.00	−0.36***	−5.39***	−0.09***	0.22***
	(0.11)	(0.08)	(0.07)	(0.00)	(0.12)	(1.42)	(0.03)	(0.08)
Governance	−3.49	−3.99**	4.92*	0.05	−9.27**	−129.50**	0.72	6.04**
	(4.35)	(1.98)	(2.86)	(0.03)	(4.33)	(60.52)	(1.10)	(2.97)
GDP growth	−0.59	0.53	1.47**	0.00	−0.60	−13.70	−0.33	−0.72
	(1.12)	(0.63)	(0.70)	(0.01)	(1.15)	(11.77)	(0.35)	(0.71)
GDP per capita	−0.00***	−0.00***	0.00***	0.00	−0.00***	−0.02*	−0.00	0.00***
	(0.00)	(0.00)	(0.00)	(0.00)	(0.00)	(0.01)	(0.00)	(0.00)
Health expenditure	1.74	0.64	−0.16	−0.00	0.14	31.01*	0.61*	−0.06
	(1.24)	(0.50)	(1.12)	(0.01)	(1.23)	(18.19)	(0.31)	(0.71)
Education expenditure	0.24	−0.82	−0.70	−0.00	0.02	6.45	0.55	0.10
	(0.75)	(0.63)	(0.47)	(0.00)	(0.98)	(13.93)	(0.54)	(0.50)
Capital formation	−0.19	−0.07	−0.20	0.00	−0.24	2.08	−0.03	0.02
	(0.30)	(0.24)	(0.21)	(0.00)	(0.35)	(4.77)	(0.09)	(0.27)
Constant	30.65**	23.03***	88.59***	0.94***	57.17***	142.27	0.78	77.75***
	(12.75)	(6.51)	(8.84)	(0.07)	(15.07)	(192.12)	(3.95)	(8.68)
Observations	84	72	85	88	90	89	73	90
R-squared	0.50	0.46	0.29	0.26	0.57	0.49	0.28	0.49

Notes: Robust standard errors in parentheses. ***$p < 0.01$, **$p < 0.05$, *$p < 0.1$

Table 11.4 Social assistance and MDGs indicators

Variables	(1) Poverty	(2) Hunger	(3) Education	(4) Gender	(5) Child mortality	(6) Maternal mortality	(7) HIV	(8) Water
Social assistance	-0.29**	-0.13	-0.02	-0.00	-0.12	-0.01*	-0.07*	0.08
	(0.13)	(0.11)	(0.10)	(0.00)	(0.12)	(0.00)	(0.03)	(0.11)
Governance	-7.40*	-5.74**	5.92*	0.04	-12.96***	-0.06	-0.30	9.11***
	(4.31)	(2.17)	(3.05)	(0.03)	(4.19)	(0.12)	(1.09)	(3.35)
GDP growth	0.83	1.54	0.73	0.00	1.41	0.04	-0.09	-1.91**
	(1.05)	(0.95)	(0.80)	(0.01)	(1.10)	(0.03)	(0.43)	(0.77)
GDP per capita	-0.00*	-0.00***	0.00	-0.00	-0.00**	0.00	0.00	0.00*
	(0.00)	(0.00)	(0.00)	(0.00)	(0.00)	(0.00)	(0.00)	(0.00)
Health expenditure	2.22**	0.28	0.11	-0.00	0.02	-0.01	0.69**	-0.15
	(1.08)	(0.55)	(1.15)	(0.01)	(0.97)	(0.02)	(0.35)	(0.77)
Education expenditure	0.08	-0.75	-0.50	-0.00	0.13	0.02	0.62	0.01
	(0.57)	(0.62)	(0.37)	(0.00)	(0.62)	(0.03)	(0.49)	(0.51)
Capital formation	-0.32	-0.24	-0.12	0.00*	-0.52	0.01	-0.13	0.07
	(0.28)	(0.28)	(0.24)	(0.00)	(0.35)	(0.01)	(0.09)	(0.23)
Constant	10.71	16.09	92.78***	0.96***	32.73**	-0.78*	-1.60	96.08***
	(12.44)	(9.67)	(10.74)	(0.09)	(14.55)	(0.39)	(4.83)	(11.25)
Observations	89	78	90	93	95	62	78	95
R-squared	0.70	0.50	0.45	0.34	0.79	0.33	0.53	0.61

Notes: Robust standard errors in parentheses. ***$p < 0.01$, **$p < 0.05$, *$p < 0.1$

Table 11.5 Labour market regulation and MDGs indicators

Variables	(1) Poverty	(2) Hunger	(3) Education	(4) Gender	(5) Child mortality	(6) Maternal mortality	(7) HIV	(8) Water
Labour market	0.75***	0.40*	0.12	0.00	0.17	0.02	-0.09	-0.15
	(0.23)	(0.23)	(0.30)	(0.00)	(0.19)	(0.01)	(0.09)	(0.14)
Governance	-9.67**	-7.62**	4.55	0.03*	-13.37**	-0.18	-0.32	5.22
	(4.56)	(2.75)	(5.19)	(0.02)	(5.42)	(0.19)	(1.08)	(3.72)
GDP growth	-1.35	-0.06	1.10	0.00	0.99	-0.05	0.28	0.28
	(1.30)	(0.98)	(1.05)	(0.00)	(1.16)	(0.07)	(0.26)	(1.27)
GDP per capita	-0.00	-0.00*	0.00	-0.00	-0.00	0.00	0.00	0.00
	(0.00)	(0.00)	(0.00)	(0.00)	(0.00)	(0.00)	(0.00)	(0.00)
Health expenditure	1.95	1.25	-1.85	-0.00	1.25	-0.05	0.40	0.08
	(1.33)	(0.75)	(1.78)	(0.01)	(1.03)	(0.04)	(0.51)	(0.89)
Education expenditure	-0.30	-1.48	-0.03	-0.00	-0.30	-0.01	0.60	0.01
	(1.08)	(1.74)	(0.41)	(0.00)	(0.45)	(0.05)	(0.42)	(0.71)
Capital formation	0.29	0.33	0.18	0.00	-0.79**	0.02	-0.14	-0.13
	(0.39)	(0.38)	(0.34)	(0.00)	(0.29)	(0.02)	(0.09)	(0.37)
Constant	-9.48	-3.30	91.15***	0.99***	22.84*	-0.67	-4.01	92.11***
	(18.07)	(9.94)	(18.15)	(0.06)	(13.11)	(0.58)	(4.69)	(15.26)
Observations	49	37	49	50	51	35	38	51
R-squared	0.74	0.65	0.62	0.60	0.87	0.44	0.43	0.56

Notes: Robust standard errors in parentheses. ***$p < 0.01$, **$p < 0.05$, *$p < 0.1$

marker regulations variable is statistically insignificant. The statistically significant results show that labour market regulations tend to increase the prevalence of poverty and hunger. While unexpected, these results could suggest that developing countries are less likely to thrive with very strict labour market regulations.

5   Conclusion

Social protection and its inclusion in the SDGs under the banner of reducing inequality is a clear signal of how the international community values the agenda of tackling inequality and vulnerability. Although the new goal is to reduce inequity, the indicator for social protection does not specify which components of social protection should be employed. This research sought to examine which mechanisms or distinct components of social protection can be associated with progress with the MDGs. Thus, using retrospective MDG data the study is able to identify which forms of social protection are contributing to achieving which MDG goals.

Our results highlight the influence of various social protection dimensions on achieving the majority of the goals even after we take account of regional effects. This finding demonstrates that social protection plays a role not just in reducing income poverty as found by Fiszbein et al. (2014) but is important in reducing other types of poverty in the form of related MDGs. While anecdotally social protection measures appeared to have helped in achieving the MDG progress, our study provides empirical evidence to support this anecdote.

Much of the literature for social protection has focused on the components of social assistance such as the efficacy of the conditional cash transfers on changing behaviours, improving wellbeing and reducing poverty. It is important to recognise that social insurance also plays an equally important role in improving development outcomes. The SDGs seek to achieve a more sustainable, equitable and inclusive world, with a particular focus on improving the livelihoods of the poor and the vulnerable. Goal 1 outlines targets towards reducing poverty and Goal 10 outlines targets towards reducing inequality. Both targets address the need for stronger social protection policies in developing countries. However, the effectiveness of social protection policies to reduce poverty and inequality depends on the coverage and adequacy of benefits. By examining whether social protection played a role in progress towards the MDGs, policymakers can be better informed about whether and how these policies can be harnessed to achieve progress towards the newly developed SDGs.

Appendix

Table 11.6 List of countries

Afghanistan	Gabon	Pakistan
Albania	Georgia	Panama
Argentina	Ghana	Paraguay
Armenia	Guatemala	Peru
Azerbaijan	Honduras	Philippines
Bangladesh	Hungary	Poland
Belarus	India	Romania
Belize	Indonesia	Russia
Benin	Jamaica	Rwanda
Bhutan	Kazakhstan	Senegal
Bolivia	Kenya	Serbia
Botswana	Kyrgyzstan	Sierra Leone
Brazil	Lao PDR	Slovak Republic
Bulgaria	Latvia	Solomon Islands
Burkina Faso	Lebanon	South Africa
Cabo Verde	Lesotho	Sri Lanka
Cambodia	Liberia	Sudan
Cameroon	Lithuania	Swaziland
Central African Republic	Madagascar	Tajikistan
Chile	Malawi	Tanzania
Colombia	Malaysia	Thailand
Comoros	Maldives	Timor-Leste
Congo, Dem. Rep.	Mali	Tonga
Congo, Rep.	Mauritania	Tunisia
Costa Rica	Mauritius	Turkey
Cote D'Ivoire	Mexico	Uganda
Croatia	Moldova	Ukraine
Djibouti	Mongolia	Uruguay
Dominican Republic	Morocco	Venezuela
Ecuador	Mozambique	Vietnam
Egypt	Namibia	Yemen
El Salvador	Nepal	Zambia
Ethiopia	Nicaragua	Zimbabwe
Fiji	Niger	

References

Barrientos, A. (2011). Social protection and poverty. *International Journal of Social Welfare, 20,* 240–249.

Barrientos, A., & Hulme, D. (2009). Social protection for the poor and poorest in developing countries: Reflections on a quiet revolution. *Oxford Development Studies, 37*(4), 439–456.

Cecchini, S. (2014). Social protection, poverty and inequality: A comparative perspective. *Journal of Southeast Asian Economies, 31*(1), 18–39.

Cecchini, S., Filgueira, F., Martínez, R., & Rossel, R. (2015). *Towards universal social protection Latin American pathways and policy tools.* Santiago: Economic Commission for Latin America and the Caribbean (ECLAC).

Elkins, M. (2014). Embedding the vulnerable into the millennium development goals: Social protection in poverty reduction strategy papers. *Journal of International Development, 26*(6), 853–874. https://doi.org/10.1002/jid.2984

Ellis, F. (2012). 'We are all poor here': Economic difference, social divisiveness and targeting cash transfers in Sub-Saharan Africa. *The Journal of Development Studies, 48*(2), 201–214.

Fiszbein, A., Kanbur, R., & Yemtsov, R. (2014). Social protection and poverty reduction: Global patterns and some targets. *World Development, 61,* 167–177. https://doi.org/10.1016/j.worlddev.2014.04.010

Fukuda-Parr, S. (2010). Reducing inequality—The missing MDG: A content review of PRSPs and bilateral donor statements. *IDS Bulletin, 41*(1), 26–35.

Guillaumont, P., & Chauvet, L. (2001). Aid and performance: A reassessment. *Journal of Development Studies, 37*(6), 66–87.

Leo, B., & Barmeier, J. (2010). *Who are the MDG trailblazers? A new MDG progress index.* Center for Global Development Working Paper 222. Retrieved from https://ssrn.com/abstract=1694138

Mesa-Lago, C. (2012). The performance of social security contributory and tax-financed pensions in Central America, and the effects of the global crisis. *International Social Security Review, 65*(1), 1–27. https://doi.org/10.1111/j.1468-246X.2011.01417.x

Niño-Zarazúa, M., Barrientos, A., Hickey, S., & Hulme, D. (2012). Social protection in Sub-Saharan Africa: Getting the politics right. *World Development, 40*(1), 163–176. https://doi.org/10.1016/j.worlddev.2011.04.004

Ortiz, I., Fajth, G., Yablonski, J., & Rabi, A. (2012). Social protection: Accellerating the MDGs with equity. In I. Ortiz, L. M. Daniels, & S. Engilbertsdottir (Eds.), *Child poverty and inequality: New perspectives*. New York: UNICEF.

Peng, I., & Wong, J. (2010). East Asia. In F. G. Castles, S. Leibfried, J. Lewis, H. Obinger, & C. Pierson (Eds.), *The Oxford handbook of the welfare state* (pp. 656–670). Oxford: Oxford University Press.

Soares, F. V., Soares, S. S. D., Medeiros, M., & Osório, R. G. (2006). *Cash transfer programmes in Brazil: Impacts on inequality and poverty*. Working Papers 21, International Policy Centre for Inclusive Growth.

12

Prosperity for the Poor: Religion, Poverty and Development in Sub-Saharan Africa

Samuelson Appau and Matthew Gmalifo Mabefam

1   Introduction

In 2014, Ghana was experiencing a mini-economic crisis and the national currency—the cedi—was falling dramatically in value against the US Dollar. At the peak of the crisis, Archbishop Duncan Williams, one of Ghana's most prominent Pentecostal pastors led his congregation to pray and save the falling cedi (Bokpe, 2014). He declared in his prayers:

> *I hold up the cedi with prayer and I command the cedi to recover and I declare the cedi will not fall; it will not fall any further. I command the*

S. Appau (✉)
School of Economics, Finance and Marketing, RMIT University,
Melbourne, VIC, Australia
e-mail: samuelson.appau@rmit.edu.au

M. G. Mabefam
Department of Anthropology and Development Studies, University of
Melbourne, Parkville, VIC, Australia
e-mail: matthewgmalifo.mabefam@unimelb.edu.au

© The Author(s) 2020
S. Awaworyi Churchill (ed.), *Moving from the Millennium to the Sustainable Development Goals*, https://doi.org/10.1007/978-981-15-1556-9_12

cedi to climb. I command the resurrection of the cedi. I command and release a miracle for the economy.

In the same year, the Ebola virus was ravaging and claiming lives in other African countries. Famous Nigerian Pentecostal pastor, T. B. Joshua sent 4000 bottles of his special "holy water", which he said can cure the Ebola virus, on a private jet to the government of Sierra Leone to distribute the water to those affected by the virus (Griffin, 2014).

What shall we make of these two stories, which may appear strange and even comical to those foreign to Africa? It has been said that the African is "incurably religious" due the perverse and seemingly eternal entrenchment of religion in every aspect of African social, economic and political life (Bonsu & Belk, 2010). There are very few people in the three countries noted above who doubt that religious deities and spirits do influence physical and material outcomes, even if it is a struggling national economy or a global health epidemic. Religion dominates the local imagination of many Africans—regardless of their socio-economic status (Appiah, 1993; Meyer, 2012). In Africa, religious agents, like pastors, are held in high veneration as experts of religious and spiritual matters, which can influence lived experience (Appiah, 1993; Ozanne & Appau, 2019). Religious practices also feature prominently in national celebrations and holidays in various African countries (Gifford, 2004; Meyer, 2012). The numbers factually punctuate Africa's religiosity; no less than 90% of people in Africa are religious (Pew Research Centre, 2017). In summary, people take religion very seriously in Africa.

But sub-Saharan Africa is also the poorest region in the world. According to the United Nations (UN), the region is home to the majority of those living in extreme poverty. The UN's Millennium Development Goals (MDG) and its successor, the Sustainable Development Goals (SDG), both have as their number one priority the goal of eradicating poverty and its related problems like hunger, poor health, unemployment and suitable accommodation with a prime focus on sub-Saharan Africa. But the MDG and SDG are only the most recent and prominent of a long history of efforts by foreign countries and global development agencies to address the canker of poverty in many post-colonial sub-Saharan African countries (Moyo, 2009). Despite all these efforts and some noteworthy achievements, poverty still affects hundreds of millions of lives in sub-Saharan Africa.

However, it is deeply surprising that despite the historically religious nature of Africans and the strong relationship between religion and poverty, little has been said about the role of religion in addressing poverty and poverty alleviation in sub-Saharan Africa (see also Togarasei, 2011). First, the fact that sub-Saharan Africans are extremely religious and poor is not too surprising, considering that many poor countries are also very religious (Awaworyi Churchill, Appau, & Farrell, 2019). Historically, poor people have been very religious and religious institutions have been very supportive of the poor, both in their teachings and philanthropic support (Geremek, 1997). The Catholic church, for example, is the largest non-state philanthropic organization in the world. Thus, it is almost egregious to not consider the role of religion and religious organizations in the conversation on poverty eradication in sub-Saharan Africa. Our purpose here, though, is not to discuss the philanthropic role of religious organizations in poverty alleviation in Africa, although this is important. Our goal here is to remind everyone that there is a harvest of unrecognized local "religious policies" on solving poverty and they are more powerful in shaping local imaginations and agency than most formal policies like the SDGs.

The purpose of this chapter is therefore to understand how religious institutions address poverty in sub-Saharan Africa using the context of the Pentecostal Christian movement and its flagship prosperity doctrine. Pentecostalism is a neo-Evangelical Christian movement that has quickly dominated the religious landscape in many sub-Saharan African countries (Anderson, 2013; Gifford, 2004). The Pentecostal prosperity gospel advances that God provides material prosperity (and eradicates poverty) for all believers who "name and claim" this wealth through monetary donations—known as "seed" offerings—to God (and the church) (Bowler, 2015; Haynes, 2012). We ask, with its materialistic orientation, how does the prosperity gospel affect and address poverty in Africa?

With regard to our research, we examine how the Pentecostal prosperity gospel has redefined poverty and wealth from economic terms into religious (spiritual) terms. We uncover how it has provided a moral agency to its adherents to engage the market economy as an arena of wealth acquisition and poverty eradication that rivals existing development discourses. We also examine the ethics and apologetics of the prosperity gospel concerning its monetary exactments from the poor as a doctrinal condition for its promises of wealth.

Although our focus is not necessarily an empirical paper, where useful to support our purpose, we employ sample data from the first authors' ethnographic study of Pentecostal religion in Ghana from 2013 to 2018. We also use additional evidence from prior research based on empirical studies of the prosperity gospel in other sub-Saharan African countries.

The rest of the chapter is organized as follows. We first provide an overview of poverty and the role of development discourses in poverty alleviation, with particular reference to the MDG and SDG. This is followed by a review of poverty and religion in sub-Saharan Africa, and Pentecostalism and its prosperity gospel in Africa. We then discuss the three main discursive roles of the prosperity gospel in poverty eradication and conclude with an invitation to development stakeholders and researchers to take religion more seriously in the conversation on development and poverty alleviation in Africa.

2   Poverty and Development: From MDGs to SDGs

The story of the world's poor has received widespread coverage and attention—in books and documentaries, popular culture and politics, and on main streets where you might meet someone trying to sign you up to donate to a charity. But often when the world's attention is aroused to the plight of the poor, it is in response to some natural catastrophe such as a tsunami in Thailand or an earthquake in Haiti. And usually the response to such disasters are as rousing as they are immaculate; the sentimental political speeches, the awakening of the sense of duty to the plight of the needy, the grandeurs of celebrities' donations and advocacy, the glittering musical concerts and the immiscible donation boxes in the airport terminals.

In the absence of and post such disasters, the life of the poor is very much no different. According to UNICEF, 22,000 children die each day due to poverty, and they "die quietly in some of the poorest villages on earth, far removed from the scrutiny and the conscience of the world" (Wronka, 2016, p. 57). Some 1.1 billion people in developing countries have inadequate access to water, and 2.6 billion lack basic sanitation. Almost two in three people lacking access to clean water survive on less than $2 a day, with one in three living on less than $1 a day. A look at these statistics could be disheartening and create a hopeless despair (Wronka, 2016).

There have been and still are important efforts aimed at alleviating and someday eradicating poverty. In 2000, the United Nations signed the Millennium Declaration bringing into force the 15-year Millennium Development Goals (MDG) to accelerate development. This declaration contained eight main goals with specific targets and indicators but the primary focus of the MDGs was the eradication of poverty. The MDGs took into consideration the multifaceted nature of poverty and made provisions for economic growth, education, gender equality, maternal health, environmental issues and global partnerships.

As part of the progress made, especially with regard to poverty, the 2015 MDG progress report indicated that "extreme poverty has declined significantly over the last two decades. In 1990, nearly half of the population in the developing world lived on less than $1.25 a day; that proportion dropped to 14 per cent in 2015". In addition, "globally, the number of people living in extreme poverty has declined by more than half, falling from 1.9 billion in 1990 to 836 million in 2015". Most progress has occurred since 2000 and "the proportion of undernourished people in the developing regions has fallen by almost half since 1990, from 23.3 per cent in 1990–1992 to 12.9 per cent in 2014–2016" (United Nations, 2015, p. 3).

Despite these notable successes, the MDGs did not solve global poverty. An examination of the MDGs progress shows that there are significant gaps that still exist regarding the poor, equality, environmental sustainability, conflicts and displacements, lack of sanitary facilities among many others (United Nations, 2015). Some rich countries did not even deliver on their promise to provide official support, which seriously derailed the MDGs objectives (Sachs, 2012). The MDG did not also account for the impact of development on the environment.

At end of the mandate of the MDGs, the UN launched another 15-year development plan dubbed the Sustainable Development Goals (SDGs) which are aimed at sustainable development that accounts for the economic, social and environmental wellbeing of all people (Sachs, 2012). The SDG was launched partly as a response to the huge criticism against the MDGs for not being holistic enough to address global poverty as well as being a top-down approach to development (Ruhil, 2015). The initiation of SDGs is anticipated to address the gaps in MDGs, thus becoming more expansive and inclusive.

But although it is too early to evaluate the SDG's viability, it adopts the same formal bureaucratic approach to development that has often been criticized as counter-productive (see Easterly, 2006; Moyo, 2009). The fact that the SDG's very primary goal remains poverty eradication just like its predecessor, unveils the undying canker of extreme poverty that continues to plague over 700 million people in the world. The experience of poverty is a painful reality of inadequacy that leads to diseases, hunger and death. The objective of this chapter is to address this issue of endemic poverty that plagues many in sub-Saharan Africa, not through the lens of pollical economic policies like the SDGs and MDGs, but through the lens of the single most dominant social institution on the African continent–religion.

3   Poverty and Religion in Sub-Saharan Africa

According to the United Nations, majority of the 700 million people still living in extreme poverty reside in sub-Saharan Africa. It is equally noteworthy that, according to the Pew Research Forum (2017), about 95% of people in Africa say they are religious and almost 90% report that religion is important in their lives. Africa being the most religious and poorest continent is by no means a fluke correlation. Gallup (2010) reported that "in the world's poorest countries—those with average per-capita incomes of $2000 or lower, the median proportion who say religion is important in their daily lives is 95%. In contrast, the median for the richest countries—those with average per-capita incomes higher than $25,000, is 47%. In short, poor countries are also very religious.

This relationship between religion and poverty is not a recent one; it is a historical marriage. Historically, religion has always glorified poverty and modest living as a pathway to piety and submission. Notable religious leaders like Jesus, Mohammed and Buddha were known for their austere lifestyles despite the abundance of wealth that surrounded them. With the explosion of market capitalism, however, the noble veil of poverty was torn, and the poor quickly came to represent the failures of this new dominant economic order (Geremek, 1997). But true to their marriage, even today, religion has been active in addressing the spread and strain of poverty as well as influencing policies aimed at poverty alleviation (Cassidy, 2013; Geremek, 1997; Togarasei, 2011). More recent research suggests that religiosity actually improves the subjective wellbeing of the poor in developing regions like sub-Saharan Africa (Awaworyi Churchill et al., 2019).

It is therefore completely surprising that in the conversation on poverty eradication, the role of religiosity, especially in uber-religious sub-Saharan Africa has remained muted. In the next section, we discuss a particularly rapidly growing Christian movement—Pentecostalism—and its flagship prosperity gospel doctrine that has as its very mandate the eradication of poverty. Presenting a parallel religious solution to the endemic poverty in Africa, the prosperity gospel reimagines the causes of poverty and offers alternative solutions that rival but overlook those proposed by political economic and development projects like MDGs and SDGs.

4   Pentecostalism and the Prosperity Gospel in Africa

Pentecostalism is a neo-Evangelical Christian movement which emphasizes spiritual gifts and experiences with God manifested through glossolalia, healing and prophecies (Anderson, 2013). Although there are many versions of this movement, including classical Pentecostalism, neo-Pentecostalism and Charismatics, we use the term Pentecostalism to denote this family of Christian movements. Pentecostalism has been traced to the Azusa Street Revival in Los Angeles (1906–1915), where Rev Seymour, an African American preacher led a series of dramatic worship meetings resulting in testimonies of miracles and other extraordinary spiritual experiences (Anderson, 2013).

Due to its emphasis on individual experiences and testimonies of God's spirit, Pentecostalism encouraged unbridled spread and experimentation of its Christian beliefs (Anderson, 2013; Appau & Awaworyi Churchill, 2019). With no central authority or organization, Pentecostalism spread globally, taking on local concerns and adapting to local needs wherever it went (Anderson, 2013; Kalu, 2008; Meyer, 2012; Robbins, 2009). Today, Pentecostal membership numbers over 500 million globally—a quarter of the world's Christian population—and has been posited as the fastest growing religious movement in the world, with a member gained every second (Pulitzer Center, 2019). But nowhere is the growth of Pentecostalism more dramatic than sub-Sharan Africa. In 2006, 12% of Africans—about 900 million people—were Pentecostals (Pew Research Centre, 2017). Today, in most Christian-dominated countries in Africa like Ghana, Nigeria, Kenya, Zambia, Zimbabwe and South Africa, about half of the population are Pentecostals and it is expected that by 2050, almost everyone in these countries will join the movement (Pulitzer Center, 2019).

Many reasons have been proffered for Pentecostalism's success in Africa (see e.g. Kalu, 2008; Meyer, 2004, 2012), but a key reason has been its flagship prosperity doctrine. The prosperity gospel—also known as the "health and wealth" gospel—declares that God provides material wealth and prosperity for all believers as well as healing from all diseases (Bowler, 2015; Haynes, 2012; Maxwell, 1998). The prosperity gospel is chiefly inspired by the Biblical scriptures of 3 John 2 that declares, "Beloved, I wish above all things that thou mayest prosper and be in health, even as thy soul prospers." In Africa, Pentecostal preachers therefore declare that God can deliver them from the spirit of poverty and bring them wealth and health (Bonsu & Belk, 2010; Togarasei, 2011). But these gains can only be precipitated through monetary offerings to God (the church); give in order to receive more—a necessary sacrifice of faith (Bonsu & Belk, 2010).

In the next sections, we examine the development implications of this doctrine that has as its very purpose the eradication of poverty (and diseases) through divinely orchestrated wealth. How does the prosperity gospel understand the causes of poverty and seek to address it? What are the ethical implications of this doctrine, considering it comes at a monetary cost to those who already have little economic means? We address these questions through three main discussions.

5 "Blessed": Eradicating The "Spirit of Poverty" through The Divine Economy

It is the blessing of the Lord that makes rich, And He adds no sorrow to it. (Proverbs 10:22)

Development studies root the source and solution to poverty in structural factors like education, free and effective markets, aid, democracy and enabling government policies (Banerjee & Duflo, 2011; Sen, 1999). The Pentecostal prosperity gospel, conversely, sidesteps the political economy and rather roots poverty eradication and the acquisition of wealth in a divine economy of blessings; those who are blessed are rich and those who are not blessed are poor (Maxwell, 1998). Poverty (wealth) is not a secular matter of economic resource distribution and acquisition; in this enchanted worldview, it is a matter of spiritual and religious capital.

Like many (Pentecostal) Christians, believers in the prosperity gospel hold that all wealth comes from God and it is God who provides material success as blessings to those who "name and claim it" in faith (Bowler, 2015; Hladky, 2012). Those who give more to God (and the church) invest in the bank of God and are bound to reap more blessings of material wealth and prosperity than those who do not (Bowler, 2015). Thus preachers encourage believers to give more money to God (the church) to engender God's blessings. Without God's blessings that bring wealth—as the above Biblical quote often referenced by prosperity gospel preachers and believers alike suggests—any individual agency or structural attempt to acquire material wealth will be futile and bring only more sorrow.

One of our informants, George, sells second-hand electronic products like used fridges, microwaves and televisions that he imports from Europe. He says, before he converted to Pentecostalism, he had been struggling with his business for many years in the past. Despite heavy cash injections into his business from his older siblings in the United States, his business kept failing and he lived on the margins of poverty. The main problem George faced was that customers would often return items they bought from him as faulty even though the items would mysteriously start working again after he had refunded the person's money. He was not making any sales and the items lost value or functionality over time causing him to lose the money he had invested in importing them. But once he became a Pentecostal, he understood that what he was missing was God's blessing over his business. With God's blessings acquired through his conversion to Pentecostalism and sowing a seed of monetary offering in church for his business, he reported a change in fortune for his business. He reflectively stated in the interview: *"If God does not bless you, even if they give you a room full of money to do business, you will still not succeed. You will burn (lose) all the money and end up in square one … you will still be poor".*

One of the longstanding debates in development is the usefulness of foreign aid (Banerjee & Duflo, 2011). To Pentecostals like George, aid, whether from foreign countries or agencies, or as remittances from family abroad is immaterial to lifting people out of poverty into wealth if it is not preconditioned by God's blessings. And these macro-level issues are not found missing in the sermons of Pentecostal preachers. Pastor Alfred of the Glorious Word Ministry (pseudonym) in Accra reflected on this to his congregation in a sermon one Sunday that the failure of aid to lift many African countries like Ghana out of poverty is because these countries are not blessed like Israel and live with the "spirit of poverty". A preacher in Maxwell's (1998, p. 360) study explained to his congregation:

> *People are trying to give help to third world persons. They find third world persons do not prosper … Billions and billions of dollars have been poured out. Hallelujah! But nothing is happening in Africa. Africa is remaining under the Spirit of Poverty.*

Poverty, Pentecostals believe, is as an evil spirit that results from sin—a transgression of God's law—because it is not the will of God for his children to be poor (Gifford, 2004; Maxwell, 1998). Pentecostals attribute sin that brings poverty to two main issues. First, Pentecostals believe that Africa's religious history of traditional religion involving totemism, ancestral worship and idolatry, which are all un-Christian and sinful, invited the curses of God on Africans. The founder of the Zimbabwean Assemblies of God Africa, Ezekiel Guti noted in one of his writings:

> *Any nation or country which worships idols or animals will have problems. Go to any nation where they worship idols or cows, these countries have problems and are poor. I say let's start with God.* (Guti, 1989)

Guti's admonition, like other Pentecostal pastors, is to adopt the Christian God and be blessed like Western countries who are rich because their history is steeped in Christianity (Haynes, 2012; Maxwell, 1998).

Thus, Pentecostals advance a need to "break from the past", a necessary rupture from their ancestral ties to rid themselves of the residue of these ancestral curses that bring poverty (Gifford, 2004; Meyer, 1998). As Naomi Haynes' Zambian informants told her, for Zambia to prosper, Zambia must be saved from the sins of the past and become a true Christian country (Haynes, 2012). At Pentecostal services like those at the Believers of Christ Church (pseudonym) in Kumasi, Ghana, where we did fieldwork, the pastor frequently led members in prayers to denounce their ancestral lineage and to "kill" every ancestral curse that was derailing their God-ordained destiny to prosper materially.

We observe here that Pentecostals do note structural causes of poverty similar to what development scholars may call a poverty cycle that results from ancestral poverty: people who are poor often come from historically poor families. Development advocates thus advance the need to help families and individuals break out of this poverty cycle that has plagued their families through education and aid (Banerjee & Duflo, 2011; Sachs, 2005). We see a parallel logic in the divine economy of the prosperity gospel here where they diagnose an (spiritual) ancestral trap—resulting from religious choice, not economic choice—that explains poverty, and similarly encourages members to break from this ancestral poverty trap through prayers. With a worldview that locates poverty and wealth in spiritual (religious) terms, we unravel a parallel religious logic that suggests that such a spiritual (religious) cause of poverty begets a spiritual (religious) solution. This is followed by a change in religious affiliations from traditional (non-Christian) religion to (Pentecostal) Christianity.

In much post-colonial African polity and discourse, Christianity, and Pentecostalism in particular, is the modern structure that necessarily usurps traditional African religions; the new overthrows the old (Appau & Awaworyi Churchill, 2019; Appiah, 1993; Mbembe, 2001). Thus, for many sub-Saharan Africans, to be Christian (Pentecostal) is to be modern (Gifford, 2004; Robbins, 2009); to be modern is to be developed (Mbembe, 2001); and to be developed is to be affluent, and not poor (Togarasei, 2011). To "break with the past" then, for the Pentecostal, is to disavow their history of poverty and the impoverishment of tradition, and to "name and claim" the present, the modern and the promise of blessed wealth.

A second source of sin that brings poverty for the Pentecostal is self-indulgence or sinful lifestyles and consumption (Appau & Awaworyi Churchill, 2019; Maxwell, 1998). These include the consumption of alcohol, smoking, gambling, and watching movies. They also include sexual indulgences like extra- and pre-marital sex, orgies, pornography, and abortion. Sin also includes socially and legally unacceptable acts like theft and murder as well as emotional excesses like greed, bitterness, envy and jealousy (Gifford, 2004; Maxwell, 1998; Togarasei, 2011). These sinful acts and lifestyles invite the anger of God and become a hindrance to the believer's blessings of wealth. Abena (pseudonym), a member at Pastor Alfred's church says that *"if you live a sinful lifestyle like drinking and sleeping with other people's husband like this lady who lives here (referring to another tenant), you can call yourself a Christian, go to church, pay offerings and everything but God will not listen to your prayers and bless you."* Thus, Pentecostals advance a moral onslaught on these lifestyles that may become barriers to their blessings (Appau & Awaworyi Churchill, 2019).

On one hand, these lifestyles—like drinking, smoking and gambling—can lead to unproductive expenditures and be a drain on income. They are also addictive and can be harmful to the body and negatively affect financial and physical wellbeing. So on one hand, reining in these lifestyles save costs and expenditures that can make low-income people even poorer, unproductive, unhappy, unable to escape their poverty or low-income or build more wealth (see also Maxwell, 1998; Togarasei, 2011). These monies can otherwise be spent on productive self and family expenses like food, education, rent and health.

On the other hand, we can also see how spending on these lifestyles and consumption can compete with giving to the church. If people are spending their disposable income on alcohol or cigarettes, then they will not have enough to give offerings in church. Thus, it is in the church's best interest to rein in such lifestyles by members, even though are no clear biblical and theological prohibitions against drinking, smoking or gambling. Regardless, the Pentecostal prosperity gospel has a loud and notable control over believers' understanding of poverty and wealth and how to escape it that at once mimics and differs from what development scholars advance.

6   God = Market? Moral Agency and the Pursuit of Wealth

On the matter of the ethics of material wealth, historically, Catholic and Protestant teachings have mostly sought to rein in the excesses of wealth accumulation and display (Sethi & Steidlmeier, 1993). They posit that even Jesus lived an austere life, with nowhere to lay his head, encouraging his followers not to pursue earthly wealth but rather store up treasures in heaven (Matthew 6:19–21). Jesus did further warn against the dangers of wealth, saying, "*it is easier for a camel to go through the eye of a needle than for a rich man to enter the kingdom of God*" (Matthew 19:24). And so did the Apostle Paul who noted in his letter to his protégé, Timothy: "*For the love of money is the root of evil*" (Timothy 6:10).

These more traditional views of Christianity have often glorified poverty and vilified the pursuit of individual wealth that is endemic in modern neoliberal global market capitalism (Geremek, 1997). In stating his vision for the church after his election, Pope Francis remarked that he desired "a poor Church, and for the poor" (Cassidy, 2013). Pope John Paul criticized the "idolatry of the market", which leads to the inequality of extreme wealth for a few and extreme poverty for many. In that same school of thought, in his first papal exhortation, Pope Francis offered an unapologetic critique of the market and capitalism stating:

> *The culture of prosperity deadens us; we are thrilled if the market offers us something new to purchase. In the meantime all those lives stunted for lack of opportunity seem a mere spectacle; they fail to move us … While the earnings of the minority are growing exponentially, so, too, is the gap separating the majority from the prosperity enjoyed by those happy few.*

The Pope ended on a call to the rich to use their resources to serve and help the poor. In some sense, the underlying ideology of development projects like the MDGs and SDGs appear to take up the Pope's exhortation to end global poverty. But even development scholars and agencies, like most economists, may not share in the papal critique of market capitalism, believing that market capitalism has done more for the poor than any other economic model before it (Cassidy, 2013; Prahalad, 2009; Sachs, 2005).

Nonetheless, the growing apotheosis of the market is not lost on reality—and seemingly not on the Pope—with the increasing global presence, power and trust in the market growing exponentially day by day (Cassidy, 2013). To many people, especially economists, the market is akin to God—powerful, self-sufficient and self-reliant, omnipresent but invisible, mysterious, and inescapable (Wood, 2015). Importantly, the market holds in its power the indeterminate ability to enrichen and to impoverish. All these attributes of the market economy and neoliberal capitalism attract and ensnare many who seek its promise of wealth at all costs (Wood, 2015); this is the idolatry of the market that past and the present pope harshly criticize.

Birthed in the globalizing echelons of American capitalism, Pentecostalism and its prosperity gospel does not share in the Catholic Church's traditional anti-market sentiments (Appau & Awaworyi Churchill, 2019). In fact, many researchers have noted that Pentecostalism and its prosperity gospel is very much a pro-market and neoliberal enterprise (Bonsu & Belk, 2010; Gifford, 2004; Haynes, 2012; Robbins, 2009). In the prosperity gospel, "Pentecostalism meets neoliberal enterprise" (Comaroff & Comaroff, 2000, p. 314).

Many Pentecostal pastors start and manage their churches (or ministries) as entrepreneurial activities that pursue entrepreneurial rewards from the marketplace of believers. They see their congregation as customers who pay for the church services with their time, money and loyalty. And they employ modern marketing and advertising techniques "with the marketing acumen of Madison avenue" through social and mass media to attract prospective customers (Grassie, 2010, p. 67). Ukah (2008) has aptly referred to the popular use of outdoor advertising on the major roads and streets of Nigeria to market Pentecostal churches as "roadside Pentecostalism". In short, Pentecostalism roundly embraces and engages in the secular market economy.

As we have noted earlier, in Pentecostal understandings, material wealth is a blessing, and poverty is sin. Pentecostal churches therefore do not share in the Pope's aspirations for a poor church. On the contrary, Pentecostals aspire towards rich churches; it is not lost on them that the Catholic Church is the richest church, and one of the richest organizations in the world. Many Pentecostal pastors themselves therefore live large; they own large mansions, fleets of luxury cars, private jets and large bank accounts (Appau & Awaworyi Churchill, 2019). They also provide entrepreneurial teachings to their congregation on how to succeed in the market (Maxwell, 1998). Despite popular criticism of this lifestyle by Pentecostal pastors, their members see these lavish lifestyles of their pastors as justified evidence of God blessing these pastors. They reason that it would be counter-evidence for a pastor to be poor and yet preach the material blessings of God to their congregation (Hladky, 2012). Some Pentecostals even believe that it is a sin to not display your wealth for the world to see the evidence of God's blessings in your life (Haynes, 2012).

Pentecostals therefore see the market as their avenue to end their poverty and gain wealth; it is the space that God uses to materially bless them for their monetary seeds and disavowal of sin. Many economists trust the market to reward those who risk their resources in the market, and certainly see it as a more effective solution to poverty eradication than, for example, aid (Easterly, 2006). Many African Pentecostals also engage the market as petty traders and investors, risking their resources, but understand the mysteries and uncertainties of the market (Lindhardt, 2009). Joel, an elder in Pastor Alfred's church remarked of engaging in the market in an interview: *"It is like a gamble, and you need to keep betting until you win"*. He understood the risk involved.

But like Joel, many African Pentecostals trust God to reward them in the market and not the market itself because they believe that God can control the market in their favour. Sowing seeds of monetary donation in church is therefore an insurance premium they pay to God to hedge their risks and investments in the market. They sow their seeds in church and reap the blessings in the market. Thus, Pentecostals who sow seeds in church feel entitled to the wealth of the market and pursue it zealously as their moral right. A Zambian Pentecostal remarked: *"We are entitled to prosperity. That is ours, this very thing, this is God's will … that we prosper. So in everything, we should prosper. We should be prospering more than non-believers"* (Haynes, 2012, p. 134). To Pentecostals, wealth is good, the market is good, and it is God's will for them to claim and flaunt the wealth that the market has to offer. It is due to this attitude towards the market that Berger (2008) calls Pentecostals "intentional Weberians".

7   Apology for the Apologetics: On the Veracity and Ethics of the Prosperity Gospel

In view of its popularity in the world's poorest subregion and continent, we must necessarily interrogate the veracity and ethics of the prosperity gospel and its promises. Does it deliver on its promise to the poor, and are its promises and practices ethical? We must begin first with the critics because they are in the majority, research-wise, that is.

Many critics observe that the Prosperity gospel has not delivered on its promises of "spectral wealth" for the poor (Bonsu & Belk, 2010; Comaroff & Comaroff, 2000; Dada, 2004; Gifford, 2004). Poor members remain poor, yet continue to make monetary donations that enrich their pastors; money that otherwise could have been spent on more productive expenditures like food, healthcare and children's education (Bonsu & Belk, 2010).

Even some African Pentecostals admit that there are charlatans—"false prophets"—masquerading as true "men of God", who only seek to enrich themselves at believers' expense (Haynes, 2012). Critics do not distinguish between authentic and false pastors; they disavow the prosperity gospel in principle because they see it as a gimmick that allows "tricksters" to take advantage of poor and desperate people looking for hope to better their situation (Bonsu & Belk, 2010).

In this regard, Gifford (2004) has poignantly linked the mass uptake of Pentecostalism in sub-Saharan Africa in the 1970s and 1980s as a period that was also the peak of post-colonial political upheaval, mass poverty and teeming youth unemployment in the region. He argues that the Pentecostal prosperity gospel's promises of wealth to believers was a key selling point—and differentiation from Catholic and Protestant churches at the time—for the many poor and religious Africans who historically did not discount divine (spiritual) interventions in their material wellbeing (Appiah, 1993; Gifford, 2004).

Consistent with their reservations, in response to the issue of ethics, critics respond in the negative. Critics challenge the ethics of a doctrine that takes the poor's little income to enrich a pastor. Because they do not accept the veracity of the prosperity gospel's promises, critics conclude that the prosperity gospel is misleading, deceptive and unethical (Bonsu & Belk, 2010; Dada, 2004).

But if it does not deliver on its promises, and is misleading, why do many still believe in it, and why is there no regulation to rein the prosperity gospel in? A simple answer to the latter question is that it is near impossible to regulate religiosity and religious beliefs in sub-Saharan Africa because almost everyone—including state officials and regulators—in the subregion is religious. On the matter of the former question, we must turn to the apologetics of the prosperity gospel.

Perhaps one of the most glaring challenges of most criticisms of the prosperity gospel is that they are not based on believers' accounts but rather on preacher sermons and books (Haynes, 2012; see also Hladky, 2012). Conversely, advocates and sympathizers of the prosperity gospel mostly use believers as their data sources (see e.g. Haynes, 2012; Lindhardt, 2009; Marshall, 2009; Premawardhana, 2012). These researchers and their informants admit that the prosperity gospel does not readily and evidently deliver on its promises of wealth but it gives members other non-monetary value (see Premawardhana, 2012).

First, the prosperity gospel gives (moral) agency to believers to work towards addressing their poverty through the market as we found. In many of the churches we studied, some believers confirmed noticing an increase in their customer base and their profits from their businesses and petty trading. Some others gave public testimonies in church about also getting a job (and promotions) and passing their exams as evidence of God's blessings for their seeds. For some, who may otherwise despair, it gives them hope to face the difficulties of poverty because the act of giving is in and of itself transformational (Premawardhana, 2012).

Notably, rather than wealth gained, members pointed to saved costs as evidence of God's blessings. Our informants noted they rarely fall sick and that saves them costly medical bills that they could otherwise not afford; this, they said, was evidence of God's blessings (see also Lindhardt, 2009). Some believers also noted that they received financial support from their church and more affluent fellow members in times of need (Bonsu & Belk, 2010; Premawardhana, 2012). Clearly, believers do not predominantly account for their blessings in the stated terms of the prosperity gospel as critics do.

But there is, however, some research which insists that the prosperity gospel does deliver on its promises of wealth. For example, Maxwell (1998) noted that his Zimbabwean Pentecostal informants actually experienced better social mobility through literacy, better financial management and industriousness in the marketplace compared to their non-Pentecostal counterparts. But his ethnographic evidence does not afford him such grand claims even if his data supports his conclusions within his context (see also Togarasei, 2011).

Another apologetic for the prosperity gospel has to do with the timeframe of expected blessings of material returns. Whereas much prosperity gospel sermons suggest that returns are immediate, many believers accept God's return blessings is temporally indeterminate; it can be gradual and it can take time (Haynes, 2012; Lindhardt, 2009). Could these all be post-hoc rationalization for their cognitive dissonance of failed promises of monetary wealth? Possibly. Marshall (2009) rather sees this as a religious technology of the self that empowers the Pentecostal subject. To the apologetics, therefore, the prosperity gospel delivers value to keep their members engaged, even if it is not always exactly what is promised.

What is our own verdict in all of this? Our own perspective is that both critics and apologetics are right. But our interest is not on the veracity or ethics of the prosperity gospel, even though these are important. Our position is that for all of its flaws and value, the prosperity gospel is not too different from many product and service offerings in the market-place. For example, the stock market, beauty products and cosmetics, self-help services, gambling and the lottery, and even University education promise much value to consumers, yet these promises elude many while only a few benefit. The ethics of these offerings invite even papal critique but their sellers and consumers mostly insist they are good value for money. Our position is that we cannot disentangle the prosperity gospel from these other service offerings in the marketplace because they are all children of the same mother—the capitalist market economy.

Perhaps critics assume a necessary separation of religious practice from the market; what has God got to do with Caesar? But even if we set aside the Biblical inspiration for the prosperity gospel, it is erroneous to assume that religion and the market have ever been separate; they have not. Certainly in Africa, long before colonialism and its ideals of separating state and market from religion, the indigenes did not so differentiate, and what is known as religion today was then and even now never separate from the market or the state (Appau & Awaworyi Churchill, 2019; Appiah, 1993). This is why local preachers believe their prayers can save the local currency from depreciation. If we can accept the intertwine of religion and the market, then we can accept that religious services like the Pentecostal prosperity gospel are market services, and we can evaluate them the same way we evaluate similar market services. And that is a necessary start for a more interesting conversation on the matter beyond veracity and ethics.

8   Conclusion

In this chapter, we have examined the relationship between the Pentecostal prosperity gospel and poverty in sub-Saharan Africa showing how the former speaks to the concerns of the poor in the region and offers its own religio-market solutions towards poverty alleviation. Regardless of the reader's position on the doctrine or its prescriptions, Pentecostalism and the prosperity gospel remind us that we cannot speak about poverty—especially in Africa—without recourse to religion. On the matter of development in Africa, as we have argued, religion always has an opinion and its influence is a soft power that can, and does, retool formal economic projects like the MDGs and SDGs for its many adherents.

There is little to suggest that religiosity will decline in Africa, regardless of its economic development. On the contrary, all factors indicate that Africa will only get more religious, and particularly sub-Sharan Africa, more Pentecostal. For all its potential flaws, religion wields the moral compass of believers, including their productivity, consumption and economic engagement. We conclude this chapter, therefore, by inviting all development stakeholders to take the inimitable role of religion in Africa seriously. In the fight against extreme poverty in Africa, there is certainly more to be gained by including religious agents and institutions than overlooking them. In Africa, no one can escape the African God.

References

Anderson, A. (2013). *An introduction to Pentecostalism: Global Charismatic Christianity*. Cambridge: Cambridge University Press.

Appau, S., & Awaworyi Churchill, S. (2019). Bridging cultural categories of consumption through indeterminacy: A consumer culture perspective on the rise of African Pentecostal-Charismatic Christianity. *Journal of Consumer Culture, 19*(1), 125–145.

Appiah, K. A. (1993). *In my father's house: Africa in the philosophy of culture*. Oxford: Oxford University Press.

Awaworyi Churchill, S., Appau, S., & Farrell, L. (2019). Religiosity, income and wellbeing in developing countries. *Empirical Economics, 56*(3), 959–985.

Banerjee, A. V., & Duflo, E. (2011). *Poor economics: A radical rethinking of the way to fight global poverty*. New York: PublicAffairs.

Berger, P. (2008). 'You can do it!' Two cheers for the prosperity gospel. *Books and Culture, 14*.

Bokpe, S. (2014). Duncan-Williams defends prayer for cedi. Retrieved June 21, 2019, from https://www.graphic.com.gh/news/politics/duncan-williams-defends-prayer-for-cedi.html

Bonsu, S. K., & Belk, R. W. (2010). Marketing a new African God: Pentecostalism and material salvation in Ghana. *International Journal of Nonprofit and Voluntary Sector Marketing, 15*(4), 305–323.

Bowler, K. (2015). Daily grind: The spiritual workday of the American prosperity gospel. *Journal of Cultural Economy, 8*(5), 630–636.

Cassidy, J. (2013, December 3). *Pope Francis's challenge to global capitalism.* Retrieved from http://www.newyorker.com/news/john-cassidy/pope-franciss-challenge-to-global-capitalism

Comaroff, J., & Comaroff, J. L. (2000). Millennial capitalism: First thoughts on a second coming. *Public Culture, 12*(2), 291–343.

Dada, A. O. (2004). Prosperity gospel in Nigerian context: A medium of social transformation or an impetus for delusion? *ORITA: Ibadan Journal of Religious Studies, 36*(1–2), 95–107.

Easterly, W. R. (2006). *The white man's burden: Why the West's efforts to aid the rest have done so much ill and so little good.* New York: Penguin.

Gallup. (2010, August 31). Religiosity highest in world's poorest nations.

Geremek, B. (1997). *Poverty: A history.* Oxford: Blackwell.

Gifford, P. (2004). *Ghana's new Christianity: Pentecostalism in a globalizing African economy.* Bloomington: Indiana University Press.

Grassie, W. (2010). *The new sciences of religion: Exploring spirituality from the outside in and bottom up.* New York: Palgrave Macmillan.

Griffin, A. (2014). Ebola outbreak: Millionaire preacher TB Joshua 'sends 4,000 bottles of'. Retrieved June 19, 2019, from https://www.independent.co.uk/news/world/millionaire-preacher-sends-4000-bottles-of-holy-water-as-ebola-cure-9674136.html

Guti, E. (1989). *The sacred book of ZAOGA forward in faith to the leaders and the Saints I.* Waterfalls: ZAOGA.

Haynes, N. (2012). Pentecostalism and the morality of money: Prosperity, inequality, and religious sociality on the Zambian Copperbelt. *Journal of the Royal Anthropological Institute, 18*(1), 123–139.

Hladky, K. (2012). I double-dog dare you in Jesus' name! Claiming Christian wealth and the American Prosperity Gospel. *Religion Compass, 6*(1), 82–96.

Kalu, O. (2008). *African Pentecostalism: An introduction.* Oxford: Oxford University Press.

Lindhardt, M. (2009). More than just money: The faith gospel and occult economies in contemporary Tanzania. *Nova Religio: The Journal of Alternative and Emergent Religions, 13*(1), 41–67.

Marshall, R. (2009). *Political spiritualities: The Pentecostal revolution in Nigeria.* Chicago: University of Chicago Press.

Maxwell, D. (1998). 'Delivered from the spirit of poverty?': Pentecostalism, prosperity and modernity in Zimbabwe. *Journal of Religion in Africa, 28*(Fasc. 3), 350–373.

Mbembe, A. (2001). *On the postcolony.* University of California Press.

Meyer, B. (1998). 'Make a complete break with the past': Memory and post-colonial modernity in Ghanaian Pentecostalist discourse. *Journal of Religion in Africa/Religion en Afrique, 28*(3), 316.

Meyer, B. (2004). Christianity in Africa: From African independent to Pentecostal-charismatic churches. *Annual Review of Anthropology, 33*, 447–474.

Meyer, B. (2012). Religious and secular, 'spiritual' and 'physical' in Ghana. In C. Bender & A. Taves (Eds.), *What matters? Ethnographies of value in a not so secular age* (pp. 86–118). New York: Colombia University Press.

Moyo, D. (2009). *Dead aid: Why aid is not working and how there is a better way for Africa.* Farrar, Straus and Giroux.

Ozanne, J. L., & Appau, S. (2019). Spirits in the marketplace. *Journal of Marketing Management, 35*(5–6), 451–466.

Pew Research Centre. (2017). *The changing global religious landscape.* Retrieved August 4, 2019, from http://www.pewforum.org/2017/04/05/the-changing-global-religious-landscape/

Prahalad, C. K. (2009). *The fortune at the bottom of the pyramid, revised and updated 5th anniversary edition: Eradicating poverty through profits.* FT Press.

Premawardhana, D. (2012). Transformational tithing: Sacrifice and reciprocity in a neo-Pentecostal church. *Nova Religio: The Journal of Alternative and Emergent Religions, 15*(4), 85–109.

Pulitzer Center (2019). Atlas of Pentecostalism: An interactive visual guide to the world's most rapidly growing religious movement. Gateway Religion and Power. Washington, DC.

Robbins, J. (2009). Pentecostal networks and the spirit of globalization: On the social productivity of ritual forms. *Social Analysis, 53*(1), 55–66.

Ruhil, R. (2015). Millennium development goals to sustainable development goals: Challenges in the health sector. *International Studies, 52*(1–4), 118–135.

Sachs, J. (2005). *The end of poverty: Economic possibilities for our time.* New York: Penguin Press.

Sachs, J. D. (2012). From millennium development goals to sustainable development goals. *The Lancet, 379*(9832), 2206–2211.

Sen, A. (1999). *Development as freedom.* Oxford: Oxford University Press.

Sethi, S. P., & Steidlmeier, P. (1993). Religions's moral compass and a just economic order: Reflections on Pope John Paul II's Encyclical Centesimus Annus. *Journal of Business Ethics, 12*(12), 901–917.

Togarasei, L. (2011). The Pentecostal gospel of prosperity in African contexts of poverty: An appraisal. *Exchange, 40*(4), 336–350.

Ukah, A. F. K. (2008). Roadside Pentecostalism: Religious advertising in Nigeria and the marketing of charisma. *Critical Interventions, 2*(1–2), 125–141.

United Nations. (2015). *Transforming our world: The 2030 agenda for sustainable development.* New York, NY: United Nations. Retrieved August 19, 2019, from https://sustainabledevelopment.un.org/post2015/transformingourworld.

Wood, F. (2015). Spirits in the marketplace: The market as a site of the occult in the South and West African supernatural and contemporary capitalist cosmologies. *Folklore, 126*(3), 283–300.

Wronka, J. (2016). Sharing my story: Representing social work at the UN and select local human rights activism. *Journal of Human Rights and Social Work, 1*(1), 50–60.

13

Building Safe and Resilient Cities: Lessons from Ghana

Festival Godwin Boateng

1   Introduction

Building collapses are becoming a common, tragic occurrence in cities in developing countries—particularly Africa and Asia (Asante & Sasu, 2018; Boateng, 2017a, 2017b, 2018a, 2018b, 2019). In Kampala, Uganda, Alinaitwe and Ekolu (2014) counted 54 building collapse deaths and 122 injuries in just four years (between 2004 and 2008). In Nigeria, Windapo and Rotimi (2012) compiled over 112 cases between December 1978 and April 2008 in Lagos alone, the largest city in Nigeria and on the African continent. To put the scale of the problem in Africa's most populous country into perspective, 29 deaths and 76 injuries were reportedly recorded from 12 building collapses across the country within just four months (February to May 2019—see Adugbo, Ibrahim, & Awka, 2019). Other countries on the continent have also recorded many of such

F. G. Boateng (✉)
School of Global, Urban and Social Studies, RMIT University,
Melbourne, VIC, Australia

© The Author(s) 2020
S. Awaworyi Churchill (ed.), *Moving from the Millennium to the Sustainable Development Goals*, https://doi.org/10.1007/978-981-15-1556-9_13

fatal incidents in recent years. For instance, a World Bank report (Moullier, 2015) noted what it referred to as a particularly strong pattern of spontaneous building collapses in Kenya over the past 20 years predominantly in the cities. Tchamba and Bikoko (2016), Alinaitwe and Ekolu (2014), to cite but a few, have reported on the situations of cities in Cameroon and some East African countries including Uganda and Tanzania.

As noted earlier, this is not a uniquely African problem. It occurs in other rapidly urbanizing parts of the developing world as well. In Asia—another hotbed for the phenomenon—some of the headline cases include the collapse of the Royal Plaza building in the city of Nakhon Ratchasima (Korat) in Thailand, which killed 137 people and injured another 227. In April 2013, an eight-story building collapsed at Dhaka, the capital of Bangladesh. The incident led to 1129 deaths and 2515 injuries (Moullier, 2015). According to Moullier (2015), in 2012 alone, India saw more than 2600 deaths and 850 injuries because of the spontaneous collapse of 2737 building structures. Feifei (2014) and Lyu, Cheng, Shen, and Arulrajah (2018) have also compiled some cases in China and the trend shows that they usually occur in urban China.

Building collapse in developing countries' cities is concerning for, not least, two reasons. First, while some may not be able to cause high enough damage at a time to meet the criteria to be categorized as "disasters" in national and international databases, according to Moullier (2015), their accumulated impacts are usually just as much if not greater than those of large disasters that result from extreme events. Second, the twenty-first century is marked by rapid growth and concentration of huge numbers of people in cities: 2.5 billion more people are joining the world's urban population by 2050, of which 90% are to reside in developing countries, particularly Asia and Africa (United Nations, 2014), where, reportedly, buildings also collapse the most. The growing number of climate-related hazards (Moullier, 2015) portends an even higher disaster-risk as more buildings could collapse in such places as a result of hydro-meteorological hazards.

It is obvious that the phenomenon constitutes one of the critical threats to a healthy and sustainable urban life, which, therefore, raises the need for an urgent conversation toward unravelling and addressing the range of agencies, motivations and causes that incentivize or propel the creation of unsafe buildings in cities in developing countries and to that end, the reason for the rampant collapses in such places. This chapter opens with the conversation on the subject from Ghana—one of the West African countries whose cities have been experiencing some of the incidents (see Asante & Sasu, 2018; Boateng, 2016; Oteng-Ababio, 2016). The chapter presents the results of extensive engagements with 32 key actors in the Ghanaian construction sector through interviews, focus group discussions, email exchanges and other mediums on what underlies the susceptibility of the West African country's cities to building collapses.

The study participants are affiliated to some of the built environment professional bodies and research institutes in Ghana, including the Ghana Institution of Engineers, the Ghana Institute of Architects, Ghana Institute of Surveyors and the Ghana Licensed Builders & Surveyors Association and the Council for Scientific and Industrial Research Building and Road Research Institute and Construction Watch–a civil society organization focused on exposing flaws in built structures in Ghana. The rest of the participants are affiliated to the Kumasi and Accra Metropolitan Assemblies—the two state bodies in charge of the management of the cities of Accra and Kumasi—the hotbeds of building collapses in Ghana (Asante & Sasu, 2018; Oteng-Ababio, 2016). The scholars the study engaged, conduct research and publish on planning and development control in cities in Ghana. They hold faculty positions in Ghana, Finland and Germany. The 32 participants apply to the study a combined experience of more than three centuries of practice in the Ghanaian construction and urban sector, and elsewhere.

Ghana is an exemplar for exploring the broader issue of building collapse in developing countries' cities because, first, as with other developing countries, urban Ghana has seen rapid growth with half of the over 24.2 million population living in urban areas (50.9% as per the 2010 census—it was 43.8% in 2000, GSS, 2012). Further, the Ghanaian construction sector, as with, most developing countries (Ofori, 2007; Wells, 2007), is dominated by informality—self-builders and small-scale enterprises (Arku, 2009). With these similarities, it was envisaged that studying Ghana could offer some insights into the case of other developing countries similarly situated.

2   Building Collapse in Cities in Ghana: What Factors are at Work?

The chapter draws on the empirical data generated from the fieldwork as well as secondary materials on the phenomenon in Ghana. Nonetheless, materials, examples and cases from other developing regions and countries are incorporated to provide a wider context for the findings, as appropriate. The following factors: informal settlement of the supply of buildings; institutional and planning failures to designate planned spaces for commercial activities; land challenges and deficient urban management emerged as critical to how the creation of unsafe buildings arise in cities in Ghana and may thus be central to establishing the grounds or structural context for the deleterious consequences of building collapses in cities in developing countries. However, urban expansions play key roles in exacerbating or worsening the scale of the problem.

The Informal Settlement of the Supply of Buildings

In Ghana, private real estate developers and the state (i.e. the private formal and public formal sectors) play limited role in building supply. The market is driven by the informal sector—self-builders and small-scale enterprises, which may be an individual (Arku, 2009; Asante, Gavu, Quansah, & Tutu, 2018). The upside is that the sector actively delivers in excess of 90% of the annual housing output in the country and mainly for lower income and poor people not targeted by the private real estate sector and government housing schemes. The downside, however, is that as in many other developing countries, unemployment is high and household income is generally low: 23.4 per cent of the population live below the poverty line, and about 8.2 per cent live in extreme poverty (Arku, 2009; Asante et al., 2018).

In absolute terms, the findings of the most recent living standards survey suggest that more Ghanaians are living in extreme poverty: the number increased from 2.2 million in 2013 to 2.4 million in 2017, based on the 2010 projections (GSS, 2018). Ghana's daily minimum wage, as of January 2019, stood at $3.05 per day, indicating an insignificant increase from $2 since 2009 (Arku, 2009). The overall point is that, the majority of the population who are the informal providers of buildings are not well off. This creates path dependency or ratchet effects by limiting their capacity to invest in safer building materials, construction, highly skilled laborers and regular maintenance. One of the study participants (a civil engineer) captured the problem this way:

> You see, because the state does little as regards to housing delivery, individuals are under pressure to put up their own building—for themselves and/or for commercial purposes. But most of the people are not in the rich class. They are in the mid class and most of them are not even all that wealthy. But still they want to put up their own buildings. And because they are not rich enough to be able to build a house but are still determined to get one, the little amount they have, they want to push it to an appreciable level. And if you are putting in the right materials, the amount the person is holding cannot get to that level but the person is still aiming at that. That explains why they want to cut cost and bring in cheap craftsmen. They do not see the problem until the collapse comes.

The problem has become even more acute in the cities as a result of increased demand for buildings triggered by rapid urban expansions. Consistent with trends in other developing countries (United Nations (UN), 2014), Ghana too is undergoing remarkable urban transformation. Census data at various times indicate a steady growth and concentration of people in the urban settings of the country. For instance, the 1960 census report indicated that Ghana had a population of 6.7 million people; 1.5 million lived in urban localities, resulting in a 23% level of urbanization. By 2005, the percentage of people living in urban areas climbed to 47.8%. According to the latest 2010 census report, the proportion of the Ghanaian population living in urban areas, as at then, stood at 50.9% (GSS, 2012).

The explosive growth in the country's urban population has come with enormous housing challenges. The 2000 Population and Housing Census indicates that the total housing stock in the country was about 2.2 million with the backlog exceeding 500,000 units and supply figures varying between 25,000 and 40,000 units per annum (Karley, 2008). The total stock of houses in the country, as per the latest census data is

3,392,745—57.7% are in the rural areas, and the remaining 42.3% in the urban areas (GSS, 2012). Urban housing deficit in Ghana, by some estimations, stood at 1.7 million as at 2015. It is projected to hit 5.7 million by 2020 (UN-Habitat, 2011). Since the public formal and private formal sectors play limited roles in housing delivery in the country, there has been enormous pressure on the informal sector to deliver even more buildings and expeditiously meet the rising demand in the cities.

The general experience, however, is that demand pressures do not just attract many producers or suppliers to engage in competitive supply for the service or commodity in dire need, but also, and even more importantly, they generate further pressures and/or incentives for hastened or speedy production (Harrison, 1994; Maskell, 1987). This has been the case with regard to building supply in the Ghanaian cities. One of the officials of the Accra Metropolitan Assembly, for instance, noted:

> *You know development is taking a different dimension [in the cities]. In putting up the building, there is some number of days you have to let it cure before [you] continue. But a lot of people are in cities and they want buildings and so little time is allowed for buildings to cure before continuing.*

A participant from the Ghana Institute of Architects shared a similar insight: "*In the urban centres, there is the rapid need for such infrastructure. So a building that is to take 6 months, they will finish it in 3 months*". The problem with speedy/hasty production, however, is the high likelihood of shoddy production—a sensitive issue, which could easily lead to unintended disastrous consequences, particularly in the construction sector where the products involved (and here buildings) require a lot of time and attention to reach the optimal healthy standard. The broader point here is that building construction is a complex, delicate, and demanding endeavour, requiring not only highly technical and professional skills but also for key inputs like concrete to reach optimal strength, they require enough time to *cure*, and, therefore, cannot be rushed through just because more people need buildings. This does not mean the construction process cannot be expedited. But in such circumstances, as the participant from the Construction Watch (a civil engineer) advised:

If you are going to do it quickly, then you have to also consider certain things. You can't just use normal concrete. If you can't wait, you have to use additives. So that you can get your building reaching its strength in [a few] days.

The problem, however is that additives are expensive and, as established earlier, at the forefront of building supply in Ghana, as with, many other developing countries (Ofori, 2007; Wells, 2007), is the informal sector—dominated by uninitiated low-income people who, as one of the fellows from the Ghana Institute of Architects observed, do "*not even know the additives to speed up the process*". Against the backdrop of expensive professional fees and/or the perception, they also employ wayside low-skilled artisans with limited knowledge on the physics of building, scientific construction procedures and practices, to do the work—and to make matters worse—with enormous haste leading to shoddy works, which then lead to inadvertent disastrous consequences. "*The reason it happens [referring to the collapses] in the urban areas*", one of the fellows from the Ghana Institute of Architects aptly noted, "*is that there is high demand and there is pressure. So the wrong thing is done hurriedly—at a lightning speed*".

The situation in Ghana is just a reflection of a rather pervasive problem in cities in developing countries where informal developers are hastily putting up buildings because of high demand. Lyu et al. (2018) show that similar dynamics underlined the collapse of four buildings in the Wenzhou City of China on October 10, 2016, which killed 22 migrant laborers and injured 6 others. Another case in point is the April 2016 collapse incident in Nairobi, the Kenyan capital, which killed close to 50 people and maimed several others. Apparently, there is high demand for buildings in Nairobi, and the owners of the facility are part of the many informal developers in the city who bypass regulations to cut down cost to maximize profit. The accounts on the incident suggest that the structure had been "shoddily" built within a few months and the 126 single rooms were being rented out at a monthly rate of $35 (£24)[1] (*The Guardian*, 2016). In Uganda, it was established that similar problems

---

[1] While this fee may not be considered exorbitant in advanced countries, in developing countries' context, it is substantial.

regarding uncontrolled speedy construction and poor workmanship led to the collapse of the BBJ building that killed 11 people and injured 26 others in Kampala, the capital, circa September 2004 (see Alinaitwe & Ekolu, 2014).

Institutional and Planning Failures to Designate Planned Spaces for Commercial Activities

The participant from the Engineering Unit of the Accra Metropolitan Assembly expressed himself on the key considerations involved in the design of buildings as follows:

> *"Every building is designed according to certain usage. I may design a building [as] a residential. The type of loading is different from a commercial building".* Nevertheless, he continued, *"people go and use the residential building as commercial buildings—as offices. These days in Ghana, that is what is happening now".*

When I suggested this to the Fellow assigned by the Ghana Institution of Engineers (GhIE) to the study, he corroborated the engineer's concerns: *"That is what is happening in Accra now. Accra is becoming like that".* The other participants made similar observations. The finding corroborates Oosterbaan, Arku, and Asiedu's (2012) claim that there is a sprawling conversion of residential units to commercial uses (service workshops, retail, and wholesale outlets) in Accra. Nevertheless, the development is not confined to just Accra. The Kumasi City authorities also expressed similar concerns: *"If you look at Adum [a suburb of Kumasi]"*, an official from the Metropolitan Assembly complained, *"Right now, they have turned every living place into commercial use".* This corroborates Adarkwa and Oppong (2005) and Cobbinah and Niminga-Beka (2017) finding that Kumasi is experiencing increasing conversion of buildings to commercial and related spaces.

The problem with the practice is that since the structures originally were not meant for commercial use, the design considerations, regarding their fit for purpose will normally not include the subsequent additional imposed loads associated with the new use. Therefore, using them commercially could exert further pressure on the structural members, cause fatigue and eventual collapse just as attempts to make the necessary adjustments to suit the new purpose, if not properly done, could also lead to structural integrity erosion and eventual collapse (Soane, 2016).

A review of the literature on urban trends and developments in Ghana (Grant, 2001; Hutchful, 2002; Konadu-Agyemang & Adanu, 2003 in Oosterbaan et al., 2012) and even elsewhere (Sutton & Fahmi, 2001; Quang & Kammeier, 2002; Barredo & Demicheli, 2003; Gough & Kellet, 2001; Coen, Ross, & Turner, 2008 in Oosterbaan et al., 2012) suggests that the practice links back to the structural reforms era in response to planning and institutional failure to designate enough planned spaces to meet the growth of commercial activities in the cities. There is no question that increasing urbanization has long been a feature of the Ghanaian economy. The evidence, however, suggests that the levels of increase during the reform era (i.e. since 1984) was remarkable. For instance, of the 10.2 million people added to the total population between 1984 and 2007, 66.7% were absorbed by the urban areas. Between 1984 and 2000, the growth rate for the overall population was approximately 2.7%, but in urban areas, the annual growth rate was 4.6% (Moller-Jensen & Knudsen, 2008).

Structural reforms attracted disproportionate shares of both public and private investments—including FDI to the cities—particularly Accra but also Kumasi, which were prioritized to serve as national icons to propel and spread growth. The unintended effect of this government cum global factors-driven spatial investment bias was a further escalation of rural to urban migration, which has since contributed to the explosive and intensified urbanization in Ghana (Oosterbaan et al., 2012). In the course of the reforms, not only did Ghana's urban populations ratchet up, also, significant number of workers suffered retrenchment, poverty levels and economic uncertainty increased, causing many urban residents to seek creative means for generating income for survival, capital accumulation, or to, simply, minimize economic vulnerability (Otiso & Owusu, 2008). Many people turned to the informal sector, the long-time source of livelihood for urban dwellers, which significantly expanded in the reform era to absorb the many formal workers who suffered retrenchment. Even some formal-sector workers invested in small businesses and acquired additional jobs, as other urban household members diversified their sources of income by engaging in multiple urban economic activities leading to increased demand for business spaces in urban settings (Oosterbaan et al., 2012).

The increased pressure on urban lands coupled with institutional and planning failures to designate planned commercial spaces/infrastructure to contain the heightened informal businesses proliferated the conversion of especially residential buildings to commercial uses. In Oosterbaan et al. (2012), one veteran city planner reminisced how the developments played out in Accra:

> *As the country's economy expand[ed], due to the reform policies, we started seeing massive residential conversion. Accra Roads Rehabilitation Project started around the early 1990s ... This was immediately coming after the commencement of economic recovery program in the 1980s. Once the infrastructure-building program was completed, small-scale activities started to spring up in most neighborhoods. People began to sell more, as retailing became the major economic activity ... it [was] one of the most intensely engaged economic activities in the city. But lack of designated commercial spaces meant that pressure [was] being put on residential property owners to convert their units into retail spaces.* (p. 56)

And with more and more people trooping into the cities, the spate of the conversion has not only been intensified, it has also been diversified in response to other social and economic needs. Therefore, today, people do not only convert buildings to commercial use, they also convert them to serve other needs such as those complained of by the study participants—churches, offices. This is not peculiar to Ghana, as many other developing countries that have implemented economic reform policies are experiencing similar pressures. The development is being felt in cities like Cairo, Lagos, Johannesburg, Rio de Janeiro, Buenos Aires, Santiago, and Hanoi Pereira and Santa Marta where significant foreign direct investment and increases in service and trade activities have created demand for commercial and retail spaces (see Sutton & Fahmi, 2001; Quang & Kammeier, 2002; Barredo & Demicheli, 2003; Gough &

Kellet, 2001 in Oosterbaan et al., 2012, for a review). Even in smaller cities like Cochabamba in Bolivia, such residential conversion to commercial uses (e.g. service workshops, retail and wholesale outlets) are said to be ubiquitous (see Coen et al., 2008).

Land Challenges-induced Inappropriate Construction

One major issue that emerged as critical to building safety challenges in cities in Ghana is land tenure insecurities. The study established that the high cost of land and land tenure insecurities do not only encourage inappropriate construction and building use practices, they also undermine compliance and enforcement of safe building regulations leading to the creation of unsafe buildings with adverse repercussions for public safety. The findings on this are presented under three subheadings.

Land-induced Building Safety Challenge 1: Noncompliance with Building Regulations

Land ownership in Ghana could be classified into two broad categories: state or public lands and customary or private lands. As pertains to other parts of Africa (see Berry, 2008; Kishindo, 2004), the traditional land-holding institutions, customary or informal tenure systems control the largest percentage of lands in Ghana—between 80 and 90 percent of the total land area in the country (UN-Habitat, 2011). However, the Ghanaian land ownership system, just as pertains to other parts of the Sub-Saharan Region, is characterized by widespread, intense disputes and uncertainty (Ayee, Frempong, Asante, & Boafo-Arthur, 2008). It is not an uncommon phenomenon for two or more people to buy the same plot of land from the same landowner or two or more competing owners. As a result, multiple people will claim ownership of the same piece of land (Arku, Mensah, Allotey, & Addo Frempong, 2016; Darkwa & Attuquayefio, 2012) with the resulting disputes undermining compliance with building safety regulations.

The Ghanaian building regulations mandate developers to acquire permits from the relevant metropolitan, municipal or district assembly (MMDA) before they could commence any project. However, once again, as with other developing countries (Lewis, 2005; Moullier, 2015), the process is long, costly and complicated—an issue about which developers have constantly complained (Arku et al., 2016; Oosterbaan et al., 2012). Institutional cultures such as corruption make the situation worse as applicants who fail to *grease palms* get their applications delayed even longer. But with the persistence of land ownership contestations, purchasers of land in especially the cities are perpetually exposed to or face huge risks of protracted litigation or loss of funds as the sellers may be incapable of transferring proper legal title.

To forestall this, developers or land buyers commence projects right after paying for lands and, thus, circumvent due process fearing that permit application may be refused or delayed unnecessarily for them to lose their lands for failure or long delay in project commencement. Thus, as some district assembly officials noted in Arku et al. (2016), although those who violate permit regulations are conscious of their actions and the consequences, the drive to safeguard their land tends to supersede the regard for building permit regulations. One of them, thus, noted

> People are afraid of losing their land to someone else so they're eager to build. The perception is "if I don't act today somebody will lay claim to the land tomorrow". Because of this urgency [the] majority of the people don't bother to fulfil the legal requirements before developing their land. (Arku et al., 2016)

The overall effect of developers' drive to build without permit, due to land conflicts and litigations, is that the authorities do not get the opportunity to comment on the proposed structure and ensure that the designs conform to public safety requirements. The regulators engaged in this study bemoaned that most structures that collapse usually do not have permit. "*So far, the buildings that are collapsing*", one of the officials from the Accra Metropolitan Assembly remarked, "*are buildings that don't have permit*". This is not surprising as the intractable land conflicts discourage developers from following building permit regulations.

Land-induced Building Safety Challenge 2: Outsourcing Jobs to Untrained Gangs

Further to compromising compliance with building safety regulations, the study also found that land ownership conflicts contribute to the prevalence of other inappropriate construction practices in the country. Challenges with multiple sale of lands; long legal processes for the resolution of land conflicts by the courts; lack of faith in the police and court systems as a result of perceived corruption and bias (Darkwa & Attuquayefio, 2012) have generated a widespread practice in Ghana—especially Accra, the capital and its environs—where land buyers or developers hire armed gangs (known locally as *land guards*—mainly young men) who engage in the use of illegitimate force to threaten and ward off competing rivals. The Ghanaian media is awash with stories about land guard activities. Recently (January 10, 2019), it was reported that some land guards had violently descended on some developers working on a project belonging to an orphanage at Dodowa in the Shai-Osudoku District of the Greater Accra Region. The workers were reportedly subjected to severe beatings by the land guards. Some of them, the report said, sustained various degrees of injury.[2] Not too long ago (March 18, 2019), there were reports that some land guards had attacked and inflicted cutlass and other wounds on building inspectors from the Ningo-Prampram District Assembly[3] at a construction site.

These are just a sample of the stories available in public sources and, as noted by Darkwa and Attuquayefio (2012), many more incidents remain unreported and inaccurately reported. Land guards, as the examples provided illustrate, threaten, maim, and sometimes kill their victims in addition to demolishing property and preventing hired laborers and city authorities from doing their job. Some of the study participants shared their ordeals with land guards:

---

[2] Dodowa Orphanage Attacked By Land Guards: https://www.modernghana.com/news/908581/dodowa-orphanage-attacked-by-land-guards.html?fbclid=IwAR3h8YIEYEd2iuZoCuPKQw0VIKqiZBXbk88N-bWpvejgapAYbpYYp-eVBm0 (Accessed: August 18, 2019).

[3] JoyNews (2019). Land guards attack: Staff of Ningo-Prampram DA left terrified following attacks. https://www.facebook.com/watch/?v=1033549370164337 (Accessed: August 18, 2019).

Because of this land guard issue, a contract we had signed, we abrogated it. We had signed contract with the client to start construction. We had mobilized materials to the site and all of a sudden we saw some guys on a motorbike— heavily built men. They asked us who gave us permission to come on the land. As we were explaining, one of them slapped my colleague. He slapped him heavily. Because of that we just moved our car from the site, we went to the office, we called the client and we just abrogated the contract. (A civil engineer)

Arku et al. (2016) found that these security concerns have made qualified engineers, architects and other trained building practitioners reluctant to take up jobs in some parts of the Ghanaian cities—especially Accra. When I suggested this to the study participants (the architects, engineers, contractors) they all corroborated Arku et al.'s (2016) claim. One of them, for instance, submitted:

Yeah, we are selective of projects. Because when these guys are coming they come with all kinds of weapons—machetes—some of them even carry guns. And they are not hesitant to shoot to kill. When we visit the site and we sense any danger of these land guards and their harassments, we just back out from such contracts.

Thus, many qualified building practitioners are reluctant to take up jobs in some parts of the cities due to the activities of land guards. Developers, however, could not wait long enough to find qualified personnel willing to brave the risk and take up such projects since they face risks of protracted litigation or loss of funds, if they delayed in commencing the project. Arku et al. (2016) found that these frustrations force land developers to outsource building construction to these same gangs, who have no training and, worse still, do it in haste. The reluctance of building owners, qualified practitioners and public inspectors to visit such sites to supervise the construction out of fear for their physical safety creates room for the gangs and their allies to put up weak buildings. Thus, land tenure insecurities create room for people without any technical competence or whatsoever to take charge of large-scale unregulated constructions. Given the prevalence of the problem in Accra in particular, it is not surprising that the city and its environs have become the hotbeds of building collapses in Ghana (Asante & Sasu, 2018).

Land-induced Building Safety Challenge 3: Appendages and Extra Floors Atop Old Structures

Human beings tend to adapt buildings to behavioral needs and/or functional requirements (Lawrence & Low, 1990). Thus, when buildings cease to accommodate behavioral and functional requirements, people seek to correct the problem through construction, renovation, or moving to a different building—which requires new land. However, in Ghana, urban lands are under enormous pressure as a result of increased demand and land title conflicts (Arku et al., 2016; Ayee et al., 2008). The implication of the high cost of lands and pervasive land ownership conflicts is increased difficulty in acquiring land for the construction of new buildings to meet the ever-escalating building needs in the cities.

Benzoni (2013) observed what he called a *"common sense response"* in Accra, the capital, where in the context of the problems noted above (rising cost of land and pervasive land ownership and tenure systems conflicts), people build up extra floors onto old structures to take advantage of what they call the free *"land in the sky"* without recourse to the city authorities, qualified architects nor engineers. The practice, however, is also rampant in Kumasi—the second biggest city in the country (see Adinyira & Anokye, 2013). Adding extra floors atop old buildings puts the structural members of buildings under enormous stress and as Salvadori & Levy noted in *Why Buildings Fall Down*, if "even the toughest rock would eventually crack under the weight of more and more stones piled up on it" (Levy & Salvadori, 1992, p. 18), how much more old buildings? The accounts of the study participants suggest that such non-engineered constructions are some of the common ways city dwellers are responding to the accelerated demand for buildings propelled by the spiraling growth in the Ghanaian urban population. Both appendage and the construction of extra floors atop structures threaded through their responses as critical to understanding building safety challenges in cities in Ghana.

One of the fellows from the Ghana Institute of Architects, for instance, noted:

Migration of low skilled people coming to the urban centres for non-existing jobs. Somebody wants to accommodate them. May be the foundation was not designed for [a] two-story but, then, he wants to exploit the situation in order to get some rents. So, he builds on the old one without taking note of the foundation—structural integrity. So people want to exploit the situation by trying to go five or more stories without doing the proper thing—in terms of structural design and soil tests.

Speaking to the worrying case of Kumasi—Ghana's second biggest city—a senior official at the Kumasi Metropolitan Assembly (KMA) made the following complaint:

You realize they have been given a permit to construct one or a two story; they end up building three stories. You sometimes realize that the design itself has been changed. They have done a whole lot of modifications to what they are supposed to do.

The situation in Accra, the capital, is even worse. An official from the Metropolitan Assembly submitted:

It is rampant [here—referring to appendages construction]. It is very rampant. And even not [only] that: you see, sometimes, they apply for a permit for may be three stories. [But] in the process of putting up the three story, you know, they think they have permit, and at your blind side, they add extra floors.

Once again, not just in Ghana, cases abound in other rapidly urbanizing parts of the developing world where population pressures, land acquisition challenges, poverty, commercial considerations, and poor knowledge in construction engendered similar non-engineered constructions leading to unintended disastrous outcomes. An exemplifying incident in point is the collapse of four (three six-stories, and one two-story) residential buildings in the Wenzhou City in the Zhejiang Province of China on October 10, 2016, which killed 22 migrant laborers and injured 6 others. Wenzhou is a major manufacturing hub for shoes and purses and has, therefore, made the city the preferred destination for many of the people in rural China who migrate to the cities in search for jobs and other opportunities. The high influx of rural migrants to the city has ratcheted up the demand for housing, which means that new spaces/ lands are required to construct more residential buildings.

However, the high rate of rapid urbanization and industrialization in the city have meant that there is pressure on the available land for housing purposes. The city's landlords responded to the situation by adding extra floors to the old structures (most of which were built in the 1970s and in floodplains) to create more spaces to meet the rising demand by the many rural migrants. It, therefore, was not surprising that the city was befell with the sad spectacle of the death of 22 people and several degrees of injuries when four of them collapsed in October 2016 (For a review, see Lyu et al., 2018).

Deficient Urban Management

The findings so far evoke a precarious construction climate where the dominance of the Ghanaian building supply industrial complex by informality; institutional failure to designate planned spaces for commercial activities; high cost of urban lands and land conflicts undermine safe construction and building use practices. The exigencies of astronomical rise in the demand for buildings triggered by rapid urban expansions accelerate these unsafe construction and building use practices leading to the creation of even more number of structurally incompetent buildings in the cites. The mandate is with the cities' authorities to uphold public health and wellbeing by bringing the development under control.

However, the insights from the participants corroborate the findings of Boamah, Gyimah, and Nelson (2012), Yeboah and Obeng-Odoom (2010), Asante and Sasu (2018) that problems like limited capacity—in terms of human resources and logistics—political clientelism and the ever-intractable issue of corruption undermine the enforcement of building safety regulations in the cities. The volume of construction developments further undermine regulatory strength and as one of the officials from the Accra Metropolitan Assembly remarked, since *"we do not have [enough] people [building inspectors] to go out [and do monitoring at construction sites], most developers take advantage and do their own thing: cut corners-use unqualified personnel; cut down material requirements; use substandard ones*". In short, the challenges of building regulations enforcement have magnified in the cities where the will to develop is undermining the need to be prudent. In the end, huge stocks of unsafe buildings are created waiting for their day.

3   Bringing it all Together

The chapter proposed to unravel what underlies the susceptibility of cities in Ghana to building collapses and gauge the implications of the findings for other developing countries similarly situated. In summary, the study has established that, first, the provision of building needs in Ghana is informal sector-driven, dominated by low income people whose socio-economic situations create path dependency or ratchet effects, and, thus, limit their capacity to invest in safer building materials, construction, highly skilled laborers. Second, the inefficiencies in the Ghanaian building permitting system (marked by corruption and delays) as well as land tenure insecurities encourage evasion, and, therefore, widespread construction of unpermitted or illegal buildings.

With the high cost of lands and pervasive land ownership conflicts, acquiring land to construct new buildings has increasingly become difficult in cities in Ghana engendering the construction of appendages and extra floors atop old buildings. Further, security concerns due to the violent activities of land guards have made qualified building practitioners reluctant to take up building construction and supervision jobs in some parts of the cities, thereby forcing developers to outsource jobs to these same gangs without any technical competence or whatsoever. All these factors play out and reinforce themselves in ways that encourage the creation of (many illegal) buildings with questionable integrity in a society with a well-documented endemic poor building maintenance culture (Obeng-Odoom & Amedzro, 2011).

It is against the backdrop of the above structural context of precarious construction climate that the country's cities are experiencing rising demand for buildings. The pressures of accelerated demand for buildings in the cities have worsened the situation by encouraging even more perilous construction and building use practices manifesting as uncontrolled speedy/hasty constructions; construction of more appendages and extra floors atop old structures and widespread conversion of buildings to (especially commercial) uses unintended in original designs. Cities' authorities would normally step in to enforce safe building regulations and guard against the practices. However, these efforts are undermined by the scale of ongoing construction works in their jurisdictions; deathly activities of land guards and institutional cultures like corruption and political interference. Add to that a dearth of building inspectors and other resources, and unsafe building practices multiply. The overall effect of all this is the creation of a flourishing climate in which the pursuit and the provision of building needs and services in the cities play out or thrive in ways that tend to undermine public safety.

Based on the foregoing, building collapse in Ghanaian cities could be said to be the contingent outcome of the inappropriate construction and building use practices influenced by the informal settlement of the provision of building needs and services in the country; undisciplined and insecure land tenure system and deficient urban management, in which the pressures of accelerated demand for buildings in the cities, triggered by rapid urban expansions, engender further incentives, causes and motivations that contribute and reinforce the prevalence of the deleterious construction and building use practices, and, hence, the widespread creation of unsafe and poorly maintained buildings in such places. The issue here is how accelerated demand for buildings, in the context of rapid demographic and economic expansions, are acting on or exacerbating the prevailing socio-economic and institutional-cultural influences of adverse construction and building use practices in the Ghanaian society in ways that lead to widespread creation of structurally incompetent buildings in the cities, with adverse repercussions for public safety.

4   Lessons from Ghana for Building Safer and Enhancing Healthy and Sustainable Urban Life

At the end of the day, every collapse incident inevitably will eventually be marked by a technical or engineering defect. And since the engineering imperatives that undergird how buildings should be or are designed, built, managed, repaired, maintained, occupied and even demolished are usually embodied in statutory and non-statutory demands: building regulations and codes (Asante & Sasu, 2018; Watt, 2007), too often, the repertoire of intervention prescriptions proffered to deal with building safety challenges in developing countries tend to center on administrative enforcement of technical or engineering regulations and codes. For instance, concerned by the pervasiveness of structural incidents in the developing world, the *Proceedings of the Institution of Civil Engineers— Forensic Engineering* published a themed issue in 2016 (Subbarao, 2016) to foster conversations on the need for "concentrated attention by governments, national and local, on initiating, legislating and enforcing measures to improve construction standards" (Soane, 2016, p. 127) in those parts of the world.

Indeed, the high incidence of building risks in developing countries as compared to the advanced world is usually explained on the account of inadequate enforcement of building regulations and codes (Berlinski, 2011; Moullier, 2015; Soane, 2016). Undoubtedly, every collapse incident would eventually be due to non-compliance and/or non-enforcement of the appropriate safety regulations underlying the construction and use of buildings. However, the problem does not seem a simple administrative issue that can easily or even mainly be remedied through the enforcement of technical or engineering regulations. What the phenomenon represents, at least as the insight from Ghana suggests, is a symptom of a complex interaction of factors including, but not limited to, exclusionary state and private sector housing schemes that disadvantage or fail to take into account the needs of lower and even middle-income people; lack of meaningful access to formal or institutionalized housing finance schemes; urban housing challenges; poverty; a political economy settlement of informal construction; land tenure insecurities; institutional and planning failures to designate planned commercial spaces/infrastructure to contain the proliferation of informal businesses in cities–just to mention a few of the underlying causes—of which compromised enforcement of regulations is only one of them.

Thus, beneath the rubble of collapsed buildings, in addition to regulation challenges, are multiple underlying causes, many of which share parallels with, and even overlap the discourses in social security and sustainable livelihoods (Bankoff, Freks, & Hilhorst, 2004; Wisner, Blaikie, Cannon, & Davis, 2003), implying, therefore, that interventions to reduce such risks must be broad, more wider-reaching and involve initiatives that address not only direct compliance and enforcement of building regulations but the structural problems that underlie and shape access and distribution of resources and the pursuit of building needs in cities in ways that generate risk or force some people to build themselves into inadvertent disasters.

For instance, the findings have underscored that an insidious dimension of the problem relates to how socioeconomic inequalities associated with urbanization processes impede low-income urban dwellers from finding safe, sturdy accommodation. This exposes them to tremendous risk, forcing them to either rely on or undertake inherently unsafe construction practices. Two issues could be addressed to ease this problem: the high cost of urban land and unfavorable mortgage and credit schemes that lock people out of accessing building or accommodation finance. Put simply, unless conscious efforts are made to address the building needs of low and middle-income urbanites, the creation of unsafe (illegal) buildings in cities cannot be prevented.

Finally, the findings show that the practice of converting buildings to uses unintended in original designs—a crucial influence of vulnerability for building collapse in cities—has an historical-institutional context linking back to the long past days of structural reforms (Sutton & Fahmi, 2001; Quang & Kammeier, 2002; Barredo & Demicheli, 2003; Gough & Kellet, 2001 in Oosterbaan et al., 2012). But, not only that. The literature on land and housing in Ghana suggests that the insecurities associated with the country's customary land tenure system (Darkwa & Attuquayefio, 2012; Juul & Lund, 2002; Sackeyfio, 2012) and its political economy settlement of informal construction (Arku, 2009; Boamah, 2010; Konadu-Agyemang, 2001)—the two most enduring structural impediments to building safety in the country's cities—were shaped and molded from the intersectionality of colonial and postcolonial modernization and recent world system market-led neoliberal housing and other urban policies of successive governments and programs of international bodies such as the IMF and the World Bank.

This historical-institutional insight raises the need for the various global, national, and local actors working on the health of cities to be more reflective of the decisions they take today about urban infrastructure, buildings/housing, land use and management for such decisions could have huge implications for development outcomes in the future and prove critical in either preventing or locking cities into unsustainable development pathways that will expose them to increasingly intense and frequent urban shocks and stresses.

5   Conclusion

The health of the many cities growing rapidly in developing countries is threatened by rampant incidents of building collapse, raising the need for conversations toward unravelling the underlying range of agencies, motivations and causes. This chapter has opened with the conversation on the subject from Ghana. The insight from the West African country suggests that informal settlement of the supply of buildings; institutional and planning failures to designate planned spaces for commercial activities; land challenges and deficient urban management are critical to how the creation of unsafe buildings arise in cities and are thus central to establishing the grounds or structural context for the deleterious consequences of building collapses in cities in developing countries. However, accelerated demand for buildings triggered by rapid urban expansions play key roles in exacerbating the scale of the problem.

Contrasted with existing engineering focal approach, which frames vulnerability for building collapse in developing countries around administrative enforcement of engineering safety imperatives, the chapter provides a deeper level of analysis that takes into account the tangle of structural conditions, including the broader political economy factors that underlie and shape access and distribution of resources and the pursuit of building needs in ways that generate risk or force some people to build themselves into inadvertent disasters. Further, the chapter goes to great lengths in amplifying the historical-institutional context of building collapse in cities in developing countries under the admittedly vainglorious presumption that the lessons may nudge the various global, national, and local actors working on the health of cities to be more reflective of the decisions they take today about urban infrastructure, buildings/housing, land use and management. This is so because such decisions could have huge implications for development outcomes in the future and prove critical in either preventing or locking cities into unsustainable development pathways that will expose them to increasingly intense and frequent urban shocks and stresses.

This study is only a first step to gaining a deeper understanding of the very much under-researched issue of building collapse in cities in developing countries. It hopes to stimulate further inquiries into the situations of other cities and/or developing countries similarly situated. Such an enterprise would be useful not just for developing a stronger understanding of the phenomenon but also for unravelling contextual differences between and among cities and countries to inform well-targeted interventions for constructing safer and resilient buildings in cities to enhance a healthy and sustainable urban life.

References

Adarkwa, K. K., & Oppong, R. A. (2005). Gentrification, use of conversion and traditional architecture in Kumasi's central business district—Case study of Odum precinct. *Journal of the University of Science and Technology, 25*(2), 80.

Adinyira, E., & Anokye, P. (2013). Illegal appendages to residential buildings in Kumasi, Ghana—A case study of North Suntreso. *Journal of Construction Project Management and Innovation, 3*(1), 511–529.

Adugbo, D., Ibrahim, H., & Awka, T. E. (2019). Nigeria: 13 building collapse incidence kills 29, injures 76 in 2019. Retrieved August 18, 2019, from https://allafrica.com/stories/201906030071.html

Alinaitwe, H. M., & Ekolu, S. (2014). Failure of structure in East Africa with focus on the causes of failures in the construction phase. In S. O. Ekolu, M. Dundu, & X. Gao (Eds.), *Construction materials and structures—Proceedings of the First International Conference on Construction Materials and Structures* (Vol. 1, pp. 76–85). Amsterdam, The Netherlands: IOS Press.

Arku, G. (2009). Housing policy changes in Ghana in the 1990s: Policy review. *Housing Studies, 24*(2), 261–272.

Arku, G., Mensah, K. O., Allotey, N. K., & Addo Frempong, E. (2016). Non-compliance with building permit regulations in Accra-Tema city-region, Ghana: Exploring the reasons from the perspective of multiple stakeholders. *Planning Theory & Practice, 17*(3), 361–384.

Asante, L. A., Gavu, E. K., Quansah, D. P. O., & Tutu, D. O. (2018). The difficult combination of renting and building a house in urban Ghana: Analysing the perception of low and middle income earners in Accra. *GeoJournal, 83*(6), 1223–1237.

Asante, L. A., & Sasu, A. (2018). The challenge of reducing the incidence of building collapse in Ghana: Analyzing the perspectives of building inspectors in Kumasi. *SAGE Open, 8*(2). https://doi.org/10.1177/2158244018778109

Ayee, J. R. A., Frempong, A. K. D., Asante, R., & Boafo-Arthur, K. (2008). *The causes, dynamics and policy implications of land-related conflicts in the Greater Accra and Eastern Regions of Ghana* (Ghana report). African Studies Centre University of Leiden.

Bankoff, G., Freks, G., & Hilhorst, D. (2004). *Mapping vulnerability*. London: Earthscan.

Benzoni, S. (2013). Did informal construction practices play a part in the Bangladesh building collapse? Retrieved August 21, 2019, from https://nextcity.org/informalcity/entry/did-informalconstruction-play-a-part-in-the-bangladesh-building-collapse

Berlinski, C. (2011). 1 million dead in 30 seconds. Retrieved August 18, 2019, from http://www.city-journal.org/html/1-million-dead-30-seconds-13396.html

Berry, S. (2008). Ancestral property: Land, politics and 'the deeds of the ancestors' in Ghana and Côte d'Ivoire. In J. M. Ubink & K. S. Amanor (Eds.), *Contesting land and custom in Ghana* (pp. 27–54). Leiden: Leiden University Press.

Boamah, N. A. (2010). Housing affordability in Ghana: A focus on Kumasi and Tamale. *Ethiopian Journal of Environmental Studies and Management, 3*(3), 1–11.

Boamah, N. A., Gyimah, C., & Nelson, J. K. B. (2012). Challenges to the enforcement of development controls in the Wa municipality. *Habitat International, 36*(1), 136–142.

Boateng, F. G. (2016). The collapse of buildings in cities in Ghana: Reasoning beyond 'scientism'. In M. Chou (Ed.), *Refereed Proceedings of TASA 2016 Conference* (pp. 7–12). Melbourne, Australia: TASA.

Boateng, F. G. (2017a). Implications of building accidents in urban settings for building safety studies. In *Refereed Proceedings of Australasian Universities Building Education Association 2017 Conference* (pp. 427–438). AUBEA.

Boateng, F. G. (2017b). Why we need to start talking about the social context of building accidents. *Planning News, 43*(8), 18–19.

Boateng, F. G. (2018a). Why the de-emphasis of wider societal factors in construction failures analysis is fatal. In *Proceedings of the Institution of Civil Engineers—Forensic Engineering*. https://doi.org/10.1680/jfoen.17.00019.

Boateng, F. G. (2018b). Exploring the collapse of buildings in urban settings. *Proceedings of the Institution of Civil Engineers—Municipal Engineer*. https://doi.org/10.1680/jmuen.17.00033.

Boateng, F. G. (2019). Knowing what leads to building collapses can help make African cities safer. Retrieved August 18, 2019, from https://theconversation.com/knowing-what-leads-to-building-collapses-can-help-make-african-cities-safer-118423

Cobbinah, P. B., & Niminga-Beka, R. (2017). Urbanisation in Ghana: Residential land use under siege in Kumasi central. *Cities, 60*, 388–401.

Coen, S. E., Ross, N. A., & Turner, S. (2008). 'Without tiendas it's a dead neighbourhood': The socio-economic importance of small trade stores in Cochabamba, Bolivia. *Cities, 25*, 327–333.

Darkwa, L., & Attuquayefio, P. (2012). Killing to protect: Land guards, state subordination and human rights in Ghana. *SUR-International Journal on Human Rights, 17*, 141.

Feifei, F. (2014). Overview of building collapses in China. Retrieved August 18, 2019, from http://www.chinadaily.com.cn/china/2014-04-04/content_17408943.htm

GSS. (2012). *2010 Population and Housing Census final results*. Accra: Ghana Statistical Service.

GSS. (2018). *Ghana Living Standard Survey Round 7: Poverty trends in Ghana (2005–2017)*. Accra: Ghana Statistical Service.

Harrison, A. (1994). Just-in-time manufacturing. In J. Storey, (Ed.), *New wave manufacturing strategies*. Retrieved from https://books.google.com

Juul, K., & Lund, C. (2002). *Negotiating property in Africa*. Portsmouth: Heinemann.

Karley, N. K. (2008). Ghana residential property delivery constraints and affordability analysis. *Housing Finance International, 22*(4), 22.

Kishindo, P. (2004). Customary land tenure and the new land policy in Malawi. *Journal of Contemporary African Studies, 22*(2), 213–225.

Konadu-Agyemang, K. (2001). Structural adjustment programs and housing affordability in Accra, Ghana. *Canadian Geographer/Le Géographe Canadien, 45*(4), 528–544.

Lawrence, L. D., & Low, S. M. (1990). The built environment and spatial form. *Annual Review of Anthropology, 19*, 453–505.

Levy, M., & Salvadori, M. (1992). *Why buildings fall down: How structures fail.* London: W. W. Norton & Company.

Lewis, J. (2005). Earthquake destruction: Corruption on the fault line. *Transparency International, Global Corruption Report, 2005* (pp. 23–30). London: Pluto Press.

Lyu, H. M., Cheng, W. C., Shen, J. S., & Arulrajah, A. (2018). Investigation of collapsed building incidents on soft marine deposit: Both from social and technical perspectives. *Land, 7*(1), 20.

Maskell, B. (1987). Just-in-time manufacturing. *Industrial Management & Data Systems, 87*(9/10), 17–20.

Moller-Jensen, L., & Knudsen, M. (2008). Patterns of population change in Ghana (1984–2000): Urbanization and frontier development. *GeoJournal, 73*, 307–320. National Building Regulations 1996, (Li 1630).

Moullier, T. (2015). *Building regulation for resilience: Managing risks for safer cities.* Washington, DC: World Bank.

Obeng-Odoom, F., & Amedzro, L. (2011). Inadequate housing in Ghana. *Urbani Izziv, 22*(1), 127–137.

Ofori, G. (2007). Construction in developing countries. *Construction Management and Economics, 25*(1), 1–6.

Oosterbaan, C., Arku, G., & Asiedu, A. B. (2012). Conversion of residential units to commercial spaces in Accra, Ghana: A policy dilemma. *International Planning Studies, 17*(1), 45–66.

Oteng-Ababio, M. (2016). Was 'Black Wednesday' avoidable? The Melcom disaster in Accra puts a generation on trial. *Singapore Journal of Tropical Geography, 37*(3), 401–417.

Otiso, K. M., & Owusu, G. (2008). Comparative urbanization in Ghana and Kenya in time and space. *GeoJournal, 71*, 143–157.

Sackeyfio, N. (2012). The politics of land and urban space in colonial Accra. *History in Africa, 39*, 293–329.

Soane, A. (2016). Learning from experience to avoid collapse. *Proceedings of the Institution of Civil Engineers-Forensic Engineering, 169*(4), 127–132.

Subbarao, H. (2016). Editorial. *Forensic Engineering, 169*(4), 121–122.

Tchamba, J. C., & Bikoko, T. G. L. (2016). Failure and collapse of building structures in the cities of Yaoundé and Douala, Cameroon from 2010 to 2014. *Modern Applied Science, 10*(1), 23.

The Guardian. (2016). Owners of collapsed Nairobi building 'had no occupancy permit'. Retrieved August 18, 2019, from https://www.theguardian.com/world/2016/apr/30/owners-collapsed-nairobi-building-kenya-no-occupancy-permit

UN-Habitat. (2011). *Ghana housing profile*. Nairobi: United Nations Human Settlements Programme (UN-HABITAT).

United Nations (UN). (2014). *World urbanization prospects: The 2014 revision, highlights*. Department of Economic and Social Affairs. Population Division, United Nations.

Watt, D. S. (2007). *Building pathology: Principles and practice*. Oxford: Blackwell Publishing Limited.

Wells, J. (2007). Informality in the construction sector in developing countries. *Construction Management and Economics, 25*(1), 87–93.

Windapo, A. O., & Rotimi, J. O. (2012). Contemporary issues in building collapse and its implication for sustainable development. *Buildings, 2*, 283–299.

Wisner, B., Blaikie, P., Cannon, T., & Davis, I. (2003). *At risk: Natural hazards, people's vulnerability and disasters*. New York: Routledge.

Yeboah, E., & Obeng-Odoom, F. (2010). 'We are not the only ones to blame': District assemblies' perspectives on the state of planning in Ghana. *Commonwealth Journal of Local Governance*, 78–98. https://doi.org/10.5130/cjlg.v0i7.1893

14

Impact of Microfinance on Poverty and Microenterprises

Sefa Awaworyi Churchill

1   Introduction

The microfinance industry, which includes services such as microcredit, micro-insurance, micro-savings, and money transfers, amongst other things, has caught the attention of a wide range of people. Microfinance over the past few decades has grown to become one of the major development programmes in the world, both in terms of the number of people targeted as well as the financial input that it receives (van Rooyen, Stewart, & de Wet, 2012). The industry has attained considerable growth around the world with the promise of helping alleviate poverty. While the truth behind its ability to alleviate poverty is still a subject of public discourse, Copestake (2002) indicates that a major reason for the popularity and growth of the industry is its 'market friendly' nature, which is characterised by flexible lending mechanisms. Some, however, remain sceptical

S. Awaworyi Churchill (✉)
School of Economics, Finance and Marketing, RMIT University,
Melbourne, VIC, Australia
e-mail: sefa.churchill@rmit.edu.au

© The Author(s) 2020
S. Awaworyi Churchill (ed.), *Moving from the Millennium to the Sustainable Development Goals*, https://doi.org/10.1007/978-981-15-1556-9_14

about the positive impact of microfinance and thus donors (both prospective and current), government agencies, policy makers, and stakeholders are showing much interest in understanding what works and what does not work in microfinance.

The most basic underlying theories of the impact of microfinance assume that a microfinance client is a sole operator of an income-generating activity, with an output that is constrained by either a high marginal credit cost relative to marginal returns or by lack of capital. Thus, access to 'cheap' capital, which eases the constraints, allows for the increase of output, profits, net income, and subsequently, the welfare of the borrower (de Mel, McKenzie, & Woodruff, 2008; Duvendack et al., 2011). Another aspect of microfinance impact theory focuses on the psychology of borrowers. Here, the assumption is that credit has the potential to affect the 'mental models' that influence the business decisions of a borrower (Nino-Zarazua & Copestake, 2008). Related to this, based on the assumption that borrowers would not borrow if credit did make them worse off (Rosenberg, 2010), research in the area of borrower psychology suggests that it is unlikely for credit to have an adverse effect on the borrower. Consequently, one strand of the evidence suggests that indeed microfinance is effective and is benefiting clients (see, e.g., Sebstad & Chen, 1996; Morduch, 1999; Khandker, 2005; Imai, Arun, & Annim, 2010; Imai & Azam, 2012).

On the contrary, the possibility that microfinance could have a negative impact has also been discussed. For instance, it has been argued that credit can be associated with various indicators of individual and household socio-economic status of the poor, and depending on which indicator, effects could be either positive or negative (Kabeer, 2005). Wydick (1999), for example, suggests that families that have access to credit and build up productive microenterprises may employ the labour of their children instead of hired labour. As a result, in the long run, while this may increase the income level of the household, it affects the child's schooling adversely. The negative effects of microfinance are thus also supported by a wide range of evidence (see, e.g., Hulme & Mosley, 1996; Hulme, 2000; Copestake, 2002; Hoque, 2005; Shaw, 2004; Nghiem, Coelli, & Rao, 2012).

Therefore, as it stands, the evidence about the impact of microfinance interventions across the world remains very controversial, and this is acting as a catalyst for development economists to conduct thorough empirical studies to ascertain the impact of microfinance. There is a need for more evidence to establish what the impacts of microfinance interventions entail, and this points to the urgent need to pull together and analyse the existing evidence on the impact of microfinance interventions. To this end, recent systematic reviews such as Duvendack et al. (2011), Stewart, van Rooyen, Dickson, Majoro, and de Wet (2010), and van Rooyen et al. (2012) conduct non-empirical synthesis of the existing literature on the impact of microfinance, and inferences drawn from these studies mainly suggest that there is no visible impact of microfinance. For instance, Stewart et al. (2010) indicate that, overall, microcredit positively influences the level of engagement of the poor in economic activities. However, there is evidence of lower income associated with microfinance clients who have been borrowers for relatively longer periods. Furthermore, this synthesis also reveals that microcredit has no significant impact on non-financial asset accumulation.

Given the findings from these systematic reviews, it is worthwhile to examine if an empirical synthesis would lead to any new conclusions. Thus, we conduct a meta-analysis of the empirical evidence on the impact of microfinance interventions on poverty and microenterprises. We focus on two measures of microfinance used in the literature (microcredit and access to microcredit), four proxies for poverty (consumption/expenditure, assets, income, and income growth), and three proxies for microenterprises (labour supply, business profits, and revenue). Here, studies that use microcredit as a measure of microfinance are those that consider the amount borrowed or loan size as an independent variable and thus examine the impact of a loan received on outcome measures. On the contrary, those that consider access to microcredit examine whether or not membership in a microcredit programme or the receipt of a loan impacts our outcome measures. We formulate four major hypotheses to guide us in this research: (1) Microcredit has a positive impact on poverty reduction (H1); (2) Microcredit has a positive impact on the performance of microenterprises (H2); (3) Access to microcredit has a positive impact on poverty reduction (H3); (4) Access to microcredit has a positive impact on the performance of microenterprises (H4). For each hypothesis, we focus on sub-hypotheses, which relate to the mentioned poverty and microenterprise measures.

Furthermore, the heterogeneity in reported findings on the impact of microfinance interventions have often been associated with various study-specific characteristics (Duvendack et al., 2011). In theory, a number of circumstances are associated with microfinance. These circumstances influence how microfinance affects economic and social outcomes. For instance, the use of different measures of poverty, female versus male borrowers, effects on the poorest versus not so poor, the level of analysis (household level versus individual level), the lending type (group versus individual), the purpose of the loan, and different effects in different countries. Thus, in our meta-regression, we examine if the impact of microfinance on our outcome variables are affected by these variations.

Specifically, this chapter makes the following contributions. First, we address the issue of heterogeneity and provide a general conclusion on the empirical evidence on the impact of microfinance interventions, poverty, and microenterprises. This is relevant given that in the presence of heterogeneity, it is difficult to draw a valid conclusion. Second, with the results from our meta-analysis, we lay a foundation for, and guide future studies in, examining areas of particular importance. For instance, we identify the need to conduct further theoretical research that would guide hypothesis formulation and promote the robustness of empirical studies that examine the impact of microfinance. We also identify the need to conduct more primary studies on the impact of microfinance interventions using various metrics for microfinance other than microcredit and perhaps adopt a standard for measuring outcomes. Third, we provide evidence of the genuine effects of microfinance beyond publication bias. In the presence of publication bias and given the disparity in the existing literature regarding the effects of microfinance, policy formulation is impeded.

Publication selection bias occurs when researchers, editors, and reviewers are predisposed to selecting studies with specific results (for example, statistically significant results consistent with the predictions of theory).

This has been considered a threat to empirical economics (Stanley, 2008). In fact, without some correction for publication bias, a literature that appears to present a large and significant empirical effect could actually be misleading. With regard to microfinance, this bias can actually extend to the predisposition to reject studies that report negatively on the impacts of microfinance interventions. However, we find no robust evidence of publication bias in the literature.

Overall, our study is an important step to dealing with the extant deadlock regarding the impacts of microfinance (whether positive, negative, or non-existent), and it also provides some explanations to how variations in the existing literature affect the nature of reported effects of microfinance.

2   Brief Overview of Concepts and Evidence

Measuring the impact of microfinance interventions is argued to be a very challenging task (Berhane & Gardebroek, 2011) because of various problems including problems of accounting for potential biases[1] (Pitt & Khandker, 1998), which may arise from self-selection and program placement (Tedeschi, 2008), amongst other things. As a result, various approaches have emerged over the years and have been used in microfinance impact assessments. There is an extensive discussion[2] on the validity of some of these approaches, with some criticisms questioning the validity of some results presented in the literature (see, e.g., Roodman & Morduch, 2013). Notably, one strand of the existing literature that examines the impact of microfinance makes use of quasi-experimental techniques and also cross-sectional data with instruments to deal with potential selection problems (Pitt & Khandker, 1998), while some adopt a randomized experimental approach (see, e.g., Karlan & Zinman, 2007;

---

[1] See Tedeschi (2008) for a review of some potential biases faced by microfinance impact-assessment researchers.

[2] For detailed discussion on impact-assessment methods used in the literature as well as arguments concerning results validity, see, Morduch (1999), Roodman and Morduch (2013), Duvendack et al. (2011) and Berhane and Gardebroek (2011).

Banerjee, Duflo, Glennerster, & Kinnan, 2009; Karlan, Goldberg, & Copestake, 2009; Feigenberg, Field, & Pande, 2010).

Overall, the common trend in the existing literature that examines the impact of microfinance on poverty is to adopt a framework that considers microcredit as an exogenous 'treatment' on households or individual borrowers to one or more indicators of poverty. A number of studies have emerged, and despite the slight differences in case studies and methodologies used, the literature on the impact of microfinance on poverty is highly debatable and point to several specific conclusions. Some of the proxies used in the literature to measure poverty include income levels, assets, and consumption/expenditure, as well as a few studies that have developed indices for poverty.

Generally, microloans are targeted towards the poor (that is, those below the poverty line); however, a number of individuals slightly above the poverty line (non-poor borrowers) also benefit from microloans as well. It is expected that borrowers above the poverty line would benefit more from microloans (Hulme & Mosley, 1996). Usually, microfinance is expected to have a long-run positive impact only if borrowers have viable investments and are equipped with the necessary skills to sustain a business. In most cases, non-poor borrowers do have such investment opportunities and the required skills. Thus, when MFIs serve such clients, the impacts of interventions are usually positive, especially on income and consumption levels. Li, Gan, and Hu (2011), using a two-year panel dataset from rural China, provide evidence to support this. Furthermore, Wood and Sharif (1997) argue that because poorer borrowers face major constraints in investing their loans into highly productive activities, they tend to benefit less from microcredit. Nonetheless, evidence (see, e.g., Banerjee et al., 2009) suggests that with the necessary support and training to the very poor borrowers, the effects of microfinance can be positive. As a result, it is generally believed that with a viable investment and appropriate training, borrowers (whether poor or non-poor) would experience increases in business productivity. However, microcredit alone is limited in effecting change in the lives of borrowers (Banerjee et al., 2009; Daley-Harris, 2009; Karnani, 2007).

Using assets and consumption/expenditure as a proxy for poverty can be misleading if the dataset used in the analysis does not cover a sufficiently long period. The underlying logic is that after MFIs provide microloans, borrowers can spread out these loans over a short period of time for the consumption or for the purchase of new items. Thus, in the short run, there is an increase in the consumption/expenditure level of borrowers, but there is a significant decline in the long run. On the other hand, some borrowers put their loans into productive use and as their income levels increase, there is a corresponding increase in assets, consumption and expenditure as well. Nonetheless, whether microloans are used for productive purposes or not, it is expected that the effects will be positive on assets, consumption, and expenditure, at least in the short run. Studies such as Pitt and Khandker (1998), Khandker (2005), Hoque (2004), Berhane and Gardebroek (2011), Li et al. (2011), Nghiem et al. (2012), Kaboski and Townsend (2012), and Imai and Azam (2012) examine the impact of microfinance on at least one of these proxies. Pitt and Khandker (1998) found that microcredit has a very significant positive impact on consumption, but mainly for female borrowers. Subsequent studies such as Khandker (2005), Berhane and Gardebroek (2011), and Imai and Azam (2012) present evidence supporting the positive effect of microfinance on consumption. On the other hand, evidence presented by Morduch (1998), Hoque (2004), and Nghiem et al. (2012) indicate that the effects of microfinance on consumption is insignificant. These studies conclude that the insignificant effect is either due to the small value of microloans issued or failure to use microloans for productive purposes. Kaboski and Townsend (2012) present evidence of positive effects on consumption and income growth in the short run but negative effects on assets.

Some studies use poverty indices to measure poverty. These indices usually capture various dimensions of poverty including those discussed earlier. Studies such as Imai et al. (2010) and Imai, Gaiha, Thapa, and Annim (2012) examine the effects of microfinance on poverty using poverty indices. In both cases, evidence supports the poverty-reducing effect of microfinance.

As discussed earlier, the general consensus is that microloans that are put into productive use impact positively on the productivity of microenterprises, especially when borrowers have the necessary skills to sustain their businesses. Copestake, Bhalotra, and Johnson (2001) and Tedeschi (2008) provide evidence to support the positive effects of microfinance on microenterprise profits. Copestake et al. (2001) further argue that it is better for clients to remain in microcredit programmes rather than leave after their first loans. This is because clients who graduate from their first loans to subsequent loans have higher returns on average as evidenced in the significant profit growth in their businesses as well as increased household income. It was also found that about 50% of clients left microfinance programmes after receiving their first loans and this category of borrowers were worse off after leaving with their first loans. However, Copestake, Dawson, Fanning, McKay, and Wright-Revolledo (2005) considered a sample from Peru and found a negative impact of microfinance on profits of microenterprises. This negative finding was attributed to the rigid nature of loan repayment schedules which, in most cases, does not give borrowers the opportunity to start receiving returns on their investment before repayments are due. This is usually the case for borrowers who invest in agriculture.

In summary, evidence from existing studies on the impact of microfinance interventions on poverty and microenterprises remain mixed.

3   Data

The data used in this study are empirical results retrieved from existing studies. In order to identify relevant literature for this study, we first searched five electronic databases—JSTOR, Business Source Complete, EconLit, Google Scholar, and ProQuest (itself containing over 30 databases), using various keywords for microfinance, poverty, and microenterprises.[3] Next we

---

[3] Keywords for microfinance include microfinance, micro-finance, microcredit, micro-credit, micro-lease, microloan, micro-Savings, micro-insurance, micro-banking, micro-bank, credit, MFI and small loan(s). Keywords for poverty and microenterprise include poverty, income, consump-

conducted a manual search process and also examined recent systematic reviews in the area (Duvendack et al., 2011; Stewart et al., 2010; Vaessen et al., 2012; van Rooyen et al., 2012) to ensure all relevant empirical studies had been included.

Given the hypotheses we aim to test, we include only studies that use either microcredit or access to credit as the measure of microfinance, and examine impacts on consumption/expenditure, assets, income, income growth, labour supply, business profits and revenue. Thus, for a study to be included in this meta-analysis, it had to be an empirical study that examines at least one of the above-mentioned variables as outcome variables and uses microcredit and/or access to credit as the independent variable. Consequently, we exclude studies that examine impacts on poverty indices (e.g., Imai et al., 2010), and those that consider micro-savings as a measure of microfinance (e.g., Ashraf, Karlan, & Yin, 2010; Dupas & Robinson, 2013). In addition, given that partial correlation coefficients are calculated to allow for comparability of studies, studies that meet the above criteria but report only coefficients and not all relevant statistics to enable the correlation coefficient calculation are excluded.

Overall, we include 25 studies, with a total of 595 meta-observations in our meta-analysis. Tables 14.1a and 14.1b present an overview of studies included in this meta-analysis.

4   Methodology

We conduct a meta-analysis of the data collected in three stages. The first stage involves the calculation of the fixed effects estimates (FEEs) for the weighted mean of the various estimates that have been reported for each study. In the second stage, to test if reported FEEs are affected by publication selection bias, we conduct precision effect tests (PETs) and funnel asymmetry tests (FATs). Lastly, we conduct a multivariate meta-regression analysis to examine heterogeneity in the literature. Details of the methods are discussed in the appendix.

---

tion, expenditure, assets, microenterprise, micro-enterprise, micro-business, small business and micro-franchise. The last search was conducted in January 2015, and thus our study captures only studies published during or before this period.

Table 14.1a Impact of microcredit (overview of evidence base per study—simple and fixed effect weighted means)

Paper	No. of estimates	Simple mean	Weighted mean (FE)	Significance	Confidence interval
Impact on Assets					
Cotler and Woodruff (2008)	6	0.0755	0.0767	Yes	(0.0547, 0.0986)
Garikipati (2008)	1	0.0829	0.0829		
Pitt and Khandker (1998)	30	0.0415	0.0408	Yes	(0.0273, 0.0544)
Takahashi et al. (2010)	6	−0.1089	−0.1097	Yes	(−0.1776, −0.0417)
	43	*0.0262*	*0.0429*		
Impact on Income					
Abou-Ali, El-Azony, El-Laithy, Haughton, and Khandker (2009)	5	−0.0397	−0.0428	No	(−0.1166, 0.0310)
Copestake et al. (2005)	2	0.1069	0.1069	Yes	(0.0568, 0.1571)
Cotler and Woodruff (2008)	3	0.0433	0.0387	No	(−0.0406, 0.1181)
Cuong (2008)	4	0.0362	0.0351	Yes	(0.0057, 0.0646)
Imai and Azam (2012)	13	0.0097	0.0076	No	(−0.0060, 0.0212)
Kaboski and Townsend (2012)	26	−0.0097	0.0063	No	(−0.0102, 0.0227)
Kouassi (2008)	4	0.0649	0.0431	Yes	(0.0019, 0.0843)
Li et al. (2011)	1	0.2425	0.2425		
Takahashi et al. (2010)	2	0.0600	0.0600	No	(−0.0599, 0.1799)
	60	*0.0131*	*0.0105*		
Impact on Income Growth					
Copestake (2002)	4	0.0766	0.0571	No	(−0.0858, 0.2001)
Copestake et al. (2001)	2	−0.0355	−0.0360	No	(−1.1040, 1.0320)
Copestake et al. (2005)	3	−0.0678	−0.0674	Yes	(−0.0880, −0.0468)
	9	*0.0036*	*−0.0263*		

Impact on Consumption/Expenditure					
Abou-Ali et al. (2009)	15	0.0222	0.0066	No	(−0.0410, 0.0543)
Alam (2012)	77	0.0081	0.0081	No	(−0.0013, 0.0176)
Augsburg et al. (2012)	5	−0.0257	−0.0257	No	(−0.0556, 0.0041)
Cuong (2008)	4	0.0426	0.0416	Yes	(0.0131, 0.0702)
Imai and Azam (2012)	9	0.0259	0.0230	Yes	(0.0115, 0.0346)
Islam (2009)	18	0.0141	0.0054	No	(−0.0095, 0.0203)
Kaboski and Townsend (2012)	24	0.0158	0.0158	Yes	(0.0099, 0.0217)
Li et al. (2011)	1	0.2556	0.2556		
Pitt and Khandker (1998)	24	0.0239	0.0237	Yes	(0.0130, 0.0344)
Takahashi et al. (2010)	8	0.0481	0.0487	No	(−0.0672, 0.1647)
	185	*0.0167*	*0.0147*		
Impact on Labour Supply					
Augsburg et al. (2012)	7	0.0213	0.0214	No	(−0.0322, 0.0750)
Pitt and Khandker (1998)	53	−0.0003	−0.0021	No	(−0.0134, 0.0092)
	60	*0.0022*	*−0.0018*		
Impact on Business Profits					
Augsburg et al. (2012)	1	0.0506	0.0506		
Copestake et al. (2001)	2	0.2310	0.2353		
Copestake et al. (2005)	1	−0.0459	−0.0459	No	(−0.9506, 1.4212)
Cotler and Woodruff (2008)	3	0.0648	0.0618	No	(−0.0021, 0.1258)
Kaboski and Townsend (2012)	4	0.0185	0.0185	Yes	(0.0009, 0.0362)
Takahashi et al. (2010)	6	0.0332	0.0339	No	(−0.0684, 0.1363)
	17	*0.0550*	*0.0268*		
Impact on Revenue					
Augsburg et al. (2012)	1	0.0575	0.0575		
Copestake et al. (2005)	1	0.0003	0.0003		
Kaboski and Townsend (2012)	1	0.0077	0.0077		
Takahashi et al. (2010)	6	0.0394	0.0406	No	(−0.0689, 0.1501)
	9	*0.0336*	*0.0178*		

Table 14.1b Impact of access to credit (overview of evidence base per study—simple and fixed effect weighted means)

Paper	No. of estimates	Simple mean	Weighted mean (FE)	Significance	Confidence interval
Impact on Assets					
Attanasio et al. (2011)	8	−0.0131	−0.0131	No	(−0.0689, 0.1501)
Garikipati (2008)	1	0.0534	0.0534		
Gertler, Levine, and Moretti (2009)	6	0.0246	0.0246	Yes	(0.0106, 0.0386)
Islam (2011)	6	0.0482	0.0458	Yes	(0.0328, 0.0588)
	21	*0.0184*	*0.0180*		
Impact on Income					
Attanasio et al. (2011)	8	−0.0115	−0.0115	Yes	(−0.0189, −0.0041)
Cuong (2008)	4	0.0394	0.0383	Yes	(0.0041, 0.0724)
Islam (2011)	12	0.0458	0.0465	Yes	(0.0290, 0.0639)
Li et al. (2011)	1	0.0550	0.0545		
Nghiem et al. (2012)	3	−0.0108	−0.0108	No	(−0.1638, 0.1423)
	28	*0.0228*	*0.0291*		
Impact on Consumption/Expenditure					
Attanasio et al. (2011)	8	0.0216	0.0216	Yes	(0.0133, 0.0300)
Banerjee et al. (2009)	23	0.0118	0.0093	No	(−0.0027, 0.0212)
Berhane and Gardebroek (2011)	8	0.1136	0.1604	Yes	(0.0218, 0.2990)
Cuong (2008)	4	0.0424	0.0415	Yes	(0.0152, 0.0679)
Gertler et al. (2009)	9	0.0299	0.0299	Yes	(0.0154, 0.0444)
Hoque (2004)	3	0.0764	0.0764	Yes	(0.0196, 0.1332)
Islam (2011)	12	0.0394	0.0476	No	(−0.0107, 0.1059)
Li et al. (2011)	1	0.0340	0.0340		
Nghiem et al. (2012)	3	−0.0358	−0.0376	No	(−0.3912, 0.3160)
	71	*0.0341*	*0.0233*		

Impact on Labour Supply					
Attanasio et al. (2011)	16	−0.0015	−0.0015	No	(−0.0100, 0.0070)
Impact on Business Profits					
Attanasio et al. (2011)	16	−0.0101	−0.0102	Yes	(−0.0160, −0.0044)
Banerjee et al. (2009)	1	0.0486	0.0486	Yes	(0.0404, 0.0774)
McKernan (2002)	46	0.0600	0.0589	Yes	
	63	*0.0420*	*0.0386*		
Impact on Revenue					
Banerjee et al. (2009)	1	0.0288	0.0288		
Kevane and Wydick (2001)	12	0.1197	0.1089	Yes	(0.0569, 0.1607)
	13	*0.1127*	*0.0739*		

5   Findings

Fixed Effect Estimates (FEEs)

Impact of Microcredit

Table 14.1a presents fixed effect weighted averages for the impacts of microcredit. From Table 14.1a, we find that four studies with a total of 43 estimates report on the impact of microcredit on assets. The FEEs for impact on assets are positive and significant,[4] except for one study (Takahashi, Higashikata, & Tsukada, 2010), with six estimates that report a negative and significant average. Based on all 43 estimates, the overall estimated weighted average is 0.0429. Drawing on inferences made by Cohen (1988),[5] we can conclude that although the effect of microcredit on assets is positive, the effect-size represents no meaningful economic significance.

With regard to association between microcredit and income, 60 estimates drawn from nine primary studies are reported. Of the 60 reported estimates, we find that about 81.67% (49 estimates) are statistically insignificant, while the remaining estimates present a positive and statistically significant weighted average. Thus, overall, based on reported FEEs, we can conclude that there is no significant association between microcredit and income. The overall estimated weighted average for all 60 estimates is 0.0105, which is also practically insignificant. For effects on income growth, nine estimates drawn from three primary studies are reported. Of the nine reported estimates, only three present a statistically significant weighted average, which is negative. The overall effect of microcredit on income growth, drawn from nine estimates, is reported as −0.0263, which also reflects a weak effect.[6]

---

[4] Statistical significance is determined by examining the confidence interval, thus studies with single estimates would not have a confidence interval in the context of out meta-analysis. Hence, we cannot indicate statistical significance for these studies.

[5] Cohen indicated that an effect can be referred to as a 'large effect' if its absolute value is greater than 0.4, a 'medium effect' if between 0.10 and 0.4 and 'small effect' if less than 0.10.

[6] It must be noted that this result emerges from a very small sample (drawn from three studies) and thus the conclusion here as well as others drawn from three or less studies must be taken with caution. This also reveals the need for more empirical studies.

Ten studies with a total of 185 estimates are reported for the association between microcredit and consumption/expenditure. Of the reported 185 estimates, 62 estimates (33.51% of total estimates) are positive and statistically significant, while all other estimates are statistically insignificant. The overall fixed effect weighted average reported for all 185 estimates is 0.0147, which also represents a weak effect.

Two studies (Augsburg, De Haas, Harmgart, & Meghir, 2012; Pitt & Khandker, 1998) with a total of 60 estimates report estimates on the impact of microcredit on labour supply. None present a statistically significant weighted average. The overall weighted average for the estimates is −0.0018, which reflects no meaningful economic impact.

The effect of microcredit on business profits is reported by six primary studies (with a total of 17 estimates). Of the 17 estimates, 11 estimates (64.71% of the total estimates) are statistically insignificant, while other estimates are positive. Overall, the weighted average for all 17 estimates is 0.0268. Similarly, we find an overall effect of 0.0178 for microcredit's impact on business revenues. This estimate is drawn from four primary studies (nine estimates).

Impact of Access to Credit

Table 14.1b presents fixed effect weighted averages for the impacts of access to credit. Four studies (21 estimates) report on the impact of credit access on assets. We find that except for one study with eight estimates (Attanasio, Augsburg, Haas, Fitzsimons, & Harmgart, 2011) that presents an insignificant average, all other studies suggest a positive and significant effect of credit access on assets. Further, the overall weighted average for all 21 estimates is 0.0180.

The association between access to credit and income is explained by 28 estimates drawn from five primary studies. We find that all reported estimates are positive and significant, except for eight estimates from one study (Attanasio et al., 2011), which show a negative and significant weighted average, and three estimates from one study (Nghiem et al., 2012), which represent an insignificant weighted average. Overall, the weighted average calculated for this association is 0.0291. This suggests a weak positive effect of credit access on income.

With regard to impacts on consumption/expenditure, we report on nine studies (71 estimates). We find that 38 estimates (53.52% of the total estimates) present statistically insignificant averages, while all other estimates are positive and statistically significant. Overall, the weighted average for all 71 estimates is 0.0233, suggesting a weak positive effect of credit access on consumption/expenditure.

We find no significant association between access to credit and labour supply. This is based on evidence from only one study (Attanasio et al., 2011) with 16 estimates. Three studies with a total of 63 estimates report on the impacts of access to credit on business profits. Except for 16 estimates drawn from Attanasio et al. (2011), which present a negative and statistically significant weighted average, we find a positive weighted average for the remaining two studies. Furthermore, the overall weighted average for all 63 estimates is 0.0386. This indicates a weak positive effect on business profits. Similar findings are made for the relationship between access to credit and business revenues. Based on two primary studies with 13 total estimates, we find a positive effect on revenue, with a weighted average of 0.0739.

Genuine Effect beyond Bias

To determine if reported estimates are fraught with issues of publication selection bias, we conduct PET/FAT and PEESE analysis to examine the robustness of reported weighted averages to publication selection bias. These analyses are performed only for microfinance-poverty/microenterprise associations that have enough observations. For instance, the tests for 'genuine effect' beyond bias are not conducted for the association between access to credit and labour supply, which is reported on by only one primary study. We report estimates using weighted least squares (WLS), clustered data analysis (CDA), and mixed-effect linear model (MLM). CDA accounts for within-study variations and thus is used to obtain robust standard errors. We use MLM as our preferred estimation method since it accounts for both between and within study variations. PET/FAT and PEESE results for microcredit and access to credit's impact are presented in Tables 14.2a and 14.2b, respectively.

Table 14.2a Impact of microcredit (PET/FAT and PEESE results)

Variables	(1) Assets	(2) Income	(3) Income Growth	(4) Con/Exp	(5) Labour Supply	(6) Profits	(7) Revenue
Panel 1: WLS Estimations							
Precision (β_0)	0.0697***	0.0037	−0.2351**	0.0090	−0.0265	0.0054	0.0013
	(0.0187)	(0.0104)	(0.0843)	(0.0112)	(0.0224)	(0.0168)	(0.0256)
Bias (α_0)	−1.0185	0.4815	4.6069**	0.3479	1.9131	1.0459	0.4275
	(0.6732)	(0.6398)	(1.8015)	(0.6551)	(1.6800)	(0.6491)	(0.5444)
Observations	43	60	9	185	60	17	9
R-squared	0.2532	0.0022	0.5265	0.0035	0.0237	0.0069	0.0004
Panel 2: CDA Estimations							
Precision (β_0)	0.0697*	0.0037	−0.2351**	0.0090	−0.0265	0.0054	0.0013
	(0.0243)	(0.0106)	(0.0440)	(0.0142)	(0.0264)	(0.0148)	(0.0095)
Bias (α_0)	−1.0185	0.4815	4.6069*	0.3479	1.9131	1.0459	0.4275**
	(0.9637)	(0.7246)	(1.3078)	(0.8187)	(2.1035)	(0.9566)	(0.1136)
Observations	43	60	9	185	60	17	9
R-squared	0.2532	0.0022	0.5265	0.0035	0.0237	0.0069	0.0004
Panel 3: MLM Estimations							
Precision (β_0)	0.0716***	0.0027	−0.2351***	0.0059	−0.0265	−0.0046	0.0013
	(0.0266)	(0.0120)	(0.0743)	(0.0117)	(0.0220)	(0.0289)	(0.0226)
Bias (α_0)	−0.9323	1.3551	4.6069***	0.6015	1.9131	1.4319	0.4275
	(0.8363)	(0.9656)	(1.5888)	(0.6913)	(1.6517)	(1.0787)	(0.4801)
Observations	43	60	9	185	60	17	9

(continued)

Table 14.2a (continued)

Variables	(1) WLS	(2) CDA	(3) MLM
Panel 4: PEESE Estimations (Income Growth)			
Precision (β_0)	−0.1265**	−0.1265***	−0.1265***
	(0.0424)	(0.0026)	(0.0374)
Standard error (α_0)	45.7769**	45.7769**	45.7769***
	(16.9981)	(8.0573)	(14.9909)
Observations	9	9	9

Notes: Standard errors in parentheses. ***$p < 0.01$, **$p < 0.05$, *$p < 0.1$

Table 14.2b Impact of access to credit (PET/FAT results)

Variables	(1) Assets	(2) Income	(3) Con/Exp	(4) Revenue
Panel 1: WLS Estimations				
Precision (β_0)	0.0282	0.0556***	−0.0021	−0.0079
	(0.0275)	(0.0193)	(0.0155)	(0.0381)
Bias (α_0)	−0.5073	−1.3989	1.6122*	1.8729**
	(1.3365)	(0.9696)	(0.9089)	(0.7784)
Observations	21	28	71	13
R-squared	0.0525	0.2415	0.0003	0.0039
Panel 2: CDA Estimations				
Precision (β_0)	0.0282	0.0556***	−0.0021	−0.0079
	(0.0228)	(0.0069)	(0.0158)	(0.0051)
Bias (α_0)	−0.5073	−1.3989	1.6122	1.8729**
	(1.6767)	(0.9635)	(0.8757)	(0.0777)
Observations	21	28	71	13
R-squared	0.0525	0.2415	0.0003	0.0039
Panel 3: MLM Estimations				
Precision (β_0)	0.0036	0.0482**	0.0033	−0.0079
	(0.0222)	(0.0229)	(0.0166)	(0.0351)
Bias (α_0)	0.7521	−1.0444	1.3698	1.8729***
	(1.0608)	(1.1680)	(0.9476)	(0.7160)
Observations	21	28	71	13

Notes: Standard errors in parentheses. ***$p < 0.01$, **$p < 0.05$, *$p < 0.1$

In addition, our preference would be to also conduct PET/FAT analysis for study clusters based on methodologies (study designs) used. For instance, we put together studies that conduct randomised control trials (RCTs) in one category, quasi-experiments in another, and possibly, other 'observational data' studies in another category. However, issues of data limitation[7] would not permit this, and thus we control for study designs in our multivariate meta-regressions.

---

[7] There are six RCTs that examine one or more of the relationships we are interested in. However, at most, only two of such studies fall into the same cluster of interest. For instance, considering access to credit and assets, only Attanasio et al. (2011) report on this relationship and it is impossible to perform a PET/FAT test for this study only. Overall, the total estimates from only RCTs examining a particular outcome (using a specific microfinance measure) are not enough for a separate PET/FAT analysis.

PET/FAT and PEESE Results

Impact of Microcredit

From Table 14.2a, based on estimates from all estimation methods (WLS, CDA, and MLM), we find that microcredit has a positive and significant effect on assets, with no evidence of publication bias. The effect size is 0.0697, which is weak according to Cohen's guidelines. This is consistent with findings presented by the fixed effect weighted average.

For the relationship between microcredit and income, PET/FAT results across all panels indicate no significant association. On the other hand, we find a negative and significant association between microcredit and income growth with evidence of bias. Controlling for this bias, PEESE estimations (Table 14.2a, Panel 4) also suggest a negative associa- tion but with a decrease in effect size. In the presence of bias, the effect size is −0.2351, and this drops to −0.1265 after controlling for bias.[8]

PET/FAT results for the entire sample suggest no significant relation- ship between microcredit and consumption/expenditure. These results are largely consistent with reported weighted averages, where close to 65% of reported estimates show statistically insignificant weighted aver- ages. Similarly, we find that microcredit has no significant impact on labour supply, business profits, and revenue. These findings are consistent across all estimation types (WLS, CDA, and MLM).

Impact of Access to Credit

From Table 14.2b, we find no significant association between access to credit and assets. Thus, overall, access to credit presents no significant effects on the assets of the poor. Similar insignificant results are observed for the effects of access to credit on consumption/expenditure as well as business revenue. These results do not differ significantly from reported weighted averages, which show effect size representing no meaningful economic impact.

---

[8] It should be noted that these results are based on only nine estimates.

Lastly, and quite robustly, results across all estimation types indicate a positive association between access to credit and income. With no evidence of bias, the reported effect size is 0.0482. This represents a weak association and thus reflects no meaningful economic significance.

Meta-Regression Analysis

This section presents results from multivariate meta-regressions that include chosen moderating variables. We estimate MRA Eq. (14.13) and provide results for WLS, CDA, and MLM. Our preferred model in this case is also the MLM. We run meta-regressions for studies that use microcredit only, and those that use access to credit only. The choices of moderating variables in our MRA are largely influenced by the factors likely to affect the effect estimates reported by the primary studies and also by the theoretical and empirical assumptions and choices made by the authors of individual primary studies. A list and descriptive statistics of moderating variables used is provided in Table 14.3.[9] Results for the MRA are presented in Tables 14.4a, 14.4b and 14.4c.

First we control for geographic location. It is observed that most of the primary studies examining the impact of microcredit consider case studies in Southeast Asia (see, e.g., Hoque, 2004; McKernan, 2002; Alam, 2012; Garikipati, 2008; Imai & Azam, 2012). Therefore in the MRAs, we control for studies conducted with Southeast Asia as a case study to see if different estimates are obtained, leaving other geographic locations as the reference category. From Tables 14.4a and 14.4c, which explain the

---

[9] Given that moderating variables represent variations in the literature, different moderating variables appear in different regressions. For instance, the relationship between microcredit and consumption/expenditure has the highest number of primary studies and reported estimates. Thus, there is a higher likelihood for more variations to exist in this cluster as opposed to the relationship between access to microcredit and consumption/expenditure, which has relatively fewer estimates. Also, some moderating variables are specific to the microfinance measure being used. For instance, productive loan amount can be controlled for in the MRA that involves microcredit studies but not in the access to credit studies. For this reason, there are moderating variables that appear in Table 14.4b but are excluded from Tables 14.4a and 14.4c, and vice versa. Additionally, given that estimates in some categories are very few, we are not able to conduct MRAs for all clusters. In the end, we ran MRAs for only the microcredit-consumption/expenditure, access to credit-consumption/expenditure and the microcredit-income associations.

Table 14.3 Summary/descriptive statistics (MRA variables)

Variables	Definition	Percent of 1s (%)	MC (%)	AM (%)
RCT	1 if PS uses an RCT, otherwise 0	20.85	3.55	44.77
Quasi-experiment	1 if PS uses a quasi-experiment, otherwise 0	38.41	61.23	6.86
OLS	1 if PS uses OLS estimation method, otherwise 0.	20.03	23.18	15.68
IV	1 if PS uses an IV estimation method, otherwise 0.	23.87	33.57	10.46
Household Level	1 if PS examines impact at household level, otherwise 0	13.31	18.68	5.88
Female	1 if PS reports impact of female loan, otherwise 0	20.58	29.55	8.17
Below Poverty Line	1 if PS examines impact on clients below poverty line, otherwise 0	3.07	4.96	1.96
Productive Loan	1 if PS reports impact of productive loans, otherwise 0	5.08	8.75	0
Land	1 if PS captures borrowers with Land, otherwise 0	9.33	0	22.22
Individual Lending	1 if PS examines impact of individual lending, otherwise 0	4.39	0	10.46
Data Period	1 if PS includes data from 2000, otherwise 0	35.12	24.11	50.33
Southeast Asia	1 if PS includes data from Southeast Asia, otherwise 0	69.82	82.03	52.94
Short Term	1 if PS examines short-term impact of microfinance, otherwise 0	55.83	55.79	55.88
Journal Rank	1 if PS is published in high-ranked journal, otherwise 0	39.64	43.03	34.97
Journal	1 if PS is a journal paper, otherwise 0	73.25	84.16	58.17
Publication Year	1 if PS is published after 2005, otherwise 0	57.48	48.23	70.26

Notes: All variables are divided by SE_{ri}

PS: Primary study
MC: Microcredit
AM: Access to Microcredit

Table 14.4a   MRA (microcredit and consumption/expenditure)

Variables	(1) WLS	(3) CDA	(7) MLM
Precision	0.0166	0.0166	0.0166
	(0.0429)	(0.0245)	(0.0411)
OLS	0.0054	0.0054***	0.0054
	(0.0139)	(0.0014)	(0.0133)
IV	0.0155	0.0155***	0.0155*
	(0.0190)	(0.0034)	(0.0182)
Journal Rank	0.1895**	0.1895***	0.1895**
	(0.0861)	(0.0340)	(0.0825)
Household Level	0.1534*	0.1534***	0.1534*
	(0.0886)	(0.0402)	(0.0850)
Journal	0.0534*	0.0534***	0.0534**
	(0.0279)	(0.0112)	(0.0267)
Southeast Asia	−0.0462	−0.0462***	−0.0462
	(0.0487)	(0.0132)	(0.0467)
Female Loans	0.0032	0.0032	0.0032
	(0.0095)	(0.0141)	(0.0091)
Below Poverty Line	−0.0166	−0.0166***	−0.0166*
	(0.0200)	(0.0022)	(0.0191)
Productive Loan	−0.0229	−0.0229***	−0.0229
	(0.0247)	(0.0000)	(0.0236)
RCT	−0.0940*	−0.0940**	−0.0940*
	(0.0537)	(0.0401)	(0.0515)
Quasi-experiment	−0.2170**	−0.2170***	−0.2170***
	(0.0857)	(0.0356)	(0.0821)
Data Period	−0.0056	−0.0056	−0.0056
	(0.0279)	(0.0070)	(0.0267)
Publication Year	−0.0165	−0.0165**	−0.0165
	(0.0162)	(0.0058)	(0.0155)
Constant	1.6309*	1.6309	1.6309**
	(0.8473)	(1.4812)	(0.8122)
Observations	185	185	185

Notes: Standard errors in parentheses. ***p < 0.01, **p < 0.05, *p < 0.1

effects of microcredit on consumption/expenditure and microcredit on income, respectively, our preferred estimation type (MLM) results reveal that the Southeast Asia dummy is insignificant. Thus, we conclude that geographic location does not affect the nature of estimates reported.

We also control for publication characteristics. First, we control for publication type and examine whether journal publications tend to report

Table 14.4b MRA (access to microcredit and consumption/expenditure)

Variables	(2) WLS	(4) CDA	(10) MLM
Precision	0.2501	0.2501	0.2501
	(0.1602)	(0.1724)	(0.1509)
Household Level	0.1049	0.1049**	0.1049*
	(0.0629)	(0.0360)	(0.0592)
Journal	0.0557***	0.0557**	0.0557***
	(0.0202)	(0.0167)	(0.0191)
Publication Year	−0.2067	−0.2067	−0.2067
	(0.1467)	(0.1410)	(0.1382)
Short Term	−0.0309	−0.0309*	−0.0309*
	(0.0248)	(0.0158)	(0.0233)
Data Period	−0.0271	−0.0271***	−0.0271**
	(0.0232)	(0.0063)	(0.0218)
Land	0.0399	0.0399	0.0399
	(0.0675)	(0.0617)	(0.0636)
Constant	−2.4001	−2.4001	−2.4001*
	(1.4964)	(2.3419)	(1.4096)
Observations	71	71	71

Notes: Standard errors in parentheses. ***$p < 0.01$, **$p < 0.05$, *$p < 0.1$

different estimates compared to working papers or theses. Controlling for publication type makes it possible to determine whether authors, as well as journal editors, are predisposed to publish papers with statistical significant estimates consistent with theory to justify selected models (Card & Krueger, 1995; Stanley, 2008; Ugur, 2013). We include a dummy for journal articles, leaving out working papers and theses as the base. From Tables 14.4a and 14.4b, it is evident across all specification and estimation types that journal articles are predisposed to reporting slightly higher estimates for the impact of microcredit and access to credit on consumption/expenditure, respectively.

Furthermore, with regard to journal articles, we examine if the reported effect sizes vary depending on the publication outlet used. Thus, we control for high-ranked journals[10] to determine if the publication outlet used

---

[10] The Australian Business Dean's Council (ABDC) and the Australian Research Council (ARC) present classifications for journal quality. Journals are ranked in descending order of quality as A*, A, B and C. Thus, we introduce a dummy for A* and A ranked journals (high quality) in our MRA, and use other ranks as base.

Table 14.4c MRA (microcredit and income)

Variables	(1) WLS	(2) CDA	(3) MLM
Precision	0.1537∗∗	0.1537∗∗∗	0.1537∗∗∗
	(0.0618)	(0.0171)	(0.0553)
OLS	0.0639∗∗∗	0.0639∗∗∗	0.0639∗∗∗
	(0.0172)	(0.0015)	(0.0154)
IV	0.0670∗∗∗	0.0670∗∗∗	0.0670∗∗∗
	(0.0181)	(0.0019)	(0.0162)
Journal Rank	−0.0961∗∗∗	−0.0961∗∗∗	−0.0961∗∗∗
	(0.0232)	(0.0037)	(0.0207)
Household Level	0.3119∗∗∗	0.3119∗∗∗	0.3119∗∗∗
	(0.0752)	(0.0143)	(0.0672)
Journal	−0.0187	−0.0187	−0.0187
	(0.0332)	(0.0142)	(0.0297)
Southeast Asia	0.0407	0.0407∗∗	0.0407
	(0.0319)	(0.0153)	(0.0286)
Below Poverty Line	0.0174	0.0174∗∗∗	0.0174∗
	(0.0260)	(0.0010)	(0.0233)
Productive Loan	0.0349∗∗	0.0349∗∗∗	0.0349∗∗∗
	(0.0143)	(0.0002)	(0.0128)
Data Period	−0.0307	−0.0307∗∗∗	−0.0307∗
	(0.0183)	(0.0017)	(0.0164)
Publication Year	−0.1764∗∗∗	−0.1764∗∗∗	−0.1764∗∗∗
	(0.0588)	(0.0142)	(0.0526)
Constant	0.0786	0.0786	0.0786
	(0.6122)	(0.4931)	(0.5475)
Observations	60	60	60

Notes: Standard errors in parentheses. ∗∗∗$p < 0.01$, ∗∗$p < 0.05$, ∗$p < 0.1$

by authors presents any variations in reported effect sizes. We find that journal quality affects the nature of reported estimates. From Table 14.4a, results show that high-ranked journals report higher effects on consumption/expenditure. We also note that high-ranked journals that report on the association between microcredit and income report slightly lower effect sizes (Table 14.4c).

Lastly, on publication characteristics, we control for publication year to examine the nature of reported estimates, given that over time, studies with larger dataset and new methodologies have been published. Specifically, we control for studies published after 2005 because we observe that there is a significant increase in the number of publications after this date, and these publications present analyses with richer datasets.[11] Based on MLM results, we find no evidence of publication year affecting reported effect sizes, except for microcredit's effect on income (Table 14.4c), where we find that studies published after 2005 tend to report lower effects on income.

Next, we control for study design and methodologies to examine what variations these categories of moderating variables may present. With regard to study designs, we control for RCTs and quasi-experiments, leaving out other study-types such as 'observational data' studies as the base. We find that the dummies for both RCTs and quasi-experiments are negative in the consumption/expenditure regression (Table 14.4a). This suggests that study designs significantly affect reported effect sizes. Using ordinary least square (OLS) and instrumental variable (IV) techniques as controls, we also find from Tables 14.4a and 14.4c, quite robustly, that the econometric methodology adopted by primary studies affects the nature of reported estimates.

Lastly, in the category of study design, we control for data period and also examine if the length of intervention (short term or long term) has any significant effects on reported estimates. We find that studies that include data after 2000 in their analysis usually report lower effects of microcredit on income (Table 14.4c) and also access to credit on consumption/expenditure (Table 14.4b). With regard to length of intervention, we control for studies that examine the impact of short-term microfinance interventions. We find that studies that examine short-term interventions tend to report negative effects on consumption/expenditure. This is consistent with the arguments presented by Copestake et al. (2001), which suggest that clients become worse off if they do not remain in microcredit programmes for longer periods.

The last category of moderating variables captures microcredit programme intervention features as well as borrower characteristics. First, we control for female loans in the microcredit-consumption/expenditure

---

[11] Our meta-analysis includes publications from 1998 to 2013 (a period of 16 years). Fewer studies are published in the first eight years compared to the last eight. And most studies that fall in the category of the last eight years (after 2005) used larger panel datasets compared to previous studies, which in most cases used cross-sectional datasets.

specification in order to examine if loans given to women affect effect sizes. This is relevant given arguments presented in favour of female borrowers. For instance, Garikipati (2008) argued that women are considered good credit risks and thus are less likely to misuse any credit they receive. Thus, some studies specifically target women while others separate outcomes by gender. In the case of the consumption/expenditure specification (Table 14.4a), we find that the female loans dummy is insignificant. This suggests that giving loans to women does not significantly alter the level of individual or household consumption/expenditure.

We also controlled for loans given to borrowers below the poverty line and found that loans given to this category of borrowers negatively affects their consumption/expenditure level. However, based on the results from Table 14.4c, we found that the loans given to borrowers below the poverty line positively affects their income. Interestingly, we found that productive loans do not affect the estimates reported for consumption/expenditure; however, they do positively affect income. These findings lend support to existing discussions that suggest putting microloans into productive use positively impacts microenterprise productivity and subsequently, income. We also introduce a dummy for borrowers that own an asset such as land. We examine if owning a piece of land alters the effects that access to credit has on consumption/expenditure. We find that the coefficient of land is not significant in the consumption/expenditure specification. This suggests that studies that capture borrowers with plots of land and have access to credit do not report results significantly different from other studies.

Finally, we capture one important characteristic of microcredit programmes (i.e., whether loans are given to households or to individuals).[12] Thus, we control for studies that report estimates on the effects of microfinance at the household level, with individual level as the base. We find from Tables 14.4a to 14.4c that results across all specifications indicate that studies that report effects at the household level tend to report positively on our outcome variables. Therefore, the evidence here suggests

---

[12] Ideally, another characteristic to capture is the lending type, whether primary studies examine individual lending or group lending. However, this is not possible given that for this dimension, fewer variations exist in the primary studies found in each microfinance-outcome variable cluster.

that microcredit given to households, and also household access to credit is more beneficial than individual-level access. This is also the case for the effect of microcredit and income.

We now determine the net effect of microfinance on our outcome variables by examining the coefficient of the precision ($1 / SE_{ri}$). After controlling for all relevant moderating variables, we find that there is no significant association between microcredit and consumption/expenditure (Table 14.4a). Similar findings are made for access to microcredit and consumption/expenditure (Table 14.4b). However, the net effect of microcredit on income after controlling for all moderating variable is positive with an effect size of 0.1537.

Robustness Checks

This section provides results from various checks that examine the robustness of our results. First, we observe that in a given cluster, weighted averages for some studies appear to be larger than those presented by other studies in that cluster. For instance, in Table 14.1a, the weighted average from Li et al. (2011) that examines the impact of microcredit on income is 0.2425, which is relatively large compared to estimates from all the other studies. Thus, we exclude studies within each cluster that are relatively large to examine if the inclusion of these studies affect the overall weighted average.

Based on the robust check results presented in Table 14.5, we observe that the exclusion of Li et al. (2011) from the microcredit-income and microcredit-consumption/expenditure clusters does not present significant variations in the overall weighted averages. For the microcredit–income association, the overall weighted average now observed is 0.0096, compared to the previously observed 0.0105. Similarly, for the microcredit–consumption/expenditure relationship, the new overall weighted average is 0.0144, which is not so different from the previously found 0.0147. Lastly, the exclusion of Berhane and Gardebroek (2011), which appears relatively large in the access to credit–consumption/expenditure cluster, reveals no significant variations as well. The new and old overall weighted averages are 0.0203 and 0.0233, respectively.

Table 14.5 Fixed-effect weighted averages (robust check)

Paper	No. of estimates	Simple mean	Weighted mean	Significance	Confidence interval
Impact of Microcredit on Income					
Abou-Ali et al. (2009)	5	−0.0397	−0.0428	No	(−0.1166, 0.0310)
Copestake et al. (2005)	2	0.1069	0.1069	Yes	(0.0568, 0.1571)
Cotler and Woodruff (2008)	3	0.0433	0.0387	No	(−0.0406, 0.1181)
Cuong (2008)	4	0.0362	0.0351	Yes	(0.0057, 0.0646)
Imai and Azam (2012)	13	0.0097	0.0076	No	(−0.0060, 0.0212)
Kaboski and Townsend (2012)	26	−0.0097	0.0063	No	(−0.0102, 0.0227)
Kouassi (2008)	4	0.0649	0.0431	Yes	(0.0019, 0.0843)
Takahashi et al. (2010)	2	0.0600	0.0600	No	(−0.0599, 0.1799)
	59	*0.0092*	*0.0096*		
Impact of Microcredit on Consumption/Expenditure					
Abou-Ali et al. (2009)	15	0.0222	0.0066	No	(−0.0410, 0.0543)
Alam (2012)	77	0.0081	0.0081	No	(−0.0013, 0.0176)
Augsburg et al. (2012)	5	−0.0257	−0.0257	No	(−0.0556, 0.0041)
Cuong (2008)	4	0.0426	0.0416	Yes	(0.0131, 0.0702)
Imai and Azam (2012)	9	0.0259	0.0230	Yes	(0.0115, 0.0346)
Islam (2009)	18	0.0141	0.0054	No	(−0.0095, 0.0203)
Kaboski and Townsend (2012)	24	0.0158	0.0158	Yes	(0.0099, 0.0217)
Pitt and Khandker (1998)	24	0.0239	0.0237	Yes	(0.0130, 0.0344)
Takahashi et al. (2010)	8	0.0481	0.0487	No	(−0.0672, 0.1647)
	184	*0.0154*	*0.0144*		

(continued)

Table 14.5 (continued)

Paper	No. of estimates	Simple mean	Weighted mean	Significance	Confidence interval
Impact of Access to Microcredit on Consumption/Expenditure					
Attanasio et al. (2011)	8	0.0216	0.0216	Yes	(0.0133, 0.0300)
Banerjee et al. (2009)	23	0.0118	0.0093	No	(−0.0027, 0.0212)
Cuong (2008)	4	0.0424	0.0415	Yes	(0.0152, 0.0679)
Gertler et al. (2009)	9	0.0299	0.0299	Yes	(0.0154, 0.0444)
Hoque (2004)	3	0.0764	0.0764	Yes	(0.0196, 0.1332)
Islam (2011)	12	0.0394	0.0476	No	(−0.0107, 0.1059)
Li et al. (2011)	1	0.0340	0.0340		
Nghiem et al. (2012)	3	−0.0358	−0.0376	No	(−0.3912, 0.3160)
	71	0.0239	0.0203		

Next, we present estimations for a smaller set of meta-observations. Although several estimates are presented by some primary studies, we extract a smaller set of meta-observation mainly consisting of primary studies authors' 'preferred' estimates and estimates capturing effect on 'total outcomes'. For instance, some studies provide a breakdown of consumption/expenditure such as food expenditure and other household expenditures and examine effects on these consumption/expenditure types as well as on total consumption/expenditure. In the smaller set of observations used for our robustness check, we consider only estimates for total consumption/expenditure. Due to data limitations, this smaller set only exists for some microfinance–poverty/microenterprise associations. Results for these estimations are presented in Tables 14.6a and 14.6b.

Table 14.6a Impact of microcredit (robustness check)

Variables	(1) Income	(2) Con/Exp	(3) Profits
Panel 1: WLS Estimations			
Precision (β_0)	0.0162*	0.0248***	0.0143
	(0.0094)	(0.0086)	(0.0099)
Bias (α_0)	1.3876**	0.0160	0.5419
	(0.5602)	(0.4621)	(0.4083)
Observations	25	85	14
R-squared	0.1148	0.0905	0.1476
Panel 2: CDA Estimations			
Precision (β_0)	0.0162*	0.0248**	0.0143
	(0.0075)	(0.0082)	(0.0082)
Bias (α_0)	1.3876*	0.0160	0.5419
	(0.6136)	(0.4770)	(0.4915)
Observations	25	85	14
R-squared	0.1148	0.0905	0.1476
Panel 3: MLM Estimations			
Precision (β_0)	0.0133	−0.0290	0.0130
	(0.0097)	(0.0207)	(0.0109)
Bias (α_0)	1.8217**	3.0586***	0.6336
	(0.7196)	(1.1472)	(0.4576)
Observations	25	85	14

Notes: Standard errors in parentheses. ***$p < 0.01$, **$p < 0.05$, *$p < 0.1$

326S. Awaworyi Churchill

Table 14.6b Impact of access to credit (robustness check)

Variables	(1) Assets	(2) Income	(3) Con/Exp	(4) Profits
Panel 1: WLS Estimations				
Precision (β_0)	0.0416	0.0686**	0.0336	−0.7858***
	(0.0260)	(0.0249)	(0.0292)	(0.1426)
Bias (α_0)	−1.5067	−2.3191	1.1970	35.6241***
	(1.2833)	(1.3530)	(1.3483)	(6.3065)
Observations	17	18	31	23
R-squared	0.1457	0.3220	0.0437	0.5913
Panel 2: CDA Estimations				
Precision (β_0)	0.0416	0.0686**	0.0336	−0.7858
	(0.0429)	(0.0208)	(0.0186)	(0.2890)
Bias (α_0)	−1.5067	−2.3191	1.1970	35.6241
	(2.2918)	(1.8008)	(0.6503)	(12.4984)
Observations	17	18	31	23
R-squared	0.1457	0.3220	0.0437	0.5913
Panel 3: MLM Estimations				
Precision (β_0)	0.0203	0.0394	0.0408	−0.5049*
	(0.0287)	(0.0312)	(0.0313)	(0.2751)
Bias (α_0)	−0.0278	−0.4233	0.8650	24.5067**
	(1.3247)	(1.6076)	(1.4814)	(12.2986)
Observations	17	18	31	23

Notes: Standard errors in parentheses. ***$p < 0.01$, **$p < 0.05$, *$p < 0.1$

From Table 14.6a, we find that our preferred estimation method results (MLM estimates) show that microcredit has no significant association with income, consumption/expenditure, or profits. This is consistent with the findings made from the larger sample. Thus, quite robustly, existing evidence suggests that microcredit has no significant impact income, consumption/expenditure, or profits.

Turning to the results for access to credit (Table 14.6b), we find that the effect of access to credit on assets and consumption/expenditure is consistent with findings from the larger sample where no significant association is observed. However, the effect on income is now insignificant in the smaller sample compared to the large sample, which is positive but with a coefficient that represents a small effect.

Overall, results from our robustness checks largely confirm results presented for both the PET/FAT and fixed effect weighted averages.

6   Discussion and Conclusion

This study conducts a meta-analysis of the empirical literature that examines the impact of microfinance on poverty and microenterprises. We consider two measures of microfinance—microcredit and access to credit—and also seven measures of poverty and microenterprises, namely consumption/expenditure, assets, income, income growth, labour supply, business profits, and revenue. Based on 595 estimates reported by 25 primary studies, we examine the following four hypotheses: (1) Microcredit has a positive impact on poverty (H1); (2) Microcredit has a positive impact on microenterprises (H2); (3) Access to microcredit has a positive impact on poverty (H3); (4) Access to microcredit has a positive impact on microenterprises (H4). First, we report fixed effect weighted averages for each study that examines our relationships of interest. Second, using precision effect and funnel asymmetry tests (PET/FAT), we examine if reported effect sizes are fraught with issues of publication selection bias. Lastly, we conduct a multivariate meta-regression analysis (MRA) to model heterogeneity and examine if study, borrower, and microfinance programme characteristics, amongst other things, affect the nature of reported effect sizes.

PET/FAT and MRA results do not support H1 for consumption/expenditure, given that we consistently find no significant effect of microcredit on consumption/expenditure. Similarly, considering our PET/FAT results, H1 is not supported for income; however, this finding is not robust to the inclusion of moderating variables, given that MRA results indicate a positive effect of microcredit on income. H1, however, is supported for assets considering our PET/FAT results, but the effect size, 0.0716, is too small to have any meaningful economic impact. PET/FAT results and fixed effects weighted averages show a negative effect of microcredit on income growth and thus we conclude that H1 is not supported in the case of income growth. Considering assets and consumption/expenditure, our results do not support H3. However, quite robustly, results support H3 for income.

Our results do not support H2 for any of the microenterprise measures. This finding is consistent across both the fixed effect weighted average and PET/FAT results. Thus, overall, we find that microcredit has no significant impact on microenterprises (labour supply, business profits, and revenues). This is also the case for access to credit, and thus H4 is also not supported.

Our results are consistent with recent systematic reviews such as Duvendack et al. (2011) that report no significant effect of microfinance on economic outcomes. Therefore, there appears to be no strong evidence at the moment to support the existing claims that microfinance has a positive effect on the well-being of the poor as well as their businesses. The mainly insignificant impact of microcredit could be as a result of the long loan-repayment time. Stewart et al. (2012) argue that, eventually, microcredit is likely to increase income; however, given that borrowers incur debts that must be repaid over time, expected positive impacts of microcredit on some economic outcomes may not be immediate. The positive impact of microcredit on assets is somewhat expected. In theory, microcredit is expected to increase the assets of borrowers, especially for use in the development of microenterprises. However, over time, the burden of loan repayments may compel borrowers to sell assets in order to pay loans quickly. This phenomenon could explain the observed weak impact.

Of course, these conclusions have been drawn from evidence that consider only microcredit and access to credit. Perhaps the implementation of other microfinance products might play a role in enhancing the effectiveness of microcredit. Within the microfinance sector, it appears the hype has been on microcredit and various lending schemes, and this has likely diverted the attention from other microfinance products as well as other potential development programmes. Arguments presented by some studies (Collins, Morduch, Rutherford, & Ruthven, 2009; Duvendack et al., 2011) suggest that the poor do not only require credit but also other financial services such as insurance and savings, as well as technical support. Several microfinance institutions provide these services, and it would be worthwhile to consider the impact of microfinance more holistically.

We concur with Duvendack et al. (2011) and propose the need for more and better research that focuses on the impact of microcredit and on the other dimensions of microfinance. In addition, for researchers to be able to design better empirical studies, there is a need for more robust and stronger theoretical motivations, which, at the moment, are relatively scarce as well. As it stands, hypotheses formulation is quite difficult given that the pathways through which microfinance can impact social and economic outcomes are complex and quite ambiguous (Korth, Stewart, Rooyen, & Wet, 2012; Levine, 2004). At the moment, most theories surrounding microfinance assume that a client's ability to borrow depends on the capacity of potential or actual business revenue to meet credit costs. A course of future theoretical research would be to also account more clearly for individual and business vulnerabilities and risk and how these affect the ability to borrow.

With regard to potential sources of heterogeneity in reported estimates, we find that differences in primary studies affect reported effect size. Specifically, we find that study design, borrower, and microcredit programme characteristics, as well as sample and data characteristics, all affect the microfinance–poverty/microenterprises relationship. Evidence from our study shows that short-term impacts of microfinance are detrimental. A course of future research is to focus more on the long-term impact of microfinance. This is crucial given that investment into some categories of microenterprises do not yield immediate returns. Thus, individuals could channel funds into investments early on, with that investment translating into increased consumption much later. This cannot be captured effectively if studies do not consider data periods sufficiently long enough. Nonetheless, this does not undermine the importance of studies that consider the short-term impact of microfinance. Some microfinance clients drop out along the line and this short-term intervention is likely to impact positively or negatively on the well-being of such clients. Thus, it is also worthwhile to examine, more thoroughly, the short-term impact of microfinance as well. In brief, there is a need to conduct more primary research, both theoretical and empirical, to understand how microfinance works and the channels through which it can affect the well-being of the poor.

A number of policy-relevant suggestions also emerge. Although we find no strong evidence of microfinance being detrimental to the well-being and businesses of the poor, we also find no evidence of a strong positive impact. However, evidence of negative impact, observed impact on income growth for instance, suggests that microfinance poses the risk of worsening the plight of the poor. Stewart et al. (2012) indicate that, in some cases, microcredit brings the risk of collateral loss and increased debt. Thus, the question of whether microfinance is a viable development tool in improving the well-being of the poorest of the poor needs to be revisited and considered seriously. Furthermore, evidence from our MRA suggests that microcredit worsens the plight of borrowers below the poverty line with regard to consumption/expenditure. This raises some major concerns, and thus caution needs to be taken in providing microloans to the poorest of the poor. Specifically, the target of microfinance services should not just be to promote financial inclusion but to also carefully consider the implications of services delivered to the very poor, in terms of potential negative effects on well-being and increased debt. Stewart et al. (2012) propose that there is less risk of microcredit causing harm if services are targeted at clients with some level of financial security or perhaps other sources of income, which makes it possible and easier to repay loans. However, such category of clients would not be the poorest of the poor in society, and this brings to question the validity of microfinance as a development tool in addressing issues of severe poverty. Related to this, Zeller, Sharma, Ahmed, and Rashid (2001) indicate that access to credit can reduce the management of risk through the diversification of livelihoods, which subsequently raises income. However, this may also not be very applicable in the case of the poorest, as they are not usually skilled enough.

Appendix: Empirical Design

This study conducts a meta-analysis of the data collected and this is done in three stages. The first stage involves the calculation of the fixed effects estimates (FEEs) for the weighted mean of the various estimates that have been reported for each study. Stanley, Jarrell, and Doucouliagos (2009) propose that FEEs are efficient given that the estimates reported by the original studies are derived from the same population and have a common mean. In addition, FEES are more reliable than simple means, and compared to random-effects weighted means, they are less affected by publication bias (Henmi & Copas, 2010; Stanley, 2008; Stanley & Doucouliagos, 2014).

Second, to test if reported FEEs are affected by publication selection bias, we conduct precision effect tests (PETs) and funnel asymmetry tests (FATs). The PET/FAT makes it possible to test if a particular microfinance measure has 'genuine effects' on the various outcome measures after controlling for biases like publication selection bias. In the last stage of the meta-analysis, we examine if variations in reported estimates can be attributed to study characteristics such as publication year and type, econometric methodology, data type, and borrower differences. Thus, a multivariate meta-regression is conducted in order to test for genuine effects on the outcome variables after controlling for various biases and the effects of moderating variables (variations) such as those mentioned earlier. This process is conducted using partial correlation coefficients (PCCs) derived from estimates extracted from the chosen studies.

PCCs are used because they measure the association between microfinance and the outcome variables while other independent variables are held constant. Basically, they are comparable across different studies as they are independent of the metrics used in measuring both the dependent and explanatory variables, and they are also widely used in meta-analysis (see for example Alptekin & Levine, 2012; Doucouliagos & Ulubasoglu, 2008; Ugur, 2013).

The PCC for each effect estimate is calculated as follows:

$$r_i = \frac{t_i}{\sqrt{t_i^2 + df_i}} \qquad (14.1)$$

Similarly, the standard error of the above coefficient is calculated as

$$SE_{ri} = \sqrt{\frac{1 - r_i^2}{df_i}} \qquad (14.2)$$

where r_i and SE_{ri} represent the PCC and the standard error of the PCC respectively. The standard error represents the variance attributed to sampling error, and it is used in the calculation of the FEEs for the study-based weighted means. t_i represents the t-statistic associated with the given effect-size estimate, and df_i represents the degrees of freedom that correspond with the estimates as reported in the studies.

For the weighted means used in this study, the approach used by Stanley and Doucouliagos (2007), Stanley (2008), and De Dominicis, Florax, and Groot (2008) was adopted. They report that weighted means can be calculated using the relation:

$$\overline{X} = \frac{\sum w_i r_i}{\sum w_i} \qquad (14.3)$$

where $\overline{X}$ is the weighted mean of the reported estimates, r_i, is the partial correlation coefficient as calculated in Eq. (14.1) and w_i, is the weight that varies depending on whether $\overline{X}$ is a random effect mean or fixed effect mean.

For fixed effect estimates (FEEs), the weight w_i is given as the inverse of the square of the standard error associated with the PCCs as derived in Eq. (14.2). Thus, Eq. (14.3) can be re-expressed as Eq. (14.4) as the fixed effect estimates for the weighted mean of the partial correlations.

$$\overline{X}_{FEE} = \frac{\sum r_i \left(\dfrac{1}{SE_{ri}^2} \right)}{\sum \dfrac{1}{SE_{ri}^2}} \qquad (14.4)$$

where $\overline{X}_{FEE}$ is the fixed effect estimate weighted mean, and r_i and SE_{ri} remain as they are above. The fixed effect estimate weights account for the within-study variations by distributing weights, such that less precise estimates are assigned lower weights, while more precise estimates are assigned higher weights. Thus, the fixed effects weighted means are more reliable compared to the simple means.

The PET/FAT analysis involves the estimation of a bivariate weighted least square (WLS) model. Egger, Smith, Schnieder, and Minder (1997) propose the following model to test for publication selection bias:

$$r_i = \beta_0 + \alpha_0 \left(SE_{ri} \right) + u_i \qquad (14.5)$$

where r_i is the effect estimate, β_0 and α_0 represent the constant term and the slope coefficient respectively, while SE_{ri} is the standard error of the estimate. Egger et al. (1997) suggest that publication bias is present if the slope coefficient is significantly different to zero. Furthermore, the model also suggests that in the absence of bias (that is the slope coefficient is not significantly different to zero), the effect estimate would randomly vary around the true effect, which is the intercept term. Nonetheless, Eq. (14.5) would not be efficient in determining whether the effect estimates are genuine since it is heteroskedastic in nature (Hawkes & Ugur, 2012; Stanley, 2008) and the variance of the reported effect estimates are not constant. In this regard, Stanley (2008) recommends that Eq. (14.5) be converted into a weighted least square (WLS) model by dividing through it by SE_{ri} to yield Eq. (14.6). Stanley (2008) demonstrates that this WLS model can be used to test for both publication selection bias (which is the FAT) and for genuine effect beyond selection bias.

$$\frac{r_i}{SE_{ri}} = t_i = \alpha_0 + \beta_0 \left(\frac{1}{SE_{ri}} \right) + \varepsilon_i \tag{14.6}$$

Here, the t-value becomes the dependent variable and the coefficient of the precision ($1 / SE_{ri}$) becomes the measure of genuine effect.[13] The funnel asymmetry test involves testing for the following null and alternate hypotheses (Eq. (14.7)) and if the null hypothesis is rejected, this means that asymmetry exists.

$$H_0 : \alpha_0 = 0 \qquad H_1 : \alpha_0 \neq 0 \tag{14.7}$$

The precision effect test, also known as the test for genuine effect, involves testing of the following null and alternate hypotheses:

$$H_0 : \beta_0 = 0 \qquad H_1 : \beta_0 \neq 0 \tag{14.8}$$

Stanley (2010) indicates that the reported estimates and their associated standard errors have a nonlinear relationship given that the FAT/PET results point to the co-existence of the presence of both publication selection bias and genuine effect. In situations like this, they propose that

---

[13] Note that the constant term and the intercept coefficient have now interchanged positions, while the error term is newly defined as ε_i.

a precision effect test with standard errors (PEESE) be conducted to account for any nonlinear relationships that may exist. They propose the following PEESE model:

$$r_i = \beta_0 + \alpha_0 \left(SE_{ri}^2 \right) + u_i \tag{14.9}$$

Dividing this PEESE model by SE_{ri}, which suppresses the constant term with the aim of addressing any potential heteroskedasticity problems, we obtain the following;

$$\frac{r_i}{SE_{ri}} = \beta_0 \left(\frac{1}{SE_{ri}} \right) + \alpha_0 \left(SE_{ri} \right) + u_i \left(\frac{1}{SE_{ri}} \right) \tag{14.10}$$

Given that $\dfrac{r_i}{SE_{ri}} = t_i$ and $u_i \left(\dfrac{1}{SE_{ri}} \right) = v_i$, we get

$$t_i = \beta_0 \left(\frac{1}{SE_{ri}} \right) + \alpha_0 \left(SE_{ri} \right) + v_i \tag{14.11}$$

Equation (14.11) tests whether $\beta_0 = 0$ and helps determine if genuine effects are present. The genuine effect in this case takes into account any nonlinear relationship that may exist with the standard error.

The use of the PET/FAT and PEESE analysis makes it possible to make precise inferences regarding the existence of genuine effects. However, these tests work with the assumption that any moderating variable that may potentially be related to specific study characteristics, or sample differences, are equal to their sample means and are independent of the standard error. As a result, the PET/FAT and PEESE do not include moderating variables. Based on this understanding, this study also conducts a multivariate meta-regression (MRA), which takes into account various moderating variables and allows us to examine the role of such variables on estimated effect-sizes. The MRA specification (Eq. 14.12) is usually used to model heterogeneity.

$$t_i = \alpha_0 + \beta_0 \left(\frac{1}{SE_{ri}} \right) + \sum \beta_k \left(\frac{Z_{ki}}{SE_{ri}} \right) + \epsilon_i + u_i \qquad (14.12)$$

where t_i is the t-value associated with each reported estimate, Z_{ki} is a vector of binary variables that account for variations in the studies, and β_k are the coefficients to be estimated, which explain the effect of each moderating variable on the estimate effect size.

Equation (14.12) is often estimated by OLS, which is a consistent estimator if the estimated effect sizes retrieved from primary studies are independent from one to another. However, given that primary studies often provide more than one estimate, this potentially brings into question the independency among estimates (De Dominicis et al., 2008). Thus, we estimate Eq. (14.13) using a multi-level model (hierarchical model) to account for any issues of data dependency. Hence, we estimate the follow model:

$$t_{ji} = \alpha_0 + \beta_0 \left(\frac{1}{SE_{jri}} \right) + \sum \beta_k \frac{(Z_{ki})}{SE_{jri}} + \epsilon_j + u_{ji} \qquad (14.13)$$

Here, t_{ji} is the ith t-value associated with the jth study and k represents the number of moderating variables. Z_{ki} remains as explained, and ϵ_j is the study-specific error term. Both error terms ϵ_j and u_{ji} are normally distributed around the PCCs' mean values such that $\epsilon_i \sim N\left(0, SE_{ri}^2\right)$, where SE_{ri}^2 is the square of the standard errors associated with each of the derived PCC, and $u_i \sim N\left(0, \tau^2\right)$, where τ^2 is the estimated between-study variance.

References

Abou-Ali, H., El-Azony, H., El-Laithy, H., Haughton, J., & Khandker, S. R. (2009). *Evaluating the impact of Egyptian social fund for development programs*. Policy Research Working Paper Series 4993. The World Bank.

Alam, S. (2012). The effect of gender-based returns to borrowing on intra-household resource allocation in rural Bangladesh. *World Development*, 40(6), 1164–1180.

Alptekin, A., & Levine, P. (2012). Military expenditure and economic growth: A meta-analysis. *European Journal of Political Economy, 28*(4), 636–650.

Ashraf, N., Karlan, D., & Yin, W. (2010). Female empowerment: Impact of a commitment savings product in the Philippines. *World Development, 38*(3), 333–344.

Attanasio, O., Augsburg, B., Haas, R., Fitzsimons, E., & Harmgart, H. (2011). *Group lending or individual lending? Evidence from a randomised field experiment in Mongolia.* IFS Working Papers: W11/20. Institute for Fiscal Studies.

Augsburg, B., De Haas, R., Harmgart, H., & Meghir, C. (2012). Microfinance at the margin: Experimental evidence from Bosnia and Herzegovina. Rochester.

Banerjee, A., Duflo, E., Glennerster, R., & Kinnan, C. (2009). *The miracle of microfinance? Evidence from a randomized evaluation.* Department of Economics Massachusetts Institute of Technology MIT Working Paper, pp. 1–40.

Berhane, G., & Gardebroek, C. (2011). Does microfinance reduce rural poverty? Evidence based on household panel data from Northern Ethiopia. *American Journal of Agricultural Economics, 93*(1), 43–55.

Card, D., & Krueger, A. (1995). Time-series minimum-wage studies: A meta-analysis. *American Economic Review, 85*(2), 238–243.

Cohen, J. (1988). *Statistical power analysis for the behavioural sciences.* Hillsdale, NJ: Lawrence Erlbaum Associates.

Collins, D., Morduch, J., Rutherford, S., & Ruthven, O. (2009). *Portfolios of the poor: How the world's poor live on $2 a day.* Princeton and Oxford: Princeton University Press.

Copestake, J. (2002). Inequality and the polarizing impact of microcredit: Evidence from Zambia's Copperbelt. *Journal of International Development, 14*(6), 743–755.

Copestake, J., Bhalotra, S., & Johnson, S. (2001). Assessing the impact of microcredit: A Zambian case study. *The Journal of Development Studies, 37*(4), 81–100.

Copestake, J., Dawson, P., Fanning, J., McKay, A., & Wright-Revolledo, K. (2005). Monitoring the diversity of the poverty outreach and impact of microfinance: A comparison of methods using data from Peru. *Development Policy Review, 23*(6), 703–723.

Cotler, P., & Woodruff, C. (2008). The impact of short-term credit on microenterprises: Evidence from the Fincomun-Bimbo program in Mexico. *Economic Development & Cultural Change, 56*(4), 829–849.

Cuong, N. V. (2008). Is a governmental micro-credit program for the poor really pro-poor? Evidence from Vietnam. *The Developing Economies, 46*(2), 151–187.

Daley-Harris, S. (2009). *State of the Microcredit Summit Campaign Report 2009.* Washington, DC: Microcredit Summit.

De Dominicis, L., Florax, R., & Groot, H. (2008). A meta-analysis on the relationship between income inequality and economic growth. *Scottish Journal of Political Economy, 55*(5), 654–682.

de Mel, S., McKenzie, D., & Woodruff, C. (2008). Returns to capital in microenterprises: Evidence from a field experiment. *The Quarterly Journal of Economics, 123*(4), 1329–1372.

Doucouliagos, H., & Ulubasoglu, M. (2008). Democracy and economic growth: A meta-analysis. *American Journal of Political Science, 52*(1), 61–83.

Dupas, P., & Robinson, J. (2013). Savings constraints and microenterprise development: Evidence from a field experiment in Kenya. *American Economic Journal: Applied Economics, 5*(1), 163–192.

Duvendack, M., Palmer-Jones, R., Copestake, J., Hooper, L., Loke, Y., & Rao, N. (2011). *What is the evidence of the impact of microfinance on the well-being of poor people?* London: EPPI-Centre, Social Science Research Unit, Institute of Education, University of London.

Egger, M., Smith, G., Schnieder, M., & Minder, C. (1997). Bias in meta-analysis detected by a simple, graphical test. *British Medical Journal, 315*, 629–634.

Feigenberg, B., Field, E. M., & Pande, R. (2010). *Building social capital through microfinance.* John F. Kennedy School of Government, Harvard University.

Garikipati, S. (2008). The impact of lending to women on household vulnerability and women's empowerment: Evidence from India. *World Development, 36*(12), 2620–2642.

Gertler, P., Levine, D. I., & Moretti, E. (2009). Do microfinance programs help families insure consumption against illness? *Health Economics, 18*(3), 257–273.

Hawkes, D., & Ugur, M. (2012). Evidence on the relationship between education, skills and economic growth in low-income countries: A systematic review. London: EPPI-Centre, Social Science Research Unit, Institute of Education, University of London.

Henmi, M., & Copas, J. B. (2010). Confidence intervals for random effects meta-analysis and robustness to publication bias. *Statistics in Medicine, 29*(29), 2969–2983.

Hoque, S. (2004). Micro-credit and the reduction of poverty in Bangladesh. *Journal of Contemporary Asia, 34*(1), 21–32.

Hoque, S. (2005). Micro-credit and empowerment of women: Evidence from Bangladesh. *Asian Economic Review, 47*(3), 411–420.

Hulme, D. (2000). Impact assessment methodologies for microfinance: Theory, experience and better practice. *World Development, 28*(1), 79–98.

Hulme, D., & Mosley, P. (1996). *Finance against poverty*. London: Routledge.

Imai, K. S., Arun, T., & Annim, S. K. (2010). Microfinance and household poverty reduction: New evidence from India. *World Development, 38*(12), 1760–1774.

Imai, K. S., & Azam, M. D. S. (2012). Does microfinance reduce poverty in Bangladesh? New evidence from household panel data. *Journal of Development Studies, 48*(5), 633–653.

Imai, K. S., Gaiha, R., Thapa, G., & Annim, S. K. (2012). Microfinance and poverty—A macro perspective. *World Development, 40*(8), 1675–1689.

Islam, A. (2009). *Three essays on development and labour economics*. PhD, Monash University, Australia.

Islam, A. (2011). Medium- and long-term participation in microcredit: An evaluation using a new panel dataset from Bangladesh. *American Journal of Agricultural Economics, 93*(3), 847–866.

Kabeer, N. (2005). Direct social impacts for the Millennium Development Goals. In J. Copestake, M. Greeley, S. Johnson, N. Kabeer, A. Simanowitz, & K. Knotts (Eds.), *Money with a mission, volume 1: Microfinance and poverty reduction*. London: ITDG.

Kaboski, J. P., & Townsend, R. M. (2012). The impact of credit on village economies. *American Economic Journal: Applied Economics, 4*(2), 98–133.

Karlan, D., Goldberg, N., & Copestake, J. (2009). Randomized control trials are the best way to measure impact of microfinance programmes and improve microfinance product designs. *Enterprise Development and Microfinance, 20*(3), 167–176.

Karlan, D. S., & Zinman, J. (2007). *Expanding credit access: Using randomized supply decisions to estimate the impacts*. CEPR Discussion Papers: 6180.

Karnani, A. (2007). Microfinance misses its mark. *Stanford Social Innovation Review, 5*(3), 34–40.

Kevane, M., & Wydick, B. (2001). Microenterprise lending to female entrepreneurs: Sacrificing economic growth for poverty alleviation? *World Development, 29*(7), 1225–1236.

Khandker, S. R. (2005). Microfinance and poverty: Evidence using panel data from Bangladesh. *World Bank Economic Review, 19*(2), 263–286.

Korth, M., Stewart, R., Rooyen, C., & Wet, T. (2012). Microfinance: Development intervention or just another bank? *Journal of Agrarian Change, 12*(4), 575–586.

Kouassi, M. J. (2008). *Microfinance and health: A study of selected countries.* PhD, Howard University.

Levine, R. (2004). *Finance and growth: Theory and evidence.* NBER Working Paper No. 10766.

Li, X., Gan, C., & Hu, B. (2011). The welfare impact of microcredit on rural households in China. *Journal of Socio-Economics, 40*(4), 404–411.

McKernan, S.-M. (2002). The impact of microcredit programs on self-employment profits: Do noncredit program aspects matter? *Review of Economics and Statistics, 84*(1), 93–115.

Morduch, J. (1998). *Does microfinance really help the poor? New evidence from Flagship Programs in Bangladesh.* Woodrow Wilson School of Public and International Affairs Working Papers. Princeton University.

Morduch, J. (1999). The microfinance promise. *Journal of Economic Literature, 37*(4), 1569–1614.

Nghiem, S., Coelli, T., & Rao, P. (2012). Assessing the welfare effects of microfinance in Vietnam: Empirical results from a quasi-experimental survey. *Journal of Development Studies, 48*(5), 619–632.

Nino-Zarazua, M. M., & Copestake, J. (2008). Financial inclusion, vulnerability and mental models: From physical access to effective use of financial services in a low-income area of Mexico City. *Savings and Development, 32*(4), 353–379.

Pitt, M. M., & Khandker, S. R. (1998). The impact of group-based credit programs on poor households in Bangladesh: Does the gender of participants matter? *The Journal of Political Economy, 106*(5), 958–996.

Roodman, D., & Morduch, J. (2013). *The impact of microcredit on the poor in Bangladesh: Revisiting the evidence.* NYU Wagner Research Paper No. 2231535, pp. 1–49.

Rosenberg, R. (2010). *Does microcredit really help poor people?* CGAP Focus Note, Number 59.

Sebstad, J., & Chen, G. (1996). *Overview of studies on the impact of microenterprise credit.* Washington, DC: Management Systems International.

Shaw, J. (2004). Microenterprise occupation and poverty reduction in microfinance programs: Evidence from Sri Lanka. *World Development, 32*(7), 1247–1264.

Stanley, T. (2008). Meta-regression methods for detecting and estimating empirical effects in the presence of publication selection. *Oxford Bulletin of Economics and Statistics, 70*(2), 103–127.

Stanley, T. (2010). Meta-regression models of economics and medical research. In I. Shemilt, M. Mugford, L. Vale, K. Marsh, & C. Donaldson (Eds.), *Evidence-based decisions and economics: Health care, social welfare, education and criminal justice* (2nd ed.). Oxford, UK: Wiley-Blackwell.

Stanley, T., & Doucouliagos, H. (2007). *Identifying and correcting publication selection bias in the efficiency-wage literature: Heckman meta-regression.* Economics Series 2007/11. Deakin University.

Stanley, T., Jarrell, S., & Doucouliagos, H. (2009). *Could it be better to discard 90% of the data? A statistical paradox.* Economics Working Papers No. SWP 2009/13. Deakin University.

Stanley, T. D., & Doucouliagos, H. (2014). Meta-regression approximations to reduce publication selection bias. *Research Synthesis Methods, 5*(1), 60–78.

Stewart, R., van Rooyen, C., Dickson, K., Majoro, M., & de Wet, T. (2010). *What is the impact of microfinance on poor people? A systematic review of evidence from sub-Saharan Africa.* Technical Report. London: EPPI-Centre, Social Science Research Unit, University of London.

Stewart, R., Van Rooyen, C., Korth, M., Chereni, A., Rebelo Da Silva, N., & de Wet, T. (2012). *Do micro-credit, micro-savings and micro-leasing serve as effective financial inclusion interventions enabling poor people, and especially women, to engage in meaningful economic opportunities in low- and middle-income countries? A systematic review of the evidence.* EPPI-Centre, Social Science Research Unit, Institute of Education, University of London.

Takahashi, K., Higashikata, T., & Tsukada, K. (2010). The short-term poverty impact of small-scale, collateral-free microcredit in Indonesia: A matching estimator approach. *Developing Economies, 48*(1), 128–155.

Tedeschi, G. A. (2008). Overcoming selection bias in microcredit impact assessments: A case study in Peru. *Journal of Development Studies, 44*(4), 504–518.

Ugur, M. (2013). Corruption's direct effects on per-capita income growth: A meta-analysis. *Journal of Economic Surveys, 28*, 472–490.

Vaessen, J., Leeuw, F., Bonilla, S., Rivas, A., Lukach, R., Bastiaensen, J., & Holvoet, N. (2012). *The effects of microcredit on women's control over household spending in developing countries.* 3ie Systematic Reviews—SR003-1.

van Rooyen, C., Stewart, R., & de Wet, T. (2012). The impact of microfinance in Sub-Saharan Africa: A systematic review of the evidence. *World Development, 40*(11), 2249–2262.

Wood, G., & Sharif, I. (1997). *Who needs credit?: Poverty and finance in Bangladesh*. London: Zed Books.

Wydick, B. (1999). The effect of microenterprise lending on child schooling in Guatemala. *Economic Development and Cultural Change, 47*(4), 853–869.

Zeller, M., Sharma, M., Ahmed, A. U., & Rashid, S. (2001). *Group-based financial institutions for the rural poor in Bangladesh: An institutional- and household-level analysis*. Research Report 120. Washington, DC: International Food Policy Research Institute.

15

Transitioning from the MDGs to the SDGs: Lessons Learnt?

Simon Feeny

1   Introduction

The signing of the Millennium Declaration in Monterrey, Mexico, by all United Nations' member states in September 2000 provided a new and important global framework for spurring global development. For the first time, the declaration committed all member states to achieving eight international goals and 18 development targets aimed at reducing income poverty and hunger, achieving universal primary education, promoting gender equality, reducing mortality rates, combatting major diseases, ensuring environmental sustainability and to developing a global partnership for development. With 2015 as the deadline for their achievement, it is appropriate to reflect on both the successes and failures of the Millennium Development Goals (MDGs) and whether the lessons learnt were applied to the current international agenda for sustainable development by 2030.

S. Feeny (✉)
School of Economics, Finance and Marketing, RMIT University,
Melbourne, VIC, Australia
e-mail: simon.feeny@rmit.edu.au

© The Author(s) 2020   **343**
S. Awaworyi Churchill (ed.), *Moving from the Millennium to the Sustainable Development Goals*, https://doi.org/10.1007/978-981-15-1556-9_15

Evaluations of what the MDGs achieved are, not surprisingly, mixed. There is broad agreement that the MDGs were successful in raising global awareness of international development issues. Moreover, the headline goal of reducing by half the proportion of people living in extreme poverty (between 1990 and 2015) was achieved early. This was largely due to remarkable reductions in the number of people living in poverty in the world's two most populous countries: China and India. Yet, other MDG goals and targets were not met and it is impossible to ascertain what would have happened to global development outcomes if the United Nations' Millennium Declaration, which brought the goals into existence, had never been signed.

The same will be true for evaluations of the Agenda for Sustainable Development and its 17 Sustainable Development Goals (SDGs). The preceding chapters of this book have demonstrated that there are a large number of important factors that policymakers need to consider in their commitment to achieving the SDGs. This concluding chapter summarises what we learnt from the global experience of the MDGs and examines the extent to which these lessons were applied to the evolution of the SDGs. It demonstrates that while some of the critiques of the MDGs have been addressed, unfortunately some of the insights we learnt from the MDGs were not applied to the SDG agenda.

2   The Scope of the SDGs

The MDGs emanated from a number of development conferences in the 1990s as well as from consultations with NGOs and civil society groups. However, the MDGs are often criticised for being devised largely behind closed doors at the United Nations with little participation from those in developing countries with respect to what should (and shouldn't) be included in the goals and targets (Haileamlak, 2014). Arguably, the MDGs lacked enough of a focus on people with a disability (Wolbring, 2011), conflict and peace (Hill, Mansoor, & Claudio, 2010), and human rights (Fehling, Nelson, & Venkatapuram, 2013) as well as the environment.

Relative to the formulation of the MDGs, the process of devising the SDGs was far more participatory, involving consultation with civil society, the private sector and the governments of a far greater number of countries. The result is a far more comprehensive list of goals which included many of the issues that the MDGs were criticised for not addressing (including *inter alia* climate change, the environment, peace and conflict, work, the oceans). However, it is often argued that the SDGs do not have enough focus on human rights (see for example Sengupta, 2018). Such a huge exercise in consensus building should be viewed positively, yet many would argue that the final list of 17 goals is far too long and unwieldly. The increased number of goals also led to a far greater number of targets (169) and indicators (more than 200). Only having eight MDGs to target efforts provided countries with a greater focus up to 2015.

It is difficult to see how any government, let alone a small, cash-strapped government of a (so-called) developing country can truly commit to achieving such a large number of goals and collecting data on so many different targets and indicators. Unless governments focus on particular goals, there is a danger that they won't achieve any. Having 17 goals rather than 8 threatens countries' commitments to achieve them and might lead to waning enthusiasm.

3   The Level of Ambition of the SDGs

It was sometimes argued that the MDGs were not ambitious enough, particularly for well-performing middle-income countries. A strong critique of the SDGs is that the goals are far too ambitious. For example, the first SDG calls for 'no poverty'.[1] The second SDG calls for the end of hunger and malnutrition and the fifth SDG to end all forms of discrimination against all women and girls everywhere. While these are admirable goals, they risk setting countries up for failure if they cannot be achieved.

---

[1] Strangely this goal is not compatible with the first SDG target of 'By 2030, reduce at least by half the proportion of men, women and children of all ages living in poverty in all its dimensions according to national definitions'.

Given the ongoing and increasing impacts of climate change and climatic shocks, it is virtually impossible to envisage nobody living in poverty and not going hungry by 2030, particularly when poverty can be measured in multiple ways. The reality is that there will be some proportion of the global population that has suffered a recent shock and has been pushed into destitution as a result. In 2030, it is important that countries are commended if they make valuable progress in reducing poverty and not labelled as failures for not eradicating it.

4   Accountability for SDG Achievement

Achieving the MDGs was largely the responsibility of developing country governments. Only the eighth goal of 'developing a global partnership for development' specified a direct role for industrialised countries in, for example, providing more (and better quality) foreign aid, sustainable debt relief and ensuring a fair-trading system. The SDGs are a clear and important departure from this, with their achievement being the responsibility of all countries in the world. While this is certainly an important improvement on the MDGs, it is still the case that the achievement of the SDGs and their targets are not legally binding. Since many of the SDGs will require actions from multiple governments, the private sector and civil society, a lack of direct accountability is likely to result in a lot of finger pointing in the post-2030 era if the goals are not achieved.

5   SDGs and Inequality

Some of the MDGs related to average outcomes without necessarily improving the living standards of everyone. Arguably, this provided incentives for policymakers to focus on the lowest-hanging fruit and to prioritise those that are easiest to reach rather than the most vulnerable such as ethnic minorities, indigenous populations and those with a disability. In this respect, the SDGs are an improvement on the MDGs by having an explicit goal of reducing inequality and an underlying philosophy to 'leave no one behind'. However, significantly reducing inequality in practice is likely to remain a significant policy challenge and many believe that the proposed targets do not go far enough.

6   Contradictions and Trade-offs in the SDGs

Possibly, the strongest critique of the SDGs is that while there are strong synergies among the different goals, there are also critical trade-offs which can undermine their achievement. For example, Scherer et al. (2018) find that pursuing social goals (such as reducing poverty and inequality) will be associated with higher environmental impacts (undermining the conservation of land, efforts at reducing carbon emissions as well as initiatives to improve access to safe and affordable water). Similarly, Fader, Cranmer, Lawford, and Engel-Cox (2018) find that various targets associated with the second SDG of zero hunger, conflict with other targets due to their resource use and threats to ecosystem services. Further, Campagnolo and Davide (2019) estimate that the commitments made under the Paris Agreement on climate change will slow down the effort to reduce poverty (4.2 per cent of people living in poverty will remain so due to the commitments). While it is true that any synergies and trade-offs will depend on individual country contexts, particularly a country's resource endowments, policy solutions to these trade-offs will need to be found quickly (Nilsson et al., 2018).

7   The Cost of Achieving the SDGs

UNCTAD (2014) estimate that to achieve the SDGs, the investment needs of developing countries alone range from $3.3 trillion to $4.5 trillion per year and that they therefore face a funding gap of approximately US$2.5 trillion. Private investment will need to increase considerably to complement public investment and the approximately US$150 billion provided in foreign aid to these countries each year. Unleashing and coordinating such financing poses a considerable challenge. Encouragingly, in comparison to the MDGs, there appears to be greater engagement and commitment to the SDGs from the private sector. However, the financing of the SDGs remains a considerable challenge.

8   Monitoring Progress towards the SDGs and Assessing their Achievement

A 2016 Centre for Global Development report notes that the availability of data was not considered during the goal and target selection, which could seriously impede SDG implementation. Of the 230 SDG indicators, the report found that just 42 per cent of the indicators have an established methodology and regularly accessible data and only 25 per cent of indicators could be found publicly online (Dunning & Kalow, 2016). It therefore becomes impossible to measure progress without baseline information. Assessing whether or not an SDG has been achieved in 2030 will be impossible in many cases. This is particularly the case for the poorest countries which do not have the resources for extensive data collection. Even when data do exist, how is it determined whether a particular SDG is achieved or not when the goals comprise of many different targets? Will they be judged to have missed the goal if they achieved all its targets except one?

9   Conclusion

The preceding sections of this concluding chapter have highlighted how the SDGs have addressed some of the critiques of the MDGs but are subject to a number of criticisms themselves. This chapter argues that these criticisms need to be taken on board but that they are not insurmountable. To address many of them, policymakers need to consider a central principle of both the SDGs (as well as the MDGs). This is to tailor the goals and targets to make them appropriate and relevant for their countries. While the UN (2015) makes this explicit, it often appears to be overlooked: "Targets are defined as aspirational and global, with each government setting its own national targets guided by the global level of ambition but taking into account national circumstances. Each government will also decide how these aspirational and global targets should be incorporated in national planning processes, policies and strategies" (UN, 2015, p. 13).

Feeny and Clarke (2012) provide a number of examples where the MDGs were tailored by countries, sometimes to be less ambitious, sometimes more so, and sometimes countries added their own goals and targets. Further, UNDP (2016) argues that one of the key lessons from the MDGs is the setting of targets that reflect people's priorities for the future.

In their assessment of 26 Voluntary National Reviews (VNRs) of the SDGs, Allen, Metternicht, and Wiedmann (2018) found that more than two-thirds of the countries reviewed had completed or were in the process of completing 'prioritisation and/or adaptation of global SDG targets and indicators'. A cursory glance of the VNRs reveals that prioritisation is far more common that adaptation.

This chapter argues that more SDG adaptation is required to ensure ongoing commitment to their achievement. In tailoring the SDGs, a number of issues must be carefully considered. Firstly, the specific goals and targets should not be cherry-picked by policymakers to strengthen political support or which are most likely to be achievable. If targets are adjusted downwards, it is important that they are still ambitious. Secondly, the process of tailoring the goals and targets must be participatory, involving all levels of government, civil society and the private sector. It should also be justified, and evidence-based. Thirdly, any tailored goals and targets must be widely publicised to other countries and international organisations to ensure that the country is not assessed with respect to the SDGs as originally specified by the United Nations. This could lead to assertions of failure when a country might have succeeded in reaching their ambition. The usual 'scorecard' that was applied at the country level to assess progress towards the MDGs is inappropriate when goals and targets are context specific. Fourthly, once tailored, to ensure an appropriate commitment to their achievement, the goals and targets should be costed and incorporated into the country's national development plans and strategies. This will raise the likelihood of members of a country uniting to achieve the SDGs and to achieve strong development outcomes beyond 2030.

References

Allen, C., Metternicht, G., & Wiedmann, T. (2018). Initial progress in implementing the Sustainable Development Goals (SDGs): A review of evidence from countries. *Sustainability Science, 13*, 1453–1467.

Campagnolo, L., & Davide, M. (2019). Can the Paris deal boost SDGs achievement? An assessment of climate mitigation co-benefits or side-effects on poverty and inequality. *World Development, 122*, 96–109.

Dunning, C., & Kalow, J. (2016). *SDG indicators: Serious gaps abound in data availability.* Center for Global Development, Washington, DC. Retrieved from https://www.cgdev.org/blog/sdg-indicators-serious-gaps-abound-data-availability

Fader, M., Cranmer, C., Lawford, R., & Engel-Cox, J. (2018). Toward an understanding of synergies and trade-offs between water, energy, and food SDG targets. *Frontiers in Environmental Science, 6*, 1–11.

Feeny, S., & Clarke, M. (Eds.). (2012). *The millennium development goals: Looking beyond 2015.* London: Routledge.

Fehling, M., Nelson, B. D., & Venkatapuram, S. (2013). Limitations of the millennium development goals: A literature review. *Global Public Health, 8*(10), 1109–1122.

Haileamlak, A. (2014). Millennium development goals: Lessons learnt and the way forward. *Ethiopian Journal of Health Sciences, 24*(4), 284.

Hill, P. S., Mansoor, G. F., & Claudio, F. (2010). Conflict in least-developed countries: Challenging the millennium development goals. *Bulletin of the World Health Organization, 88*, 562–563.

Nilsson, M., Chisholm, E., Griggs, D., Howden-Chapman, P., McCollum, D., Messerli, P., … Stafford-Smith, M. (2018). Mapping interactions between the sustainable development goals: Lessons learned and ways forward. *Sustainability Science, 13*, 1489.

Scherer, L., Behrens, P., de Koning, A., Heijungs, R., Sprecher, B., & Tukker, A. (2018). Trade-offs between social and environmental sustainable development goals. *Environmental Science & Policy, 90*, 65–72.

Sengupta, M. (2018). Transformational change or tenuous wish list?: A critique of SDG 1 ('End poverty in all its forms everywhere'). *Social Alternatives, 37*(1), 12–17.

UN. (2015). Transforming our world: The 2030 Agenda for sustainable development. New York: United Nations General Assembly.

UNCTAD. (2014). World investment report 2014: Investing in the SDGs: An action plan, United Nations Conference on trade and development. New York: United Nations.

UNDP. (2016). *From the MDGs to sustainable development for all: Lessons from 15 years of practice.* New York: United Nations Development Program.

Wolbring, G. (2011). People with disabilities and social determinants of health discourses. *Canadian Journal of Public Health, 102*(4), 317–319.

Index[1]

---

[1] Note: Page numbers followed by 'n' refer to notes.